Planning the City upon a Hill

Planning
the City
upon a Hill

....

Boston since 1630

Lawrence W. Kennedy

The University

of Massachusetts Press

Amherst

Copyright © 1992 by Lawrence W. Kennedy
All rights reserved   Printed in the United States of America
LC 91–43645   ISBN 0–87023–780–2
Designed by Mary Mendell   Set in Berkley Old Style
Printed and bound by Thomson-Shore   This book is published with the
financial support and cooperation of the Boston Redevelopment Authority and
the University of Massachusetts at Boston.

Library of Congress Cataloging-in-Publication Data
Kennedy, Lawrence W., 1952–
Planning the city upon a hill : Boston since 1630 / Lawrence W. Kennedy.
p.   cm.
Includes bibliographical references and index.
ISBN 0–87023–780–2 (alk. paper)
1. City planning—Massachusetts—Boston—History.   2. Boston (Mass.)—Social
conditions.   3. Boston (Mass.)—Economic conditions.   4. Urban policy—
Massachusetts—Boston—History.   I. Title.
HT168.B6K46   1992
307.1′2′0974461–dc20   91–43645 CIP
British Library Cataloging in Publication data are available.

Frontispiece. Boston, 1880. Lithograph by Beck and Pauli. Courtesy of Historic
Urban Plans, Ithaca, New York.

Contents

....

Maps and Illustrations
....

Acknowledgments

....

To acknowledge everyone who has helped me write this book is to express my gratitude to so many who have helped me to learn and grow over the last five years. Of all the people who have touched my life, the most important is my wife, Judith McCarthy Kennedy, to whom I dedicate this book. She has been loyal, patient, and loving, and without her support and assistance I never would have completed this effort. Our sons, Patrick and Paul, have been a source of inspiration and joy. I am grateful to them for allowing me the time and peace to work and the opportunity to share in the more important things in life.

The Boston Redevelopment Authority (BRA), under Director Stephen Coyle, sponsored my research and allowed me the time and independence to pursue my own path through this endeavor. I deeply appreciate the director's enthusiasm for the work, his willingness to provide backing for publication, and the time he gave me. I wish to acknowledge the support of Clarence "Jeep" Jones, present chairman of the BRA, and Robert L. Farrell, his predecessor. I am also grateful for the backing of other board members, James K. Flaherty, Michael F. Donlan, Francis X. O'Brien, Consuelo Gonzales Thornell, and former member Joseph J. Walsh. Mayor Raymond L. Flynn set the tone under which a study such as this could be undertaken and he deserves credit for his support.

Alexander Ganz, longtime director of Policy Development and Research at the BRA, originally suggested that I investigate the topic of Boston's planning history as part of the comprehensive research program he established in the agency. Alex led the way in expanding the scope and scale of the research and in the decision to secure publication by a scholarly press. His role in the development of this work was crucial. Gregory W. Perkins and John Avault, both deputy directors in the research department, have been helpful in providing information, sources, and counsel. Richard Henderson and Milton Abelson read early drafts of this book and patiently prodded me to do better. Richard played a particularly important part in formulating my thoughts on the shaping of Boston. Peter Neitz of the BRA drew the wonderful set of maps that illustrate the story of Boston's growth. His contribution to the book is immeasurable and enduring. I enjoyed working with Pete and am thankful for his good humor, patience, and interest, in addition to his skill.

Over the years I have learned much about Boston history from Thomas H. O'Connor and other historians at Boston College, especially Andrew Buni, Mark Gelfand, and Alan Rogers. They each have inspired me and I am grateful for their continued support. Tom O'Connor's careful reading of an early draft of the manuscript was, as always, helpful. My debt to him and appreciation for all he has done are great and I look forward to his forthcoming book on the "New Boston." Mark Gelfand's corrections and thoughtful comments on Chapter 6 were of great value, and his writings on urban history are models of erudition and insight. Long ago, Father Thomas Grey, S.J., guided my first research paper on Boston, introducing me to the joys of historical scholarship. In the even more distant past Marvin Rintala enthralled me with his understanding of the study of politics. As he reads this work I hope he recognizes the effect he has had upon my career.

In writing this book I also experienced the help of the larger community of scholars. At a crucial point Sam Bass Warner, Jr., made a huge difference by encouraging me to continue my research and to seek publication. His suggestions and recommendation helped me achieve the goal of reaching a wider audience. For his generous assistance I am most grateful. Similarly, the interest and critiques of Bernard Frieden and Martha Wagner Weinberg helped broaden and strengthen my work. Later, I profited from the insightful reading and comments by Stanley Schultz and Arnold M. Howitt.

There are a number of other people who also encouraged me in this endeavor. Ian Menzies of the John W. McCormack Institute of the University of Massachusetts at Boston was an early supporter. My cousin Ann Louise McLaughlin, Lynn Wehnes, and Les Larson all shared their enthusiasm for Boston with me, read early drafts, and in a variety of ways helped me to hold my course. Frank Costello aided me in my scholarly pursuits and has been a good friend. Jill Gambon helped clarify some key points about contemporary politics and planning. Judy Jack labored long and hard through this book, editing several drafts and generously devoting untold hours to helping me learn about writing, word-processing, and much more. I send a special thanks to her for her unwaning interest and moral support.

The staff of the area libraries that opened their doors, books, and archives to me provided a level of service and assistance that helped my research and made my life more pleasant. I appreciate the kindnesses of the people who work in the Boston Public Library, the Thomas P. O'Neill, Jr., Library of Boston College, the Massachusetts State Library, and the Library of the Boston Athenaeum. George Sanborn of the State Transportation Library was very helpful and I also wish to acknowledge the assistance of Philip Bergin, Librarian of the Bostonian Society. Staff members of the Boston Redevelopment Authority offered various forms of assistance and I especially want to thank Bob Arnold, Janet Carlson, Sue Hannon, and Kevin Morrison. Dan Moon, Laurie Onanian, Ed Roche, and Veronica Quirk Young all helped with illustrations, as did Larry Gillis and Ed Quill of the City Archives. The staff of the BRA Library has been most helpful; Elaine Happnie assisted with photographs and Maxine Strickland has been helping cheerily for several years. All the past and present members of the BRA's Policy Development and Research Department with whom I have been associated deserve special thanks for their interest, especially Bob Amatruda, Andrew Foley, and Louise Wright who hold it all together and have done so much to support my efforts. Paul Wright, the Boston editor of the University of Massachusetts Press, helped turn a manuscript into a book. My thanks also goes to managing editor, Pam Wilkinson, and to copyeditor, Elizabeth T. Fowler, for their suggestions and assistance.

All the people who consented to be interviewed and generously gave of their time are listed, but I am especially grateful for the opportunity to discuss Boston's history with Mayors John F. Collins, Kevin H. White, and Raymond L. Flynn. Ed Logue has been helpful with discussions about planning, past and present, and I want to express my debt to him and to the many others who have, in a more casual setting, shared their recollections and opinions about how Boston was shaped. I have enjoyed hours of conversation with countless people who are intrigued by this city and have shared information, insights, and opinions with me. To all who have contributed to enriching this book, named or not, I offer my thanks.

**Planning
the City
upon a
Hill**

Early one Sunday morning in the fall of 1987, their abandoned cars lining the Massachusetts Turnpike Extension in Boston as far as the eye could see, thousands of Bostonians congregated to watch the demolition of the Travelers Insurance Building on High Street. It was an exciting moment, evoking images of summer evenings when cars park along Storrow Drive and concert-goers flock to the banks of the Charles River for the Boston Pops Orchestra. But on that morning, only the disappearance of part of the city's skyline could justify the scores of cars stopped along the busy interstate highway and the crowds gathered behind the blue and white police barriers.

As the building collapsed inward upon itself, it took with it the dreams of an earlier generation of Bostonians for whom the now-dated structure had represented the hope for a new and better Boston. More than a slice of the city was wiped out in those few stunning minutes. The demise of the twenty-eight-year-old Travelers, along with the spectacular dynamiting and demolition of the Hotel Madison that same decade, represented the shunting aside, during an era of economic boom, of the ambitions and plans cherished by previous generations of planners. Just as the Travelers had heralded the building of the "New Boston" in the 1950s and 1960s, the Madison (originally the Manger) represented the vibrant redevelopment of the North Station region in the 1920s. Each building had, at its inception, embodied the idea of a revitalized Boston; yet each was sacrificed to a succeeding generation's vision of what the city could and should be.

Such constant tinkering with Boston's cityscape has characterized the city almost from the moment of its founding in 1630. Since that time, Boston's topography has undergone more alterations than that of any other comparably sized city. Boston has been endlessly reshaped, its hills cut down to fill in harbors, mudflats, rivers and channels, its streets and avenues endlessly redirected. Throughout its history, political and business leaders and ordinary citizens have made decisive choices about the physical growth, shape, and appearance of the city. Unencumbered by any rigorous, official definition of urban planning, earlier generations of Bostonians—like their present-day counterparts—nevertheless engaged in the endeavor, and Boston looks as it does today largely because of planning, the inherently political process of allocating land and regulating its use. The history of planning in Boston demonstrates the tremendous impact of political choices on the physical city.

Planning is fundamentally and inherently a political process because it involves, as political scientist Harold Lasswell once said, who gets what, when, and how.[1] Modern planning, when defined as the use of government power to advance the economic interests and alter the physical appearance of a city, is concerned with the allocation of resources in a defined area and time period. As such, it entails mediating needs and balancing the interests of innumerable forces and persons. Primarily, planning addresses economic rather than aesthetic or cultural needs, and the prime mover of planning is hence economic.

American cities provide social, cultural, and educational opportunities, but there should be little doubt that, as historian David Schuyler writes, "cities are first and foremost economic institutions. They exist primarily to serve the demands of commerce."[2] Since city planning influences a variety of interests in a private-market economy, it is by nature a multifaceted process, involving contradictory capital interests and competing social and economic goals.[3] This competition can create confusion and the results have not always been pretty. Sam Bass Warner, Jr., points out that the "private market's demand for workers, its capacities for dividing land, building houses, stores and factories, and its needs for public services have determined the shape and quality of America's big cities."[4] This tradition, which Warner calls "privatism," has all too often kept American cities from meeting other needs more effectively. But increasingly in the late nineteenth century, planning as a self-conscious activity emerged not solely to aid private development, but also to address matters ignored by the private sector. Such public-sector planning first turned toward practical matters such as transportation, water, and sewage. Gradually government planning came to be accepted for parks and playgrounds, which citizens viewed as healthful, practical and necessary. Before long, planning involved regulating the size and location of buildings. Thus planning was fairly advanced by the late nineteenth century although its true extent was not immediately apparent.[5]

A modern text in the discipline defines planning as "the deliberate, organized, continuous process of identifying different elements and aspects of an organism, determining their present state and interaction, projecting them in concert throughout a period of future time, and formulating and programming a set of actions and plans to attain desired results."[6] Quite apart from the question of whether Melville C. Branch's definition can be said to describe the activity of any city, corporation, or other human organization, such an all-encompassing formulation could not fairly be said to have characterized Boston's growth over the centuries; moreover, the definition is not suitable for evaluating the past because it rests on contemporary assumptions regarding the professionalization and institutionalization of urban planning.

One of America's leading urban historians, Stanley K. Schultz, offers another more helpful perspective on planning in his recent book, *Constructing Urban Culture*. Observing that for most historians, modern city planning began in 1909 with the First National Conference on City Planning, Schultz argues that "comprehensive" city planning was a product of the entire nineteenth century, not simply a phenomenon that developed suddenly at the turn of the twentieth century. Schultz states:

> Cities are the accumulation of human experience. They are the manufactured containers, the physical expressions, of human culture. In that sense, all cities are planned environments. They are the results of cultural decisions about the most appropriate physical uses of land and the residential distribution of people. Urban form encapsules time and space. At any moment in time, the physical landscape of the city reveals countless decisions of bygone days about the "best" uses of space—"best" means those individual or collective values and judgments about the quality of life made by citizens in the past, judgments that affect the lives of those in the present—and the future. Urban forms reveal what was and was not important to their builders and residents in any given historical moment.[7]

Considered within this framework, the history of Boston's development suggests that Bostonians did indeed plan their city upon a hill. As society became more complex, urbanized, and technological, the scope of planning grew and its nature and definition changed.

Today, planning involves real estate developers, city planners, bureaucrats, politicians, technical experts, preservation advocates, and community groups. It incorporates architectural design, land-use zoning, plans for transportation and streets, and the construction of public works and spaces. It is a process dominated by government agencies and characterized by hefty documents, reams of supporting materials, hours of hearings, and a plenitude of illustrations and models depicting yet another masterful scheme for altering the city. This form of city planning is, however, only the most recent phase of a long-established tradition that originated in the seventeenth century and that reflects a continual interplay between the private and public sectors. The history of planning in Boston since 1630 thus records how Bostonians interacted with one another, both individually and collectively, and with their environment to fashion a great city.

In the early years of the seventeenth century, the physical community and built environment simply evolved from the aggregate of decisions made by individuals. Private citizens designed homes and workplaces; private partnerships provided basic services; and the extent of government involvement in city planning was limited to the Great and General Court of the Commonwealth, which enacted the necessary legislation. Private entrepreneurs orchestrated major developments, such as filling in the shoreline and building the early wharves. Similarly, the provision of water, fire protection, and the disposal of sewage were all private concerns for many years.

In the eighteenth century, initiative and money continued to come from the private sector, and planning by groups of merchants began to dominate political life. Town meeting members, for example, gladly allowed merchants to plan and construct seawalls that extended the shoreline, made trade easier, and gave the merchants more property. Later, although skeptics abounded, Peter Faneuil provided the funds to build the hall that now bears his name and that he intended to serve both public and private interests. In the case of Faneuil Hall, both the town and the merchants profited: the site not only provided commercial space for the merchants, but also office space and meeting rooms for the local government.

The beginning of the nineteenth century heralded the visionary collaboration between the great architect Charles Bulfinch and the shrewd businessman (and later mayor of Boston) Harrison Gray Otis. These two men did more to purposefully shape the emerging town than anyone else; to them we owe the State House, as well as the residential districts of Beacon Hill and South Boston. Moreover, the career of Harrison Gray Otis illustrates the powerful way in which private interests contributed decisively to the planning of Boston. Otis lined up financial partners, selected a brilliant architect, Charles Bulfinch, obtained the requisite legal authority from both town meetings and the state legislature, and set about developing and expanding the city.

The dramatic changes in Boston in the nineteenth century challenged the municipal government to an unprecedented degree. The Town of Boston incorporated itself as a city, expanded its land mass into the surrounding harbor and Back Bay, and acquired additional territory by annexing adjacent towns. Revolutionary advances in transportation, communications, and building methods altered the city beyond anything early settlers could have imagined. Historian Kenneth T. Jackson argues that "the shape of cities, indeed their very existence and growth, is in large measure a function of technological development."[8] This is certainly true of Boston, especially with regard to transportation. Over the last two centuries technological advancements allowed Bostonians to transport tons of fill required to fill in large amounts of land in the Back Bay, the South End, and South Boston. Successive revolutions in transportation have determined other facets of the city's development. The railroad created the Back Bay and allowed suburban growth that molded the patterns of living in and around Boston.

Technology is clearly a major factor in shaping the city but, as historian Eric Monkkonen argues in a recent book on American urban development, of "far greater historical and contemporary importance than the shaping power of transportation technology have been the enormous political, social and economic efforts by government—local, state, and federal—to promote them and make them functional." Monkkonen further observes that "without a social or political system willing to make the appropriate innovations, no technology has inherent utility."[9]

In the nineteenth century, it became obvious, in large part because of technological developments, that the municipal government would have to assume more responsibility for the well-being of the city and its residents. Three of Boston's ablest mayors, all named Josiah Quincy— father, son, and great-grandson—moved the city further along the path of increased government involvement in planning. In the 1820s, "the Great Mayor" (the first of the Josiah Quincys) energized the municipality to clean the streets, provide for the poor, and develop a new and grand public marketplace to supplement Faneuil Hall. In the 1840s, the second Mayor Quincy led the drive to acquire a reservoir for city residents, and in the 1890s the last Mayor Quincy presided over both the dedication of America's first subway and the construction of public bathhouses.

Boston flourished between the election of the first and last Quincy.

During these decades the government moved along the track of ever-increasing involvement in planning, but private interests, as always, still powered the engine. The government continued to respond to the needs of the private sector, for example, by allowing corporations the right to establish and build on reclaimed land. Moreover, while the South End typified city initiative and the Back Bay represented state planning, most of Boston's territorial expansion took place when the new streetcar lines—built by private corporations—allowed city dwellers to move out to the suburbs. Roxbury, Charlestown, and Dorchester, populated by former residents of Boston proper, stretched the city boundaries. Roads were laid out and paved. Boston gobbled up street systems of a bewildering variety, planned by towns, street car companies, or developers; the city had no way of truly integrating them.

It was not the chaotic street system, however, that most sharply illustrated the need for a greater government role in planning. Water supply and sewage disposal were at the heart of many political battles of the nineteenth century, and new government agencies were established to deal with the provision and maintenance of water, sewer, and park systems. In the 1880s, Boston's municipal government created one of the premier water and sewage systems in the nation, and the state soon incorporated Boston and surrounding towns into a metropolitan network to centralize control of these services.

The late nineteenth century was a time of innovative and far-reaching change. Citizens demanded new services from municipal government and municipal government responded. In the decades after the Civil War, Bostonians committed to realizing a civic vision supported a variety of public endeavors, including the grand new Public Library at Copley Square, the founding of the Boston Symphony Orchestra, and the park system conceived by Frederick Law Olmsted. Strung together on an "Emerald Necklace" that still runs from central Boston to its neighborhoods, Olmsted's parks brought together disparate elements and sections of the city. Bostonians of one hundred years ago, sensing the growth to come, planned public spaces, parks and playgrounds for the enjoyment of posterity.

Private enterprise continued to serve as the engine driving the development of Boston, but local government had at last begun to take a more active role. Expected to provide its citizens with social services, to function as the regional center for the utility, water and sewer systems, and to promote the port of Boston, the city had to learn to deal with a larger and more diverse population, cooperate with neighboring towns, and compete with other ports and cities. All these efforts were complicated by ethnic and political shifts within the city.

In the last decades of the nineteenth century and the early years of the twentieth century, Boston City Hall was taken over by the immigrant Irish in the Democratic party, a political development that had serious consequences for urban planning by both public and private decision-makers. It marks, in fact, a turning point in the relationship between the public and private sectors. When the former ruling elite—the Boston Brahmins— lost control of political power in the city, they displayed Yankee ingenuity and created new ways to check the power of the emerging Irish. The state government, at that time still thoroughly dominated by the Republican elite, introduced metropolitan planning, in part to rationalize the provision of government services but more importantly to retain some control of Boston's political bosses. The mayoral victories of John F. Fitzgerald in 1905 and James Michael Curley in 1914 signaled the end of the alliance between the private and public sectors which had done so much to shape the city over the past century. Thereafter, as private-sector interest in promoting the growth of Boston declined, public-sector involvement in planning grew.

Ambitious planning efforts and a prolonged period of economic stagnation characterized the thirty-five years of Boston politics dominated by the colorful James Michael Curley. Reformers had created a city planning agency in 1914, but private investment plummeted as Bostonians became painfully aware that their fortunes were tied to regional and national economic trends. Boston's economic stagnation between the 1930s and the 1950s, which resulted from the private sector's distrust of Curley as much as from the Great Depression, had a profound impact on urban development. Curley, who served four terms as mayor of Boston and one term as governor of Massachusetts, was famous for creating public works projects to put constituents to work. Eventually, the public sector replaced the private sector as the main stimulant to economic growth.

Boston's economic decline continued into the second half of the twentieth century. As the city teetered on the edge of bankruptcy in the late 1950s, the public and private sectors came together for the first time in a half century to begin a new era in Boston planning. Important private groups attempted to bridge the gap between the public and private sectors, reflecting a growing awareness of the need for a new approach to planning, one in which the two sectors could work together to improve the city. The resulting "New Boston" campaign of the 1960s, supported by an aggressive local government and bolstered by federal funds, spurred private development, but all through the 1960s the engine of growth remained governmental. Edward J. Logue, director of the Boston Redevelopment Authority, working with Mayor John F. Collins, epitomized the new style of planning, which stressed government action primarily to stimulate private-sector investment.

As the new approach succeeded, fresh problems emerged and communities began to demand greater involvement in the planning process. In the late 1960s and 1970s neighborhood and community groups began to assert a far greater role in the process of shaping Boston, often halting or greatly altering government plans. Although the old public-private sector relationship had been restored and the two forces now worked hand in hand, social conditions and attitudes had changed dramatically, introducing a new element into the planning process. No longer could planning be done exclusively in corporate boardrooms and government offices; it now had to take into account the wishes of ordinary citizens.

Kevin White succeeded John Collins as mayor and vowed to restore attention to the city residents who felt cut out of the planning process. The White years, however, were marked more by fantastic growth in downtown office and hotel space than by neighborhood planning and growth. The city, which could no longer count on federal largesse to fuel its growth, offered tax and other incentives to downtown developers. The "New Boston" came to fruition, and by the end of the 1970s, the old city possessed a dramatic new skyline. With its unique blend of the old and the new, Boston became a "world-class city" admired by many as a desirable place to live and work.

Mayor Raymond Flynn followed White to City Hall, and his administration contended with new problems in the second half of the 1980s as Boston endeavored to adapt to its sudden prominence. With Boston's success came an increasing awareness of the disparity between prosperous areas like Copley Place in fashionable Back Bay and the declining neighborhood near Dudley Square only a few miles away. Boston's popularity and rapid growth required new initiatives and strategies, and the issue of affordable housing came to the forefront. Under Flynn, the city attempted to stimulate the production of housing for residents previously excluded from the booming 1980s economy. The Flynn administration also redirected some of the benefits accruing to the city from the downtown development bonanza to aid ailing neighborhoods, in the process introducing new zoning laws and encouraging increased participation of community groups in planning. Progress in meeting these goals was made during the economic boom of the first Flynn term but, with a dramatic downturn in the national and local economy, these issues remain ongoing concerns.

The focus of this study is on the changing role of local government in city planning. Boston's municipal government holds the primary responsibility for guiding the growth of the city, and the following chapters concentrate on that fact. The city's political leaders have always needed to work with partners in the private sector, and in the twentieth century have found it increasingly necessary to cooperate with federal and state agencies as well. Although the roles played by the federal and state governments—like that played by the private sector—are crucial to the story of Boston, I consider them here primarily in relation to city government. This book is not, then, a comprehensive account of all planning done by government agencies, but an attempt to examine the process of planning and uncover some of the patterns at work. Planning Boston has been a sustained activity for nearly four centuries; what follows is the story of the continuous evolution of both an idea and a city.

1

A City
upon
a Hill

In 1630 when John Winthrop proclaimed to his fellow passengers aboard the *Arbella*, "We shall be as a City upon a Hill," he did not have the site of Boston in mind. Although Boston literally sat upon several hills, only one of which remains, Winthrop was speaking metaphorically; his words describe the religious mission of the Puritan voyagers to New England. The founders of the Massachusetts Bay Colony envisioned a "Godly Commonwealth" that would serve as a spiritual beacon to the rest of the world.

John Winthrop's notion of a model community became an enduring part of Boston's heritage. His band was not the first to settle the Bay Colony—others had already built rudimentary homes and settlements along the shore of Massachusetts Bay before his party of Puritans first landed at Salem—but it became the most important. As soon as Winthrop and his successors nestled into the peninsula, with hills dominating the western side and land narrowing to a long southern neck which connected it to the mainland, Boston became conscious of its role as a model to others seeking a spiritual pattern for living. Winthrop went beyond aspiring simply to social harmony; he envisioned "a city in a literal, physical sense, a place where arrangements involving land, property, and status would be planned and organized around a central community institution, the church."[1]

But Boston was molded as surely by its physical setting as by the ideology of its Puritan founders. In fact, Boston has always developed in response to the dynamic interaction between ideals and other factors—

topographical, economic, demographic, and political. The story of Boston is partly that of the evolution of a frontier settlement into an internationally acclaimed city, but it is also the story of how its citizens embraced new ideas about the role of government. During the colonial era the government distributed property, defended its people against both the sea and the enemies who sailed it, and protected them from dangers within their community. Bostonians soon established a distinct pattern in which the public and private sectors collaborated; this partnership has characterized Boston planning for centuries. In a brief look at the first century and a half of urban development, we will see how the appearance of the city and the way Bostonians planned it both arose from this unusual partnership.

Boston had a specific and self-conscious origin. Winthrop founded Boston in an unlikely location, and its topography has always been influential in planning both town and city.[2] Located on a 750–acre peninsula with numerous inlets and marshes, and dominated by a trio of hills, Boston in 1630 gave little promise of becoming a great metropolitan area. Originally occupied by the reclusive Reverend William Blaxton, the Shawmut Peninsula—as it was then known—was soon overrun by hundreds of settlers, among them Governor Winthrop and his band of Puritans. Shawmut had purer drinking water than that found in Charlestown, their original settlement, and the peninsula also provided greater safety from hostile Indians and wild animals. Most important, the peninsula possessed a harbor where ships could enter easily and safely.[3]

Bostonians of the colonial era built their city as none have been able to do since. They began with the raw material of land in the wilderness and followed their fancy as they laid out streets, house lots, wharves, meetinghouses, and markets. The salamander shape of the town remained unchanged in the seventeenth and eighteenth centuries, although the edges of the peninsula were modified by landfill. Early settlers also created the eccentric street pattern that survives to charm and frustrate today. Despite the legend that wandering cows were responsible for the city's maze of streets, Boston was actually laid out on the English pattern, with the focus on the market area, now the vicinity of the Old State House.[4] Furthermore, the first proprietors took pains to adapt their public ways to the local topography, and Boston's original street plan was no more confusing than those of some of its neighbors, notably Salem and Ipswich.[5]

Boston's setting on a hilly peninsula jutting into a harbor protected by numerous islands was both fortuitous and restrictive. The fledgling town depended on the ocean for its survival and growth, yet Boston was hemmed in by the hills, the shore, and the sea, which made expansion

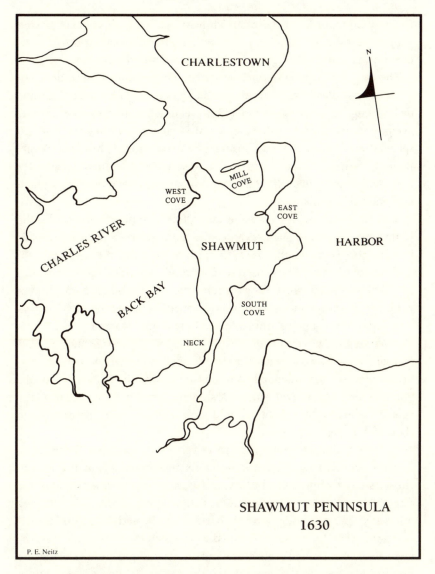

CHARLESTOWN

N

MILL
COVE

WEST
COVE

EAST
COVE

CHARLES RIVER

SHAWMUT

HARBOR

BACK BAY

SOUTH
COVE

NECK

SHAWMUT PENINSULA
1630

P. E. Neitz

Map 1.1 Shawmut Peninsula, 1630. Boston in its earliest form during the colonial period. The narrow neck connecting it to the mainland was gradually expanded over the next several hundred years and all the coves noted on this map were also filled in. Virtually no water's edge was left untouched.

difficult. People and produce came to and from Boston principally by water throughout the seventeenth and eighteenth centuries because there was only one road in and out of town along the Neck to Roxbury, and that flooded at high tide, turning the town temporarily into an island. In 1631 the General Court inaugurated a ferry to Charlestown. In 1638 the

General Court ordered the establishment of a ferry to connect Boston with Winnissimmet (Chelsea) and Noddle's Island (East Boston), a connection maintained into the middle of the twentieth century.[6]

The early townspeople conceived no grand plan for physical development but steadfastly went about creating an entirely new town, building by building. Responding to topography as much as to present economic needs and community values, colonial Bostonians wasted no time on speculation and projections of future growth patterns. As historian Daniel Boorstin writes of them, "perhaps because their basic theoretical questions had been settled, the Puritans were able to concentrate on human and practical problems."[7]

Sam Bass Warner, Jr., uses the term "folk planning" to describe the settlement process in such seventeenth-century New England towns as Boston.[8] He suggests that for a period of time the medieval English tradition of town planning fused with local religious ideology to create an informal consensus concerning the religious, social, and economic framework for the burgeoning community. Nevertheless, as the town and its population grew, a more unified form of planning became necessary, and the role of local government expanded. Bostonians also formed public-private partnerships, created charitable institutions, civic centers and marketplaces, and contended with the Colony and the Crown. Throughout this period, as ever since, Bostonians argued—and occasionally agreed—about what the city should look like and how they should go about achieving their vision.

From a twentieth-century perspective, government involvement in community affairs may appear relatively insignificant, but the Massachusetts Bay Colony and the Town of Boston shared responsibility for directing local growth throughout the colonial period. Massachusetts Bay originally operated under a royal charter that allowed the colony virtual autonomy. The founders established a representative system of government with a bicameral legislature and an elected governor. During the first two decades of the colony's life the General Court evolved into a legislative body representing all the towns of the colony. Boston was the seat of government and, like all towns, subject to the authority of the colonial government. Bostonians conducted their community's affairs in open town meetings, with the execution of decisions assigned to various elected officers. Between meetings seven to nine selectmen, elected annually, assumed the executive function. Most government action was in response to emergencies and conflicts, and so did not require far-reaching planning or close study of the community's needs. In the beginning, however, in keeping with their vision of a city upon a hill, Boston's founders hoped to follow a detailed scheme for mapping out their new town.

The Massachusetts Bay Company hired Boston's first professional "city planner," Thomas Graves, originally of Kent, England. Sent to New England to "lay out" the community where Winthrop and his thousand followers were to settle, Graves journeyed first to Salem, then, in 1630, to Charlestown. There he laid out a model town, allocating a two-acre plot to each individual or family.[9] The community soon moved across the Charles River to the Shawmut Peninsula, but there is no record of Graves' repeating his planning work for the settlers.[10]

Although the Shawmut Peninsula numbered 750 acres, the colonial government also granted the Town of Boston control of the lands of present-day Chelsea, Winthrop, Revere, Braintree, Quincy, Randolph, Holbrook, Brookline, and East Boston as well as Roxbury, Dorchester, and other parts of the current city. By 1639, the total area under town authority exceeded 43,000 acres.[11] By 1794, however, the various additions, with the exception of East Boston, had been stripped away. Mount Wollaston split off to become Braintree in 1640, Muddy River to become the Town of Brookline in 1705, and Tumney Marsh to become the Town of Chelsea in 1739. Other towns followed suit, and by century's end, Boston was once again reckoned a land area akin to its original size—logging in at just 783 acres.

Nevertheless, the land mass controlled by the settlers throughout the seventeenth century was quite large, and once the founders had settled on the site of contemporary Boston, they determined, through their local government, a great deal of the town's early appearance. Assignment of house lots in the community was a civil matter and occupied the town's authorities for the first half-century of Boston's existence. In the early years the town set a maximum on the amount of property one person could own and would not grant any land unless the potential recipient was considered a likely candidate for permanent acceptance into the Puritan congregation. (A 1638 law, for example, specified that land was to be allocated on the condition of "inoffensive carriage.")[12] Legislation enacted by town officials in 1635 allowed houses to be erected only on sites approved by town overseers, who themselves were charged with "avoyding of disorderly building to the inconvenience of streets and laynes" and with "the more comely and commodious ordering of them."[13] The penalty for any builder caught disregarding this order was the forfeiture "of such sum as the overseers shall see fitting."

Town officials designated land for streets and meetinghouses but important patterns of land allocation also arose from private enterprise and the search for wealth. Harvard historian Bernard Bailyn observes that land speculation has always been a major preoccupation of ambitious people in America, and that by 1675 politically influential individuals in Massachusetts had been "granted personal gifts by the legislature totaling 130,000 acres, in parcels far larger than any conceivable personal use could justify and beyond any possible personal use by their children or grandchildren."[14]

In the seventeenth century, the local authorities who allocated land tended to be liberal in granting farmland on the mainland west of the peninsula, but conservative in assigning house lots on the peninsula itself. The colonial legislature granted Governor John Winthrop, for example, numerous properties in eastern Massachusetts, including Winthrop's most cherished possession, Tenhills Farm, a 600-acre property in what is now Medford, and his total holdings in the colony amounted to no more than two or three thousand acres.[15]

Much of the early settlement of Boston took place in what is now known as the North End. Streets were given sensible names like Fore, Middle, and Back to correspond to their locations. Now known as North, Hanover, and Salem Streets, they were then the target of an early street-widening project. In what may have been the first local use of the power of eminent domain, after a fire in 1676 the legislature stipulated that Hanover Street be broadened to a uniform width of twenty-two feet.[16]

Fire was an ever-present danger in the wooden town and prompted the expansion of government power as both the town authorities and the Massachusetts General Court took steps to protect Bostonians from tragedy. Within a year of Boston's founding the government passed the first of many fire regulations. The law was fairly simple: no one was to build a wooden chimney or to have a thatched roof.[17] Another law in 1653 required each home to be equipped with a ladder long enough to reach the roof.[18] The great fire of 1676 proved a milestone in Boston's planning history. After the fire, the selectmen not only passed more rigorous fire codes, but also moved toward street planning on a larger scale. The selectmen persuaded the General Court to require any new house construction to be of stone or brick, covered with slate or tile. The penalty for violating this law was a fine equivalent to the value of the building, unless the selectmen granted an exception. This measure, however well intended, proved unenforceable and was quickly suspended.[19] Wooden houses continued to be built, including "Paul Revere's House," which still stands in the North End and survives as a popular tourist attraction.

After the 1676 fire, the legislature granted the selectmen permission to stake out streets in the burned areas and to require all new buildings to conform with the new lines. The General Court passed an even more important measure in 1692–the first zoning law, which limited commercial activities to designated areas in the town. The legislation allowed boards of health to assign certain places for the exercise of "any trade or employment which is a nuisance or hurtful to the public health, or is attended by some noisome odors," and allowed the board of health to "prohibit the exercise thereof within the limits of the town or in places not so assigned."[20]

In addition to establishing streets and regulating building materials, Bostonians also involved themselves in laying out and building wharves and docks. As early as 1634 an ordinance required a beacon warning, constructed of stones and logs, near every landing place. A law granting property rights to the low-water mark led to considerable land reclamation by providing an incentive to fill in marsh and extend property.[21] Also in 1634, the colony's leaders sanctioned a common landing place on the north side of the great cove. In 1641 the town went a step further and gave title to all the wastelands in the vicinity of what is now Faneuil Hall to a group of merchants for the purpose of building wharves and warehouses.[22] The town granted the merchants' association the right to charge vessels landing on these wharves, and thus Boston gained a more convenient town cove created at private expense.

Just two years later, in 1643, the town granted a group of partners the area of the North Cove facing Charlestown on condition that they erect and maintain one or more corn mills for milling wheat and cereal. These developers were allowed to cut a waterway through the marsh along the present Blackstone Street in order to operate the mill or mills they established. Private citizens further altered the shoreline in 1673 when the town authorized a group to create a seawall, which the colony had suggested as a defense precaution. A special town meeting declined to vote the needed funds but offered to give the mudflats between the town and the proposed wall to private builders, who could then construct their own warehouses, wharves, and docks adjacent to the wall. Over forty subscribers stepped forward to build lengths of the wall from 20 to 150 feet long. Despite the town's success in getting the wall built, the developers' profits were meager and they allowed the wharves to decay.

Commercial interests exercised an ever-increasing influence in shaping the young town. By 1687 merchants with large investments in English and West Indian trade and those engaged in shipbuilding and distilling controlled 66 percent of the town's wealth. Five of the nine selectmen were sea captains, while the presence of Deacon Henry Allen on the Board was "a tangible indication of the continuing influence of the church."[23]

Control by commercial interests expanded in the next century and extended well beyond matters of trade. Enterprising Bostonians of the early eighteenth century helped Boston reach out to surrounding areas.

In 1707 Elisha Cooke, son of a prominent town leader, organized a group of other young merchants to develop the Neck—a narrow strip of land running from Boston to Roxbury. The town meeting approved their plans to widen and fill in portions of the Neck and granted them exclusive rights to the land for twenty years.[24] Similarly, in 1710 and 1711, entrepreneurs built Long Wharf, a public facility. Captain Oliver Noyes and associates took charge of this massive project, an extension of King (now State) Street from the Town House into the harbor. The lengthened wharf allowed merchants to load and unload the largest ships of the day, and formed a picturesque road to the sea. Long Wharf prospered and eager traders quickly lined its half-mile span with rows of warehouses and shops, to which Noyes and his associates gained exclusive rights for forty years.[25]

Despite the importance of commerce, for more than a century Boston had no permanent public market. In fact, Boston exercised only limited and ineffective control over local trade during these years. The town was unique among large communities in Europe and America for having no market, no strict market regulations, and no set market day. Other colonial governments exercised their economic powers by setting prices, wages, and standards of quality, but Bostonians preferred the freedom to choose among tradespeople roving the streets and to buy on all weekdays.[26]

The eighteenth-century battle over the construction of a public market signals an important shift away from the laissez-faire tradition in Boston. A pamphleteer argued against the project by claiming that tradesmen would refuse to bring their provisions to a central market in Boston, preferring to sell only in the unregulated towns of Roxbury and Charlestown.[27] However, Boston was suffering an economic decline in comparison with other seaports, and by the 1720s many citizens were convinced that the time had come for the town to establish more regular trading and market practices.[28] But the battle was only beginning. In 1733 the town meeting voted first in favor of building a market, then against the proposal.

The following year a compromise among the various geographical interests established not one but three markets in Boston, to be located in the north, south, and central districts of the town. Still the issue was not settled: additional legislation actually weakened the existing commercial regulations, and the town refused to pay officials to patrol the new markets. Bostonians, fearing the new markets as an extension of government authority, boycotted them. Then, after a long, cold, and hungry winter, a mob attacked and burned the wooden markets in March 1737. Town authorities ordered the damaged buildings closed permanently the following month.

Three years later Peter Faneuil, a prominent merchant, offered to construct a central market of brick at his own expense. He stipulated that once the market was opened, the town could "legally authorize, regulate and maintain it."[29] Faneuil also offered to provide public space in the new building, including rooms for town offices and a meeting hall. The market issue was still so controversial that the town meeting only narrowly approved this generous proposal by 367 to 360, with the understanding that strolling vendors would continue to be free to operate throughout the town.[30] As a result, many stalls in Faneuil Hall, which was finally built in 1742, stood empty for thirty years.[31]

Among the least controversial and most noteworthy steps taken by local government in the colonial era was the purchase of land for the creation of America's first public park. The forty-five acres of land for Boston Common, purchased by the town in 1634 for thirty pounds from the Reverend William Blaxton,[32] served as a cow pasture for two centuries and as a training ground for the militia until the Civil War.

Then as now, public institutions for criminals and for the poor were a serious concern. In 1657 the town meeting instructed the selectmen to construct a house of correction for anyone who might be "debauched and live idly."[33] Voters advised the selectmen to finance the penal institution with the sale of wastelands, and once again the town financed a public facility without resorting to direct taxation. In 1738 the town also constructed a workhouse for the poor between the Granary Burying Ground and the Common.

As Bostonians made these and other decisions they still depended upon the General Court to make laws, and on six different occasions between 1650 and 1677 sought greater autonomy by petitioning for a municipal charter incorporating the town into a city. Each time provincial authorities killed the proposal. In the eighteenth century, however, Bostonians themselves came to oppose a municipal charter, in part because of a general fear of public authority. Advocates of a municipal charter resumed agitation, however, immediately after the American Revolution, contending that a city form of government, with correspondingly increased powers, would be better for promoting trade, paving streets, and preventing crime. Sam Adams, leader of the Boston Tea Party, spearheaded the opposition to this move. He argued against any change in the charter "from its present democratic plan, in order to build up a new fabric approximating more nearly an aristocratical or monarchical government."[34]

Other neighborhoods of present-day Boston became independent towns during the colonial era and embarked on independently conceived municipal plans. Originally part of land granted to Boston, for example, Roxbury became an independent township and in 1652 appointed a commission to lay out streets. Within eleven years twenty streets were in place, including the present Washington, Tremont, Dudley, Parker, Boylston, and Heath Streets.[35] The streets of Charlestown were also surveyed for the first time in 1670, and the records indicate that both present-day Main Street and Rutherford Avenue were in existence at that time. In 1713 and 1766, the town government of Charlestown again surveyed the streets. In another innovative stratagem for avoiding taxes for public improvements, the legislature in 1760 granted Charlestown permission to hold a lottery to finance the paving of Main Street. The town sold six thousand tickets and awarded 1,245 prizes, retaining 10 percent of the proceeds. Not long after, the opening salvos of the American Revolution and the fires resulting from the Battle of Bunker Hill destroyed all but fifteen houses in Charlestown, which required extensive planning and rebuilding.

By the time of the Revolution, then, Boston and neighboring towns had considerable experience in managing their affairs and in determining their physical appearance. In the colonial era, Boston used a variety of approaches to meet community needs, setting constraints on the location and material of residences, assuming some control over the operations of merchants, undertaking responsibility for public transportation, and drawing on a combination of public and private funds for major improvements to the town. Town officials recognized community needs and steered a pragmatic course to secure their objectives while exercising a limited amount of government control.

Although the legislature of the colony also made laws regulating some aspects of building and street patterns, the most significant decisions were often made by individuals who wanted to develop certain projects they believed would enhance their wealth. These men used the town meeting to advance their goals, making certain that the town authorized and subsidized their individual or collective actions by granting publicly owned land. In all of this, although there were factions and conflicts, there was a certain unity of purpose. Developers built places of commerce that benefited the townspeople. The interests of the entrepreneurs and the town were essentially the same.

Moreover, class interests did not diverge much when it came to developing the emerging metropolis. It was an article of faith that both entrepreneurs and town profited by the sort of public-private partnerships common at the time. Given that Boston's economy depended on its seaport, these arrangements generally related to matters of commerce like building wharves and warehouses. In the post–Revolutionary era, however, public attention increasingly turned to coping with the town's transformation into a city, and to the residential development of Boston's shoreline. These goals required greater governmental leadership, as well as a new order of public-private collaboration.

2
....
The
Great
Selectman

At the turn of the nineteenth century, Charles Bulfinch's new State House capped Boston's skyline and the town took on its now familiar appearance of brick and granite. The shoreline edged out into the water and the town grew steadily. It was a time of energy, prosperity, expansion, and gifted leadership. Charles Bulfinch—an architect, developer, and elected official—exerted unprecedented influence in shaping Boston during this period. The old colonial town evolved into "Bulfinch's Boston" not only because of the architectural gems he created, but also because of his vision of what the city could be.

In his triple roles as architect, entrepreneur and leading town official from the late 1780s until 1817, Bulfinch—along with lawyer-turned-developer Harrison Gray Otis, Uriah Cotting, and others—left his mark on Boston by grasping the opportunities inherent in the economic revival following the Revolution. The turmoil of independence ushered in a new era of government, significant population growth, and the need to rebuild for a new century. Acutely aware of what they were about, these men created much of the Boston we know today. Unlike the colonial period when ad hoc decision-making satisfied the needs of the town, the Federal period placed greater demands on the community's leaders as the pace of growth accelerated. That these men achieved so much was perhaps inevitable; that they did it so well was not.

Boston had been severely damaged by the Revolution. British occupying forces ripped pews from churches and cut down fine old trees on Boston Common the morning before they evacuated on March 17, 1776.[1]

The decade of the 1780s marked a period of depression for the seaport, but the new Federal Congress, meeting in 1789, enacted protectionist trade legislation which favored Massachusetts. Boston's commerce boomed in the next decade, the era of the China trade.[2] The economic success of the town's merchants and shippers expedited the transformation of Boston in the 1790s and early 1800s. Yankee entrepreneurs resumed the West Indian trade and reached out to open routes to South America, the northwest coast of North America, the Hawaiian Islands, and China. The Boston vessel *Columbia*, the first American ship to circumnavigate the globe, inaugurated this trade. Carrying furs from the Pacific Northwest, the *Columbia* and other ships journeyed to Canton. After a three-year voyage the *Columbia* returned to Boston Harbor in 1790, her holds loaded with tea, porcelain, and other goods from exotic ports.

By 1800 the port of Boston enjoyed unprecedented prosperity. Wealth ushered in an era of conspicuous consumption, both public and private. Historian Samuel Eliot Morison aptly compares Boston's merchants of this epoch to those of Renaissance Italy who "wished to perpetuate their names and glorify their city by mansions, churches, and public buildings of a new style and magnificence."[3] Charles Bulfinch stood ready and able to fulfill their dreams. The construction of banks, insurance offices, and shipping facilities symbolized the new affluence. State Street became the center of a burgeoning financial district and adjacent areas boomed. The port itself, source of the new wealth, was improved by the establishment of a federal government shipyard at nearby Charlestown in 1797, following the government's purchase of an unpromising 43-acre mudflat for $39,214. A landmark facility was under way.[4]

Charles Bulfinch was born to wealth during the revolutionary era and matured as the town prepared to take its place in the nation under the new federal constitution written in 1787. Boston's losses during the Revolution became Bulfinch's opportunities. He graduated from Harvard and traveled in Europe. He returned in 1787 expecting, as a gentleman of leisure, to devote himself to the service of his hometown. Financial reverses, however, robbed him of the life of ample means he had anticipated, and for the next thirty years he earned his living as an architect, developer, and town official. Although he never recouped his fortune, his architectural legacy is unsurpassed. Bulfinch designed acclaimed state capitols for both Massachusetts and Connecticut as well as Harvard's University Hall in Cambridge. Surviving structures in Boston designed by Bulfinch include the State House, St. Stephen's Church in the North End, the old Charles Street Jail, several residences for Harrison Gray Otis, and

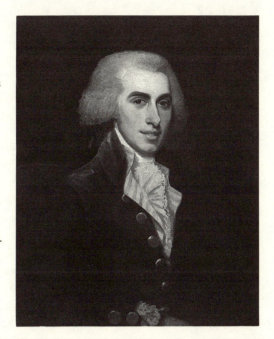

Figure 2.1 Charles Bulfinch, the "Great Selectman." Bulfinch as a young man preparing for a life as a gentleman-architect. Financial reverses launched him on careers as Boston's leading public servant in the early years of the republic and its most famous architect. Portrait, oil on canvas, by Mather Brown 1761–1831. (Courtesy of the Harvard University Portrait Collection, Harvard University, Cambridge, Massachusetts. Gift of Francis V. Bulfinch, 1933.)

the remodeled and expanded Faneuil Hall. One account of Bulfinch's work concluded that "he put his imprint upon Federalist Boston as completely as Bernini did upon Rome."[5] When he began Boston was a town of wood; when he left thirty years later, it was a city of brick.

In addition to these outstanding buildings, Bulfinch's legacy rests on his extensive city planning. In one way or another, he was involved in virtually every significant alteration in the appearance of Boston from the 1780s to 1817, when he left Boston for Washington, D.C. Inspired by the British example of city planning, Bulfinch dreamed of rebuilding Boston in the image of cities in mid–Georgian England.[6] He developed the area of present-day Franklin Street, now part of Boston's financial district; planned a new development to run from Park Street to Beacon Hill; supervised the filling of land and extension of streets from Haymarket to the site of today's Boston Garden, the sports arena, and along the Roxbury Neck out through the South End.

Bulfinch also played a pivotal role in the evolution of the idea of city planning in Boston. As a member and longtime chairman of Boston's Board of Selectmen, Bulfinch was in fact, if not in title, Boston's first city planner. Voters elected young Charles Bulfinch to the board on March 30, 1791. Except for a four-year hiatus from March 1795 to March 1799, he was reelected annually until he left for Washington, D.C., in December

1817 to become the architect of the U.S. Capitol. Bulfinch was chairman of the board and thus the town's chief administrator for nearly nineteen years.

Planning in Boston at that time originated primarily from proposals put forth by individuals and real estate syndicates who wanted to extend the shoreline along the town's peninsula. The democratically organized town had to approve any plans that might alter the original shoreline, whether by fill or by constructing wharves or bridges. As a result, a handful of power brokers packed these meetings and controlled most planning decisions.

Until Boston's incorporation as a city in the 1820s, the annual town meetings decided policy and left enforcement to the selectmen, who were unpaid officials. Their meetings, held weekly and sometimes more often, usually focused on issues of street widening, schools, hospitals, and charitable institutions. Members of the Overseers of the Poor and the Board of Health often attended these meetings as well. Customarily, board members constituted a majority of those present.[7]

This situation gave town officials and developers considerable latitude. They made little distinction between private and public interests, adhering to the generally accepted belief that the town's physical growth was best accomplished by private enterprise. This was the traditional manner of expansion and nothing in the experience of late-eighteenth-century Bostonians indicated the need for any other approach. Privately funded expansion allowed the town to reap the benefits of tax revenues without having to pay the capital expense of filling in land.

Not all planning of this period was, however, devoted to expanding the town. There were other opportunities to rebuild the town from within, such as the great fire of 1794, which offered a chance to create a better town early in Bulfinch's career on the board. This conflagration destroyed nearly one hundred homes, ropewalks, and other buildings.[8] In the wake of the fire the town decided to compensate some owners of the economically important ropewalks and institute some small-scale "rezoning" at the same time. In the days of sail, manufacturers produced the rope in long structures called ropewalks. When fire destroyed the old ropewalk in the region of Pearl Street, the town granted the ropemakers land along the edge of the Common where the Public Garden is now located. This move segregated land uses and ensured residential rather than industrial use of the Pearl Street area. Furthermore, by stipulating that the ropewalk proprietors build a seawall in the Back Bay, the town also benefited.[9]

Under Bulfinch's leadership, the selectmen enacted building code ordinances. A law passed in 1803, for example, required any building over ten feet high to be erected of brick or stone with a roof of slate or other noncombustible material. The most recent such law stipulated only that the largest side or both ends of private houses were to be made of brick or stone. Unlike the innumerable fire codes of earlier days, this one was enforced. Bulfinch, in his multiple roles as head of both the police and the selectmen, and as the town architect, was in a unique position to enforce it.[10]

Fires aside, Boston in the 1790s clearly needed extensive planning. Reverend Timothy Dwight, president of Yale, observed in a visit to Boston in 1796, "Had ten open squares been formed at the proper intersections of the principal streets . . . or had some other plan . . . been completed, Boston would even now have been the most beautiful town that the world has ever seen."[11] Bulfinch was better prepared than anyone else to supply the vision for which Dwight called. On the whole, although Bulfinch dedicated his municipal service to planning the physical growth of the community, it is his work as a private real estate developer and architect of the famous Tontine Crescent that best exemplifies his achievement as a city planner. All that remains of this development today is the graceful curve of Franklin Street; the homes were razed after fifty years when the area succumbed to commercial expansion. The Tontine Crescent "was remarkably advanced for its time and not only in Boston" and won great acclaim for Bulfinch.[12] The financial realities of the entire project were another matter, however, and reduced Bulfinch to bankruptcy.

The Tontine Crescent was actually part of a larger plan for Franklin Place. In 1793 Bulfinch's brother-in-law purchased an estate on Summer Street at the edge of town and persuaded the architect and other investors to join in developing the tract of land as a residential neighborhood. Bulfinch designed sixteen houses along 500 feet of the new Franklin Street. He planned a corresponding row along a curve with an oval-shaped park between. The new houses, of brick painted grey (a Bulfinch innovation), were Boston's first residences built in a deliberately planned group rather than constructed individually.[13] Not content merely to be the architect for these homes, Bulfinch went on to plan, for the first time, a distinct, carefully conceived district called Franklin Place. With its mixture of land uses it was a "microcosm of what Bulfinch dreamed Boston might be."[14] Franklin Place set a pattern for Boston's later development and, as architecture critic Jane Holtz Kay writes, it was here that the "Boston of the town house, park, and city place became the ideal."[15]

Bulfinch envisioned a coherent, planned subdivision which would attract investors and well-to-do residents. In the Tontine Crescent, he directed an ambitious project which entailed housing design and con-

Figure 2.2 The Tontine Crescent in 1857. Designed by Bulfinch, it is shown here looking down toward Arch Street from a location near Washington Street. Filene's is now located to the right. (Courtesy of the Boston Athenaeum.)

struction, opening a new neighborhood, providing public spaces, and creating new streets. Bulfinch designed a park and donated space in his buildings for the Massachusetts Historical Society and the Boston Library Society.[16] In addition, he designed and supervised construction of Boston's first real theater, an integral part of the Tontine Crescent.

Contemporaries saw the Boston Theater as a triumph of the "new social spirit," made possible only by the timely repeal of the old Puritan ban on such buildings.[17] As recently as 1792, with the blessing of Governor John Hancock, the sheriff of Suffolk County had broken into an illegal performance by a troupe of actors performing in a stable converted into a theater.[18] The ensuing riot literally brought the house down. This sorry episode contributed to the repeal of the ban on theaters and led to the creation of the Boston Theater. Vice President John Adams, merchant Thomas H. Perkins, and others backed this project by buying shares in the theater, which was originally estimated to cost $20,000.[19] The actual theater building designed by Bulfinch ended up costing twice as much. It opened on Federal Street in 1794, burned four years later, and was rebuilt more simply.

Despite the grandness of Bulfinch's vision and the beauty of his design, the Tontine Crescent attracted only half the number of investors it needed. Internal and external problems delayed it until Bulfinch was financially ruined. With remarkably poor timing, Bulfinch and his brother-in-law pursued the project despite the fact that the Commonwealth never officially incorporated the enterprise. When his brother-in-law began selling off his shares in 1794, young Bulfinch assumed a staggering debt to finance construction. European wars now threatened to involve the United States and Boston's consequent trade slump made money temporarily scarce; investors and buyers all but vanished. The houses were slow to sell and by 1796 Bulfinch slipped into insolvency. Though a financial disaster for Bulfinch, the Tontine Crescent soon proved a great success for his creditors, the shrewd Harrison Grey Otis and David Sears, who took a long-term view of development and had the financial wherewithal to remain solvent until sales picked up.[20] Never again did Bulfinch have the kind of control over private development that he initially exercised in the creation of Franklin Place, but he had ample opportunity to plan the city according to his ideas for another two decades, particularly as his relationship with Otis grew.

After making his first fortune by exploiting Bulfinch's problems with the Tontine Crescent, Otis again and again carried out plans conceived by Bulfinch for the development of new parts of town. Unfailingly, it was Otis who reaped the rewards while Bulfinch barely scraped by, in part by drawing on commissions for architectural work on these Otis-run projects. In addition, Bulfinch designed three successive residences for Otis, all of which are still standing (on Cambridge, Mount Vernon, and Beacon Streets). The relationship was more complex than that of a real estate developer capitalizing on the expertise of a talented and popular architect, or of one business partner exploiting another.

This strange partnership, sustained for over a decade, never solved Bulfinch's financial woes; on the contrary, Otis continually profited from the ideas of the architect and planner while sharing relatively little with Bulfinch. For example, Bulfinch retained title to the West Boston mud flats along the Charles River during his financial crisis of 1796. He began filling the area in 1805 but the trade embargo imposed during the Napoleonic Wars and the lingering recession a few years later slowed sales. In 1810 Bulfinch placed the land in the hands of trustees. As in the Tontine

Figure 2.3 Harrison Gray Otis in 1809 after over a decade of entrepreneurial development of new Boston neighborhoods, including Beacon Hill and South Boston, and two decades before his election as mayor of the city. "Harrison Gray Otis (1765–1848)," by Gilbert Stuart (1755–1828), oil on wood panel. (Courtesy of the Society for the Preservation of New England Antiquities. Photograph by David Bohl.)

Crescent project, Otis and his associates grabbed the land and Bulfinch failed to profit because he couldn't maintain the necessary cash flow.

Another Bulfinch-Otis project in the 1790s turned out more happily for Bulfinch, however, and reveals the architect's vision of a new shape for Boston. Beacon Hill, the highest spot in Boston, was eminently suitable for Bulfinch's great achievement. His plans for Beacon Hill resembled those for Franklin Place, where Bulfinch transformed what might have been an isolated building scheme into something far more grand. His design for the Massachusetts State House atop Beacon Hill is his most visible and famous work, but his plans for the surrounding area and his years of work to improve it are equally important in tracing the evolution of the city and the process of planning.

In order to understand the planning of Beacon Hill, however, one must first turn to the story of Harrison Gray Otis, who joined the ranks of Boston's wealthiest men through development schemes that swelled his estate from nothing in 1786 to a "considerable fortune" in 1810.[21] Otis's career clearly indicates that Boston's growth in this period was planned, rational, and capitalistic, and not just the accidental result of haphazard natural evolution.[22] Otis, whom his nephew described as "easy, polished, courtly," was born with the proverbial silver spoon in his mouth, the scion of a prominent Boston family: his uncle James Otis was the famous orator of the American Revolution and his aunt was the poet Mercy Otis Warren. Unlike most others who sought their fortunes in Boston at this time, young Otis looked to the land, not the sea.[23] Otis and his associates repeatedly obtained inside information, influenced official decisions, bought land which would appreciate in value, and reaped handsome profits.

The siting of the Massachusetts State House and subsequent development of Beacon Hill reveals Otis's modus operandi. Soon after the American Revolution, the Commonwealth of Massachusetts decided to build a new state house and placed the project in the hands of a special commission in June 1787. Young Bulfinch promptly drew up a plan for the building and submitted it to the commission. Financial and political problems, however, delayed the project until the next decade. The Town of Boston, anxious to retain its status as the state capital, tried to resolve some of the financial problems by building the seat of government largely at its own expense. It succeeded in doing so, and also persuaded the state to grant the town title to both the old State House and the Provincial House. Early in 1795 a state commission was authorized to procure the necessary land for the project. Otis belonged to both the legislative commission which decided to locate the new State House on Beacon Hill and the town committee that purchased the land. Thus he knew in advance that land prices would jump, and cashed in on the opportunity to make early and profitable investments in surrounding properties. This episode in Boston politics clearly "illustrates the relationship between private interests and political leverage," and shows that the development of Beacon Hill as a fashionable residential district, "far from being inevitable, was to a considerable extent the result of deliberate promotion."[24]

At the same time the state adopted Bulfinch's design for the capitol and appointed him one of three agents responsible for executing the plans.[25] Bulfinch received $600 for his design of the State House and as agent earned another $800 for supervising the work on the building, which was finally ready for occupancy in 1798.[26] The region around the beautiful new State House, no longer on the fringe of town, became an attractive area for investment, and Harrison Gray Otis stood to realize an immense profit on his dealings in the area. Back when the town purchased land for the new State House from John Hancock's estate, Otis and his cronies, armed with inside information, had quietly purchased the adjacent property belonging to the famous expatriate artist John Singleton Copley. This land was upland pasture with three wooden houses on eighteen and one-half acres. Copley, who had paid $3,000 for the property and was now living in London, sold it to Otis through an agent for $14,000, making a profit of several hundred percent.[27] But when he learned of the State House plans and realized that the land was suddenly worth much more, Copley decided he had been swindled and sent his son to regain title to the land. The Copleys failed to win back the property but because of the dispute Otis and his associates maintained only a shaky claim for many years.

This legal battle and other outside circumstances delayed profits for the Mount Vernon Proprietors, a syndicate established to sponsor the Beacon Hill development, but all except Bulfinch could afford to wait. The proprietors' foresight and ability to influence events was crucial to their success, for the land was not automatically valuable once the hill was chosen for the State House. Rather, it took a great deal of planning, manipulation, salesmanship, and hard work to make the Beacon Hill development a going concern. It was, from the first, intended as an exclusive residential neighborhood, and so Bulfinch prepared plans for spacious lots with freestanding houses.[28] The Mount Vernon Proprietors built some of the earliest houses for their own use in an attempt to promote the area as a fashionable district and to encourage others to purchase land. Bulfinch also wanted to reserve a large site, 450 by 250 feet, as a private and exclusive garden for owners. He and the Mount Vernon Proprietors tried to retain the rural charm of the hill by requiring that houses along Mount Vernon Street be set back from the street, but within several years this requirement was already being ignored.[29]

In 1799 the proprietors abandoned Bulfinch's proposal for the continued development of the residential section of the hill, and instead adopted the plans of Mather Withington, which maximized profits for the investors but resulted in the more crowded arrangement that predominates today. As a result, Beacon Hill came to connote "horrid crowding upon sites that had once been shaded by great trees" to Bulfinch and others who survived into the 1840s and 1850s.[30] In part external factors caused the changes in the Beacon Hill plan. International problems stemming from the Napoleonic Wars led President Thomas Jefferson to impose a trade embargo in 1807 which virtually shut down Boston's trade. This especially hurt the mercantile classes of Boston, limited the availability of credit, and hindered the development of Beacon Hill as Otis and others felt the pinch in their real estate interests.[31]

Nevertheless, the street pattern clearly demonstrates that the proprietors were anxious to maintain the exclusive character of the neighborhood. Withington's plan aimed to minimize north–south traffic because lower-class families occupied the northern slope of the hill, which was also the home of a long-established African-American community.[32] Similarly, Otis and his associates decided that the nearby red-light district had to go. Appropriately known as Mount Whoredom, the area adjacent to their development was notorious for its bawdy houses and raucous inhabitants. The Mount Vernon Proprietors purchased the land and moved the commercial operations to a more remote section down the hill in the vicinity of the West End. They expected the old district, once vacated of its previous residents, to become an attractive area and a profitable investment. Harrison Gray Otis wrote whimsically to a friend that "we are taking down Mt. Whoredom. If in future you visit it with less pleasure, you will do so with more profit."[33]

The syndicate that developed Beacon Hill recognized the desirability of the Park Street area with its superior height, view, and space, even converting Boston Common from a cow pasture into a public park suitable for fashionable promenades. By removing the town's charitable and penal institutions from the front side of the hill, where the State House stands, the developers furthered their scheme to preserve Beacon Hill as a neighborhood for the well-to-do. In 1737, the town had built a public granary on the present-day site of the Park Street Church (adjacent to the cemetery which still bears the name Granary Burial Ground) to store foodstuffs that the destitute could buy at a price just above cost.[34] Later that century, town planners transformed the area around the granary and today's Park Street from a district of public institutions for the poor into Boston's most exclusive residential section. In 1795 the town voted to sell the granary as part of the plan to build the State House on Beacon Hill. Enterprising Bostonians, precursors of today's preservationists, removed the building to Dorchester and reconstructed it as a tavern. Another public institution, the almshouse, stood at the top of today's Park Street on the site of the Amory-Ticknor House, across from the new State House. It had been built in 1686, with wings added later for the aged and infirm. In 1795, after several years of controversy, the town meeting voted to remove the almshouse as well. Workmen tore the building down and the town sold the land, along with an additional five acres of the Common, to finance construction of a new almshouse on Leverett Street.

These decisions by the town meeting offered abundant development and architectural opportunities for Bulfinch. In 1805 he designed Park Place, a row of four townhouses, each five stories high, for a site located on Park Street just down the hill in front of the State House and bordering Boston Common. In 1810 Bulfinch also proposed his famous Colonnade Row on part of the Common that the town had sold, along Tremont Street from West Street to Mason Street. Bulfinch also planned the new almshouse which was constructed on Leverett Street near the Suffolk County

(Charles Street) Jail, yet another Bulfinch-designed public institution. Bulfinch designed a promenade along the west side of the Common, where he also planned the extension of Charles Street in 1803. In 1812 he supervised construction of a gravel walk, six feet wide, to run the entire length of the Charles Street boundary of the Common. The War of 1812 halted this project. On the Tremont Street side of the Common a mall ran from Park Street to West Street.[35] Then as now it was a popular spot where pushcart and food vendors hawked their wares. Early-nineteenth-century vendors congregated near a wooden fence to sell lobsters, oysters, dough-nuts, cookies, and waffles, as well as ginger beer, spruce beer, and lemon-ade to quench the thirst of pedestrians.[36]

Bulfinch's considerable planning efforts assured the reputation of the territory around the State House as the town's most fashionable address, although one of the most exclusive sections of Beacon Hill, Louisburg Square, got off to a rather shaky start. S. P. Fuller drew up the plan for the Square in 1826 but no one purchased any land for another eight years because of the continued threat of a legal battle over land north and west of the Square. Once sales began, furthermore, purchasers of the land preferred to keep the streets private, despite the proprietors' plan to cede the streets to the city in order to create an open square.[37]

As an architect, Bulfinch was instrumental in changing the old town into a new city, designing and building churches, banks, schools, hospi-tals, and offices. Although Beacon Hill is one of his best-known achieve-ments, he is also credited with making State Street into a financial center by converting it from an avenue of brick-faced shops into "an impos-ing thoroughfare with granite banks and insurance houses."[38] Less well known but crucial to the development of Boston as a whole was Bulfinch's role in developing the land south of the city.

South of the Common, Roxbury Neck (also known as Boston Neck) led to Roxbury by way of Washington Street. Bulfinch's plan to develop the Neck was unusual in that the town government attempted the project by itself, without recourse to private investment. In 1801, the selectmen, under Bulfinch's chairmanship, proposed to develop the Neck into streets laid out in a rectilinear pattern. This proposal was similar to the Beacon Hill plan in that it featured a central square, and tried to avoid the haphazard street planning of earlier years.[39] The selectmen broke the monotony of the plan with Columbia Square, an oval grass plot bounded by four streets, with Washington Street in the center.[40] The proposal in itself was not at all innovative. It was a standard gridiron pattern, first used in Philadelphia at the end of the seventeenth century. Though typical of urban plans in all parts of America from the early days of the

Republic to the 1890s,[41] the grid was not the only alternative. Pierre Charles L'Enfant's ambitious plans for the nation's capital were well known but not easily imitated. New York's gridiron plan of 1811 was famous and widely copied, but the city fathers accepted it only after rejecting the city architect's proposal with its public squares, public structures, and wide boulevards.

Historians take differing views of the gridiron plan. One suggests that New York's grid system embodied the principles of republican simplicity and demonstrated the revival of classical taste.[42] Others argue that in New York, as elsewhere, the simple grid prevailed over more ornate concepts because it was more attuned with "the new urban realities of minimal government responsibility, rampant land speculation, and minimal interference with private property."[43] As Laurence Gerckens notes, the gridiron plan is "the most dramatic expression of the commercial forces that have shaped American development."[44] Boston is no exception, as can be seen in the development of the South End.

When Boston sold off land in the area now known as the South End, its civic leaders expected considerable profits and charged a committee to "lease and manage said sales in such a manner as shall appear to them for the interest of the town."[45] However, the town realized only $13,000 in the first decade of sales, and interest in the district declined even further before reviving in the middle of the century. Here, as in the Tontine Crescent, Bulfinch's timing was off. His work, however, was not wasted; it provided the basis for development fifty years later. Meanwhile, in his private capacity as an associate of Otis, Bulfinch worked on other areas of the town; districts which competed with and undercut the development in the South End.

Otis and others planned the private development of several newer sections of town. In all of these ventures—Front Street, South Boston, Broad Street, India Wharf and the Mill Pond—the local government was intimately, albeit secondarily, involved. Private enterprise took the lead, and the town allowed certain developers to plot the future; in fact, these entrepreneurs controlled the town meeting. And the system worked: where the publicly planned development of Boston Neck failed, these privately planned developments succeeded.

The first of these, all of which blossomed in a remarkably short time, was Front Street, described a century ago as "the first systematic and cooperative enterprise having in view the enlargement of the limits of Boston by making new land."[46] Along what came to be called Harrison Avenue, this project added nine acres of land to the town. The proprietors filled mud flats on the periphery of the town, from Front Street to the shoreline, at a cost of $65,000. They began work in 1804, completed the project a year later, and incorporated the land into the town in 1809. An innovative feature of this project was the owners' stipulation that no structure be erected less than ten feet from the line of the street, thus guaranteeing wider avenues.[47]

The next scheme encompassed an even larger territory. South Boston, long known as Dorchester Neck, was part of the still independent town of Dorchester. The 560-acre site east of today's Dorchester Avenue and 9th Street beckoned to Harrison Gray Otis, who, along with others, recognized that this hilly peninsula could be the next major development. Although Dorchester Neck was some distance across the harbor and mudflats from Boston, Otis's associates succeeded in annexing it to Boston in 1804. They promptly laid out a street plan and constructed a bridge to join the land to Boston.

Dorchester Neck (which Otis renamed South Boston) had been occupied, but barely, since 1673. Between 1700 and 1800 the number of families rose from three to ten. Early in the nineteenth century Otis quietly amassed property there just as he had on Beacon Hill. In 1803 he surreptitiously petitioned the town of Boston to annex Dorchester Neck, circulating a story that the ten families living there had sold their property to a gentleman from the West Indies who, seeking a better climate for his health, wanted to live on the peninsula. The truth soon came out: the "West Indian gentleman" was actually a Boston syndicate headed by none other than Harrison Gray Otis. It included Jonathan Mason, Joseph Woodward (another of the Mount Vernon Proprietors), and others, who now owned the valuable land.[48] Otis recognized that competing real estate interests could muster strong opposition to his plans in the town meeting, and so prudently withdrew his petition for annexation. He opted instead to go straight to the legislature, which overrode opposition in both Dorchester and Boston town meetings, and enacted the appropriate legislation in March 1804.[49] Dorchester received no compensation. The Otis syndicate completed a bridge seventeen months later, and, as expected, land values rose sharply.[50] With its height and sea breezes South Boston appeared a natural spot for growth and Mather Withington, the town's leading surveyor and the man who laid out Beacon Hill, was hired to plan South Boston. He laid out the main streets running north and south, while the cross streets ran east and west.

In 1805, rivals of Otis petitioned the General Court for permission to build a dam or additional bridge to connect the town of Boston to South Boston. The petition shows that Bostonians of the time were not only aware of city planning, but actively engaged in it. In arguing the need to build a second bridge, the writers articulated (however insincerely) concerns about the cost of housing, the quality of life, and the dangers to the health and morals of the working classes residing in Boston, stating:

> Already the land within the peninsula and within a convenient distance for business, is too dear for the laboring classes of the people. Rents absorb an undue portion of their industry, and throw a burden upon our productive labour. The prices of rent abridge the comforts, and expose the health of the poor. The population already accumulates too much in straitened dwellings, confined inclosures, and narrow avenues. A due regard to their health, their morals and their comforts, requires a wider space, and a purer atmosphere.[51]

The petitioners' remedy was intended to make South Boston more accessible to the working classes and less desirable to the potential residents Otis had hoped to attract. They also noted that problems among the workers led to "disadvantageous competition with our sister cities" and contended that Boston has "a deep interest in her manufactories and mechanic arts," many of which could be conducted with "as great advantage and at smaller expense, in the environs than in the centre of the city." In developing plans for the city's growth these petitioners cast their eyes not only on South Boston; they also asked, "Who can behold the narrow and crowded peninsula of Boston and then turn his eyes on the adjacent hills of Charlestown and Dorchester, without saying that a gracious and beneficient Providence has given these ampler fields to counteract the evils of a confined territory, and a crowded population?"[52] These petitioners were not alone in seeking to fulfill a regional version of manifest destiny.

Like other toll bridges, Otis's Dover Street Bridge—which connected Boston and South Boston—was built by private corporations; unlike the others, it failed, mainly because of its poor location and the fact that in 1810 there were still only 350 people in South Boston. Both the bridge and the residential development failed because for once Otis was outmaneuvered politically. The commercial interests of the competing Front Street district prevented the Otis group from building their bridge in the most convenient location, thus discouraging people from settling in South Boston. A second, toll-free South Boston bridge, built in 1828 at the more convenient Federal Street site, delivered the final blow to the South Boston Bridge Corporation. The Otis bridge paid no dividends and the owners finally sold it to the city in 1833, which immediately opened it for free travel.[53]

In 1805, while Otis and his syndicate were opening their South Boston bridge, another group led by Uriah Cotting, and including Otis and Francis Cabot Lowell, planned the development of Broad Street down to Fort Hill (near today's South Station). The Board of Selectmen, chaired by Bulfinch, considered a street development plan prepared for the Broad Street Association by private citizen Bulfinch. In June the plan was approved and Bulfinch, the chief selectman, hired workmen to stake out the street and tear down old buildings.[54] In a project which may be regarded as a forerunner of urban renewal, Bulfinch and the town transformed both India Wharf and the area between Batterymarch and State Streets.

Bulfinch also drew on both roles in his final project of the first decade of the nineteenth century. The area between Haymarket and North Station is now known as the Bulfinch Triangle in recognition of the man who laid out the streets and designed the original buildings. At one time a mill pond generating water power for various grain mills, the area had long since fallen into disuse and become a notorious breeding ground for disease.[55] Many developers set their sights on extending the downtown region by filling in the pond. Not surprisingly, Harrison Gray Otis led the group that ultimately won the development rights.

In March 1804, a group of businessmen created the Mill Pond Corporation and floated a proposal which aroused more controversy than any other in this crucial decade. It took several turbulent town meetings for the voters to approve filling the pond, partly because it was so close to the heart of Boston.[56] Otis sweetened his plan by promising to use only gravel from Beacon Hill to fill in the Mill Pond and by persuading six of Boston's leading physicians to attest to the healthfulness of this idea. As time went on, however, the Mill Pond was filled with anything the developers could find, including oyster shells and rubbish.

The 1807 agreement between the Mill Pond Corporation and the town is a prime example of a mutually beneficial public-private partnership. Coinciding interests and decision-makers facilitated their cooperation, but such arrangements were not always smooth. The Otis group agreed to fill in the Mill Pond within twenty years and give the town one-eighth of the newly created land.[57] The agreement furthermore stipulated that the proprietors should accommodate several Baptist churches which had settled along the pond for convenience in practicing total immersion in the rite of baptism. The town also specified "that Streets shall be laid out and completed fit for paving according to a plan delineated by the Chairman of the Selectmen."[58] Bulfinch, in both his public and private roles, was—like Otis—neck-deep in most of these schemes. Although several competing sets of street plans were prepared for the new Mill Pond site,

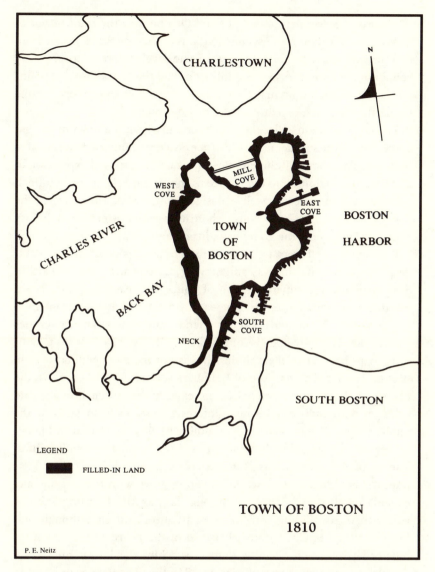

LEGEND

█ FILLED-IN LAND

TOWN OF BOSTON
1810

P. E. Neitz

Map 2.1 Town of Boston, 1810. The filled-in land is shown here all along the edges of the original Shawmut Peninsula. The focus of the town had long been in the North End (the appendage between the Mill Cove and East Cove and the area along the harbor). The great amount of commercial activity is seen in the many piers and fingers of land with wharfs extending into the water on the harbor side.

the town chose Bulfinch's design and workers began the job at once under his supervision as chairman of a special committee of selectmen.[59]

The Mill Pond project marked the end of the Bulfinch-Otis partnership and the close of an expansionary era. Although Bulfinch remained head of the Board of Selectmen until 1817 and Otis became the third mayor of Boston in 1829, their greatest contributions to shaping the city came from their private roles as architect and real estate developer, respectively. They could not have wielded so much influence had they not possessed political power, yet their roles in the planning and development of Boston came primarily from their activities in the private sphere.

The concentration of local power (particularly in the town meetings) conferred an unusual degree of influence on a few committed persons like Bulfinch. The phrase "Bulfinch's Boston" is no exaggerated expression of admiration. In addition to his service as the "Great Selectman," Bulfinch was the chief of police, as well as designer of the State House where the law was enacted, the Court House where it was administered, and the city and state jails where the guilty were incarcerated.[60]

Bulfinch himself went to jail for failing to pay his debts in July 1811, despite the fact that he was still serving as chairman of the Board of Selectmen and the superintendent of police. He reappeared at a board meeting on August 7 after his debt was financed, and no further mention was made of the matter. That his friends, supporters, and colleagues would allow this to happen is somewhat mystifying.[61] Despite his talents, or perhaps because of them, Bulfinch was not the most popular man in Boston. His son Thomas said of Bulfinch's service on the board, "In the course of these improvements he necessarily was often brought into collision with individuals whose interests were made to yield to the public exigency."[62] In their study of Bulfinch's Boston, Harold and James Kirker assert that Bulfinch often opposed the commercial and political leaders of the town in his effort to create a modern city.[63] The facts indicate, however, that he worked hand-in-glove with most of the successful capitalists of the time; his problem lay more in alienating ordinary voters than in colliding with influential figures. Indeed, although Bulfinch's colleagues elected him chairman of the Board of Selectmen for nineteen years, each year the voters gave him the lowest number of popular votes of any town official. In 1815 the electorate even failed to give him one of the nine seats on the board. The elected members, however, refused to take their seats unless the town held a new election and elected Bulfinch.[64] Considering all the political and financial problems he faced, it is not surprising that he finally left Boston in 1817 to accept the post of architect of the U.S. Capitol.

In his many years of service to the town, Bulfinch was able to affect the shape of Federal Boston, not only as an architect and hopeful real estate developer but also through his active service in local government. Bulfinch was not especially successful as either a businessman or a politician, but when the two roles coincided he accomplished enough to make the town his own. He clearly understood the possibilities of creating new neighborhoods on old sites or newly filled-in land, and while some of his most noteworthy projects, such as Park Street, the Bulfinch Triangle, and State Street, were constructed under his supervision, others like the South End remained for successors to implement years later.

In his public and private personas, Bulfinch is a transitional figure. In serving both the private sector which spurred Boston's growth and the public sector which began to channel speculative forces, he left his mark as much on the process of shaping the city as on the physical city itself. The local government only partially determined the direction and volume of development but that it did at all is largely because of Bulfinch's expertise and interests. By his preeminence in architecture and urban vision he made greater government involvement in the planning process palatable and even desirable. This, however, owed more to his singular abilities and personality than to any consensus about the proper role of government.

Bulfinch is crucial in the history of planning in Boston because he saw the emerging city in comprehensive terms. Throughout the seventeenth and eighteenth centuries the town planned on an ad hoc basis, usually accepting the initiative and efforts of whoever wanted to build wharves, walls, and streets. No one before Bulfinch conceived whole sections of the town or understood their relationships to one another so well. He laid out streets, created entire neighborhoods, and designed buildings appropriate to specific land uses. Bulfinch did not resort to zoning, but by being so intimately involved in every aspect of development, he paved the way for a new conception of planning as a comprehensive activity appropriate to government.

Although Bulfinch established the precedent for active government involvement in developing the city, it was not until Josiah Quincy, "the Great Mayor," took office in the 1820s that Boston was shaped by an individual whose influence derived solely from public office. Boston became a very different city in the Quincy era as local government assumed a greater role in planning, but it will forever bear the imprint of Charles Bulfinch, "the Great Selectman."

3

....

The Growth

of a

Metropolis

The half century after Boston became a city in 1822 was a time of terrific change. The period saw an unprecedented expansion of the geographical borders of the city, in part made possible by technological advances that led to the creation of the new South End and the filling in of the Back Bay. At the same time, a tremendous influx of immigrants and the first exodus to the suburbs altered forever the city's demographics. Against all of this swirled the immense political ferment of the mid-nineteenth century. The nation was wracked by sectionalism and the threat of violent fracture, but the city grew. In the five decades from the 1820s to the 1870s, Boston reshaped itself not only by filling in the Back Bay and the South End, but also by annexing the land and population of several neighboring towns: Roxbury, Dorchester, Charlestown, Brighton, and West Roxbury.

Bostonians found that the expansion of the functions and nature of municipal government was no less dramatic than the rapid extension of the city's land mass. From the creation of Quincy Market to the elaboration of plans for a vast South End to the magnificent scheme for the Back Bay and the destruction of the old Fort Hill, city and state government moved toward new ideas about the nature of planning.

Economic growth continued to influence Boston's evolution. Great textile fortunes were made and mill towns sprang up. During the War of 1812 Boston merchants turned from commerce to industry and in subsequent years established ever greater enterprises. Francis Cabot Lowell's career illustrates this transition—experienced in Boston as in the nation—from commerce to manufacturing. Lowell started out as a merchant, then diversified. From 1801 to 1806 he invested in a distillery, a bridge located in Springfield, Massachusetts, and land in Maine. His principal investments, however, were in Boston real estate. Associated with Otis, Cotting, and others, Lowell was a speculator in the Batterymarch Street Associates, India Wharf, the Broad Street Association, and Wheeler's Point Wharf Company.[1]

Lowell, along with Nathan Appleton, a fellow merchant, transformed the expanding local factory system from a threat to Boston's commercial elite into an asset, partly through planning.[2] Instead of making their fortunes by importing manufactured products, they made goods in new factories and founded the Boston Associates to develop the planned industrial cities of Lowell and Lawrence. Along with a few other closely linked corporations, the Boston Associates turned New England into the textile center of the nation by utilizing the waterpower and capital available in the region. Few mills were built in Boston itself but the mill owners invested their textile fortunes there, fueling the growth of the city throughout the nineteenth century. A new class, dubbed "Brahmins" by Dr. Oliver Wendell Holmes, emerged and set the standards for Boston for decades to come.

The economic shift from commerce to manufacturing altered the shape of Boston in the nineteenth century. Textile industries in the outlying regions required new storage facilities and wharves in Boston; warehouses grew to hold the products of the mills; and enterprising Bostonians expanded commercial quarters and built new docks.[3] Commerce also retained some significance in determining the character of the town. Close by in Charlestown, for example, was the wharf of Frederick Tudor, an enterprising Yankee who conceived the idea of selling ice to habitants of warmer climates. By 1833 Tudor was marketing his ice as far away as Calcutta, India; he had staked out yet another significant export for Boston. Throughout these decades Boston commerce with the Mediterranean, China, India, California, and South America, supplemented by the American coastal trade, produced fortunes and fame. It also created capital which could be invested in the city.

Shipbuilding emerged as a great enterprise in this period. Most famous of all shipbuilders was Donald McKay, whose East Boston shipyards set the standard of excellence for sailing vessels in the middle of the century. Spurred by the desire for speedy travel to California in the Gold Rush of 1849, McKay and others produced a series of beautiful clipper ships. During the five years from 1850 to 1854 various shipyards in East Boston produced these swiftest of sailing vessels. Most celebrated was McKay's *Flying Cloud,* which averaged 101 days in the journey from New York to

San Francisco. These ships soon lost preeminence as steamships and railroads rendered the clippers obsolete in the years after the Civil War.

Similarly, Boston was eclipsed as a center of commerce and finance in those same years. The great wealth created by the shipping and textile magnates in the first half of the century paled in comparison to the fortunes amassed by industrialists in other regions of the country in the second half of the century. Boston money was conservative, its guardians preferring certain but limited dividends. Consequently, Boston capital was less productive in the years of explosive technological and economic change. Proper Bostonians continued, however, to be people of great wealth, especially compared to the immigrants who began populating the city during the middle of the century. Throughout this era the Brahmins who controlled Boston capital constructed luxurious new homes, clubs, churches, and cultural institutions that did much to change the face of the city. Most important, the well-to-do were able to maintain their business interests in Boston yet move their residences away from the core city when trains allowed them to commute between home and office.

The transportation revolution of the nineteenth century created a new and expanded city as Bostonians spread into the suburbs and then annexed these outlying regions. These transportation networks were planned by corporations which secured approval from state and then local governments. Thus, although there was little governmental or official planning, the public sector often supported these projects indirectly.

In addition to the extensive network of tracks, private corporations also built several bridges to allow greater access to Boston from markets and growing suburban areas north and west of the town. The most famous of these, the Charles River Bridge, opened in 1786. Ferries connecting Boston to Cambridge and to Charlestown had limited capacity and use because of their size and the vagaries of weather. Thus, the state legislature readily agreed when a group of entrepreneurs, "The Proprietors of the Charles River Bridge," proposed a bridge across the harbor to Charlestown in 1785. The state authorized the proprietors to build a bridge (according to detailed specifications) and to collect tolls. Harvard College was compensated for its loss of revenue; by statute the ferry had contributed a portion of its profits to the school since early in the previous century. Interestingly, passengers could still discern the Puritan influence in the double tolls charged on Sunday.[4]

The bridge, 1,470 feet long and 42 feet wide, opened on Bunker Hill Day in 1786 and met with immediate success. Travelers from north of Boston found their overland trip halved or better. Farmers coming from Medford, for example, no longer had to journey thirteen miles through

Cambridge, Brookline, and Roxbury; now the distance totaled only five miles.[5] The advantages of bridges crossing the Charles were obvious and in 1793 the West Boston Bridge to Cambridge opened. Commerce boomed, tolls poured in, and Harvard skimmed money from the profits of both bridges. But by the 1820s, as the economy underwent revolutionary change, the public came to see such exclusive charters as a hindrance rather than an aid to business, and representatives of the new wave proposed construction of a toll-free bridge to Charlestown.[6]

The legislature approved the new bridge, which opened in 1828 and collected tolls for six years before becoming a free crossing in 1834. In the meantime, the proprietors of the original Charles River Bridge went to court and fought a lengthy and losing war against the Warren Bridge project, which the U.S. Supreme Court finally concluded in 1837. The Supreme Court ruling against the Charles River Bridge was a landmark decision in constitutional law: it established the principle that charter rights granted by the state were not absolute and exclusive. A new and more flexible outlook on property rights prevailed in the aftermath of this ruling. Generally, government authority to establish these speculative building companies lay with the Commonwealth, not the local government, and the construction and operation of bridges and other transportation systems were private affairs. However, when they proved business failures, as did Harrison Gray Otis's South Boston Bridge, the municipal government would often take over responsibility. (This pattern repeated in the limited government supervision of railway transportation, also the result of entrepreneurial rather than municipal planning.)

In the mid-1820s horse-drawn coaches ran on set schedules along routes to Boston from Roxbury, Charlestown, and Cambridge and by the 1840s the first commuter rail opened up more distant areas as residential suburbs. The Boston and Lowell, the Boston and Worcester, and the Boston and Providence railroad companies all began operations in 1835. The three railroads were originally designed for longer journeys but their managers soon recognized the lucrative possibilities of shuttling people over short distances. Between 1839 and 1845 the railroads requested and secured facilities to accommodate suburban travelers.[7] Boston was thus serviced by some form of rail, either steam-locomotive or horse-drawn streetcars, both of which continually expanded. Suburbanites' promotion of free bridges, omnibuses, and commuter rail lines triggered a revolutionary change in mobility and transformed suburban expectations about work, residence, shopping, investment, and government.[8]

Boston itself was transformed by the political developments of the 1820s. Most notably, the old town became a city. The town meeting form

Figure 3.1 Josiah Quincy, the "Great Mayor." Quincy led Boston's government to develop the marketplace behind Faneuil Hall and later served as president of Harvard University. Quincy's son and great-grandson both became mayors of Boston. (Courtesy of The Bostonian Society/Old State House.)

of local government had survived until 1822 when, after many attempts, Boston finally incorporated itself as a city and adopted a charter providing for eight aldermen and a forty-eight-member common council. The council appointed city department heads, and the mayor had little to do but appoint committees.[9] The first mayor, John Phillips, represented a compromise between the forces supporting Josiah Quincy and those backing Harrison Gray Otis. Mayor Phillips exercised only a minor role as mayor during his year in office, perhaps acknowledging the concerns of those who feared the power of the new system of governance.[10]

Josiah Quincy, descendant of a well-known family, was elected the second mayor of Boston in 1823. Although the new mayor harbored misgivings about the city form of government, expressed in his inaugural address,[11] he exercised the power of the mayoral office without reservation. To overcome the weaknesses of the charter, he placed himself at the head of all important committees of the Board of Aldermen and resolved to appropriate as much of the municipal function as possible.[12] In assuming greater power than the charter stipulated, Quincy seized the authority necessary to accomplish his goals for the city, but his maneuver ultimately called down severe criticism and led to his departure from office.

During his reign, Quincy appointed a marshal of the city to oversee the police and public health, supervised a rigorous streetcleaning campaign, and brought sewers under municipal control. He presented a study to the city council on the issue of supplying pure water to Boston and although no action was taken he has been credited with the conception and instigation of a plan for adequate municipal water facilities.[13] Mayor Quincy also established a House of Industry to replace the almshouse and instituted prison reforms by founding a House of Reformation in South Boston. Over the years, this district accumulated so many institutions for the poor, the criminal, the sick, and the insane that residents of South Boston protested in 1847 that the city government was turning their peninsula into a dumping ground.[14]

Quincy was an activist whose sense of duty propelled him into leading a raid on Boston's notorious center of vice, known as "the Hill," in the West End. The brothels, dance halls, and gambling houses located there enjoyed a lively business, seven days a week, and drew the ire of neighbors, perhaps concerned as much about property values as morality.[15] A mob had already destroyed several brothels in 1820 before Quincy launched his successful posse-style attack on the West End. In 1825, residents of the North End, apparently feeling slighted by the mayor's concern for another part of town, took matters into their own hands in the so-called "Beehive Riot" against a brothel in their district. For the most part, however, Mayor Quincy was not charged with neglecting to wield power.

Quincy's most important and famous project, Faneuil Hall Market-place, is popularly known as Quincy Market. No one doubted the need for new market space and improvements in the district, but few were eager to do anything about it. With only 14,000 square feet of stall space for the commerce of this growing city, Faneuil Hall was in drastic need of renovation or replacement. Conditions were deplorable. The farmers' market was cheek by jowl with all the other food markets and butcher shops. Dealers in fish and vegetables were exposed to the winter weather and vulnerable to sickness. The streets had always been narrow, crooked, and heavily congested, but it took the death of one child and the mutilation of another in traffic accidents in 1824 to spur the city to action.[16] In the first attempt to relieve traffic congestion in 1811, the town had required all trucks and sleds to be numbered and registered.

Economic prosperity encouraged Mayor Quincy not only to address public health issues but also to dream of constructing new buildings on land reclaimed from the sea and from the demolition of old, dilapidated structures. Quincy spearheaded Boston's earliest foray into publicly funded urban renewal. He demolished old buildings, constructed new ones, expanded the town's land area, and created new streets, all in one fell swoop. He modestly claimed many years later that the project was "probably without a parallel in the history of any other city."[17]

The mayor supervised as many parts of the operation as possible. Beginning in 1823 he and a committee prepared to acquire land in the area around Faneuil Hall and the adjacent town dock by sizing up the various holdings and conferring secretly with each owner over a period of months.[18] The mayor insisted on secrecy to prevent the owners from realizing what was going on and raising their prices. Owners, however, were reluctant to reveal the estimated value of their land for fear that assessors would use the information to increase their taxes. By the end of the year negotiations collapsed.

Quincy then reluctantly decided to go public with his plans and use the power of eminent domain, an important innovation in the development and planning of Boston. Previously this power had resided with the surveyor of highways, but by earlier assuming other facets of this office, Quincy had laid the groundwork for usurping yet more legal authority. On January 24, 1824, the mayor produced a plan showing the improvements he had in mind. Although he received overwhelming support for two motions—to extend the markets toward the sea, and to exercise the power of eminent domain in obtaining the necessary land—opposition was not long in coming.

The *Boston Patriot* of January 13, 1824, criticized the project because it ran counter "to the spreading-out tendency" of the city.[19] (What we often think of as a twentieth-century issue concerned Bostonians at the beginning of the nineteenth century as well.) Naturally, there was neighborhood competition. Some residents of the North End and investors in the rival Boylston Street Market believed Quincy's projects harmed their property values. Nevertheless, in the next election Quincy and all the aldermen were reelected with almost no opposition. The mayor won 3,867 votes out of 3,950 cast. Quincy interpreted the results as a mandate and credited voters in the districts near Faneuil Hall for welcoming the prospect of the new market.

After the election the project moved along swiftly. The city purchased the land and commissioned Alexander Parris to design the structures. By July 1824, all land that could be negotiated for had been acquired, including property belonging to Harrison Gray Otis and to Governor Eustis. A few other sales were consummated after arbitration. At first Quincy thought of extending Faneuil Hall itself, but instead decided to create the linked structures known today as Faneuil Hall Marketplace. Alexander Parris designed the 535-foot Greek Revival markethouse and two flanking rows of granite-faced, brick buildings. The city built the market in the center and sold lots to investors who then built the other buildings in accordance with strict design criteria. The buildings had to be of brick or stone, cover the entire lot, have a cellar, slated roof, and granite front, and line up with adjoining stores. Only a close examination reveals that both the North and South Markets are composed of separate structures integrated in one unified design rather than each being a single massive building. After the city acquired the land, cleared any intruding structures away, and filled in part of the cove, construction was ready to begin. The land was auctioned off in April 1825, twenty-five lots on the north side and twenty-two on the south. Construction proceeded according to city-mandated regulations and Parris's plans.[20]

This early mix of public and private sector development is a truly remarkable achievement. Quincy's market project involved the government in acquiring property, clearing it, placing public structures and new street plans in the area and selling other parcels to private developers who had to conform to established criteria. The project cost the city $1 million, but by 1826 downtown Boston was completely transformed.[21]

The central granite building is Faneuil Hall Market, long referred to as Quincy Market in tribute to the mayor. Just before its dedication in August 1826, one commentator said that "Boston has long enjoyed the reputation of a neat city, [and] it bids fair indeed to gain the reputation of a handsome one."[22] Caleb Snow wrote effusively in 1828 that the project exceeded all others "in boldness of design, in promise of publick benefit, and in energy of execution."[23] In 1872 Samuel Adams Drake wrote in *Old Landmarks and Historic Personages of Boston* that the market was a monument to Quincy's genius and perseverance. He added that "any other man would have succumbed to the obstacles he had to encounter, but he pressed on to the accomplishment of his purpose. He invested the sluggish town with new life, and brought into practical use a new watchword—progress."[24]

After the success of this project, however, Quincy became increasingly embroiled in municipal controversies and in 1828 lost his bid for another term as mayor. He accepted the presidency of Harvard in 1829 and served until his retirement in 1845 at the age of seventy-three, shortly before his son and namesake became the eleventh mayor of Boston. The first Mayor Quincy died in 1864 at age ninety-two, leaving among his many descendants a five-year-old great-grandson and namesake who would become Boston's thirty-second mayor.

One controversy that dogged the first Mayor Quincy involved the supply of water to the city. Private water companies like the Aqueduct Corporation had been bringing water to Boston in pipes of pitch pine from Jamaica Plain and other sources since the 1790s. This water provided fire protection and supplemented domestic wells, but both the poorer and the less densely populated sections of the city long remained without the benefit of this service. Quincy was unable to persuade his city to take a more active role but his son later championed the cause successfully.

Over time, Bostonians came to accept the provision of water as a legitimate function of city government. Although as late as 1857 a private corporation was formed to supply the towns of Roxbury, West Roxbury, and Brookline with water, legislators and voters became convinced that only an agency not interested in profit could supply water consistently and fairly.[25] A municipal referendum in 1836 approved the concept of municipal ownership of Boston's water supply but the Panic of 1837 and ensuing fiscal crises delayed action until the next decade. The issue of water supply continued to be controversial and the center of several mayoral elections.

In the 1840s, the second Mayor Josiah Quincy finally persuaded the city to authorize creation of a reservoir and pipes to supply the city's water. Groundbreaking for the Cochituate Reservoir and pipe project took place in 1846, and just over two years later water began flowing to Boston Common. Despite its $4 million pricetag, the project was deemed a success because of Quincy's skillful management of the enterprise and its financing. The new system included an aqueduct capable of delivering eighteen million gallons daily from Lake Cochituate in Natick to a reservoir in Brookline.[26]

It was Harrison Gray Otis, however, who immediately succeeded the Great Mayor in 1829. Otis was now at the end of his long career in public service. Born in 1765, Otis could remember watching British troops march off to meet the Minutemen at Lexington in the opening days of the American Revolution.[27] Since then, in addition to being a successful real estate speculator, he had served as a member of the U.S. Congress and as both Speaker of the House and president of the Senate in the Massachusetts state legislature. He also lost an election for the governorship before at last winning the Boston mayoralty in 1829. He had moved, then, from national to state and finally to local government office.

Boston's economy boomed during Otis's mayoralty, and with prosperity the city widened many streets, installed new sewers, and began replacing whale oil street lamps with gaslight. In 1830 the city government moved from its seat in Faneuil Hall to new quarters in the Old State House. But most important for our story is Otis's impact on the evolution of city planning. He began his term in the mayor's office by setting forth his ideas about shaping the city and pleading for some type of city planning. In his inaugural address of 1829 he correctly observed that the new form of transportation, the railroad, created conditions which required government planning. He feared that unless the city took action "the streams of our prosperity will seek other channels." In other words, the government should be in the service of private capital. In his next two inaugural speeches Otis called for harbor improvements, which were soon carried out, and the filling in of the Back Bay, which he described as "an immense morass . . . a receptacle of seeds of disease."[28]

The geographical extension of the city inaugurated in the early nineteenth century by Harrison Gray Otis and other developers had stalled after the first decade. Bulfinch's South End plan remained in limbo because the area was only sparsely settled and not even completely filled in. Part of the sluggishness in growth resulted from the byzantine sales procedures, which at first required the city council to approve individual sales; a semi-annual public auction was instituted in 1825, but sales remained slow.[29]

The city never made much money from the South End project, a primary motivation, so in 1829 Mayor Otis created an Office of Land Commissioners with the power to lay out streets and sell the land. The year before, S. P. Fuller had set forth a new plan for developing the South End. Whereas the original 1801 plan called for a large block pattern, Fuller made a rectangular block formation by adding through-streets parallel to Washington Street, and by substituting row houses for the freestanding ones which were the ideal of an earlier age.[30] Since the plan covered an area still largely under water, little actual development took place.

The municipal government mapped out the street plan for the region and then turned the entire project over to private developers. In 1833, the South Cove Company was established to extend streets in the South End to the east of Washington Street. This development had a novel and striking purpose. Whereas previous landfills were matters of convenience— rocks from a hill being leveled had to go somewhere, or the material sold in order to reduce the town debt—here in the South Cove the city deliberately assigned private developers the task of providing space for a growing population.[31] The principal objective of the South End landfill was to accommodate more residences.

In the early 1800s, people had begun abandoning the city by leapfrogging over the South End to other towns served by horse-drawn streetcars and the new means of transport, the railroad. Once bypassed by the rail systems, the South End faced an uphill battle in attracting new residents, and the city failed to respond to this problem for nearly twenty years. The private sector, however, did respond, and focused on more promising areas than the South End. In the 1830s a group of Democratic party politicians headed by David Henshaw briefly attempted to develop South Boston into a resort but ultimately abandoned their plans.[32] Subsequently industry took over much of the area. Developers also turned to East Boston in the 1830s. The East Boston Co. formed in 1833 to sell off the land, but the establishment of a railroad terminus in 1836, the Cunard Line pier in 1840, and the increasing number of shipyards producing world-class clippers in the 1850s marked the real beginning of growth for the former Noddle's Island.

The celebrated "war of the cows" on the Common drew far more attention during Otis's administration than development of new land. The city charter of 1822, which forbade the sale of the Common, protected the revered park. Additional statutes placed restrictions on adjacent buildings and roads but now residents of the swank new homes on Park Street challenged the time-honored tradition of cows grazing on the Common. Otis led the attack, arguing that preserving a pasture for a mere 65 cows in a city with a population of sixty thousand "is an anomaly for which it will be difficult to find a parallel in any City of the world."[33] After a series of fierce battles, numerous protests, surveys and politicking, Otis won and drove the last cow off the Common in 1830. Boston's most fashionable citizens could now stroll through the park without fear of stepping in cow dung. Despite this victory, the aristocratic Otis decided that he no longer cared for municipal governance and declined to run for a fourth term in 1831.

The Boston that emerged over the four decades after Otis left office was far different from the city he governed. Boston planning in the decades after Harrison Gray Otis retired from the mayoralty was not dominated by individuals like Bulfinch and Quincy; rather, it was characterized by dramatic change in both physical shape and the functions of the city government. While the nation sprawled over vast western regions, created a national communications and transportation network, and fought a Civil War, Boston was transformed by demographic, physical, technological, and economic change. The city's population swelled from 61,000 in 1830 to a quarter million in 1870, mainly due to immigration and the annexation of surrounding towns and cities. The old city increased from an area of approximately 1,000 acres to a metropolis of 30,000 acres as hills were cut down, shorelines filled in, and the adjacent communities of Dorchester, Brighton, Roxbury, Charlestown, and West Roxbury were added to the city. Despite this explosive growth, the city

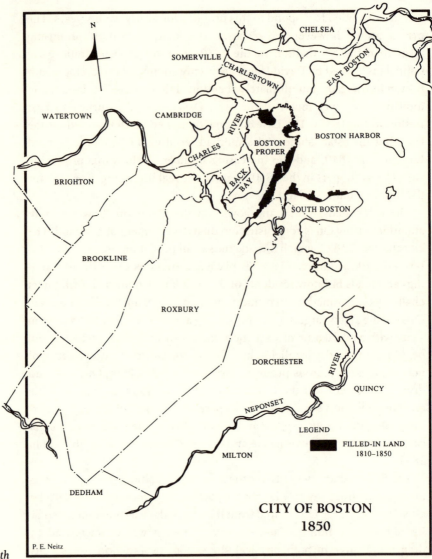

CHELSEA

SOMERVILLE

CHARLESTOWN

EAST BOSTON

WATERTOWN

CAMBRIDGE

RIVER

BOSTON
PROPER

BOSTON HARBOR

CHARLES

BACK
BAY

BRIGHTON

SOUTH BOSTON

BROOKLINE

ROXBURY

DORCHESTER

RIVER

QUINCY

NEPONSET

LEGEND

FILLED-IN LAND
1810–1850

MILTON

DEDHAM

**CITY OF BOSTON
1850**

P. E. Neitz

....
*The Growth
of a
Metropolis*

54

Map 3.1 City of Boston, 1850, showing landfill. The original Shawmut Peninsula
is shown in relation to other towns which emerged in the first two centuries of
Boston's existence. The filling of land continued, most notably in the old Mill
Cove and along the southeastern section of the peninsula. The development of
South Boston is also begun.

began to lose economic strength relative to other American cities but
from the 1830s to 1870 Boston was too preoccupied with its own expansion to notice the decline.

To a large extent, as always, private capital determined the form of the

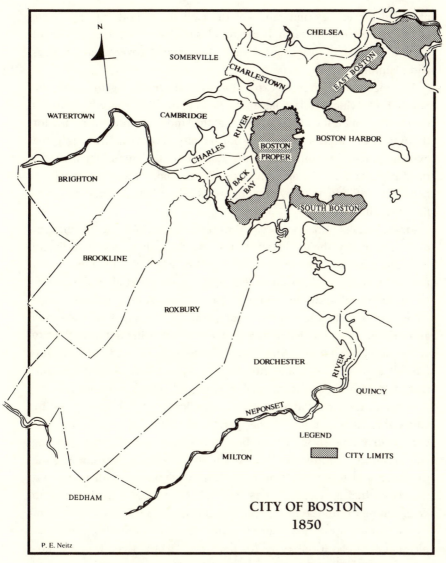

CITY OF BOSTON
1850

P. E. Neitz

Map 3.2 City of Boston, 1850, showing political units. By this time Boston included not only the original Shawmut Peninsula, but also South Boston and East Boston, both early examples of highly planned private development.

city throughout the nineteenth century. As William Pease and Jane Pease write, "Boston's economic leaders—be they directors or independent merchants and manufacturers—relied on entrepreneurial skills and private capital to guide and finance urban development."[34] The interesting thing about this era, however, is the degree to which the government began to direct the course of development. It is true that the private sector provided the energy and much of the capital but both city and state governments took increasingly active roles in channeling the direction of growth, ultimately fostering the idea of expanded government services and planning.

The inexorable surge of expansion in mid-century again led to the South End, which at last began to flower. In 1848 the city council's Committee on Public Lands argued that the land could provide homes for thousands of citizens as well as bolster city revenues. Criticizing the existing practice of land sales in the South End, the committee invited a third plan for the development of the South End, which was drawn up between 1848 and 1850 by city engineers Ellis S. Chesbrough and William Parrott.[35]

Mayor Josiah Quincy, Jr., began the process by authorizing the filling in of the South Bay, the grading of tracts, and the laying out of streets and lots. Under his successor, Mayor John Bigelow, a sewage and drainage system was installed and city engineers designed a number of small squares. In addition to dotting the area with parks and planning additional side streets for greater variety, other urban planning extras included: alleys to allow service wagons hidden access; a horsecar trotting out from the city center along Washington Street; and fountains, trees, and wrought-iron fence.[36] Furthermore, numerous restrictions were placed on the height, materials, setback, and manner of dwelling permitted in the squares.[37]

Whereas the Back Bay represented a radical shift in Boston planning and architecture, the South End, patterned on London, continued "the conservative English-influenced Boston tradition of residential planning and architecture found on Beacon Hill and the areas surrounding the Common and the Public Garden." Margaret Supplee Smith points out that city officials, from Charles Bulfinch on, played a critical role in determining the appearance of the South End. These officials were influential in four areas: first, through the design, modification, and implementation of various plans for the street layout; second, by exercising municipal control over building through incentives and covenanted deeds; third, by encouraging high-class occupancy through the use of certain streets and squares as focal points; and fourth, by reserving tracts of land for public institutions like the Boston City Hospital. The decision to incorporate a number of squares appeared in the plans of 1848–1850. The streets of the South End had been laid out wide enough so that the elongated parks called "squares" were relatively easy to insert. Where necessary, the city bought back land from abutters.[38]

As the nineteenth century progressed and urban poverty and crime increased, escape from the city became a desirable choice for many. As

Stanley K. Schultz writes, "native residents, both wealthy and working-men, who felt oppressed and endangered by the immigrant presence could flee Boston proper," while within the city's borders "the walls of residential segregation by occupation, income, and class began to rise in the 1850s."[39] The South End development was conceived as a government strategy to counteract the suburban exodus, but the city's own efforts to provide affordable housing torpedoed the plan to retain wealthy residents in the South End. The demolition of lower-class housing in the Fort Hill area and the Commonwealth's development of the Back Bay further

Figure 3.2 Bird's-eye View of Boston. This 1850 view shows the first stages of the fill of the Back Bay in the foreground. Beacon Street is to the left with numerous bridges over the Charles River to Cambridge and Charlestown where the newly built (1825–1843) Bunker Hill Monument looms over the Boston Navy Yard. The Bulfinch-designed State House is to the left of the Boston Common at the top of Beacon Street which runs down alongside the Public Garden and begins to cross the Back Bay. The upper right corner of the view shows a part of the South Boston peninsula. The business district and the harbor are in the center. (Lithograph by John Bachman. Courtesy of Historic Urban Plans, Ithaca, N.Y.)

lessened the prospects for the South End. First, in the mid-1850s Mayor Jerome V. C. Smith deliberately encouraged persons of moderate means to settle in the still-young neighborhood by selling the land at public auction and by establishing more favorable loan terms for purchasers. Smith asserted that "enterprising men of limited means" could not afford to build on city lands because the size of the down payment on the purchase of the land, 10 percent, was too high. He called for lowering the deposit to 1 percent along with an annual interest rate of 5 percent. These praiseworthy goals came, oddly enough, from the same man who recommended selling Faneuil Hall Marketplace and erecting a tower on Beacon Hill for the use of the police and fire departments.[40] Moreover, Smith's proposals ran counter to the earlier intention of the South End planning: to make the district attractive to well-to-do Bostonians tempted to leave the city for suburbs like Newton which were developing at this time.

The decline of the South End also stemmed from the large-scale urban renewal project carried out in the late 1860s at Fort Hill (near today's South Station). Earlier in the nineteenth century the Fort Hill area was home to merchants such as Thomas Handasyd Perkins, but it soon declined as a residential neighborhood because of its proximity to the business district. Many old-time residents moved away, allowing the encroachment of trade and real estate speculation, and accelerating Fort Hill's deterioration into a slum for Boston's immigrants.[41] These immigrants were for the most part Irish peasants, especially in the famine period of the 1840s and 1850s. In that decade, the immigrant portion of the city's population jumped from 22 to nearly 46 percent.[42] Oscar Handlin points out in his classic study, *Boston's Immigrants,* that the population growth after 1840 "violently upset the process of physical adjustment," and refers to the example of Fort Hill as a once fashionable region taken over by speculators and allowed to deteriorate.[43] Old mansions and warehouses were converted to house large numbers of Irish immigrants. Gardens disappeared under shanty dwellings as every square yard of space yielded to human habitation. The quarters were expensive, crowded, and unhealthy. A committee investigating conditions in the 1840s concluded that the Broad Street district, with 3,131 inhabitants, had an average of thirty-seven people per house and an average area of seven square yards per person. The committee concluded, "Here is a density of population surpassed, probably, in few places in the civilized world."[44]

In the fall of 1866 the city began clearing the Fort Hill area. Reports held that some hill-dwellers clung to their homes "until the roofs were taken off, and their rooms laid open to the city," but by 1872 the entire hill was leveled and the dirt used, in part, to fill in the new Atlantic Avenue.[45]

Figure 3.3 Taking down Fort Hill, 1869. Currently near the site of International Place and adjacent to the Central Artery, this site has been transformed many times since it played a part in Boston's colonial defense system. (Courtesy of The Bostonian Society/Old State House.)

Not for the last time an urban renewal program forced poor immigrants to seek new housing. Many of those displaced moved to the nearby South End and contributed to its decline as a fashionable residential neighborhood. The relocation of poor residents to allow extension of the downtown business and commercial district foreshadowed slum clearance efforts in the West End neighborhood in the twentieth century. Once again, the powers that be allowed a residential district to deteriorate until it became a serious health and fire hazard, and could be cleared to make way for downtown commercial and financial interests.

Neither the city's affordable housing policy under Mayor Smith in the 1850s, nor the policy decision of his successors who removed the poor from Fort Hill in the 1860s, nor the financial panic of 1873 were responsible for the fate of the South End; above all else, it was the proximity of a more appealing residential alternative. Just as the slum dwellers of the Fort Hill section gravitated to adjacent territory in the South End, upper-class citizens naturally filled in the Back Bay, conveniently sited next to Beacon Hill, home of the city's elite. The Back Bay, which was also close to the downtown centers of commerce, was a fairly natural and logical choice of residence once it came into being. Thus, although the South End was fashionable until the early 1870s, it did not appeal for long to the upper classes.

In *The Late George Apley*, John P. Marquand portrays the snobbishness that led "proper Bostonians" to withdraw to the Back Bay. Apley's father purchases a home in the South End "under the impression that this district would become one of the most solid residential sections of Boston." One morning the senior Apley observes his neighbor emerge from his house in shirt-sleeves. The next day Apley sells the house and moves the family to Beacon Street: "Father had sensed the change; a man in his shirt sleeves had told him that the days of the South End were numbered." The neighborhood, no longer the preserve of a suitable class, quickly degenerated into "the region of rooming houses and worse."[46]

It is worth noting that the decision to create the Back Bay as a residential area was a state matter beyond the control of city leaders, who had no opportunity to limit competition between city- and state-sponsored projects. Sadly, public policy—embroiled in the state's development of the Back Bay—must be recognized as the crucial factor in the decline of the South End district.

One of the greatest land reclamation projects of America until the twentieth century, Back Bay was literally a bay in back of the town. The Back Bay's 580 acres, mostly mudflats at low tide, were filled in and transformed into one of the most beautiful and architecturally important areas of Boston, and indeed the country. The Back Bay was not, however, a highly planned enterprise. It developed gradually throughout the entire nineteenth century. As incredible as it may seem now, this neighborhood noted for its stately homes was originally intended as an industrial district.[47]

Uriah Cotting conceived the idea of a great mill dam stretching across Back Bay in 1813. He envisioned numerous mills located along the dam to allow American industry to fill the gap in manufactured goods during the war with Britain. Cotting joined with others to form the Boston and Roxbury Mill Corporation, which defeated other proposals to win legislative approval of its plan. The project met delays and Cotting died but

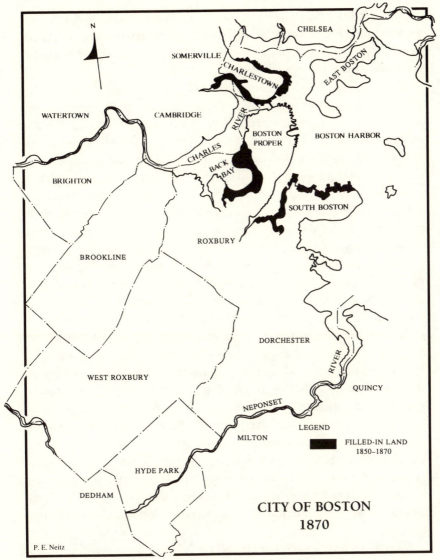

Map 3.3 City of Boston, 1870, showing landfill. The Back Bay is beginning to fill in from the Public Garden as is the South End along the edges of the Neck. Both Charlestown and South Boston continue to fill in and diminish the distance between themselves and Boston. The extension of what would become the Fan Pier is apparent as the largest piece protruding from South Boston's mudflats.

others completed the mill dam and it opened as a thoroughfare in 1821. At first called the Milldam, then Western Avenue, and finally Beacon Street, it cost $600,000 and extended one and a half miles from the foot of Beacon Hill to Sewall's Point in Brookline.[48] Several factors proved the undoing of the mill project: the war with Britain ended and trade in manufactured goods from abroad picked up; new mill towns proliferated along the Merrimack River; and by the 1840s steam power had rendered water-powered mills superfluous.

The obsolete Mill Corporation spun off a new Boston Water Power Company, with neither parent nor offspring doing well. The water power was never as strong as expected and the construction of railroad trestles across the Bay in the 1830s and 1840s decreased it further. Indeed, trains transformed the Back Bay into the land mass we know today. New economic interests controlled the legislature and established railroad routes along the Bay, although any modern environmental impact review would have revealed the injurious consequences of constructing such rights-of-way. The water no longer flowed in and out with the tide but settled in stagnant pools; refuse and waste soon created a stinking bog.

Undeterred by the mess, a number of visionaries drew up plans to develop the Back Bay. Robert Fleming Gourlay, a native of Scotland who visited Boston and New York in the 1840s, prepared the most notable of these proposals. After only a few months in Boston, Gourlay submitted a report—in the form of letters, notes, and elaborate plans for developing the city, including the Back Bay.[49] Long before the 1903 construction of the Charles River Dam allowed development of a park along the edge of the river, Gourlay called for the creation of such open space. His predictions for population growth over the next century were amazingly accurate, to within one tenth of one percent.[50] He also suggested routes for railways and tunnels, foreshadowing twentieth-century transit systems. Gourlay conceived and mapped out a system remarkably like the contemporary Red Line of the Massachusetts Bay Transportation Authority, which runs from Cambridge to Dorchester, and the Green Line, which trundles from North Station to Tremont Street and out along Boylston Street.

Gourlay believed "no other city on earth has such opportunity, such materials to work with, such a field to improve, such a subject for profitable speculation, and certain gain." He imagined being on top of the State House, viewing the finished work after the city had been rebuilt according to his blueprint. From his perch he envisioned a grand crescent in the distance and a city of wide boulevards. On nearby Boston Common he proposed a five-story pagoda with a flower garden.[51] Further afield, and most important for actual development, he saw an improved Charles River. Gourlay planned a Charles River Basin with a tree-lined boulevard, but no one paid any attention to Gourlay or his plans, and he washed his hands of Boston.

Figure 3.4 A view of the Back Bay from the State House, prior to 1858. This is almost a reverse view of figure 3.2. It shows the Public Garden on the left and Beacon Street extending across to today's Kenmore Square. Back Bay is crossed by several railroad lines which obstructed the flow of water and made its fill necessary. (Courtesy of The Bostonian Society/Old State House.)

Meanwhile the Back Bay still stank, and in 1849, David Sears outlined a plan for filling it in. He proposed leaving a seventy-five-acre oval lake which would maintain the flavor of a more pristine Back Bay. This proposal served only as a starting point for discussion. Finally, in 1852, a legislative commission formally proposed filling in the Bay, but the city and state argued for several years over ownership. Inevitably the state won—it acquired the area by eminent domain—and distributed parts to the City of Boston, the Mill Corporation, and the Water Power Company, retaining the largest section for itself, then selling it for a substantial profit.[52] The state created a commission to oversee the landfill project, but proceeded "with singularly little coordination with what the city was doing in the South End."[53] Bainbridge Bunting, in his *Houses of Boston's Back Bay*, blamed the city for failing to cooperate with the state but noted

Figure 3.5 Back Bay landfill in the 1850s. This photograph was taken from the corner of Beacon and Charles Streets. The emerging Public Garden is to the left of the sidewalk and trees. Behind it is a train which has carried gravel from Needham to fill in the flats. A closer look reveals the unloading platforms, stone-crushers, and pile-drivers used in the operation. (Courtesy of The Bostonian Society/Old State House.)

that the commissioners "were still determined to lay out the land held by the Commonwealth with all possible dignity and impressiveness."[54] Bunting summarized the commissioners' goals succinctly: to create a district that was spacious, homogeneous, and ornamental.

Architect Arthur Gilman, inspired by the French approach to city planning, laid out a well-devised sectional street system with broad thoroughfares running East–West and cross streets running North–South. He also specified sixteen-foot alleys at the rear of house lots for deliveries by the butcher, the baker, and the grocer.[55] Gilman achieved the spaciousness the commissioners sought by plotting five broad avenues of widths varying from 90 to 200 feet. The Commonwealth ensured the homogeneity of the district by placing restrictions on the property: buildings had to be at least three stories high and constructed of masonry and, except for minor appendages, a building's facade could not project beyond a uniform line set for each street. These restrictions applied to property sold by the state. The Boston Water Power Company and the Boston and Roxbury Mill Corporation set similar restrictions on their lands.

Although the new Public Garden had a long way to go before it became the tree-filled beauty it is today, it clearly helped attract people to the Back Bay. Its story is important, and begins in 1837, when Horace Gray and a crew of horticulturists petitioned the city council for permission to use the site for a public botanic garden.[56] Two years later the council granted their request. These enthusiasts began to prepare the site, but Gray lost his fortune in 1847 and work halted. In 1850 a city council committee recommended using the land for housing, but fortunately the idea was discarded. The state, to the contrary, enacted legislation that forever committed the Public Garden to park space, leaving open, however, the possibility that the land might be used for a new city hall. A special committee of the city council appointed George F. Meacham to draw up a plan for the Public Garden. James Slade, the city's engineer, modified the plan, and the Public Garden began to bloom.

Another interesting aspect of planning for the Back Bay was the consideration given to the creation of a so-called cultural district. In 1859 the Committee of Associated Institutions of Science and Arts organized to petition the state legislature to reserve a tract of land for educational, scientific and cultural institutions. In 1861 the legislature went so far as to set aside one block for the Museum of Comparative Zoology and the new Massachusetts Institute of Technology.[57]

The Commonwealth sold one section of the Back Bay at a time, using the proceeds from the sale of one block to fill in the next and netting a total of $3,442,205 after expenses.[58] The state laws regulating the Back Bay set a fixed minimum price which ensured upper-class occupancy.[59] As with the South End, people were slow to buy in the new area. Unlike the South End, however, the responsible government, in this case the State, chose to preserve the area for the well-to-do. Although the state initially sold a number of lots at discount prices on Commonwealth Avenue to prominent gentlemen who promised to construct their own homes in the new district, the official rationale—that because these men were taking a risk on a new district, they should receive a discount—held. The maneuver succeeded and ensured the neighborhood's snob appeal.[60] This conscious planning choice meant that while the city and private entrepreneurs were planning the "rival" South End the state was undercutting it.

In the years after the Civil War, the success of the Back Bay quickly became apparent, and one of the great visionaries in Boston planning, Robert Copeland, formulated further development schemes. He published *The Most Beautiful City in America: Essay and Plan for the Improvement of the City of Boston* in 1872. Copeland, a "landscape gardener" with offices in Philadelphia, was among the first in the United States to use the term "city plan," and his book offered Bostonians a careful consideration of how to segregate the industrial and residential sections of an urban area. Copeland's plan, according to John Reps, a leading historian of city planning in the United States, was "no mere abstract design for a vacant site but a serious and clearly thought out proposal for the redevelopment of a great city." As such, it "should be recognized as the first modern city planning study, a forerunner of the thousands to come later and the superior of most in literary quality and logic of presentation."[61]

Copeland suggested that planning a city was "a problem which admits of division into parts, of discussion and measurement" but conceded that "we have not been accustomed to plan in this way." He recognized that many would see municipal planning as interfering with private property, but argued that it was a better alternative than the all-too-familiar situation "when the necessity comes to drive an avenue through a man's factory, close up his business by indicting it as a nuisance, cut down the road in front of his house, leaving him to get down as best he may, or raise his house into the air to be got onto only by a ladder."[62]

Copeland was inspired by the work of the great Baron Haussman in redesigning Paris and offered specific suggestions to Bostonians for a government center, a park system, an embankment along the Charles River, and a system of wide boulevards. He envisioned a large common surrounded "by the city and state buildings of the future" and proposed a traffic circus around the State House from which six radial boulevards would lead to all sections of the city.[63] Copeland also imagined an enlarged Charles River basin containing a lagoon with two islands named "Circus Island" and "Elysian Fields." A railroad and parallel boulevards would follow the sweep of the basin.

Copeland found Boston picturesque and wanted to preserve its beauty, which he believed was as important as its commercial and financial core. He was less concerned about the downtown than about expansion into the newly acquired suburbs, where he thought surrounding hills should be preserved like landscape gardening on an estate. Rather than level the hills, he proposed crowning each summit with groves of trees and gardens. By contrast he saw South Boston, with its two waterfronts and two railroads, as "particularly well adapted to commerce and manufactures," predicting accurately that speculators would fill in the flats for these purposes. Copeland also predicted that by "reserving the South Boston heights as suitable and sacred to good dwelling, we may expect that the entire waterfronts and the Dorchester Neck will become densely populated with warehouses and workshops."[64]

Copeland's park system—which called for both large and small parks near densely settled sections of the city—was designed especially to help the poor. He wrote that "if it is possible to provide by restrictions, or regulations, for the erection of cheap and comfortable houses near the chosen land for the poorer classes, the great purpose of the park would be more certainly secured." Though sensitive to the costs of his various proposals he denied that they would require higher taxes. Instead, he proposed that the city condemn and acquire unused land and assess adjacent owners for the cost. The money required to develop the public lands, asserted Copeland, would be appropriated "by posterity as they want to use them, and will be no addition to the burdens of today."[65]

Copeland's work, along with that of Gourlay and Sears, was visionary, yet it had little immediate impact. Although these men (and others like them) stimulated Bostonians to think about shaping the city, they usually failed to persuade anyone to adopt their plans. Economic and technological change rather the vision of planners held sway—along with countless business and personal decisions, the population movement out of the city, and the concomitant polarization and separation of classes.

Most Bostonians in the early nineteenth century lived in mixed-income areas. Segregation by class awaited fulfillment of the transportation revolution, which dramatically sped the flight from the city, and the advent of the streetcar suburb, defined by Sam Bass Warner, Jr., as "an attempt by a mass of people, each with but one small house and lot, to achieve what previously had been the pattern of life of a few rich families with two large houses and ample land."[66]

A frequently cited reason for the retreat to the suburbs is the arrival of masses of immigrants. Another, the advance in technology that allowed people to live far from their place of work, may have been even more significant than the push of poor immigrants. At any rate, the implications for Boston were immense. Aside from the immediate health, sanitation, and crime problems bred by the slums, long-term problems result, including increasing suburban flight, cultural conflict, and political struggle. In planning for its growth, Boston has long had to contend with the ramifications of a tense situation that first developed when a new ethnic group overwhelmed the old city and eventually seized political power.

Paradoxically, the great period of annexations to Boston also took place during the middle of the nineteenth century. No sooner did people move

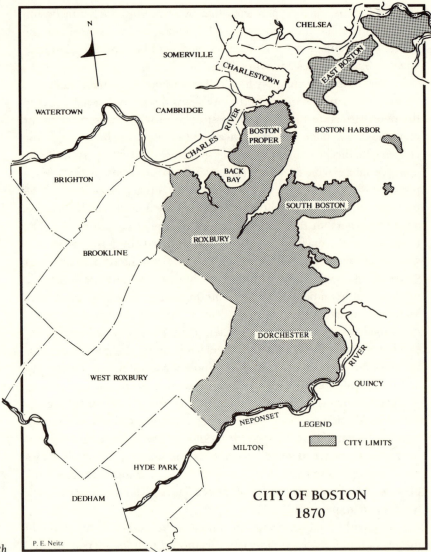

N

CHELSEA

SOMERVILLE

CHARLESTOWN

EAST BOSTON

WATERTOWN   CAMBRIDGE

CHARLES RIVER

BOSTON
PROPER   BOSTON HARBOR

CHARLES

BRIGHTON   BACK
BAY

SOUTH BOSTON

ROXBURY

BROOKLINE

DORCHESTER

RIVER

WEST ROXBURY

QUINCY

NEPONSET   LEGEND

MILTON   CITY LIMITS

HYDE PARK

CITY OF BOSTON
1870

DEDHAM

P. E. Neitz

Map 3.4   City of Boston, 1870, showing political units annexed since 1850. This was an era of tremendous growth for the city as neighboring Roxbury was annexed in 1868 and Dorchester in 1870. These towns had their own street systems and services which had to be integrated with Boston. Note the separate Town of West Roxbury had split off from Roxbury in 1851 and remained independent for several more years before it followed the path of its parent town and was annexed to Boston. Another new political unit was the Town of Hyde Park, created in 1868 when Dedham, Milton, and Dorchester each ceded land for this purpose.

to the suburbs than they wanted to make the suburbs part of the city. But annexation required the approval of the state legislature. Roxbury was the first to vote for annexation in 1867. Dorchester followed two years later, while in 1873 Charlestown, Brighton and West Roxbury voted likewise. Essentially, these areas joined the city in search of municipal services, a quest which could cut both ways. Suburban voters wanted the city to provide the services but the city was at times reluctant to accept new expenses. In 1856, for example, the state legislature authorized Boston's annexation of Chelsea, but the voters of Boston, fearing the costs of extending water and sewerage, rejected the move.[67]

Roxbury was a different story. The Town of Roxbury, named in 1630, had already become a city in 1846. During the expansion of the nineteenth century the legislature approved the annexation of Roxbury in 1867 but required voter approval in both Boston and Roxbury, thus giving Roxbury greater control of its fate than had been accorded the other towns annexed in the same period.[68] During the ensuing campaigns numerous advocates of union argued that the only way to solve the town's water and sewer problems was to join Boston. Others pointed to improved streets as a reason to favor annexation. Voters in Roxbury approved annexation by a three-to-one vote while the margin favoring it in Boston was even greater. On January 6, 1868 Roxbury formally became a part of Boston.[69]

Opponents of annexation in Dorchester in 1869 appealed to Yankees' ethnic and class solidarity by arguing that annexation would allow an influx of Irish Catholics displaced by the Fort Hill demolition project. One speaker at an anti-annexation rally charged that the Irish "would not make very desirable neighbors."[70] George D. Tucker maintained that "the laboring men of Dorchester were a higher class than those in Boston." Despite such arguments, Dorchester voted for annexation 928 to 726 and the town was officially annexed to Boston on January 3, 1870.

West Roxbury, originally part of Roxbury, was set off as an independent town in 1851, but remained separate for less than a generation. The annexation issue in West Roxbury hinged on water supply. The level and quality of water in the town was deteriorating and residents feared that Boston might acquire access to good water and thereby thwart West Roxbury's efforts to secure an independent source. After years of study and debate West Roxbury voters approved annexation and finally merged with the city on January 5, 1874.[71] Today's neighborhoods of Jamaica Plain and Roslindale emerged with their own strong identities distinct from West Roxbury, their parent district. This explains why people have difficulty determining the precise borders between Roslindale and West

Roxbury. The reason is the "border" never existed except in the minds of postal employees who identified a Roslindale district in the early 1870s, or later in the hearts of the district's residents.[72]

Brighton, an independent town since it split from Cambridge in 1807, was annexed January 5, 1874, along with Charlestown, which was settled in 1629 and incorporated as a city in 1847.[73] The Town of Brookline remained steadfastly independent but in 1874 ceded land to Boston along Commonwealth Avenue to permit the recently acquired Brighton district to be joined to the rest of Boston by a narrow strip of land.

Largely as a result of the annexation movement, Boston's population jumped from 140,000 in 1865 to 341,000 ten years later. Boston contained a mounting proportion of the area's total population until 1880, and thereafter showed a decline. In 1880 the city's population of 362,839 was 45.5 percent of the population of what was later identified as the Standard Metropolitan Statistical Area.[74]

Regional problems and solutions have been part of the Boston experience ever since. Brookline's 1874 vote against annexation was the first significant defeat for the consolidation movement in Boston and the nation. According to historian Kenneth T. Jackson, after this "virtually every other Eastern and Middle Western city was rebuffed by wealthy and independent suburbs."[75] In the cases of Dorchester and West Roxbury, however, it became clear that although some feared and opposed annexation, others felt that the serious problems of life in a new industrial age required the assumption of more public responsibility than could be provided by a small town government. Economic and technological changes necessitated choices, and all of these factors affected Boston's growth.

To accommodate this growth, the local government laid out major arteries. Atlantic Avenue, which Walter Muir Whitehill cited as a classic example of over-optimistic planning, took more than four years to construct starting in the late 1860s and cost $2.5 million, but created a great thoroughfare.[76] One casualty, however, was a series of Bulfinch-designed warehouses on India Wharf. At the same time, the city spent a million dollars extending Broadway across Fort Point channel to Albany Street and another half million widening Federal Street, the principal route to South Boston.[77] Huntington Avenue was laid out in 1872, following Columbus Avenue and Commonwealth Avenue as the third great artery to the west and south.[78]

In 1872 Boston celebrated its fiftieth anniversary as a city, a period marked by phenomenal expansion. The focus throughout these decades, once Quincy Market was constructed, was on expansion away from the downtown. The city grew by landfill and by annexations of neighboring towns. Economic forces, demographic changes, and technological developments fueled this expansion but local government took on an ever-increasing role in planning and developing the city. This greater role started with Mayor Josiah Quincy, who created a vibrant new commercial center in support of the private sector, and continued with Mayor Smith in the 1850s. Smith used the sale of city lands to engineer the social composition of the community. The city's aggressive efforts to develop the South End indicated an enlarged notion of the appropriate role of government in shaping the city. Still, private economic interests continued to predominate. The new and powerful railroads inadvertently affected the city's topography by placing railroad tracks across the Back Bay. By cutting off the tidal flow the railroad made the mammoth landfill operation inevitable. The manner in which the state chose to accomplish this reclamation in turn shaped the social development of the South End.

Social and demographic forces of the mid-nineteenth century increasingly determined how Boston evolved. The influx of immigrants introduced new pressures on the old city and pushed the city's population outward from the center. People were no longer compelled to work and live within the confines of a small walking city. The railroad allowed them to distance themselves from the crowded urban center by moving out to garden suburbs from which they could commute easily to town. Once in the suburbs they demanded water, schools, and fire protection on a level their new communities could not provide. This need drove the movement to annex outlying towns to Boston, expanding and revolutionizing the city.

More immediately, Boston had to focus on downtown, which suffered its worst fire in 1872. The task of rebuilding the core city revealed the constraints on local government in its planning efforts. Private investors, though glad for municipal assistance in expanding the city, opposed city intervention and regulation of existing property and street patterns. Public power had renewed the market area in the mid-1820s but failed to rehabilitate the commercial district of the 1870s.

4

....

Building
Downtown
and around
Town

Downtown Boston reached toward the sky while parks and streetcars spread around town at the end of the nineteenth century. The United States industrialized and cities mushroomed so fast after the Civil War that a new term, "urbanization," was coined to describe the phenomenon.[1] Boston shared in this growth and developed manufacturing sections, notably South Boston, Roxbury and East Boston. By 1900 South Boston boasted such large firms as Gillette Razor, New England Confectionery, and Metropolitan Coal Company. The largest wool trade in the country was located in "handsome warehouses" just across the Summer Street extension bridge not far from the newly constructed South Station.[2] These warehouses stood at the edge of industrial South Boston, which extended from the Fort Point Channel area toward Edward Everett Square and Dorchester. In Roxbury cordage factories, iron foundries, carpet factories, lithography, suspender and shoe factories hummed alongside cigar manufacturers and breweries. Although ship overhaul and repair continued to dominate East Boston, warehouses, garment and shoemaking plants, and cotton-weaving factories also figured in the local landscape.

But most astounding were the demographic changes in Boston in the last three decades of the nineteenth century. Immigration and the annexation of other towns not only created a population explosion, but also brewed a totally new ethnic mix. The population of Boston in 1870 was 250,526, but after the city swallowed West Roxbury, Charlestown, and Brighton in the next decade, the population jumped another 112,313, a

45 percent increase. The 24 percent growth rate of the 1880s brought the population to 448,477; the 1890s growth rate of 25 percent made for a total population of 560,892 in 1900.

Despite all the negative impressions about cities in the late nineteenth century, places like Boston met the challenges of the new era. Boston's services probably surpassed those of any European city; the Hub could boast "the world's largest and grandest library, as well as a park system designed by Frederick Law Olmsted, the first subway in America, an innovative system of intercepting sewers," plentiful water, and "renowned public schools."[3] In addition, Boston provided public baths, municipal lodging houses for the indigent, and relief payments to noninstitutionalized poor.

All this required a great public investment, and yet the last quarter of the nineteenth century marked a period of fiscal conservatism for American cities. Expansion itself brought in the necessary new sources of revenue, keeping municipal debt under control and tax rates as low as possible.[4] Boston, which proved one of the most able borrowers of all the major American cities, was well-financed and relied heavily on special assessments placed on abutters to finance street improvements. In the second half of the nineteenth century, the city committed between one-third and one-half of its annual budget to projects and services directly affecting real estate.[5] Moreover, considerable public monies went into adapting to social and technological change, and Boston spent more per capita on public services than any other city in the country.[6] Indeed, the city budget at this time routinely exceeded that of the entire Commonwealth of Massachusetts.

Modern city government emerged in the final third of the nineteenth century and the public gradually accepted the concept of deliberate government planning. Business, civic, and political leaders came to agree with reformers on the need for a more explicit and positive role for government, yet the precise definition of that role remained open to question and, at times, heated debate. In the past the people leading and planning growth in Boston came from a shared background with certain common assumptions, and planning was more or less a gentleman's pastime. Entrepreneurs competed among themselves and influenced officeholders to support profit-making schemes for developing Boston. Emerging technological, economic and social realities, and the continuing change in the city's demographic makeup rocked the foundations of politics and planning. In addition to the Yankees and Irish, other groups, including African-Americans, who had a long-established community, became increasingly visible and important in city politics. Immigrants from southern and eastern Europe arrived in the United States and Boston in ever-increasing numbers in the 1890s and the first decade of the twentieth century, forever altering the shape of the city.

The North End reflected the shifting nature of Boston's ethnic makeup. Once the home of Yankee merchants, Paul Revere, and sailors, the North End was an Irish enclave by 1863 when John F. "Honey Fitz" Fitzgerald was born there. By the time Fitzgerald became the ward boss of the district in the late 1880s it already possessed large Jewish and Italian settlements. The various ethnic groups shared the North End, albeit in sharply defined areas. One resident recalled, "we recognized the different areas and walked with caution should we have to go through there."[7]

The North End Jewish community, made up of immigrants from Russia, Poland, and elsewhere in Europe, reached its greatest numbers in the late 1890s to the 1920s. At one point the neighborhood had five synagogues in addition to kosher markets, restaurants, Hebrew schools, and a loan society. The Italian community on the east side of Hanover Street divided itself along the lines of the immigrants' native towns, with Sicilians in one section, Genoese in another, and so on. In 1890 there were approximately 5,000 Italians in Boston along with 4,000 Jews. By 1910 over 30,000 Italians lived in the North End alone while 40,000 Jews crowded into the neighboring West End. Poles, Lithuanians, Greeks, and many other ethnic groups also moved into Boston during this era.

The official declaration by the U.S. Census Bureau that the great American frontier disappeared in 1890 had an enormous psychological impact, leading many Americans to fear for the future of their country. The older Anglo-Saxon nation seemed doubly threatened by the influx of foreign people with strange tongues and unusual costumes, food, and religion because there was no longer a "safety valve" in the West. Catholic and Jewish immigrants transformed the Protestant nation, especially cities such as Boston, within a few years. As one of America's leading historians of religion comments, "few events did so much to weaken the evangelical empire in the United States as did the rise of the city."[8] Boston Yankees responded with alarm, projecting their fears and disappointments onto the immigrants. These Bostonians believed that, with their inability to speak English, "their wrongheaded religion, and their inappropriate culture, the new immigrants were the source of all difficulties— unsanitary, overcrowded housing, low wages, shoddy work, vulgar entertainment, ignorance, promiscuity, unruly children, lawlessness, and political corruption."[9]

In facing the challenges of the new urban age, Boston planning for the downtown remained limited by old constraints, but the city's develop-

ment of parks and new forms of transportation showed genuine progress and leadership. The Great Fire of 1872 offered Bostonians their greatest opportunity for revamping the downtown area, but they failed to achieve consensus over the use of government power. Up to this point in the city's growth Bostonians ordinarily agreed that the government did a good job in distributing vacant or filled-in land. But when it came to government reallocating land to make the street system more rational, the true nature of the relationship between the public and private sectors was revealed. Boston's property owners and investors gladly used government power to expand the city but steadfastly opposed its use, even in search of the common good, when it threatened application to their property. This stance was commonly held by nineteenth-century American capitalists, but perhaps even more tenaciously by Bostonians at this time. In the immediate post–Civil War years they had eagerly spent vast sums changing the city, and so were particularly reluctant to part with new or upgraded property.

Right after the Civil War, business interests invested huge sums of money in revitalizing the downtown commercial area, once a residential district for the wealthy and the site of Bulfinch's Tontine Crescent. The great volume of development spurred the nascent preservation movement, and although John Hancock's house was destroyed in 1863, Bostonians managed to save the landmark Old South Meeting House from destruction.[10] Boston's Old City Hall, designed by Gridley J. F. Bryant and built on School Street in 1862, was among the most striking buildings in the new business district and one of the first Boston structures to evidence the French influence in architecture. Investors built a number of five- to seven-story buildings containing stores and factories along Washington Street between Winter and Summer Streets. These commercial structures were usually faced with granite or cast iron and topped with Mansard roofs made of wood. Few were fireproof and many had wood-lined elevator shafts and stairways.[11] In 1866 and again in 1867 Fire Chief John S. Damrell asked for control over the construction and alteration of buildings but each time the city leaders denied him the power to set and enforce building codes, a policy they were soon to regret.

Figure 4.1 Bird's-eye View of Boston, Showing the Burned District, 1872. This lithograph shows the harbor in the forefront, Quincy Market to the right, and Old South Meeting House on the right edge of the burned district. The steeple of Park Street Church, the Boston Common beyond and the State House are visible in the upper right corner. The South Bay with a ship sailing in it is apparent to the left. (Lithograph by Currier and Ives.)

The Great Fire, which destroyed much of the downtown and exposed the weakness of government planning in Boston, began on Saturday evening, November 9, 1872. Starting in a building on the corner of Summer and Kingston streets, it went unnoticed by the fire department for a full quarter of an hour after observers in Charlestown had spotted it.[12] Steam engines, which had replaced the old hand-tubs only in 1860, were called into action. The fire spread quickly as a result of the highly combustible materials of the structures. Moreover, the fire department was handicapped by the scarcity of hydrants, and because many of its horses were ill and unavailable.

The fire destroyed some sixty-five acres of downtown property at a cost of seventy-five million dollars. If not for a combination of factors, even more of the city would have gone up in flames. The most dramatic happening was the result of the fire chief's authorization to allow Boston's postmaster, a former Civil War general, to use explosives to demolish buildings. These planned demolitions, and the fact that the new post office was fireproofed, halted the spread of destruction.[13] It was a close call. Among the few downtown buildings spared was the famous Old South Meeting House, saved by the dedication of firefighters who pumped water through one thousand feet of hose extended from the harbor.[14] South of the city, the gaping scars left by the recent demolition of buildings on Fort Hill served as a firebreak, and stopped the conflagration.

At first Bostonians saw an opportunity to reshape the downtown and responded with zeal.[15] Thoughtful citizens wanted to rebuild this part of the city to address such long-standing problems as congested streets, insufficient drainage, and limited space. As they set about reconstruction, however, they soon realized they were hampered by an assortment of difficulties, including conflicts over the proper role of government in planning, disputes between different branches of government, economic competition, and personal squabbling. Although Robert Copeland's grand plan for Boston had been published earlier that year, for many reasons 1872 did not prove a time of great municipal vision and action.

Many powerful political, technological, and economic factors blocked optimal redevelopment.[16] Private interests and fears predominated over public cooperation, and the initial consensus disappeared. Consequently, although some streets were widened, intersections improved, and Post Office Square created, the opportunities for many improvements slipped away.[17]

Intragovernmental conflict was devastating. Concerned government agencies had strictly defined jurisdictions but lacked any mechanism for integrating or reconciling goals. Boston's board of street commissioners,

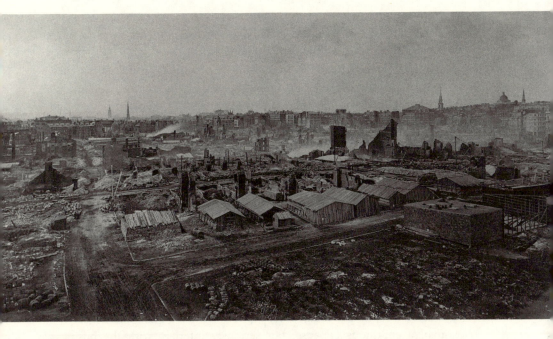

Figure 4.2 View of the Ruins of the Great Fire of 1872. This view, ascribed to James Wallace Black, shows the State House in the upper right corner, the steeple of Old South to its right (on the edge of the burned district), and Park Street Church to its left. Settled among the ruins are some sheds in the foreground which mark the beginning of the rebuilding effort. Also seen are street markings. (Courtesy of the Boston Public Library, Print Department.)

board of aldermen, and common council all had designated responsibilities in planning the rebuilding of the burnt district. At first, prospects for change looked good. The street commissioners and the joint committee on streets leaned toward taking the whole territory by eminent domain, a procedure that required state approval.[18] They moved quickly: a mere three days after the fire the city surveyor produced a proposal for a new street pattern for the destroyed section of the city.

Objectors soon appeared, however, complaining about the unconstitutionality of the method and the cost of compensation. One major obstacle was the state law which prohibited the use of city funds to aid the owners of private property in any ambitious redevelopment scheme. Another was that the city proved unable to give good title to the land it sought for the project.[19] Other protestors feared delay and the possible loss of business to New York while Boston rebuilt. Most important, property owners feared a complete takeover and redistribution of land in which the original 1872 owners might not be able to afford to buy a comparable piece of property for their businesses.[20] Owners of the *Boston Post,* whose property survived the fire but was threatened by street realignments, were the most politically powerful of the early opponents.

By the November 18 meeting of the city council, several weeks later, the city had already rejected the eminent domain approach. Alderman Clark reported for his colleagues on the special committee that had initially considered requesting legislative authorization for taking the whole burned area and laying out plans such as the city surveyor had proposed. His statement was simple: "Upon mature consideration, it was found that such an arbitrary disposition of the territory was open to very serious objections."[21] Newly elected Mayor Henry L. Pierce agreed, saying "the best form in which we can commemorate the great disaster which has overtaken us is by establishing wider streets in the district covered by the fire, and by improved methods in the construction of buildings through- out the city."[22] Pierce, a businessman of some vision, successfully devel- oped Walter Baker's chocolate factory in Dorchester Lower Mills into the largest plant of its kind in America.[23] But as for a total remapping of the affected area, he declared, "the adoption of such a plan would not only involve enormous expense, but seriously interfere with the business interest of the city."

Even a modest proposal for street reconstruction and widening became embroiled in political conflict. Though agreeing to limit the scope of the project, Mayor Pierce suggested extending Washington Street to Hay- market Square, and Devonshire Street to Dock Square. As this would mean going beyond the burnt district, the plan engendered serious busi- ness opposition and was rejected out of hand by the aldermen. After months of debate, however, advocates of street widening won some success. Washington Street between Summer and Milk Streets was wid- ened to sixty feet, while Federal, Hawley, Arch, and Pearl Streets were all improved and Post Office Square was laid out at a cost of over $100,000.[24]

This new square, the greatest planning feat in the post-fire era, was the achievement of Boston's postmaster, General William L. Burt. As might be expected, even this accomplishment had its critics, who felt Burt had re- sorted to "unusual political machinations and grandstanding techniques outside regular governmental channels" in order to force the hands of decision makers.[25] Powerful elements in Boston resented the federal intervention and complained about Chicago's better treatment in the aftermath of the 1871 fire there.

Overall, the burnt district returned to its previous street pattern largely because rival commercial interests were pitted against one another and in opposition to the public interest of improving the street system. Abutters

Figure 4.3 The City of Boston, 1873. This bird's-eye view of the city shows a fuller picture of the South Bay than is shown in figure 4.1. South Bay, to the left, is traversed by a railroad track which heads out to the emerging piers built on the mudflats between Boston and South Boston known today as the Fort Point Channel district and Fan Pier. Bunker Hill Monument, to the right, dominates Charlestown. The Back Bay has largely filled in but the mudflats in the center-left background posed a problem solved by Frederick Law Olmsted, who created the Fenway. (Lithograph by Currier and Ives, Courtesy of Historic Urban Plans, Ithaca, N.Y.)

opposed the tax increases they would have had to pay for an improved street, while owners of property on other streets feared the improved street would draw business at their expense. Christine Rosen, in her study of Boston's response to the Great Fire, describes this as "a political competition in which the most politically and economically powerful private interests typically got what they wanted, regardless of the costs to others and the community as a whole."[26]

The wrangling over rebuilding the fire-ravaged downtown opposed hopes of rational street planning against questions of legal title, one

Figure 4.4 Boston: Bird's-eye View from the North, 1877. Another of the popular bird's-eye views of the rapidly changing city. Fan Pier takes shape in the rear as South Boston gradually loses its peninsular shape. Bridges crossing the Charles to Charlestown and Cambridge are in the forefront. (Site of the proposed Scheme Z bridge-crossings for the Central Artery/Tunnel Project). The State House and Boston Common are reference points to the right. (Lithograph by Louis Prang prepared from a view by John Bachman. Courtesy of Historic Urban Plans, Ithaca, N.Y.)

branch of government against another, and one level of government against another. It also raised the issue of whether the public would agree to develop and fund the infrastructure necessary to run an important part of the city. The results showed the dominance of the private sector, for all its contentiousness, and the limits of public-sector planning.

The Boston fire of 1872 thus did not stimulate a rationalization of commercial, industrial, and residential land use such as had just occurred in the much larger fire district in Chicago.[27] The result in Boston was conservative change. Boot and shoe businesses moved south, toward the future South Station, where they were joined by leather and drygoods wholesalers. The old commercial district shrank because of street widening and because most new buildings were limited to four stories rather than the previous norm of five. The influx of banks, brokerage houses, and insurance businesses into the fire district also limited space.

Private property owners often made costly improvements when they rebuilt their properties. The interiors of new buildings were more comfortable, providing central heating, more efficient lighting, and plumbing.[28] New building codes further improved Boston's buildings, but this, too, proved controversial. Even the popular mansard roof design became

Figure 4.5 View of Boston, 1880. This lithograph shows another perspective on the post–Civil War city. The Back Bay is mostly filled and partially built upon, as seen in the upper left portions of the view, but the Fenway remains to be named and developed by Frederick Law Olmsted. Railroad tracks and warehouses on the Fan Pier are visible in the forefront. (Lithograph by Beck and Pauli. Courtesy of Historic Urban Plans, Ithaca, N.Y.)

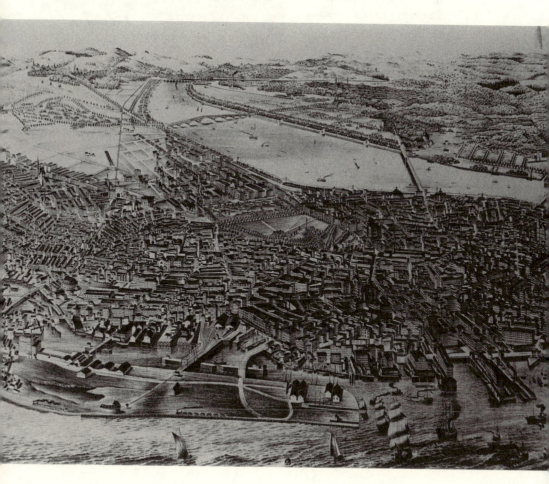

Figure 4.6 Copley Square. The foreground of this photograph shows the foundations of the Boston Public Library, designed by McKim, Mead, and White (built 1887–1895), being put in place. H. H. Richardson's Trinity Church is across a Copley Square divided by the beginning of Huntington Avenue. City planners ever since have contended with the difficulties of the spot. (Courtesy of The Bostonian Society/Old State House.)

a source of conflict, for it was thought by some to be a fire hazard that hastened the spread of the Great Fire. Public outcry turned the roofs— which were built of wood and covered with tin, iron or slate—into a scapegoat, despite testimony given by local architects to a state investigatory commission that combustible materials, not the roof design, were responsible. Eventually a new building code was hammered out in a series of new statutes and ordinances, modified occasionally over the next several decades. The result was a hodgepodge of regulations, and the beneficial effects of the code were further diluted because city departments, which did not coordinate their activities very well, divided responsibility for enforcement.[29]

The creation of Copley Square also evidences the limited power of city planning in the late nineteenth century. This now-famous site has posed a challenge and opportunity to Boston planners for over a century and, as a case study, "reveals the difficulty that Americans have had—and continue to have—in determining how their public spaces ought to be formed, and what purposes such spaces should serve."[30] The square itself is more the result of accident than design, a by-product of the lack of coordination between city and state in planning the development of the Back Bay and South End earlier in the nineteenth century.[31]

Construction of the Back Bay was just underway in 1860 when the future Copley Square, located on the edges of the Back Bay and the South

....

Building
Downtown
and around
Town

84

End, was nothing more than a series of pie-shaped pieces of land owned separately by the Commonwealth of Massachusetts and the Boston Water Power Company. Though the land's market value was comparatively low, two different groups began thinking about ways to explore the potential of this area.[32] Both offered proposals in the 1860s. One, by the Committee of Associated Institutions, proposed a Conservatory of Arts and Sciences. The other, by several city engineers and surveyors, suggested a "St. James Park." It took twenty years, however, for Copley Square to appear.

The Great Fire of 1872 proved a boon for the development of Copley Square because a number of important cultural institutions decided to rebuild there. Fortuitously, Huntington Avenue was laid out in 1872 and created an important intersection with Boylston and Dartmouth Streets. In 1876 the Museum of Fine Arts opened on the site of the present Copley Plaza Hotel and between 1872 and 1877 H. H. Richardson's masterpiece, Trinity Church, rose to dominate the scene. Contemporaries compared it to other Back Bay churches, claiming it occupied " a more advantageous site than any other, allowing an irregular and picturesque disposition of the accessory chapel and cloisters."[33] That irregular siting, however, with Huntington Avenue running diagonally across the open space in front of the church, posed a host of problems for succeeding generations. More than a century later Bostonians were still trying to create a suitable public space in front of Richardson's jewel. The grand new Boston Public Library, built in the late 1880s, faced the church and defined another side of the Square. The firm of McKim, Mead, and White designed this beautiful structure in the Italian Renaissance style as a people's palace. In conjunction with the Museum of Fine Arts it fulfilled plans made a quarter-century earlier for a cultural enclave in the Back Bay.

Another measure of the success of this new section of the city was the location there of residential hotels serving an upper-income clientele.[34] Yet their very presence posed a problem, because the land of the future Copley Square was still vacant and real estate promoters were eager to acquire it from its several owners. Only a last-minute response by the city stopped construction of a hotel directly in front of Trinity Church, on the section east of Huntington Avenue. The City of Boston scotched the hotel plan in 1882 by purchasing several parcels of land from the Commonwealth, the Massachusetts Institute of Technology, and the Museum of Fine Arts for $39,000 and combining them to create a new public space. The site was named Copley Square the following year, but the controversy continued.

The oddness of the site posed difficulties for all who had a hand in planning Copley Square. Had it acted in an earlier era, the city might have determined transportation, cultural, and private uses of the land. However, other issues during the Civil War years and during the postwar rush to develop more promising areas overshadowed plans for this site, and the city lost its opportunity to shape an important public space. Thus, when the city finally did act, it confronted a space determined by previous land uses. The result has never been wholly satisfactory. Until the 1960s automobiles continued to bisect the land now covered with grass, trees, and walkways. Proposals for the site popped up in every decade of the twentieth century, culminating in a horrendous concrete bowl which marred the square from the late 1960s until the end of the 1980s, when an architectural competition and an onslaught of bulldozers invented yet another face for Copley Square.

Despite the prominence of the Copley Square site and the attention given to it, the greatest challenge facing Boston in these years was the growth of the recently annexed towns of Dorchester, Brighton, Roxbury, West Roxbury, and Charlestown. In *Streetcar Suburbs,* a classic of American history, Sam Bass Warner, Jr., examines the process of growth in three of these communities—Roxbury, Dorchester, and West Roxbury—in the late nineteenth century. Warner demonstrates that the development of these suburban areas from 1870 to 1900 resulted from a partnership between large institutions and individual investors and homeowners, none of whom were bound by any organization or zoning law, and by precious few regulations. Nevertheless, the suburban growth followed a regular pattern and produced fairly homogeneous districts.

The contrast with earlier periods is instructive. The Back Bay, Beacon Hill, Pemberton Hill, the North Cove, and the South End had all been developed by big syndicates, a necessity for leveling hills and filling in marshes and mudflats. Similarly, South Boston and East Boston required bridges, ferries and extensive public facilities, all of which were built by private companies, while the Back Bay required state supervision. In contrast, no big corporations predominated in the streetcar suburbs; rather, the actions of thousands of decision-makers shaped this environment.

A more recent study accepts Warner's thesis that the pattern of suburban settlement in the nineteenth century was indeed characterized by many individual decisions but argues that greater emphasis should be laid on fundamental decisions made possible by government sanction, such as providing "transport access and utilities, and subdividing the farms and woods for small-scale builders to purchase." These decisions "are also part of the suburbanization process," and indicate how government and "large-scale developers—the subdividers of land rather than the actual builders of dwellings—have had an important influence on the form of the suburbs, as well as garnering a large portion of the profits generated."[35] Big developers and utilities may have put forth and implemented the actual plans, but they could proceed only with government approval and cooperation; thus are fundamental planning decisions made through the political process.

Some 22,500 new dwellings were constructed by 9,000 individual builders in the three towns Warner studied, yet the suburbs attained a great uniformity of land plans and architecture. Warner's study showed how these three areas "were built by a strict discipline of nineteenth-century conditions which organized the structures and their builders into patterns which, in their way, were as rigid as any modern development statutes."[36] Further, the rate of growth was unprecedented. West Roxbury, for example, experienced a building boom in the last fifteen years of the century, as scores of middle-class homes were constructed along streets following the basic grid pattern.

Boston's government played its part in the growth of the streetcar suburbs, primarily by developing streets. It also created an elective Board of Street Commissioners in 1870, a feeble attempt to cope with the challenge of tremendous growth. No systematic plan was followed, however; streets were laid out haphazardly by real estate developers and the street commissioners did little more than accept or reject the work of the private sector.

Many services arose from public–private partnerships. The municipal government provided water and adopted the new sanitary engineering of the late nineteenth century, for example, but private corporations provided utilities. Gas was available from the 1840s, while electricity and telephone service dated from the 1890s.[37] As the city bargained with the gas and electric companies to extend its own lighting, it often worked on behalf of residential customers as well. Installation charges for new utilities and streets were held below cost, with a great deal of the expense carried by taxation and normal service rates. The homes constructed during this era were usually soundly built and equipped with indoor plumbing.

City professionals who took part in the suburban expansion produced high quality work. City engineers were nationally esteemed and Boston, along with New York and Chicago, was often at the forefront in embracing new technology and engineering techniques to solve municipal problems.[38] Growing pains, however, were inevitable. It was not uncommon during these decades for the city to put in water mains and sewers and pave the road only to have a street railway or gas company come in and tear everything up to place rails or pipes. Overall, however, the public–private partnership was able to meet the needs created by the dramatic expansion. As Professor Warner writes:

> Though in today's terms there was no planning in late nineteenth century Boston, the largely successful effort to give new services to the whole jurisdiction with its consequent aid to private development was a conscious policy designed to achieve the ends of society. By providing equal service to all citizens, by extending as rapidly as possible to the whole geographic jurisdiction, Boston's public agencies hoped to give the greatest scope to the workings of the capitalists. Education, health, transportation, and plentiful land were tools to encourage individuals to work effectively as private profit makers. The works of the individual profit makers were to be the return for the public costs and efforts.[39]

The expansion itself, then, was no triumph of public planning, but the subsequent effort to incorporate these districts fully into the city turned into one of the signal achievements of planning. The result may not be pretty, but this is the nature of planning: responding to the forces of growth.

The creation of the city's far-flung and celebrated park system, undertaken during the same period, offers a clearer example of successful, advance planning, as well as the pleasing results of this process. The idea of a park system to connect the city's disparate neighborhoods won gradual support during the late nineteenth century and is widely considered a great triumph of civic endeavor. The park system that emerged is inextricably linked to the work and name of Frederick Law Olmsted, whose impact on Boston is justly famous. Evolving under his supervision from 1879 to 1895, the park system ultimately incorporated over 2,000 acres of land throughout the newly enlarged city, and stands as one of the most massive public projects ever undertaken by Boston's municipal authorities.

The story of the park system begins in 1868 when a citizens' group petitioned the city council to reserve space for a large park or several smaller parks within the city limits. The rationale—to preserve public health and morality in an era ravaged by industrialization, and to confirm Boston's status as a first-class city—proved compelling. In 1875 the city created a three-member Park Commission to deal with two tasks: establishing a park system and solving the problem of drainage in the Back Bay. This Park Commission, which can be viewed as the city's first municipal planning board,[40] faced myriad problems and soon called upon Frederick Law Olmsted for help.

The distinguished landscape architect and "father of American city planning" was already famous for planning and developing New York's Central Park. Olmsted had also served as a leader of the U.S. Sanitary Commission during the Civil War and held strong convictions about the need for developing healthful cities.[41] He was far more than merely a designer of attractive landscapes. Olmsted's Central Park, for example, serves not only as a model of design but also of the planning process itself. He advocated business methods of study, specialized responsibility, the concentration of planning authority in a small group, and government independence for park planning agencies.[42]

For Olmsted, park design was essential to a comprehensive city plan. According to Cynthia Zaitzevsky, author of *Frederick Law Olmsted and the Boston Park System,* he believed that "a park was never an ornamental addition to a city but an integral part of its fabric and a force for future growth on several levels: geographic, economic, social, and cultural."[43] Open spaces would give city residents the opportunity to refresh themselves in nature. As historian Thomas Bender writes in *Toward an Urban Vision,* Olmsted's park ideal "represented an attempt to harmonize the economic and cultural possibilities of urban living with a somewhat idealized heritage of New England town life that emphasized the ideas of organic social relations, community, and natural beauty."[44]

Although Olmsted's ideas and achievements place him among the

Figure 4.7 Frederick Law Olmsted before he assumed direction of Boston's parks and created a system of open spaces and thorough-fares to connect the newly annexed portions of the city to the downtown via the new Commonwealth Mall. Estimated to be 1878. (Courtesy of the National Park Service, Frederick Law Olmsted National Historic Site.)

earliest and most significant urban planners, his reputation is still contro-versial among historians. Like many other reformers of the time, the great landscape architect relied on the introduction of the countryside into the city as a remedy for social and physical ills. He argued that parks human-ized and democratized great cities and could bring social classes together in harmony. Geoffrey Blodgett, Stanley Schultz, and others acknowledge Olmsted's contributions but point out that Olmsted shared the disdain of many reformers for the working classes and immigrant poor. Blodgett observes that Olmsted shared a "profoundly conservative concept of reform" along with Henry Adams, E. L. Godkin, and Charles Francis Adams, Jr. Like them, Olmsted had an "urge to focus professional intel-ligence on goals of social order and cohesion." Blodgett further notes that Olmsted and members of this "reformist gentry" held in common "as-sumptions about the design of a good society, where hierarchy, deference, and skilled leadership might impose tranquility on a contentious, egali-tarian people. Schultz puts it more strongly when he writes that Olmsted "was one of the earliest antiurban planners, a leader of those who de-nounced the trend of cities becoming too big, too crowded, too dirty, polluted, too filled with strange foreigners, too rife with class hostili-ties."[45] Melvin Kalfus recently defended Olmsted, conceding that while Olmsted shared most of the basic assumptions of his peers in the gentry and employed their language in enlisting support for his urban design projects, the parks he designed "have endured as triumphs of urban design because they were energized by the validity of Olmsted's vision, deriving from his own deeply felt inner needs—a validity in human terms, not class or gender terms."[46] Whatever the limits of his egalitarianism or sources of his vision, Olmsted's contributions to Boston and city planning are undoubtedly extraordinary.

Olmsted's consulting work for Boston began with a report to the Parks Commission in 1880, and extended over many years, but he at first maintained his home base in New York, only gradually deciding to relocate. In fact, he summered in Brookline for three years before deciding to move there permanently. Surprisingly, it was not the summer charms of this leafy suburb that decided Olmsted. Rather, while on a winter visit in 1881 to H. H. Richardson, his friend and collaborator, Olmsted, amazed at the speed with which a snowplow came to do its job, concluded, "this is a civilized community. I'm going to live here."[47] Brookline's efficiency was fortunate indeed for Boston because Olmsted settled here for the remainder of his life and left an unequalled mark on the parks and roadways of the city.

Olmsted did not build Boston's park system single-handedly, nor did he ever use the term "Emerald Necklace" so often associated with his work. Rather, Olmsted was a refiner of ideas and a shrewd manipulator of public opinion. His first step in Boston was to reconcile conflicting goals for the Back Bay Fens area. Boston's newly appointed Park Commissioners faced three problems in this western edge of the Back Bay: flooding; polluted water; and the ugliness of a neglected area. The first two posed no major problem but the third gave Olmsted, the artist, "momentary pause."[48] The commissioners were principally concerned with creating a storage basin for flood waters from the Muddy River and Stony Brook, but Olmsted urged the commission to scrap plans for a park on top of Parker Hill and instead develop the area which he called the Back Bay Fens. Under his guidance the region was transformed from an undesirable and nondescript border area into a lovely landscape which pleased the eye and provided a safe conduit for flood waters.

His proposal for the Back Bay Fens was only the beginning of the Emerald Necklace. This strand of roadways connecting parks and outlying sections of the city with the original peninsula helped beautify and unify the city that Boston had become after the annexations of the 1860s and 1870s. It was not conceived in the abstract; Olmsted worked with what was available and molded it to his vision, but always within the parameters established by political and economic realities. And in this he did a magnificent job. As Geoffrey Blodgett writes, in creating the Emerald Necklace, Olmsted "engaged the resources of the city in a remarkable mix of public and private enterprise. The system developed in a pattern of fruitful interaction among wealthy Back Bay and suburban landowners, museums, colleges, and other cultural institutions which migrated to the edges of the park chain."[49] Even a casual examination of previous park plans shows that connecting links were proposed, but only Olmsted succeeded in transforming ideas into reality.[50] As one scholar wrote, that Olmsted created the system "attests to his development from writing about what should be, to recognizing what could be, to getting it done."[51]

Olmsted's plan called for connecting the Back Bay Fens to the proposed West Roxbury Park and labeling the sections along the route as Fenway, Riverway, Jamaicaway, and Arborway. The Fenway was built in the 1880s and the remainder during the next decade. The city soon changed the name of West Roxbury Park to Franklin Park in honor of Benjamin Franklin in order to secure a portion of his estate. Franklin's will stipulated that one hundred years after his death part of his estate should be given to a worthy cause, and the city succeeded in persuading the estate that this park was just such a cause.

Olmsted believed that this and other parks should be reserved for passive use and serve to restore the city dweller to health by creating a natural environment, but Boston's Parks Commissioners soon abandoned this view and allowed all kinds of sports and recreational uses.[52] Some parts of Olmsted's plan were forsaken and others, such as the development of Columbia Road as a parkway through Dorchester, were never achieved, but Olmsted's interest and work on Boston's park system continued through the 1880s and 1890s. Though his last years brought severe mental illness and hospitalization before he died in McLean Hospital in Belmont in 1902, Olmsted's parks flourished. Over time his son and the Olmsted firm assumed greater responsibility for Boston's parks; the great man's work was also continued by his spiritual heirs, Charles Eliot, a landscape architect, and Sylvester Baxter, a journalist, who created the metropolitan park system.

Eliot, son and namesake of Harvard's longtime president, trained under Frederick Law Olmsted before setting up his own office in 1886 at the age of twenty-six. Just as Olmsted expanded both the park system and the popular understanding of planning, so too did the young Eliot. He and other landscape architects of the period popularized the notion of public planning in their insistence on seeking a satisfactory relationship between humankind, space, and nature in the urban community.[53] Eliot was also foremost among those who realized that future population increases

Figure 4.8 Two views of the Riverway which was created by Olmsted. The upper photograph, in the late nineteenth century, shows how the water was channeled between Boston and Brookline and paths created alongside. Thirty years later vegetation creates the artful impression of undisturbed nature in the midst of the city. (Courtesy of the Archives of the City of Boston.)

Figure 4.9 The Emerald Necklace. This plan by the Olmsted firm shows what came to be called the Emerald Necklace connecting Boston's downtown with outlying neighborhoods. This 1894 version of the plan traces the park system connecting the Boston Common and Public Garden to Franklin Park. The system includes the Charles River Basin, Charlesbank, the mall along Commonwealth Avenue, the Fens, improvements to the Muddy River, what is now called Olmsted Park, Jamaica Pond, the Arborway, and Arnold Arboretum. (Courtesy: National Park Service, Frederick Law Olmsted National Historic Site.)

would deprive the region of open spaces, and he organized the Trustees of Public Reservations to lobby for government action.[54] Eliot also gathered together members of local park commissions in 1891 to petition the legislature for a metropolitan park authority; the group succeeded in getting a legislative commission formed to study the issue in 1892.[55] Eliot's friend Baxter drummed up support for the movement and in 1893 they persuaded the state legislature to create the Metropolitan Park Commission.

The first chairman of the Metropolitan Park Commission was Charles Francis Adams, grandson of John Quincy Adams. Under Adams's experienced hand the commission moved quickly to meet its mandate. Within its first year the five-member commission acquired five reservations with over 7,000 acres.[56] It promptly acquired Revere Beach, the lower banks of the Charles River, and land for parkways from the Blue Hills to the edge of Boston. By 1902 the Metropolitan Park Commission controlled about 15,000 acres, thirty miles of river frontage, ten miles of ocean shoreline, and twenty-two miles of right-of-way for parkways, an impressive achievement for one decade's work.

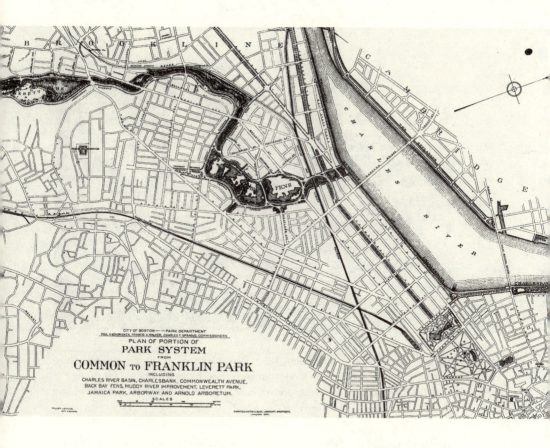

CITY OF BOSTON——PARK DEPARTMENT
PAUL H KENDRICKEN, FRANCIS A WALKER, CHARLES F SPRAGUE, COMMISSIONERS.
PLAN OF PORTION OF
PARK SYSTEM
FROM
COMMON TO **FRANKLIN PARK**
INCLUDING
CHARLES RIVER BASIN, CHARLESBANK, COMMONWEALTH AVENUE,
BACK BAY FENS, MUDDY RIVER IMPROVEMENT, LEVERETT PARK,
JAMAICA PARK, ARBORWAY AND ARNOLD ARBORETUM.
SCALES

This public concern for parks represented an important step forward in acknowledging how seriously population growth and crowding worsened life for many city dwellers and how important open space was to promoting public health.[57] Likewise, the public began to perceive that water and sewers were a "city's lifeline" and as such "were too vital to be left to either the good intentions or the caprices of the private enterprise game."[58] Thoughtful Bay Staters soon recognized that they could secure an adequate supply of water to the city and dispose of sewage most efficiently by instituting regionally defined efforts similar to those of the Metropolitan Park Commission. Massachusetts thus not only led the nation in establishing a metropolitan park system; it also maintained that leadership by creating metropolitan districts for water supply and sewage.

Then as now, sewage treatment was a costly and controversial issue in urban politics. The first sewers in Boston dated from the seventeenth century and were privately installed. Government first regulated them in an ordinance of 1701.[59] Over the years, with the extension of the shoreline into the harbor, old outlets were cut off and sewer extensions with little or

Figure 4.10 Charles River Basin, 1893. Portions of the retaining wall shown in this photograph may still be seen from James Storrow Memorial Drive along the Charles River today. The homes shown here face Beacon Street. (Courtesy of The Bostonian Society/Old State House.)

no slope resulted. These were almost invariably below the high-tide level and provided with tidegates. Sewers became an expensive item in the city budget, especially because of the annexations of the streetcar suburbs, which required the expansion of the sewer system. Expenditures on sewers in the city increased from $18,760 in 1864 to $227,827 in 1873, and this was only the beginning.[60]

Boston's residents considered neighboring communities natural partners in developing an expanded sewage system; as early as 1874 a state commission proposed a metropolitan sewerage authority[61] that would link the city and neighboring towns. This controversial proposal, an alternative to further annexations, provoked heated debate. Fifteen years, two additional commissions, and one Board of Health report later, the state finally created the Metropolitan Sewerage Commission. Meanwhile, the city could not wait to discharge its sewage, and so began its own main drainage system in 1876. Completed in 1884–1885, it was the first such project in the entire country.

The state legislature now turned its attention to the provision of water.

Predictably, another state commission was created to consider the issue and the result was another metropolitan solution. An act of 1895 created the Metropolitan District (defined as the area of eastern Massachusetts) and the Metropolitan Water Board.[62] In 1901 the state combined the water and sewer boards in the hope of gaining efficiency and economy. In 1919 the Metropolitan District Commission (MDC) consolidated the operations and functions of the Metropolitan Park Commission and the Metropolitan Water and Sewerage Board, unifying the parks, water supply, and sewage disposal systems.[63]

A broad spectrum of people found the metropolitan solution attractive for a variety of reasons. Some believed that Boston alone was incapable of handling municipal growth adequately. Others alleged great waste in spending ever since the annexations of West Roxbury, Dorchester, Brighton, Roxbury, and Charlestown, which had not been accompanied by comprehensive planning. Still others sought the metropolitan solution because Boston was now coming under the control of the Irish-dominated Democratic party, and extending the metropolis would dilute their power base. And there were those who saw all these factors as an undivided trinity. The metropolitan solution accorded its proponents the opportunity to retain control over the capital city of the old Bay State, although the Yankee Protestant element was now a minority.

As in many other cities around the country, ethnic cultural and political conflict heated up in the 1890s and immensely complicated the formulation of public policy. In Boston, the Irish took to politics with great passion. Politics offered personal power and social advancement to the leaders, and services to the followers. Whereas the newly arrived Irish voters were looking to the government to help them acquire food, clothing, shelter and jobs, established Bostonians took an entirely different view.[64] The Bostonian of Yankee background looked for a government to set and enforce rules, operate the financial system frugally, and guarantee high-quality leadership. The differences in these views became more apparent over time as the city faced new problems in transportation, education, and recreation.

The conflict came to a head when Bostonians elected the first Irish-born mayor, Hugh O'Brien, in 1884. O'Brien, who came to Boston from Ireland as a boy, rose through the ranks in the newspaper business to become the owner and publisher of a shipping journal. He was also a bank president, leader of many charitable activities, and chairman of the Board of Aldermen. In many ways the mayoralty of Hugh O'Brien marks the emergence of Boston as a modern city. This was not due to any force of character on his part but to an unusual convergence of forces and political change. During his watch the legislature strengthened the office of mayor, making the position central to Boston politics.

In addition, however, O'Brien had a deep sense of Boston's history and deserves recognition for anticipating and planning for the growth of the city.[65] He firmly believed that the city could do a much better job of preparing for the future, pointing out that street systems had been laid out without any coherent plan or regard for future needs. His ideas on planning ranged across topics from the mundane to an impressive vision of the twentieth century. His inaugural address in 1885 reveals this range. The new mayor was happy to note that the sewer drainage system, opened the year before, was a great success; with the sewage now disposed of near Moon Island in the outer harbor, he observed that the "offensive odors formerly prevalent over the city during the summer were not noticed this season."[66]

O'Brien thought seriously about the process of growth, speculating how it would affect Bostonians a half-century in the future. Estimating that Boston's population in 1885 was about 410,000, which meant that over the past fifty years it had increased fivefold, he projected this same rate of increase into the future and predicted that by 1935 the city's population would be two million. Although the 1930 census showed his estimate to be wrong (Boston had 781,000 in that year) the metropolitan area population was nearly in line with O'Brien's prediction, which had been based on the assumption that annexation would bring most of the neighboring towns (which he termed "little more than outlying districts") into the city borders.[67] He urged Boston to prepare for the future and demonstrated unusual foresight by proposing that the city acquire parkland while the property was undeveloped. Outlying districts like Brighton, Hyde Park and West Roxbury still had large tracts of undeveloped land in the final decades of the nineteenth century; these huge swaths can still be discerned on contemporary maps indicating the locations of Stony Brook Reservation, George Wright Golf Course, and numerous cemeteries. O'Brien's interest in purchasing some of this land for future parks revealed his keen sense of business: a fiscal conservative, he wanted the city to get the land for the lowest possible price.

O'Brien was also instrumental in subduing the antagonism that initially developed between his newly appointed Parks Commissioners and Frederick Law Olmsted. Parks were the great planning issue of the time and the new commissioners, aiming to control the park system, fired Olmsted in the spring of 1885. A political ruckus ensued. Charles Eliot Norton lamented to his friend Olmsted over "the disgraceful procedure of Mayor

O'Brien and the Common Council" and observed that "the Irish dynasty has fairly settled itself on the throne in Boston and although there may be spasmodic revolts against it, I do not look to see a successful revolution."[68] There was no revolution, but ethnic and cultural conflict continued to disrupt Boston politics and planning.

Fear of corruption and incompetence led Yankee reformers to counter the Irish in city government by both strengthening the mayor's office and requiring greater accountability. The mayor had largely been a figurehead with the power to appoint committees of the city council, where real power lay, but O'Brien now enjoyed greater authority over department heads, albeit within a more limited sphere. The price for greater power was responsibility for more problems, and in O'Brien's final campaign of 1888 he was attacked on the one hand for allowing too much control to a "City Hall ring" that wasted money and on the other hand for not spending enough money. More ominously, ethnic and religious conflict marred the election and Hugh O'Brien lost his bid for reelection. Anti-Catholicism once again surged forward in Boston politics and swept away even a moderate and respectable leader like O'Brien. Boston's Irish failed to elect one of their own to the mayoralty until 1901.

Such political conflict was just one aspect of the transformation of Boston during these years. Ethnic conflict, along with the economic depression of the early 1890s, slowed Boston's planning efforts but technological change continued to affect the old city. Steel construction and elevators allowed the first "skyscrapers," while the telephone, typewriter, and electricity revolutionized the world of business. In the final third of the century streetcars and subways transformed cities. The street railways expanded prolifically throughout the second half of the nineteenth century. By 1900 commuters could travel six miles on streetcars in an hour and the old walking city no longer bound all but the very rich. Thousands of Bostonians of all classes moved to the periphery of the city yet continued to work in the core.

In many ways, streetcar service was the key to the development of Boston during this period. Essential city planning came about through the efforts of privately owned transportation companies and the land speculators behind them. Yet by the turn of the century the private sector could no longer provide all the services Bostonians wanted, particularly in downtown transportation. Hence the City of Boston stepped forward and engineered the extension of the public transportation system through subways and elevated rail, taking a giant step in changing both the appearance of the city and the idea of planning. In the nineteenth century, the heyday of laissez-faire government, transportation nevertheless proved the exception; technological change of this order required political change as well.

Government moved to regulate business, and regulation of streetcars came first. In 1869 the Commonwealth of Massachusetts created the Board of Railroad Commissioners to regulate both railroads and streetcars. Although this board was not the first regulatory agency in America or even the first state railroad commission, it is widely considered "the most important regulatory pioneer" in the United States.[69] The state board, however, dealt more with railroads than streetcars, and focused on the incorporation of various companies rather than on the routes assigned them. Boston's Board of Aldermen theoretically retained the power to grant franchises for specific streetcar routes, but in reality, developers took the initiative, setting routes not to serve the public's needs but to encourage people to buy land owned by streetcar companies. All of this made for confused planning and exacerbated rivalries among some twenty streetcar companies in the Boston metropolitan area.[70] The result was overbuilding, fragmentation of routes, and multiple fares, climaxing in the 1880s in a crisis for Boston's transportation system.[71] Ultimately the government took charge but in the short term one of Boston's greatest real estate developers and entrepreneurs, Henry Whitney, resolved the city's transportation problems by buying and consolidating the various streetcar companies within his West End Street Railway Company.

After chartering the West End Street Railway as a subsidiary to his land development company, Whitney gained the street rail franchise for the area he was developing in Brookline, west of Boston. Whitney wanted no competition and resolutely devoured the Highland, Charles River, Cambridge, Metropolitan, South Boston, and Middlesex streetcar companies. By 1887 the West End Street Railway had over 3,700 employees, 1,700 cars, 8,400 horses and 200 miles of track. Boston now boasted the first unified public transit system in a major American city and the largest single streetcar system in the world.[72]

Whitney's streetcar system succeeded because of innovations in service. His company standardized the fare at a nickel, abolished zones, used color codes to identify routes, and posted signs identifying the car's destination. Public relations experts, had they existed, would have labeled it "user-friendly." The late historian Samuel Eliot Morison, for example, described the old horse-drawn streetcars of his youth as a convenient means of transportation that stopped wherever necessary, not just at corners: "The conductors knew everyone along the route, and the residents knew their names, and even those of the horses."[73]

The West End Street Railway was also the world's first system to

....
Building
Downtown
and around
Town
100

electrify. By 1888 one third of the system was electrified, four years later two thirds, and in 1894 over 90 percent. The system carried 137 million passengers in 1894, an increase of fifty-nine percent over 1886. With the free transfer system, in 1896 a Bostonian could travel to all parts of the metropolitan area for a nickel.[74]

Whitney's career in Boston demonstrates the primacy of land speculation in planning and developing Boston. In creating a streetcar system, he provided transportation to land he had purchased for residential and commercial development, operating as a speculator seeking to ensure the value of his investment. Transportation was merely a means to an end. The result was galloping suburbanization and the creation of an immense metropolitan region. One may compare the sea change of Whitney's era with the years immediately after World War II, when the federal highway system again swelled the suburbs. However, a critical difference exists: in Whitney's day the private sector led the way while in the later period government constructed and maintained the transportation network.

The West End Street Railway created a uniform system of streetcars in Boston but the company failed to meet the urban transportation requirements of the 1890s when great crowds of passengers had to be funnelled through the downtown. The critical factor in this failure was Whitney himself. After he left Boston late in 1893, heading west to undertake new enterprises, the West End Company's creative role in planning the city's transportation network declined while the government's intensified. In the 1890s, traffic congestion in the downtown was the key transportation problem facing Boston, and forward-looking Bostonians proposed both an elevated railway and a subway as solutions. As early as 1879 an elevated railroad had been proposed but rejected by the state legislature. In 1890 Whitney had proposed an elevated structure contingent upon the city laying out new streets to make way for it. Although the legislature approved the plans, abutters and those opposed to government aid to private enterprise successfully opposed the West End Street Railway, and by 1891 Whitney's El proposal was dead.[75]

The governor then appointed a commission to investigate the issue of elevated trains in Boston; it recommended a system with four different elevated railroads throughout the city and a subway under Boston Common. Meanwhile, Mayor Nathan Matthews, a Yankee Democrat in coalition with the Irish Democrats, won legislative approval to appoint a Rapid Transit Commission. This group, too, was charged with recommending either subways or elevated railroads. In its 1892 report the Rapid Transit Commission recommended the elevated option with one short tunnel underneath the Common. The commission favored public construction

....
*Building
Downtown
and around
Town*
101

of the new transit system but urged that it be operated by private enterprise.[76]

The commissioners also suggested the creation of a three-person state
board (similar to those for parks, water, and sewer) to build a metropolitan transportation district and then lease the lines. A number of
competing interests obscured the issues and in 1894 the legislature enacted a compromise bill to protect the value of the West End Company,
establish a new Boston Elevated Railway Company, and set up a new
Boston Transit Commission to replace the Rapid Transit Commission.
The bill also stipulated that a subway should go under the Common and
an elevated train along Washington Street. Boston voters who had the
final say narrowly approved the proposal in a special election.[77]

One of the great success stories of city planning ensued as the new
commission built the first subway in the United States. Work began on
March 28, 1895 at the Public Garden. The $5 million, three-year project
proceeded quickly and the first section, Park Street to Boylston Street,
opened on September 1, 1897. The entire original project stretched two-
and-one-half miles from North Station to Tremont Street near Broadway.
The subway was an immediate success and freed downtown streets of
much traffic. Where 200 trolley cars an hour had previously rattled along
Tremont Street, the new subway carried 282 cars an hour; rush hour
traffic and capacity doubled along the route and over 50 million riders
took the subway in its first eleven months of operation.[78] This success
spurred planning for the elevated line, and construction started early in
the twentieth century.

Boston's transit system in 1900 was a private monopoly under public
control. The public sector financed construction and maintained ownership of the rapid transit lines, but leased the administration and management of the system to private interests. The West End Company leased the
line for twenty years and paid the city over $200,000 rent per year,
enough to service and amortize the city debt incurred for the transit
system. The era was a true watershed in Boston's planning history. It
evinced, as Charles W. Cheape writes, "a formal recognition of the industrial metropolis' need for a coordinated transit system and for an active
public role in its development."[79]

An energetic new mayor presided over the subway opening in 1897 and
inaugurated an activist administration which soon stretched the definition of planning in other ways. During the 1890s the state legislature
decided to lengthen the term of office for Boston's mayor from one to two
years. The first man elected for this lengthened term was Josiah Quincy,
dubbed "the last of Boston's Brahmin Democrats."[80] The third of that

....

Building

Downtown

and around

Town

102

name to hold the office, he was the great-grandson of the "Great Mayor" of the 1820s and the grandson of the 1840s Mayor Quincy. The 1896 Quincy was a Democrat, former state legislator, and ex-Assistant Secretary of State.

His reign over City Hall was energetic and innovative, as befitted his name and heritage, and he helped Boston become a modern city; however, his administration also revealed some of the constraints on planning. Quincy worked hard to ameliorate the physical and social problems of the poor, but he soon ran into a wall of opposition that forced him out of city hall after four years with much of his agenda unrealized. He could mobilize political support for public works projects such as parks and subway lines—which served major financial interests—but his efforts to prod the government into assuming greater responsibility for the quality of life of Boston's poorer citizens were less successful. Nevertheless, during Quincy's administration Boston made substantial headway in developing a modern, scientific approach to urban planning. For example, Quincy established the nation's first municipal bureau of statistics and brought in a Johns Hopkins Ph.D. to direct it. More important, Boston built bathhouses, schools, and other municipal facilities besides the subway. Many of these accomplishments were largely due to fortuitous circumstances. As the debilitating depression of the early 1890s receded, Bostonians were primed for growth. Both the public and private sectors invested in the expansion of the city. Capital planning and construction naturally won support from ward bosses, contractors, builders, workers, and voters.

In contrast, the housing issue continued to be a controversial part of the political agenda. Serious overcrowding in certain sections of the city stimulated debate over the proper mix of public and private initiative in remedying the situation. In times past most people agreed that "private capital should provide shelter but that its quality should be regulated by public authorities."[81] Up to this time the public regarded urban land and housing as commodities subject to the laws of supply and demand, but by the end of the century Americans were "less confident that market disciplines would suffice. The influx of workers and immigrants together with the creation of new cities challenged the traditional private enterprise system beyond its ability. Consequently, planners, housing reformers, and others launched a search for norms of public intervention."[82]

Considering that the overwhelming majority of Bostonians in this decade were renters, some new government action was bound to develop. In 1890 the national average in cities with populations over 100,000 was 77 percent tenants while in Boston it was 82 percent. By comparison, 94

....

*Building
Downtown
and around
Town*

103

percent of New York's population and 58 percent of Milwaukee's were tenants.[83] The major concern at this time was not home ownership but the quality of housing, with sanitary problems paramount. Quincy modeled his approach to the housing problem on the New York slum-clearance strategy, under which the Board of Health condemned and razed unsanitary housing, leaving the land to the owner. Quincy won passage of a similar law in Massachusetts and more than 230 buildings were demolished within several years.[84] Regrettably, however, the law made no provision for replacement housing. Quincy made greater head-way in planning and building baths and swimming areas, particularly after recruiting Robert A. Woods, the famous settlement-house worker, to serve as the city's Commissioner of Public Baths.[85] Bathhouses were especially important to poor people who lived in cold-water flats because the facilities provided them with an opportunity to use soap and hot water.

Mayor Quincy also earned favorable reviews for his part in the move-ment to build playgrounds for children. Reformers had long wanted to relieve the squalor and overcrowding in the West End and North End, and although people like Joseph Lee and members of the Massachusetts Emergency and Hygiene Association are usually credited with establish-ing playgrounds in Boston, Stephen Hardy, in *How Boston Played,* argues that neighborhood groups and politicians actually led the campaign; only later, he asserts, "did genteel reformers exalt the movement with sophisti-cated theories about play, child development, and social behavior."[86] The first two playgrounds were located in Franklin Park and along the Charles River. In 1889 the Boston Parks Department converted a ten–acre tract on the Charles to an open-air gymnasium for residents of the nearby densely packed West End.[87] Under Mayor Quincy the city began a comprehensive playground program in 1898, at which point twenty parks were already in existence or underway and another twenty were authorized.

To accomplish as much as he did, Quincy learned to negotiate with various groups of political and financial leaders, illustrating again that Boston's traditional partnership between the private and public sectors was essential to planning. Quincy dealt with Boston's Democratic ward bosses, who were mostly Irish and wholly divided, by establishing a "Board of Strategy," an informal advisory group that allowed the bosses direct input on neighborhood projects and so provided a base of support for Quincy. It also assured that party leaders retained control over money and patronage. Moreover, to keep the bosses happy, the city council appropriated $25,000 to each ward for street improvements no matter how good or bad the roads were.[88] To reach the Republican power base

....

Building

Downtown

and around

Town

104

Mayor Quincy established the Merchants' Municipal Committee in 1896, which represented six leading commercial organizations in the city.[89] This alliance shored up business and legislative support for his administration but could not protect Quincy from the threat posed by his fellow Democrats.

Despite his many efforts to provide services and jobs, Quincy's progressive administration could not survive forever without clashing with the ward bosses.[90] In his last years in office Quincy was increasingly criticized as a spendthrift and a socialist. His greatest "crime," however, was attempting to consolidate power in the mayor's office and circumvent the city council. In his valedictory address to the council, the mayor denied the charge "that the present admitted stringency in our municipal finances has come about chiefly through extravagant expenditures for baths, gymnasia, public convenience stations, music, lectures, children's excursions, ice-water fountains etc." Quincy maintained that his program, "characterized sometimes as municipal socialism," was not inordinately expensive.[91] The real issue, however, was not the amount spent but who was to control the city budget. By 1899, unrelenting battle with the legendary Martin Lomasney, boss of the West End, forced Quincy out of public office and ended an extraordinary era in Boston's growth.

In the last decades of the nineteenth century, city planning became a formal and recognized function of city government. Industrialization—with its accompanying economic, technological, and demographic shifts—required new responses from Boston's city government, which took significant steps to enlarge its role in shaping the urban environment. Although city planners lost an unusual opportunity when they failed to replan the downtown area after the Great Fire, a great deal happened in Boston between 1872 and 1897 when the first subway opened. In many ways, the aftermath of the Great Fire revealed the limits of planning: there was no city planning agency and businesses would not permit the government to reorganize the street system in the burnt district. Business cooperation had not yet reached the level at which the common good, even of the merchants themselves, would be allowed to interfere with individual property rights.

As so often in the history of planning in Boston, individuals played a prominent part in showing the city how to use government power effectively. Frederick Law Olmsted's pioneering work in designing the city's park system was momentous in that it signaled the acceptance of a more positive and active role for government in determining the appearance of the city. Olmsted pointed the way to a new conception of planning: because his vision was not restricted to a single area, he saw the need for

....

Building

Downtown

and around

Town

105

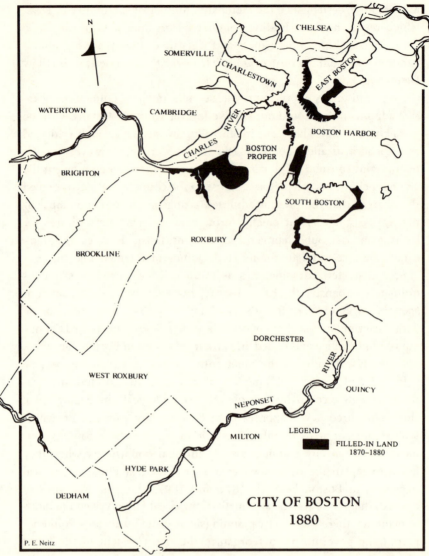

Map 4.1 City of Boston, 1880, showing landfill. The filling of the Back Bay has largely been accomplished, although not all built upon. The Fan Pier in South Boston is shown. (For another perspective see figure 4.5.) East Boston also continues to edge into the inner harbor and to develop wharfs.

....

Building

Downtown

and around

Town

106

parkways to weave the city together; moreover, he saw the need for—and built—a coalition to support his plans. In creating the Emerald Necklace, Olmsted broke the path for other government action. The Boston park system set an important precedent that led to the metropolitan park, sewer, and water systems of the 1890s. Furthermore, Olmsted's under-

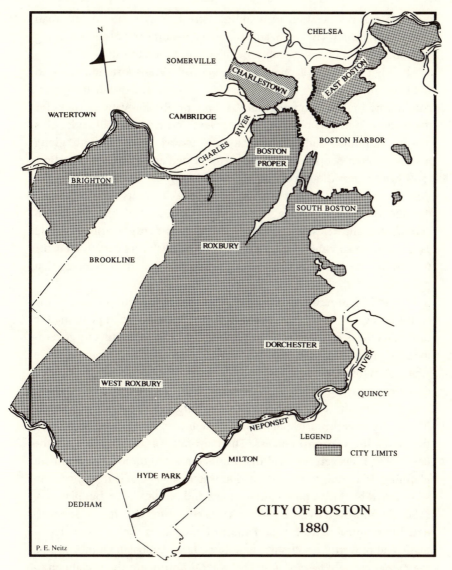

N

SOMERVILLE

CHELSEA

WATERTOWN

CAMBRIDGE

CHARLESTOWN

EAST BOSTON

BOSTON HARBOR

CHARLES RIVER

BOSTON PROPER

BRIGHTON

SOUTH BOSTON

BROOKLINE

ROXBURY

DORCHESTER

RIVER

WEST ROXBURY

QUINCY

NEPONSET

LEGEND

CITY LIMITS

MILTON

HYDE PARK

CITY OF BOSTON
1880

DEDHAM

P. E. Neitz

Map 4.2 City of Boston, 1880, showing annexed areas and political boundaries. The 1870s brought another decade of explosive growth to Boston. Charlestown, Brighton and West Roxbury were all annexed to the city on January 5, 1874. That same year Brookline, which until 1705 was owned by Boston, bucked the annexation trend and voted 706 to 299 to remain independent of the growing metropolis.

standing of the need to connect the old peninsular city with outlying districts was mirrored by the private sector's massive construction of streetcar lines. Henry Whitney, a private-sector visionary, greatly affected the shape of Boston through both his land developments to the west of the old city and his creation of a unified streetcar system. No less than Olmsted, Whitney saw the need to connect distant parts of the emerging metropolis. And no less capably, he made his dream a reality.

Although no such visionary appeared on the transportation scene in the 1890s, the collective efforts of the city, the state, and the local business community built a technologically and politically innovative system for the construction and operation of subways and elevated railroads. This mixture of public- and private-sector efforts was consistent with a long history of such cooperation, a pattern repeated again and again in Boston's history, but the novelty of the situation in the 1890s was twofold. First, technological advances in railways and electricity allowed—even demanded—new strategies, new partnerships. Second, the downtown commercial and real-estate interests recognized that government could assist them in solving their problems. Twenty-five years earlier, after the Great Fire, the business community was not prepared to embrace that possibility.

Responding to new challenges and meeting new needs are part of the continual evolution of a more powerful government role in planning the future. As the need for systematic planning became apparent, city government began to show success in adapting to change, and a new attitude emerged. This new view recognized the benefits of local government doing more to shape the city than simply distributing land and planning streets. With the city now involved in building a magnificent public library, a pioneering park and sewer system, and America's first subway, the possibilities seemed endless. The mayoralty of Josiah Quincy in the late 1890s, however, revealed that limits remained on local government planning. Planning to provide parks, water, sewers, and transportation was backed by the predominant business and political elite, but planning to secure improved living conditions was either unsupported or subordinated to political patronage and strained budgets. It took a more charismatic and powerful leadership than that offered by Josiah Quincy to lead the city effectively toward a greater role in improving the social conditions of Boston's poor.

....
Building
Downtown
and around
Town

108

5

....

"A Bigger,
Better, Busier
Boston"

The idea of city planning as a profession budded during the first two decades of the twentieth century when Bostonians enthusiastically promoted the City Beautiful movement, aimed at transforming the physical and political body of the city. Changes in the physical city were, however, restricted to developing the port facilities and imposing limits on building heights, matters of considerable concern to the city's business leaders. Problems of health and housing, education and recreation confronted thousands, but—as Mayor Josiah Quincy's frustrated attempts to address these issues in the 1890s showed—there was still no effective coalition to support sustained municipal activity in these areas. In part this was due to the transfer of political power from the Yankees to the Irish, which reduced business's faith in local government, but even more important was the persistent ideology of limited government. Power wielders used government activity to promote business interests while those who wanted the government to enhance the physical and social welfare of Boston's citizens were forced to wait.

Boston basked in general commercial and economic well-being in the last years of the nineteenth century. Textiles, improved rail connections to the West, and increased production of local goods raised the level of Boston's exports so that by the end of the century it was the second leading U.S. port in foreign trade. Much of this growth resulted from private-sector development of new land specifically to service trade. The Boston, Hartford, and Erie Railroad bought over two and one-half million square feet of South Boston mudflats and solid land from the Boston

Wharf Company in 1868, and spent over a million dollars in the next ten years filling and improving the area, building new warehouses and grain elevators and enlarging piers in the section now known as Fan Pier and the Fort Point Channel District.

Bostonians invested in a number of important new businesses at the end of the nineteenth century. Although Boston as a secondary source of capitalization declined relative to other cities, in some areas it led the way. The Boston Fruit Company, founded in 1885, was part of an 1899 merger that created United Fruit. General Electric, a New York firm founded in 1892, rested on a strong Boston Brahmin presence. In 1899 Louis Brandeis, a Boston lawyer, arranged a merger that created the United Shoe Machinery Corporation. American Telephone & Telegraph Company was initially a Boston concern, with Brahmins named Forbes and Higginson prominent among its directors. In the early twentieth century, however, control of AT&T shifted to New York—a move that symbolized Boston's shifting fortunes.[1]

The changing composition of international trade also hurt Boston in the years around the turn of the century. In the late nineteenth century immense quantities of grain, cereal, and meat moved through the city on the way to Europe, but in the early twentieth century agricultural trade declined. Manufacturing products, which now dominated United States trade, were more likely to move through the ports of New York, Philadelphia, and Baltimore.[2] Boston underwent a serious dislocation, losing ground in most industries, but managed to keep its position in the wool and leather trades. During World War I Boston was the biggest wool center in the world and the largest exporter of boots and shoes, but overall the city dropped from second in foreign shipping in 1901 to fourth in 1908 and sixth in 1920.

After 1860, the new method of packing fresh fish in ice spurred the growth of Boston's fishing fleet, but the city became more of a marketing center than a fishing port. Fishing activity centered on Commercial Wharf until 1884, when it moved to T Wharf (so named because of its shape). Pier No. 5 and a nearby fish pier opened in 1913 and major fish dealers moved to South Boston in 1914, leaving the Atlantic Avenue wharves to deteriorate.[3]

The port's decline in the beginning of the twentieth century concerned many Bostonians. Because the city lay farther from the source of raw materials than its competitors, Boston needed to improve its transit and shipping facilities dramatically if it were ever to reduce the cost of handling goods and materials.[4] The federal government stepped in, dredging a channel from Charlestown to the sea in 1902 and building the largest

....

*"A Bigger,
Better,
Busier
Boston"*

110

stone and concrete drydock in the world at the Boston Navy Yard in 1905.[5] Other harbor improvements before World War I included the opening of Commonwealth Pier in 1911.

Significant changes also took place in the city's political life as the Irish moved into a clear ascendancy and progressive reformers tried to remedy the ills of urban life. These two developments had a great effect on the story of planning as social, ethnic, and partisan strife sharply reduced the likelihood of cooperation between business and political leaders. The Progressive movement had a variety of goals, one of which was to correct the ills and abuses in urban society and to impose some order on a nation experiencing rapid and confusing change.[6] Members of the traditional elite, threatened with the loss of status and power, sought new ways of maintaining both, as well as advancing the interests of the community as they saw it.[7]

The Progressive movement in politics, which followed hard on the heels of the enthusiastic reception accorded the Federal Civil Service Reform, came to the fore in the 1890s. Reformers founded the National Municipal League in 1894, the same year the first National Conference for Good City Government met and a coalition of academics and reformers attempted to strengthen city governments through a variety of methods.[8] Reform mayors replaced bosses and broke up political machines as Progressives experimented with new forms of administration, special commissions, and city-manager government in cities such as Toledo, Detroit, and Milwaukee. Many Bostonians shared this passion for reform, but others, particularly the now-embattled Brahmins, seized upon administrative changes and institutional reforms as a way of keeping "undesirable members" of the Boston Irish community out of political life "in favor of those middle-class professionals—doctors, lawyers, businessmen, financiers—who were more acceptable to the local advocates of good government."[9]

A "respectable" Irishman, Patrick A. Collins, stepped forward to succeed Mayor Josiah Quincy in 1899, but the Republican candidate, former Mayor Thomas Hart, won. Two years later Collins took office. The Irish-born Collins, a Harvard Law School graduate, former state legislator, U.S. Representative, and diplomat, won the respect of Bostonians of all ethnic groups.[10] Like former mayor Hugh O'Brien, Collins was a fiscal conservative, and fiscal conservatism was the norm in these years. In fact, Boston's per capita outlay dropped between 1880 and 1902 by a remarkable 31 percent, from $51 to $35.[11]

Collins sought fiscally responsible government yet was committed to capital planning. He vetoed relief programs for the poor and drastically

....

"A Bigger,
Better,
Busier
Boston"

111

cut street improvement budgets, but approved construction projects for playgrounds and bathhouses. He proposed construction first for schools and then for the creation of a road from Fort Point Channel to the northern portion of the docks on downtown Boston's waterfront. In addition Collins stressed the importance of renovating the harbor and building a new city hall. Collins's promise to the city council "that Congress will make adequate provision for the improvement of our great harbor" has a familiar ring to it: federal influence, especially in transportation, was already important.[12] This was but one shift in planning; limiting building heights was another.

Whereas in the previous century the city had continually exerted its power to expand the community, in the beginning of the twentieth century it began to constrict growth. City planning, as a profession, developed in an era when Boston began taking some of the most significant, yet restrictive measures in its history. Although the first building-height limitation was adopted by the U.S. Congress in 1899, prohibiting the construction of any building above the height of the U.S. Capitol, the same spirit predominated in Boston: no structure could rise above the golden dome of Bulfinch's elegant State House.

Tall buildings were physically impossible until the years after the Civil War, when technological developments (including the typewriter, the telephone, and electric lighting) created a new type of business environment which required more space, while at the same time advances in construction methods allowed office buildings to rise above the four- or five-story limit of the past. In 1868 the Sears Building at the corner of Washington and Court Streets was the first building in Boston to have an elevator. In 1887 the ten-story Fiske Building rose to a height of 183 feet, while in 1889 the fourteen-story Ames Building near the Old State House reached 190 feet. The Winthrop Building, constructed in 1893–1894, was the first steel frame building in Boston.[13] Bostonians criticized these structures, along with the eleven-story Exchange Building (1889–1891), for a number of reasons, but especially for stealing light and air from neighboring structures and from the street.[14] Opponents also complained about traffic congestion and fire hazards.

More important, however, to the outcome of the building-height debate were reservations articulated by the real estate developers themselves. Fiscally conservative property owners in Boston feared the office market would become overbuilt. When several of the first skyscrapers were slow to yield a return on their investments, the owners' fears were confirmed.[15] They persuaded the state legislature in 1892 to allow Boston to set a maximum height of 125 feet, with the exception of spires of

....

"A Bigger,

Better,

Busier

Boston"

112

churches.[16] In the next year William Minot, Boston's largest landowner, rewrote the city's building code, which incorporated this state limit, although Minot was said to have preferred an even lower maximum height of 100 feet.[17] Business interests wanted government regulation to protect their property.

Over the next several years the legislature placed more restrictions on certain sections of the city, such as Commonwealth Avenue, Copley Square, and Beacon Hill. These restrictions, however, were based more on aesthetics than finances. Haddon Hall, for example, an apartment house of eleven stories located on Commonwealth Avenue at the corner of Berkeley Street, "seriously marred the established scale of townhouse streetscapes."[18] Angry neighbors' complaints led to the imposition of height limitations on Commonwealth Avenue. The legislature also passed a law in 1896 which allowed the city's Park Commission to impose a building-height limit of seventy feet along the edges of parks and parkways.[19] The legislature's 1898 enactment of a one hundred-foot limit on the north side of Copley Square and ninety feet on the other three sides, however, was quickly challenged.[20]

The restrictions on Copley Square came in response to the proposal for a ten-story apartment house on the southeast corner of the square. Legislators acted only after construction had already begun, but the developer agreed to modify the building to a height of ninety-six feet, six above the maximum. Opponents were not satisfied by this compromise and launched a multitude of commissions, investigations, lawsuits, and appeals which eventually reached the U.S. Supreme Court. The builder was finally forced to lower the building to ninety feet by removing the offending six feet of terra cotta frieze, but the city had to pay $350,000 in compensation.[21] Ironically, today the sixty-story John Hancock Tower rises 790 feet above the site.

The legislature protected its own home against shadows by establishing a limit of seventy feet in the vicinity of the State House on Beacon Hill in a series of laws passed between 1899 and 1902.[22] Two years later Massachusetts enacted the first comprehensive height-of-buildings law in the nation. This law imposed a height restriction of forty-five feet on wooden buildings in Boston and set two different height limitations for business and residential districts labelled "A" and "B," respectively. The maximum height allowed in the business district was 125 feet, the maximum in the residential district, eighty.[23]

The tower added to the U.S. Custom House in 1913–1915 proved an exception to the new limits. The Custom House at the foot of State Street, originally designed by Ammi Burnham Young as a Greek temple, was

....

"A Bigger,

Better,

Busier

Boston"

113

Figure 5.1 The Custom House built on State Street, 1837–1847, did not have its now-famous tower (see figs. 6.2 and 7.4) until the federal government added it on between 1913 and 1915. A portion of a ship may be seen in the lower right corner. (Courtesy of the Library of the Boston Redevelopment Authority.)

....

"A Bigger,

Better,

Busier

Boston"

114

completed in 1847. In the early twentieth century the federal government decided to add a sixteen-story, 500-foot tower designed by the architectural firm, Peabody and Stearns. Boston's building-height limits were in this case ineffective since the federal government is not subject to local legislation. The controversial tower rose above the old interior rotunda and clashed with the design of the original structure. Purists who opposed the building for its intrusion on the city's skyline and damage to an earlier masterpiece would find it ironic that this same tower has since become a famous and revered Boston landmark.

Massachusetts' building-height limitation served as a model for other cities until New York's comprehensive zoning ordinance of 1916 succeeded it, and the era of restrictive height limits ended nationally. Boston, however, incorporated the maximum height law in its zoning laws of the 1920s and retained such restrictions until the 1960s. Such legislation and zoning cast the city in an essentially negative role. The motivation was, in part, aesthetics, but more important, the protection of established property interests. The height-limitation movement demonstrates a basically conservative attitude, although it was, in fact, an extension of municipal power to meet the new reality of the twentieth century. Ironically, building-height limits paved the way for further government power, which some believed should be used to plan for the growth of the city rather than the limitation of it. These people were the first so-called "city planners," many of whom began their work in the "City Beautiful" movement.

Activists in the City Beautiful movement in the United States, inspired by the beauty and planned unity of the Chicago's World Fair of 1893–1894, envisioned the city as a work of art.[24] Daniel Burnham, a prominent architect, led a team that included Louis Sullivan and Frederick Law Olmsted, in planning a brand-new sparkling-clean city on the Chicago lakefront. Over twenty-seven million people came to see the great "White City"—so named for its numerous white buildings—the grounds of which were laid out by Olmsted. Called the Columbian Exposition, in celebration of the four hundredth anniversary of the discovery of the New World, this spectacle came to symbolize the city in America, and was influential in stimulating others throughout the nation to follow suit. The fair exhibited agricultural and industrial technology, offered fantastic entertainment, and "lured spectators into an idealized future and a ro-manticized past"; most important of all, the exposition demonstrated what planners could do if offered the chance.[25]

Fifteen years later, the Burnham Plan for Chicago showed the breath-taking possibilities of planning. Burnham's motto was "Make no little plans . . . Make big plans; aim high in hope and work." His 1909 proposal for the great Midwestern city was a milestone and continues to serve as a reference point for planners throughout the country, although few other cities could match its scope. The Burnham Plan dealt with transportation and recreational needs, and prepared for future development; in contrast, most other City Beautiful projects consisted of little more than new public buildings and civic centers, and cosmetic attempts to make com-mercial districts more attractive and profitable.[26]

Critics have charged that such civic centers, monuments, boulevards, and fountains were "an exercise in vanity on the part of the upper classes" and in part were intended "to instill the citizenry with respect for country, culture, and capitalism."[27] Historian Paul Boyer, on the other hand, puts more emphasis on the social, moral, and physical challenges facing plan-ners than on government concern for inculcating mass support for cap-italism. He writes that "the conviction that an intimate link existed between a city's physical appearance and its moral state—and that Amer-ica's cities were sadly deficient on this score—was central to the 'city beautiful' movement."[28] In referring to the 1909 plan for Chicago, Boyer

....

"A Bigger,

Better,

Busier

Boston"

115

Figure 5.2 View of the Charles River Esplanade, taken in 1912; compare to fig. 4.9. These well-dressed Bostonians stroll along what all too quickly became Storrow Drive. Beacon Hill is in the background. (Courtesy of The Bostonian Society/Old State House.)

singles out the fundamental object of Burnham's proposal: "to restore to the city a lost visual and aesthetic harmony, thereby creating the physical prerequisite for the emergence of a harmonious social order." Burnham felt that "the city planner's great opportunity—and solemn obligation—was to wage battle against the external disorder that was both a symptom and a cause of the city's spiritual malaise."[28]

The completion in 1900 of Boston's majestic South Station, then the world's largest railroad terminal, was but one manifestation of the spirit of the City Beautiful movement. In Boston the private Metropolitan Improvement League, founded in 1904, published a monthly bulletin, *The Better City,* and undertook such beautification projects as tree planting along Beacon Street, park improvements, commemorative monuments, improvements of the Fens, and development of the Esplanade along the Charles River. Although the creation of a park along the Charles sounds attractive and appealing, it provoked a battle because Beacon Street residents on the water side feared a new street would rise to obstruct their views; they claimed even not to mind the flooding of their cellars, the wharf rats, and the unbeautiful sight of the low-water flats.[29]

The state's Metropolitan Improvement Commission was another manifestation of the local City Beautiful movement, although the five-member

....

"A Bigger,

Better,

Busier

Boston"

116

commission, created in 1907, tended to concern itself more with the economy than aesthetics. Charged with improving the transportation capabilities and maritime position of the city, the commission upheld the view that the waterfront "affords the highest possible opportunity and promise for commercial and industrial development. . . . Nothing further should be done by the public in the way of takings for park purposes or otherwise which will divert any portion of this great waterfront from its potential use for commerce and industry."[30] Few statements could be more plainly opposed to the planning priorities that emerged in Boston during the 1980s.

A second major concern of the Metropolitan Improvement Commission was the creation of a civic or government center. In a study appended to the 1909 report, consultants argued against the public perception that an undertaking of this magnitude was beyond Boston's ability, and cited ambitious nineteenth-century projects—from Quincy Market, South Station, and the Back Bay to Commonwealth Avenue and the Emerald Necklace—to prove that such large public enterprises were feasible. The commission suggested several possible locations for the civic center. One was the Public Garden, although they acknowledged legislative restrictions on the site. Another was Copley Square, on the site of either the old Museum of Fine Arts (which had moved further out Huntington Avenue

Figure 5.3 View of the Charles River Esplanade, taken from the West Boston Bridge in 1915. The Back Bay is in the distance and Beacon Hill to the left. (Courtesy of The Bostonian Society/Old State House.)

....

"A Bigger,

Better,

Busier

Boston"

117

along with other cultural and educational institutions) or the nearby Boston and Providence railroad property. Coyly avowing that it did not regard it "a duty to urge definitively any one site," the commission favored the Public Garden site as the "cheapest as well as one where great results could be obtained," even while acknowledging that public opinion "probably opposed it."[31]

Transportation was a third major concern of the Metropolitan Improvement Commission. Arthur A. Shurtleff,[32] a landscape architect, attached a study of Boston's roads to the commission's report and proposed a system of radial highways for the region. He was not the last to lament "the bewilderment of strangers who view for the first time the unusual street system of Boston."[33] Shurtleff proposed a circumferential road around the metropolitan area but this proposal and others of the commission were long ignored. (Decades later, the circumferential road idea again generated a mountain of controversy, adding another chapter to Boston's planning history.)

The first years of the twentieth century were marked by other equally ill-fated ideas. In 1907, for example, a special committee of the Boston Society of Architects (BSA) weighed in with a number of bizarre proposals for the Boston of the future. The architects' report consisted of a series of disparate suggestions and made numerous impracticable suggestions based on comparisons of Boston with European and other American cities. The committee's avowed task was to "collect and study any plans that we can find for making Boston now, and as it grows larger, more convenient for its inhabitants, better adapted for commerce, and more beautiful in appearance." It began by reviewing "fatal errors that have been committed" in Boston in the recent past, an intriguingly contemporary catalogue of planning blunders that included the failure to coordinate a court house and city hall buildings with the State House on Beacon Hill; the construction of both North and South Stations without any "grand or stately effects"; and the inadequate public space at Copley Square. The committee also deplored the fact that "our parks are defaced by a fringe of cheap tenements" and the "waters of our harbor are defiled with sewage."[34]

The architects' committee, concerned about Boston Harbor and developing facilities for ocean commerce, put forth an especially mind-boggling proposal to construct piers extending from what is now Carson Beach in South Boston. They wanted to fill in Old Harbor five hundred feet out from shore and extend nine-mile-long piers nearly to Thompson's Island. Each pier would be three hundred feet wide and bear two rows of four-story warehouses and four railroad tracks connecting to the Old

....

"A Bigger,
Better,
Busier
Boston"

118

Colony Railroad. Fortunately, the only part of this scheme carried out was the construction of Old Colony Avenue. Another fanciful idea advanced by the committee was the construction of an island in the Charles River between Boston and Cambridge.[35]

The same committee echoed Arthur Shurtleff's proposal for the construction of circular boulevards. One, called the "Inner Boulevard," was to run from Andrew Square in South Boston to the Fenway and over to Cambridge. The other, "Outer Boulevard," would wind from Fields Corner in Dorchester through Roxbury, Brookline, Allston, and into Cambridge.[36]

In articulating its multifarious plans, the BSA committee implied that Boston's chief problem was the shackles placed on the private sector by local government. It blamed the standstill in construction not only on the shortage of space, but also on the city's "too restrictive building laws, both as to height and material."[37] Although little came from either of these 1907 reports, the BSA spurred debate, more of Boston's leading citizens joined in the discussion, and the concept of planning the city grew in popularity.

The beginning of the twentieth century was an era of a self-conscious civic-mindedness. Local reformers established a Good Government Association in 1903 to oppose the "City Hall circle" which continued to reap unmerited benefits during Mayor Patrick Collins's administration.[38] Although they did not challenge Collins's personal integrity and motives, they did not refrain from attacking the integrity of a longtime ward boss who succeeded to the mayoralty when Collins died in office in 1905. The first term of John F. "Honey Fitz" Fitzgerald nourished an even more strenuous effort by the reformers.

John F. Fitzgerald, political boss of the North End, had served in the city council, Massachusetts legislature, and U.S. Congress before becoming mayor. Like Josiah Quincy, Fitzgerald was an activist mayor. A maverick among the ward bosses, he cut deals with them while simultaneously forming alliances with the city's conservative businessmen.[39] Also like Quincy, he failed to reconcile the two worlds.

Fitzgerald's campaign call for "A Bigger, Better, Busier Boston" shrewdly appealed to all who would profit by promoting the city's growth. Fitzgerald's booster spirit was already well-known and he faithfully served the business sector through projects aiding commerce and promoting Boston. As a Congressman in the late 1890s he played a key role in bringing the U.S.S. *Constitution,* "Old Ironsides," to Boston. He also aided the port by securing a deeper channel, a lighthouse, and a drydock.[40] Mayor Fitzgerald cared deeply about the city, and made meeting the transportation needs of both his time and the future a primary goal. He once gave a re-

....

"A Bigger,
Better,
Busier
Boston"

119

Figure 5.4 Campaign photograph of John F. Fitzgerald, which was borne on a hand-card given to voters as they entered polling places in 1905. The back of the card promised that Fitzgerald's election means a "Bigger, Better, Busier Boston." (Courtesy of Gerard F. Burke.)

markable speech anticipating the importance of air travel but was laughed at for saying that "Perhaps . . . airships may be invented to sail from this country to other parts of the world." His vision also found expression in more concrete terms: during two mayoral terms he oversaw the building of the City Hall Annex (later the School Department headquarters at 26 Court Street), the City Point Aquarium in South Boston, and the Franklin Park Zoo.[41] These impressive accomplishments must be set, however, against the pattern of corruption in city construction projects, a low point in Fitzgerald's first administration. The city lost hundreds of thousands of dollars in inflated land deals and the purchase of superfluous goods and services, and an odd assortment of new city posts such as Tea Warmers, Wipers, Rubberboot Repairers, and City Dermatologist proliferated.[42] The public reacted furiously and Fitzgerald himself called for the creation of the Finance Commission to consider the charges.

Perhaps Fitzgerald viewed the involvement of such a commission as inevitable; perhaps he hoped it would clear his name. As Doris Kearns Goodwin, chronicler of the Fitzgerald and Kennedy families, writes, he may have assumed that this committee "would merely run its course with an occasional meeting, sporadic interviews and a dull report, and in the meantime its very existence would provide a release of tension."[43] But

....

"A Bigger,
Better, Busier
Boston"

120

Fitzgerald had no such luck. The state-chartered Boston Finance Commission displayed extraordinary zeal investigating the city and newspapers ate it up. The negative publicity proved ruinous to the mayor and he lost a reelection bid in 1907. The first Fitzgerald administration provided plenty of evidence, to those who sought it, of the need for controlling Boston politicians and had implications far beyond the immediate political future of "Honey Fitz," John Fitzgerald Kennedy's grandfather.

In fact, the shift in political power from Yankee Republicans to Irish Democrats played a significant part in determining the future of metropolitan reform. Progressive reformers and others realized there were only two ways they could control Boston's city government, either by diluting the power of Boston politicians through a metropolitan government plan which would incorporate Boston with adjoining cities and towns, or by maintaining Boston's independence but placing it under stricter state control. Since the legislature held absolute authority over the city's existence, reformers could dismiss Boston's feelings in the matter and devote themselves to winning legislative support for either approach. Somewhat paradoxically, ethnic conflict served as both a motivation and a deterrent to these efforts. The Republican, Yankee-dominated legislature sought to control Boston and limit Irish power by making the city more directly answerable to the state while at the same time representatives from adjacent communities worked assiduously to maintain separate town identities.

The one exception was the town of Hyde Park, which welcomed its annexation to Boston in 1912. Hyde Park had been created in 1868 from land grants by Dorchester, Dedham, and Milton.[44] Alpheus P. Blake and his "Twenty Associates" bought the farmland just before the Civil War and drew up plans for a residential subdivision, but few people moved there until after the war ended in 1865. During the Civil War, the first black regiment called to arms trained in the Readville section of Hyde Park along with thousands of other troops at Camp Meigs. The 54th Regiment, led into battle by the young Robert Gould Shaw, is memorialized by the famous Saint-Gaudens bas-relief on the edge of the Boston Common across from the State House.

Hyde Park grew in the last third of the nineteenth century largely due to the influx of Irish, Italian, and Jewish workers looking for work in mills along the Neponset River. The town's population mushroomed from 1,512 in 1887 to 15,000 in 1912, the year it was annexed to Boston. Robert Bleakie, owner of a local woolen mill, led the movement for annexation. His supporters were mainly immigrants; opposition came from the Yankee population. Longtime Hyde Park residents recall the split

....

"A Bigger,

Better,

Busier

Boston"

121

taking form along religious as well as ethnic lines, since Protestant churches opposed joining Boston while the Catholic church was for it.[45] The size of the newer, immigrant population made annexation inevitable; after a vigorous debate Hyde Park voters approved the move by a two-to-one margin in November 1911. Boston officials coveted the tax revenue the city would gain from the factories in Hyde Park and despite the town's $10 million debt formally accepted the acquisition in early 1912. This annexation was a singular case in the twentieth century, however, and is explained by the unique fiscal and ethnic situation of Hyde Park. All other adjoining towns managed to avoid being absorbed by Boston, with its despised Irish politicians and immigrant masses.

Since annexation or metropolitan government was doomed, the Republican legislature turned to the alternative—strict state control of Boston and continual state interference with Boston's electoral and political system. The Good Government Association, representing Yankee financial interests, easily persuaded the legislature to create a watchdog group, the Boston Finance Commission, and to revise the Boston city charter in 1909. Reformers pinned their hopes of controlling Boston on the charter reform of 1909, which separated the legislative and executive functions of the city more clearly, extended the mayor's term to four years, and substituted a unicameral council with nine at-large members for the unwieldy Common Council and Board of Alderman.[46] Imposed by the state, the charter reform of 1909 was intended to weaken the power of ward bosses by establishing a stronger mayoralty. Reformers assumed that the voters would choose a suitable Yankee as mayor. Reformers also tried to eliminate political parties from municipal elections by instituting nonpartisan balloting. Last, they established a permanent Finance Commission for Boston and required that all municipal department heads, although appointed by the mayor, be approved by the State Civil Service Commission.[47] The charter reform, clearly aimed against the likes of Fitzgerald, was an immediate failure: in 1910 Boston voters rejected the reform candidate, James Jackson Storrow, and returned "Honey Fitz" to office. The long-term value of the charter reform was equally doubtful to the city's Republicans who, because their numbers are so few, are almost never able to place a candidate in the November mayoral elections. Under nonpartisan voting Boston customarily has two Democrats facing off in the final selection.

In the short term, however, Fitzgerald triumphantly returned to City Hall and surprised the reformers by attempting to work with them and the city's business leaders to promote Boston's economic prospects. Fitzgerald genuinely wanted to cooperate, but the poor reputation of his previous administration earned him the enduring hostility of the good-government types, and they proceeded on their own. The reformers included James Jackson Storrow, Fitzgerald's 1910 opponent, in the leadership of an ambitious crusade to make over the old city by the year 1915.

Edward A. Filene, Louis Brandeis, and others organized the "Boston–1915" campaign early in 1909, a program that became the most important and well-known component of the City Beautiful movement in Boston. Filene and his associates announced their agenda at a dinner meeting of several hundred civic leaders on March 30, 1909, and set up an office, a board of directors, and a speakers' bureau the next day. The organizers believed that the city's physical, economic, social, and political problems had to be dealt with as a whole. Accordingly, they gathered financial data, formulated plans for a federated metropolitan area, and prepared studies on health, education, and physical changes in the city. Paul Kellogg, one of the nation's most prominent planners, expressed the vision of many when he wrote "it is not merely the . . . community of 1915 for which these men are working, but for the city imperishable."[48] With an all-encompassing program and rhetoric like this the Boston–1915 movement was vulnerable to attack. Cynics derided both Edward Filene, the organization's chief sponsor, and its target date of 1915 by anticipating the arrival of "the Filennium."

Filene and his associates acknowledged the ambitious nature of their goals and set about gathering as much support as possible for their movement. In 1910 they began publishing *New Boston,* a magazine that aspired to be "A Chronicle of Progress in Developing a Greater and Finer City Under the Auspices of the Boston–1915 Movement." In addition to sponsoring these large-scale public efforts, they invited some 1,600 agencies throughout the city to send representatives to the movement. They divided the representatives into groups of business organizations, charities and correctional agencies, educational institutions, health organizations, civic organizations, cooperative organizations, women's clubs, and youth organizations. The membership was further divided into special committees to deal with various issues ranging from an Olympic-like "Boys Games" and a "Saner Fourth of July" to the quality of the city's housing. One such group was the "City Guard" of boys and girls, "who shall be military scouts for reporting to the department or organization concerned all offenses against good city housekeeping."[49] Although in retrospect some of these programs may appear humorous or quaint, Boston–1915 was serious and its leaders understood the crucial elements which shaped the city.

New Boston proclaimed that "fundamental to all city development is the

....

"A Bigger,

Better,

Busier

Boston"

123

question of housing," and reported that the movement's Housing Committee was conducting "an investigation into present conditions of congestion, and into possible means of remedy." The committee focused on the economics of the situation, pointing out that owners could charge higher rents because so many people were crowded into their buildings. Land values rose, with the result that poor people could meet the rising costs only through further crowding. At the same time, land values in South Boston and Charlestown were decreasing. The committee thus complained of "illegitimate congestion" in the North and West Ends and concluded that housing conditions in these neighborhoods had deteriorated so badly that "a gradual moving-out process" was necessary.[50] By clearing out the West and North Ends property values would be equalized and housing and costs would be more rationally distributed. Nearly half a century later, the city's leaders followed a somewhat different line of reasoning but with the same result: the people of the West End were evicted and their homes demolished. In the 1950s, city planning became synonymous with failure and insensitivity, but at this early stage the profession was filled with hope.

In the early twentieth century, professional planners stepped forward to assert both the ideals and name of the profession. Many were engineers, architects, or landscape architects only now assuming the title of city planner. Local planning agencies were a recent innovation—the first pair appeared in New Haven in 1907 and Chicago in 1909. The idea of city planning boards in America stemmed, in part, from the City Beautiful movement, whose projects often began as private ventures but ended by turning to government powers to fulfill their goals.[51] Planners held the first national conference on planning in Washington, D.C. in 1909, the same year that the first course in planning was offered at Harvard and the first text in the field was published.[52] Frederick Law Olmsted, Jr., was a leading light in the movement and articulated the vision of the city planner at the second national conference on city planning in 1910. Olmsted argued that the idea of the profession was one in which "all the planning that shapes each of the fragments that go to make up the physical city shall be so harmonized as to reduce the conflict of purposes and the waste of constructive effort to a minimum, and thus secure for the people of the city conditions adapted to their attaining the maximum of productive efficiency, of health, and of enjoyment of life."[53]

Locally, John F. Fitzgerald discussed the need for municipal planning in an article on "The City of the Future" in New Boston. He wrote, "I believe that we in America shall cultivate the art of town planning more and more and perhaps in time go as far as the European cities, with results equally

....

"A Bigger,

Better,

Busier

Boston"

124

admirable."[54] Before Boston could do anything of the sort, however, it first had to set up a planning board. By 1914 the city had such a board but not without a great battle over the creation of a larger, metropolitan planning board, one of the primary goals of the Boston–1915 movement. Backers of the idea drew support from a variety of interests, including Boston's Chamber of Commerce, which issued a 1911 report fully articulating the arguments for a metropolitan planning board. The premise was evident in its title, *"Real Boston": The 'Get Together' Spirit Among Cities and Towns.* The chamber argued that the forty cities and towns in the region were actually one city. With a total population of one and a half million people, this city extended from Salem to Cohasset and included the western towns of Lincoln, Lexington, Wayland, Framingham, Sherborn, and Canton. As such it constituted the fourth largest city in the nation.[55]

The Chamber of Commerce introduced the "Real Boston Bill" which promised "cooperation not annexation" but created a metropolitan district to be named "The Federation of Metropolitan Boston." The plan for this district was modeled on the Greater London Council and authorized a metropolitan planning board which would review local plans and be invested with the power to delay a town's action for a year. Independent cities and towns wished to remain autonomous, however, despite inducements such as having the state pick up part of the cost for improvements. The Metropolitan Affairs Committee of the state legislature killed the "Real Boston Bill" in April 1912 and the Boston–1915 movement collapsed.[56] The reformers had staked considerable prestige and clout on the metropolitan scheme, and when they failed to attain even this goal the leaders lost heart and support withered.

Mayor Fitzgerald attacked the towns of Newton and Brookline for their "parochial shortsightedness and lack of enlightenment" in rejecting such metropolitan plans. He told the fourth national conference on city planning, meeting in Boston in the spring of 1912, to look around them because "the environs of Boston afford an excellent missionary field for your association."[57] Fitzgerald himself, of course, and the ethnic power he represented, were important reasons that suburban towns refused to join with Boston in any such metropolitan scheme. Consequently, Fitzgerald and other advocates of increased government planning had to content themselves with planning restricted to the Boston city limits. This led to the most important legacy of the Boston–1915 movement, the creation of a Boston planning board.

Before Boston established this board, however, the state created the Homestead Commission in 1911 to develop homesteads in the suburbs for workers and their families.[58] The commission survived only until

....

"A Bigger,

Better,

Busier

Boston"

125

1919 but its brief life was notable: it developed a long-range, comprehensive housing program concerned with both design and site planning, and demonstrated an acute sense of regional planning.[59] It also helped bring Boston's Planning Board into existence. The 1913 report of the Homestead Commission argued that all families should be housed in "a wholesome home" and that the numbers living in squalor menaced the stability of government. Furthermore, the death every year of ninety-four out of one thousand children under the age of five in certain districts was "a reproach to the intelligence and conscience of the community." The commission's goal was intelligent city planning that would enable the worker to raise a family with the necessities of pure water, light, and air, while also enjoying recreation and education. The commission complained about the lack of planning which led to a "haphazard, unsystematic development of our cities," and concluded that while most cities grow by chance, without conscious design, direction, or supervision, "the only sensible method of procedure" is to deliberately plan a city's development, thus avoiding an "incalculable waste of effort, efficiency, health, and wealth."[60] Consequently, the commission recommended legislation requiring planning boards in each town or city with a population over 10,000. As far as housing was concerned, however, the commissioners relied upon private associations to plan and construct low-cost suburban homes.[61] The enabling legislation authorizing planning boards passed in 1913 and the Boston Planning Board was established under a city ordinance in 1914.[62] Boston's planning activities now had a focal point.

With this step Boston became one of only fourteen American cities to have a planning agency, almost all of which were advisory in nature. They never received much financial support and few planners or city officials were committed to large-scale planning activities. Boston's five unpaid members (by law at least one of whom had to be a woman) were appointed by the mayor and subject to confirmation by the city council. The board was kept on a tight leash, restricted to a budget of $3,000, and initially allowed only a single staffer.[63] This first staffer, however, proved to be a magnificent choice. A great deal of credit for the work of the board must go to Elisabeth M. Herlihy, who was associated with the Boston Planning Board for nearly forty years. She served as the secretary for more than two decades and then as a board member for the rest of her life. The board itself lasted only a few years beyond her death in 1953.

Elisabeth Herlihy was born in Wilton, New Hampshire, in 1880 and attended Bryant and Stratton Business School in Boston. Her municipal career began in 1910 as a stenographer in the mayor's office and in 1914 Mayor James Michael Curley placed her on the Planning Board staff. Miss

....

"A Bigger,

Better,

Busier

Boston"

126

Herlihy not only served Boston faithfully; she also quickly assumed a leadership position among city planners. She was the first woman member of the American City Planning Institute and served as a director of that organization and of the American Society of Planning Officials. After twenty-two years on the staff of the Boston Planning Board, she was appointed the first chairperson of the new State Planning Board by Governor Curley. It was a remarkable career, especially in a profession dominated by men, but it had its limits, just as the activities of city planning boards were limited.

The pioneering period in the planning profession began in the 1890s with the notions and ideals of the City Beautiful movement. At first strong and committed business leaders were devoted to public service. A rash of committees, commissions, and organizations appeared and attempted to improve the political, physical, and social city and metropolitan area. This drive to improve the city came just as professional city planners created a self-conscious and "scientific" approach to shaping the city, but it was doomed because of politics. Planning and politics have always been intimately connected but the negative aspects of the relationship and the missed opportunities for cooperation are especially obvious in first two decades of this century.

Mayor Fitzgerald's call for "A Bigger, Better, Busier Boston" showed his willingness to cooperate with business leaders in fostering their economic fortunes along with those of the city, but the social and political gap was too wide. When James Michael Curley succeeded Fitzgerald the ethnic chasm widened, with dire results for city planning. For at least the next third of a century, conflict replaced the traditional cooperation between the public and private sectors, and planning in Boston was severely constrained. National factors also placed limits on the development of both the physical city and the idea of planning, but the war between Yankees and Irish, and between business and political leaders, was singularly responsible for the relative decline in Boston's fortunes until the city's revival in the 1960s. Capital, which had always guided the development of the city through government, soon migrated elsewhere and Boston languished for decades.

....

"A Bigger,

Better,

Busier

Boston"

127

6

....

James
Michael Curley
and the
Old Boston

James Michael Curley, a near-mythic figure who symbolizes either the best or worst of Boston politics to many people, is the least understood figure in Boston's planning history. "Both the product of his harsh environment and the creation of his own creative imagination, Curley's image ranges from the rogue saint of his . . . self-description in his autobiography, *I'd Do It Again*—where he is the 'champion of the oppressed and underprivileged'—to the exploitative man of power without vision in William V. Shannon's *The American Irish*."[1] Curley's persona loomed large over City Hall for thirty-five years, and he—more than anyone else—was responsible for shaping Boston from 1915 to the middle of the century. In an era when the private sector abandoned its traditional role of meeting the housing and transportation needs of the community, Curley and the city stepped forward and transformed planning in Boston. The private sector laid out the streetcar lines and the new suburbs of the nineteenth and early twentieth centuries, but by the time of the Great Depression the expansion of Boston's public transportation network and streetcar suburbs had come to a halt. The automobile eliminated the incentive to invest in new rail lines, and the housing market plummeted as well. The depression of the 1930s ended the preeminent position of the private sector in shaping Boston, and while influential business interests sought to focus the city's attention on traffic congestion downtown, city planners focused on zoning. The government, which had always worked in partnership with, and largely in the service of business, now became the

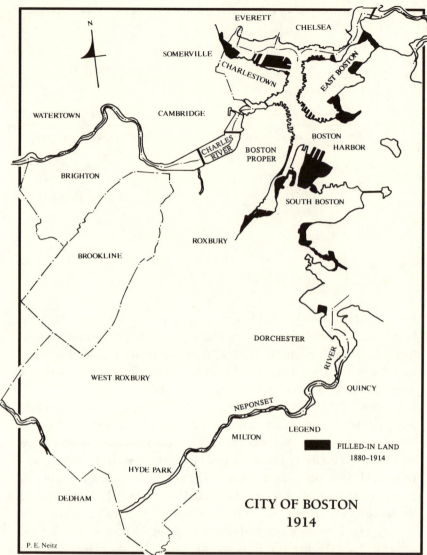

N

EVERETT

CHELSEA

SOMERVILLE

CHARLESTOWN

EAST BOSTON

WATERTOWN

CAMBRIDGE

BOSTON HARBOR

CHARLES RIVER

BOSTON PROPER

BRIGHTON

SOUTH BOSTON

ROXBURY

BROOKLINE

DORCHESTER

RIVER

WEST ROXBURY

QUINCY

NEPONSET

MILTON

LEGEND

FILLED-IN LAND
1880–1914

HYDE PARK

DEDHAM

**CITY OF BOSTON
1914**

P. E. Neitz

S

····

*James
Michael
Curley
and the
Old Boston*

130

Map 6.1 City of Boston, 1914, showing landfill. East Boston is connected with Breed's Island. Charlestown continues to expand to meet the needs of commercial shipping, and South Boston's Commonwealth Flats become solid land. The old South Bay is narrowing and Columbia Point bears a sewage pumping station and fill.

major force in planning the city. And, increasingly, "the government" came to mean Curley.

Curley rotated in and out of the mayor's office from 1914 to 1929, but with his return for a third term in 1930 and the deepening depression he

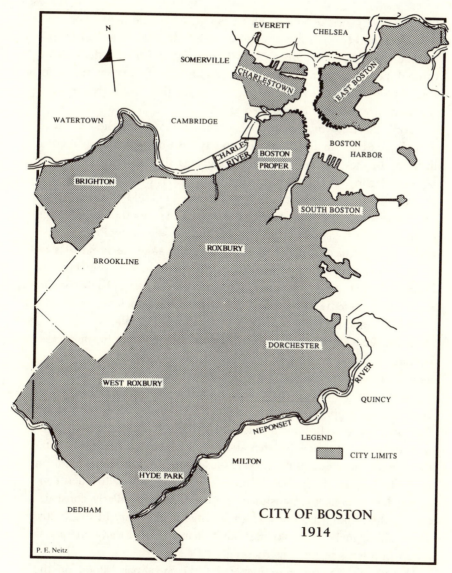

Map 6.2 City of Boston, 1914, showing political borders. Boston reached its fullest extent since the colonial period with the annexation of Hyde Park in 1912.

seized the opportunity to make government a more powerful force in planning. No abstract desire to shape the process or the city motivated Curley. Rather, his immediate objective was to provide relief for Boston's poor. Curley initiated an ambitious public works program to put people to work, and in the process substantially redirected the role of local government in building the city. Nevertheless, it should also be stressed that the emergence of motorized transport, economic depression, the New Deal, and two world wars, along with immense social and demographic changes, did more to alter Boston fundamentally than all of Curley's programs combined. Moreover, although the mayor was often held responsible for Boston's stagnation during this era, the reasons for economic decline were far more complex.

During the third of a century that Curley dominated the city, little growth took place in any older Eastern city. Like most of urban America in these decades, Boston suffered through the throes of economic and political decline. The flight of the textile industry to the South hit New England hard and the wealthy were not inclined to build office and retail space in downtown Boston. During the thirty years after the stock market crash, the twenty-six story Hancock and the ten-story New England Life buildings were the only major additions to Boston's skyline. From 1930 to 1960 the city languished in depression. Although the core problem was economic, an attitude of depression infected Boston like a plague and the city was dismissed as a "shabby, brokendown, bluestocking, politically corrupt city and the subject of satire and national ridicule."[2]

In the 1920s, however—an exciting and optimistic era in America—Boston was far more dynamic than is generally recognized. All across the nation, skyscrapers like the Empire State Building sprang up, "as certain an expression of the ebullient American spirit as the Gothic cathedral was of medieval Europe."[3] Although no office building as tall as the Empire State towered over Boston, luxury hotels, office buildings, and a major redevelopment project at North Station abounded in the 1920s. The Ritz-Carlton, a new edition of the Parker House Hotel, and the Hotel Madison at North Station all opened in this decade, and Sears, Roebuck constructed an imposing establishment on the Fenway. Similarly, construction of the hulking Boston Garden belongs in the story of the 1920s. Thus, although Boston's skyline didn't change dramatically, there was plenty of private-sector construction.

These private-sector investments, for the most part, stood on the periphery of downtown Boston. In the public sector, Curley also diverted funds away from downtown and toward city neighborhoods, thereby straining municipal finances and widening the chasm between the downtown and outlying districts. As historian Thomas H. O'Connor notes:

> [while Curley] built playgrounds in Dorchester and Roxbury, Scollay Square turned into a place where ugly tattoo parlors and sleazy burlesque houses blighted the historic landscape. While he planned extensive bathhouses in South Boston, the docks along Atlantic

Avenue's waterfront section rotted on their pilings. While he laid out miles of paved sidewalks in Charlestown and East Boston, the cobblestones of Beacon Hill fell apart and the lampposts came tumbling down.[4]

For thirty-five years after 1914, Curley paid particular attention to neighborhood recreational, cultural, and health facilities even as city planners focused on creating a zoning plan for Boston.

Indeed, Curley may have dominated politics, but other forces controlled city planning. Planning as a professional activity, which had developed in Boston in the years after the creation of the Planning Board in 1914, was still a new profession throughout the Curley years. No school offered a curriculum in the field until 1929 when Harvard offered a three-year program leading to a master's degree, followed shortly thereafter by MIT, which established a graduate program in 1934 and created a Department of City Planning in 1937.

Lack of funding, traditional ideas of limited government, and the youthfulness of the city-planning profession imposed limitations on Boston's planning board from its inception, but it was able to carve out an early identity by focusing on the city's housing problems. It surveyed East Boston in 1916 and the North End in 1918 and recommended block improvements, street widenings, and playgrounds to relieve overcrowding.[5] World War I soon interrupted progress on the housing front in Boston as well as the rest of the country. In many areas of the nation, the housing shortage impeded war-related production, and the federal government began providing public housing through the U.S. Shipping Board's Emergency Fleet Corporation. The government built, sponsored, or controlled a number of housing projects for war workers in places such as Camden, New Jersey and Wilmington, Delaware—but not in Boston.[6]

Shortly after the war the city council asked the Boston Planning Board to consider whether there was a housing shortage, whether it had worsened, and what the city could do in the absence of private capital investments in housing. The board concluded that there was indeed a housing shortage but reasoned that the only appropriate local-government response would be to aid in the delivery and transportation of goods for housing.[7] That is to say, the planning board would concern itself solely with traffic and economic development, a decision in marked contrast to what might have been expected of the emerging planning profession, given its initial high-flying rhetoric.

The immediate postwar years were crucial for the city-planning profession throughout the United States. Before the First World War the planner was most often a social reformer in alliance with other reformers; after the war the city planner became a technical expert dealing with matters relating to zoning, law, finance, capital expenditure, and transportation, but one largely excluded from social-policy decisions.[8] Paul Boyer points out that, like the City Beautiful movement, city planning "must be viewed against a background of profound apprehension about the moral fate of the city"; moreover, he suggests that belief in the moral potential of city planning was short-lived.[9] In the 1920s bureaucratization set in and the focus of the profession narrowed. Planners in the Jazz Decade sought to assure the public that they had abandoned the "sweeping pretensions of their predecessors" and now were almost exclusively technical experts. The Progressive Era had run its course, the broad base of support for reform had evaporated, and 1920s-era planners focused more narrowly on the technical, scientific aspects of their field. National planning conferences began to shift attention from aesthetics toward land-use issues and street and transit systems.[10] Boston's planning board's interest in maps and roads, building heights, parks, and playground space now characterized planning; the cardinal issue was zoning.

Zoning—the fundamental framework for controlling private development—was established in the United States during the 1920s. German cities had pioneered the idea of zoning at the beginning of the century, and although some Californian cities had developed nuisance-zones for businesses such as slaughterhouses, saloons, and dance halls, not until New York passed a zoning plan for the entire city in 1916 did the idea become popular in the United States. New York's plan categorized three types of land use—residential, commercial, and unrestricted—and five kinds of height districts. This had obvious advantages, such as separating homes from smelly, noisy, and noxious factories, but in some ways this law impeded the city-planning movement because it encouraged people to accept zoning as a substitute for planning.[11] By 1920 twenty-five cities had zoning laws and by 1930 nearly one thousand cities had followed New York's lead. Under Secretary Herbert Hoover, the U.S. Department of Commerce published a model zoning statute in 1924 and the Supreme Court sanctioned this type of law two years later. (Pre-1925 ordinances generally were limited to keeping business and industry out of residential areas while later laws also regulated the height and volume of buildings.)

Rudimentary zoning legislation in Massachusetts, dating from the seventeenth century and separating certain commercial land uses from residential areas, was in place, but little else was done until the twentieth century. Private covenants were sometimes employed, as in the Back Bay and streetcar suburbs, to regulate the use and appearance of an area, but

....

James
Michael
Curley
and the
Old Boston

134

the city government itself steered clear of such devices.[12] In 1917, the year after New York adopted its zoning plan, the Massachusetts Constitutional Convention assigned the General Court power "to limit buildings, according to their use or construction, to specified districts of cities and towns."[13] In 1920, the legislature granted cities and towns other than Boston the right to zone.

Boston's zoning code, in contrast, had yet to be approved by the legislature; in the interim, the state capital remained subject to state law. Nevertheless, the way for zoning in Boston was opening, even if it was not yet clear, and the Boston Planning Board and a Zoning Advisory Commission began work on a comprehensive zoning plan under the direction of Arthur C. Comey, Consulting City Planner.[14] Board members also began an intensive lobbying effort on Beacon Hill and commercial, civic, industrial, and professional groups mounted an aggressive campaign to support the zoning plan which Mayor Curley introduced to the legislature in January 1924. Boston's zoning advocates sponsored public hearings and meetings, took out advertisements, and placed newspaper articles in support of the bill. Their work paid off: the legislature approved the bill in June 1924.[15]

The new zoning plan divided the city into various districts: single and general residence; local and general business; industrial; and unrestricted districts. The plan eliminated the old two-tier system based on building heights—except for special areas around the State House and Copley Square—and over time became the city's vehicle for managing growth as well as height. Interpretation and enforcement of the plan fell to the city building commissioner but the board of appeal could grant variances. Furthermore, a board of zoning adjustments could change the boundaries of the various districts, though these lines were generally adhered to (by 1930 the board had granted only 64 of 219 petitions for zoning adjustment).

The old animosity between city and state persisted. The fact that Boston was the only municipality in Massachusetts whose zoning code was a state statute rather than a local ordinance clearly indicates the state's continuing reluctance to allow Curley and the city much autonomy. Although Curley's support of the zoning plan demonstrated that he and the business community could cooperate, the conservative goals of the plan suggest the limitations of that cooperation. Frederic H. Fay, chairman of Boston's planning board at the time, made no bones about the limited and conservative essence of the zoning code. The aim of the 1924 plan, in his words, was "to guide the growth of the city with the least possible disturbance of established conditions."[16]

....

James
Michael
Curley
and the
Old Boston

135

This smug contentment with the status quo on the part of the business community, however, did not mean they wouldn't tinker with the machinery of zoning. In fact, business leaders backed a number of changes in building-height limits even before the 1924 code was enacted. The legislature, for example, raised the business district building-height limit from 125 feet to 155 feet in 1923.[17] The state allowed even taller office buildings in 1928 by passing a "pyramid" zoning law which traded higher buildings for less density near the top; the resulting structures often resemble pyramids or wedding cakes. The pyramid design limits the creation of high-walled canyonlike streets and the obstruction of light and air to other buildings.[18] An example of these modest high-rises is the twenty-four story United Shoe Machinery Corporation Building, with its vertical blocks which "step back progressively toward a central tower capped by a truncated pyramid of tile."[19] Renovated and rechristened "The Landmark" in the late 1980s, this impressive structure was built in 1929 and is Boston's first example of the Art Deco skyscraper.

Early planning commissions, according to Sam Bass Warner, "continued the old American tradition of businessmen taking an active role in persuading the public and the municipal corporation to improve the commercial environment of the city."[20] In the 1920s Boston's downtown financial interests were more worried about the impact of traffic than building heights and, in keeping with a nationwide trend, were eager to improve the traffic circulation at public expense. Historian Marc Weiss points out that "beginning in 1914, the attention of city planning began to shift dramatically away from the downtown and onto the peripheral growth of metropolitan areas"; the debate over proposed public improvements moved from civic centers to major streets and highways.[21]

The unprecedented and phenomenal increase in motor vehicle traffic in American cities in the 1920s created a nightmare for drivers and planners. At the beginning of the decade nine million automobiles were registered in the United States; by the end there were twenty-six million. In 1910 only 10,100 trucks were registered in the United States; by 1920 there were 1.1 million, and in 1930 nearly 3.7 million.[22] Although these figures reflected a national trend, in 1930 Boston's planning board claimed "there is probably no city in the United States where traffic congestion on the streets of the downtown business section [is] so near the saturation point as [it is] here in Boston today." Elisabeth Herlihy, secretary to the board, continued, "a crisis in traffic congestion is fast approaching and the next few years will of necessity witness the adoption of a variety of radical measures for the relief of the travelling public." Herlihy estimated that the value of downtown real estate dropped $34

....

James
Michael
Curley
and the
Old Boston

136

Figure 6.1 Aerial view of Boston. Taken in 1930, this photograph shows the new Boston Garden to the right and the new United Shoe Machinery Building off to the left. Note Storrow Drive has not yet been added to the Esplanade. (Courtesy of the Archives of the City of Boston.)

million between 1925 and 1930 because of traffic congestion, while the total value of real estate in the city had increased by $110 million.[23] The planning board made solving Boston's traffic woes a priority but even then Bostonians feared the city's character would be lost in the struggle to accommodate the automobile. Boston had no preservation movement in 1929, but a concerned Bostonian warned citizens not to ascribe "all wisdom and foresight to the city planners and street commissions," because year by year, "structures with priceless associations are destroyed by the hands of progress; streets endeared by their very narrow crookedness are made wide and straight for a generation in a hurry."[24]

Transportation specialists, who remain a crucial force in city planning, initially worked for the local government. When state and federal governments first undertook the construction of roads, they supported rural post roads and ignored the cities. By 1930, for example, Washington had poured some $10 million into Massachusetts for two hundred road projects totaling 700 miles, but not one dollar reached the city of Boston. The Commonwealth also discriminated against cities after it created the state highway fund in 1925. Even a gasoline tax in 1928, which brought in $2 million the first year, didn't help Boston. In 1930, of the 1,600 miles of state highway, only one and a half miles were located in Boston: the section of Washington Street in West Roxbury from LaGrange Street to the Dedham line. Consequently, during the 1920s the City of Boston shouldered the responsibility for hundreds of miles of streets as well as sixty-two bridges and two ferries. In 1929, furthermore, the state authorized the city to construct, operate, and collect tolls for an East Boston tunnel.[25]

Members of the Good Government Association (labeled "Goo-Goos" by Curley) attacked the new tunnel as a boondoggle even though the incumbent Republican mayor, Malcolm Nichols, supported it. In 1929 the electorate returned Curley to City Hall for his third term.[26] Meanwhile, Boston's Planning Board continued to struggle with the city's traffic problems. Its first task, a traffic survey begun in 1927, concluded in 1930 with a *Report on a Thoroughfare Plan for Boston*. The report was largely the work of consultant Robert Whitten, president of the American City Planning Institute, who advocated a total of ten major and fifty-six lesser transportation projects for Boston.[27] The main projects included the East Boston Tunnel, which was quickly constructed; the Central Artery, long delayed but finally built after World War II; and a "radial highway" to be extended from the Central Artery (between North and South Stations) to the Blue Hills. The shadows cast by these ideas are easily recognizable. The city has constructed not only the original tunnel, but a second, built in the 1950s; a third tunnel is slated for the year 2000. The Central Artery, now considered an eyesore and traffic nightmare, is supposed to be converted to an underground roadway, and although plans for a radial highway through the southwestern sections of the city were killed in 1972, a rapid transit line and park opened along this route in 1987.

In 1930 planners believed the Central Artery would be an attractive and absolutely essential solution to downtown Boston's traffic woes. Architect William Stanley Parker, chairman of the City Planning Board, originally suggested some sort of elevated highway in 1923.[28] The concept, adopted by numerous other American cities, is merely an adaptation of the practice of building elevated train tracks on city streets. At the time planners had no fear of blighting Atlantic Avenue, the route much of the Artery would travel, because this major thoroughfare along Boston's waterfront already had an elevated train along its path (and would continue to do so until the El was torn down in 1938).

....

James
Michael
Curley
and the
Old Boston

138

Whitten's 1930 plan described a six-lane highway along two miles with a capacity of sixty thousand vehicles a day traveling an average speed of thirty miles an hour. By drawing off forty percent of the vehicles clogging city streets, Whitten believed the new road would prove an economic boon to the city. He concluded that "the proposed express roads and other projects are costly, but they are not nearly as costly as the present condition and delay."[29] Despite this warning, Whitten's elevated artery didn't get off the drawing boards (or ground) for decades, and planning board reports continued to praise the proposal and propose new sources of funding. The 1938 report of the board, for example, recommended that the city pool its money with metropolitan and state sources to construct the project, but the necessary cooperation and political support for such an undertaking were missing.[30]

The planning board was fond of calculating the economic losses caused by traffic congestion in Boston. It used this line of reasoning to bolster both the Central Artery project and an underpass proposed for Forest Hills in 1929. "Based on a time saving of one minute for each vehicle entering the intersection at Washington Street and South Street, and valuing this time saving at two cents a minute, it is estimated that the aggregate annual economic saving due to the construction of the underpass would be $107,700."[31] The city council approved, but Mayor Nichols vetoed the project because it cost $350,000. Twenty years later an overpass was built through the Forest Hills section of Jamaica Plain instead of the proposed underpass.

We can also trace another contemporary planning issue to the 1920s. When the city decided it needed a municipal airport, the planning board grappled with the problem of site selection. A small landing field in East Boston was finally chosen; it has since swelled into Logan International Airport, one of the busiest airports in the country. The site added a great deal of land to the city because the airport's voracious appetite for property pushed it out into the harbor, expanding the boundaries of East Boston. Interestingly enough, the East Boston site narrowly edged out an alternative location, Columbus Park on the South Boston-Dorchester line, a choice which certainly would have meant filling in the water between Columbia Point and South Boston. Columbia Point today boasts the John F. Kennedy Library, the University of Massachusetts at Boston, and the campus of Boston College High School, but at the time it was a combination swamp, dump, and ideal landing place for rum-runners. After idea of an airfield at Columbus Park failed, Mayor Curley created the famous Strandway along the mudflats of South Boston and developed Castle Island for recreational uses.[32] Curley's decision in favor of recre-

....
James
Michael
Curley
and the
Old Boston
139

ational rather than industrial or commercial uses of Boston's waterfront ran directly counter to most established thinking yet fulfilled Olmsted's original plan for Boston.

The mudflats on the other side of South Boston, between the peninsula and South Station, an area known as the Commonwealth Flats, had already been filled. By 1930 the area contained the world's largest wool market and city planners presciently believed the location was "destined to be the seat of thriving industrial plants, as well as warehouses and railroad yards."[33] The city's fishing fleet, which had its glory days in the 1920s, was also based on the western side of South Boston. Fishermen and longshoremen daily poured into the area, accounting for a significant proportion of the city's employment base. The port of Boston, although past its heyday, still mattered to the health of the city's economy, and city government alone bore the responsibility for the port. In 1929 the Mas-

Figure 6.2 View of Atlantic Avenue skyline, 1925. This photograph shows the dominating status of the Custom House Tower, completed in 1915. The federal government was not bound by Boston's building-height limitations. (Photograph of Boston Harbor Docks by Fairchild Aerial Survey, Inc. Courtesy of the Boston Public Library, Print Department.)

Figure 6.3 James Michael Curley and Franklin Delano Roosevelt in 1931. This photograph of the mayor and the future president was taken at the North Shore estate of Col. Edward M. House, a one-time confidante of Woodrow Wilson. Although Curley was in the forefront of mayors supporting the New York governor's presidential aspirations, a strained relationship hurt Boston's recovery under the New Deal. (Courtesy of the Boston Public Library, Print Department.)

sachusetts legislature created the Boston Port Authority but the city continued to meet all expenses of the authority until 1939 when legislation provided that the Commonwealth assume half the costs.[34] The state assumption of at least part of these costs shows that leaders on Beacon Hill recognized the need for some government involvement in developing and planning the port but they remained loathe to grant Curley or the city of Boston the requisite power. Earlier legislatures had used metropolitan commissions to get around such problems but now the state used special authorities to deny local governments the power or money to deal with new problems.

Curley, with his theatrics and inflammatory rhetoric, remained Boston's dominant political figure, in or out of office. He also remained the target of the state's wrath. It is difficult, but important, to separate the Curley legend and reputation from the facts. Unfortunately, the numerous stories, seemingly countless campaigns, and endless controversy surrounding his terms of office obscure Curley's considerable impact on planning Boston. Part of the difficulty in assessing Curley's achievements (or failures) derives simply from the longevity of his political career—it spanned more than half a century. He first ran for office in 1899 and made a final run for mayor in 1955. Curley won the Boston mayoralty for the first time in 1914 and for the last in 1945. He served four terms in the U.S. House of Representatives, four terms as mayor, and one term as governor.

Figure 6.4 Mayor Curley and an immigrant at the 1933 dedication of the Prado, the North End park later renamed the Paul Revere Mall. According to his son, this was Curley's favorite picture of himself. (Courtesy of Frank X. Curley.)

Curley also served two terms in jail, the first time when he took a civil service exam for a constituent. Cannily turning the infraction to his own account, he gained the undying support of generations of Bostonians in this celebrated case because "he did it for a friend." The idea of assisting the needy quickly became an essential part of the Curley appeal and legend. To thousands of Bostonians James Michael was a latter-day Robin Hood who stole from the rich and powerful to help the poor and needy.

Curley was indeed a mayor of the poor. He not only provided city hall scrubwomen with handles for the mops so they could get off their knees; he also directed the power of the city away from the downtown to those who needed it in the neighborhoods. Throughout most of his career Curley was a social reformer, and his policies had a lasting and significant effect on Boston's planning and development. Historian Charles Trout notes that "in an era when progressives were beginning to speak of 'blighted' neighborhoods and were discovering the slums, Curley opposed construction of elevated lines in every part of Boston on the grounds that these unsightly structures not only created unwanted noise, but defiled the neighborhoods of the poor."[35] Curley's objective was to win votes and his strategy worked: poorer residents of Boston had a champion in city hall.

Predictably, the rich found Curley loathsome. His critics believed Curley was "an ignorant and venal spoilsman, the practitioner of a loutish, brutal, opportunistic, offensive political style."[36] Curley provided his critics with ample evidence of his populist inclinations. Immediately upon assuming office as mayor, he set out to upset his Yankee opponents. One day after his inauguration he proposed selling the Public Garden, bordering the Brahmin preserves of Beacon Hill and Back Bay, for ten million dollars and using half the proceeds to construct a park more accessible to the general public. He further outraged public opinion by proposing a water-pumping station for the Boston Common. These mischievous suggestions indelibly established the lines of conflict and it became clear that the "Brahmin aristocracy would never cooperate with a political leader who mocked their institutions and trifled with their proud historical heritage."[37] Ironically, Curley merely revived and modified a proposal of the Yankee-dominated Metropolitan Improvement Commission, which in 1907 had suggested that a new city hall be built on the Public Garden. So thoroughly does ethnic conflict color Boston's history, however, that Curley's proposal quickly became notorious.

Despite many such attacks on the "codfish aristocracy" and "the State Street wrecking crew," Curley decided to invade Jamaica Plain, at the time a Yankee preserve, and build an eighteen-room brick Georgian colonial on the Jamaicaway. As many have observed, "to signal his arrival—and his defiance—Curley had shamrocks cut in the 30 white shutters."[38] The luxurious features and furnishings of the house soon raised the question of how the mayor, with a $10,000 salary, could afford a $50,000 mansion. An investigation by the Boston Finance Commission was thwarted by a wall of silence, and the smell of corruption lingered. In 1988 the city of Boston bought Curley's home from the Oblate Fathers to whom his estate had left it for $1.2 million, inspiring Professor Shaun O'Connell to comment, "only the churlish would point out that the city had by then paid for the house *twice*: once through builders' kickbacks, in return for city contracts during the Mayor Curley era, then again through direct purchase in Mayor Flynn's day!"[39]

In his own day, Curley learned to cope with the hostility of Boston's banking community, after a fashion. The mayor claimed that when the president of the First National Bank of Boston refused to loan the city money to meet its payroll, "I decided a bit of political banditry was in order." According to the story, the mayor told the banker, "there's a water main with the floodgates right under your building. . . . You'd better get that money up by 3 P.M. or those gates will be opened, pouring thousands of gallons of water right into your vaults."[40] He got the money, along with more enemies.

The financial community and investors deplored Curley's manipula-

....

*James
Michael
Curley
and the
Old Boston*

143

tions in assessing real estate taxes because there appeared to be a dual tax system, based on low valuations in residential sections of the city, where voters were plentiful, and higher rates downtown where there were none. Hotels and department stores were always hit with the heaviest tax increases. In 1946, for example, the first year of Curley's final term, the assessed value of the Statler Hotel was raised $1 million while Filene's valuation was increased by $950,000 and Jordan Marsh's by $615,000. One businessman's reaction was typical: "We've had rosy plans for the future, but what do you think a hike in assessments on investment property like this is going to do to these plans? Certainly it won't encourage new construction."[41] A further twist was that the high tax rate on commercial properties could be whittled down through an extensive and expensive appeal process which enriched the lawyers who fought the cases. During the Curley years, it was common for 30 to 40 percent of commercial property owners to file for abatements every year; politically connected attorneys were, of course, the best choice for arguing on behalf of property owners.[42]

In his autobiography Curley bragged of manipulating tax assessments when he related the story of the tax rate on the Herald-Traveler building. The *Boston Herald* had denounced the construction of the Sumner Tunnel in the late 1920s as an example of "Curley extravagance," but the mayor got his revenge "when I raised the assessments of the *Herald-Traveler* paper, along with other businesses in Boston which had not been paying their share of the tax burden."[43] Many urban historians and political commentators cite such reprisals to explain the decades-long lack of investment in Boston, but the stagnation in the real estate market cannot be laid entirely at Curley's door: other conditions militated against growth in Boston during the 1930s and 1940s.

Over the years, even as Curley's critics found him more reckless and increasingly given to demagogic appeals, his supporters found that he continued to deliver entertainment, emotional affirmation, and jobs. Most of all, his administration produced numerous facilities for the lower-income neighborhoods of Boston.[44] In the course of four mayoral terms Curley enlarged Boston City Hospital, established neighborhood clinics, and developed beaches, roads, and tunnels, all of which not only improved the ethnic neighborhoods but created the jobs his backers badly wanted. This was Curley's real contribution to Boston planning—the use of government power primarily for the benefit of its citizens rather than to serve either the private sector or abstract notions of aesthetics.

As a strong leader, Mayor Curley was in an enviable position to set the municipal agenda during his various administrations (1914–1918, 1922–

....

James
Michael
Curley
and the
Old Boston

144

1926, 1930–1934, 1946–1950). His veto could not be overridden, and all city appropriations, except the school budget, had to originate with him. The state revised the city's charter in 1924 and replaced the nine-member city council with a twenty-two-member body, one from each ward. Despite their greater geographic spread, the ward councilors in the expanded body soon came under fire for having too narrow a focus.[45] (In 1949, during Curley's last term, another charter reform restored the nine-member council; later, during the 1980s, yet another "reform" created a larger council with a combination of at-large and district councilors.) The council could reduce or reject an item in Curley's budget but could not add or initiate one.[46] The state continued to set the ceiling on city taxes and budgets but Curley fought this control and displayed typical creativity in financing construction. For example, construction of the Paul Revere Mall in the North End was financed by the privately endowed George Robert White Fund. The fund, dedicated to municipal improvements and under city control, was also used to finance seven new health units.[47] Curley's approach has since become standard procedure and the White Fund was used in the 1988 purchase of Curley's home on the Jamaicaway.

Curley was defeated in 1918, after his first mayoral administration, but returned to City Hall in 1922 for a second term. His opponents on Beacon Hill then passed a new state law, directed against Curley, to prohibit Boston's mayor from succeeding himself, so he waited until 1929 to run again. He served as mayor from 1930 to 1934 and as governor for a two-year term in 1935–1936. In some ways, then, the thirties was the most successful and important period in Curley's career, particularly in terms of his influence on city planning. From 1914 to 1929 Curley had pushed his program of neighborhood improvements and services, but his efforts were deflected by the City Planning Board's focus on downtown problems such as traffic and zoning. During the thirties, however, pressure built up for a different approach to city planning, and Curley was willing to take the lead.

In 1929, the stock market crash ushered in the depression, and confronted city government with the need to provide relief and jobs for Boston's poorer citizens. Curley began his third mayoral term in 1930 enthusiastically advocating an activist approach to government. Although he called for dozens of building projects he secured neither state or federal backing nor local support, so these projects never left the drafting room of the Boston Planning Board.[48] It was not just a Republican-dominated state legislature that hindered his efforts; rather, personal and political conflicts with city councilors, a Democratic governor, President

....
James
Michael
Curley
and the
Old Boston
145

Roosevelt, and his ever-present foes in the downtown financial clique stymied his plans.[49]

A city councilor denounced the mayor as "a Santa Claus" who built "antelope houses with the people's money at Franklin Park while people starved"; Governor Joseph Ely responded by damming the flow of money from Beacon Hill to the city.[50] After the election of Franklin Delano Roosevelt, Curley, the first big-city mayor to endorse Roosevelt's presidential campaign, looked to Washington for aid, but FDR kept his distance. Roosevelt dashed Curley's hopes for the post of secretary of the navy, offering instead the ambassadorship to Poland. Legend has it that FDR told associates he offered the Polish post because there was nothing there that Curley could steal. Not only was Curley disappointed in his hopes for an important federal position but Boston, too, was penalized: the city did not reap as much federal largesse as expected.[51]

Such relief efforts as the federal government did sponsor in Boston came through a succession of "alphabet agencies." First was the Public Works Administration (PWA) created in June 1933, followed by the short-lived Civil Works Administration (CWA) and the Works Progress Administration (WPA). The City Planning Board administered many projects funded by these agencies. In 1933, the first year of the PWA, the board spent just under $300,000, and by January 1934, 461 people were on the payroll.[52] The chief accomplishment was the official map survey project of 1935 which supplemented the 1926 city map and ended up costing $1 million. Other relief money went to hiring workers to prepare land-use maps and inventories of real property in the city, conduct surveys of business and industrial buildings, and undertake income and cost surveys. Despite this record level of activity, Charles Trout reckons that political squabbles between Curley and other Democrats cost the city as many as 10,000 CWA jobs, the benefit of any PWA money until 1935, a serious delay in the start-up of the WPA, and a year-long delay in the payment of unemployment compensation provided by the Social Security Act of 1935.[53]

New Deal programs challenged the business ideology of limited government and low taxes, and represented a seismic shift in ideas about the proper role of government in economy and society. As mayor, Curley was active in this transformation but faced significant opposition during the 1930s from downtown real estate interests, which blocked both PWA projects and housing proposals whenever city funds were required to match federal grants.[54] (Only later, when they sniffed the possibility of profit for themselves, did American business leaders accept the need for federal expenditures in urban development.)[55]

Despite bitter opposition and obstructionist political quarrels, a number of federally sponsored projects were in fact undertaken in Boston. Curley's shopping list for federal funding was often designed to shore up his political support in areas where it was weakest. The Huntington Avenue subway, the second largest WPA project ever completed in the country, cost $7 million and transported Back Bay voters to the Museum of Fine Arts.[56] Curley also built new schools in both West Roxbury, then a Yankee stronghold, and South Boston, a largely Irish neighborhood, and initiated a major artery, later called the Truman Highway, from Hyde Park to Milton.[57] Other depression-era projects that changed Boston's appearance include Storrow Drive along the Charles River and the Leo Birmingham Parkway in Brighton.[58]

The New Deal expanded government responsibility into new areas, of which housing is—along with transportation—the most significant. Housing was a sick industry: between 1928 and 1933 national construction of residential property dropped 95 percent, and the 1930 census revealed that 25 percent of the houses in the nation's cities did not meet minimum standards. As the economy collapsed in the early thirties, people lost their homes at an alarming rate: by 1933 banks were foreclosing on a thousand homes a day.[59] The housing problem in Boston was no less severe than elsewhere. In 1930 the city's population reached nearly 800,000 and conditions for many were deplorable. Standards in the North End were particularly low; a 1929 investigation revealed that only half the dwelling units had a toilet and a mere 81 of 5,030 rental units had mechanical refrigeration.[60] The neighborhood was packed with 799 persons per acre, compared to 167 residents per acre in the Back Bay.

New Deal remedies for such problems began with the housing division of the Public Works Administration, which authorized construction of "low rent housing and slum clearance projects." At first private enterprise supervised these efforts, but after February 1934 the federal government took control. For the first time the federal government officials became directly involved in housing and city planning, although the extent of their involvement was limited by a Supreme Court decision in 1935 requiring all federal aid to be funneled through state or local government agencies.[61] Boston led the way in securing federal money for housing. Old Harbor Village (now the Mary McCormack) in South Boston, the city's first public housing project, was also one of the first fifty-one projects in the country built by the PWA. The Planning Board proposed more than one thousand units for the thirty-three-acre site in Representative John McCormack's district.[62] The contractor, Matthew Cummings, was a favorite of Mayor Curley, and conditions seemed propitious until this political

....

*James
Michael
Curley
and the
Old Boston*

147

favoritism and wrangling invited criticism from former governor Joseph Ely and the City Planning Board, who delayed the project.[63]

Opposition from both was in part a traditional political power struggle and in part a reflection of different ideological responses to the economic and social problems facing Boston and the nation. The Planning Board wanted more local (Yankee) financial control than federally funded operations would allow, and so recommended creation of a city housing committee and a state board of housing. The legislature went along with the suggestion and created the Board of Housing, which was authorized to purchase or take land to relieve congestion and provide homesteads.[64] Furthermore, the state authorized the mayor and city council to create a housing authority, which was done in October 1935. But the Boston Housing Authority (BHA) did not really get underway until the Wagner–Steagall Act of 1937 created the United States Housing Authority and authorized USHA to take over all PWA projects.[65] Federal involvement in housing evolved from this modest beginning and thereafter the Boston Planning Board was only indirectly concerned with the housing issue.

Federal law contained an important "equivalent elimination" provision which required that one slum unit be destroyed for each unit of public housing built. Senator David I. Walsh of Massachusetts (a former Bay State governor) inserted this provision into the Wagner–Steagall Act in a misguided attempt to prevent middle-class families from moving into housing needed by the poor. Walsh wanted both slum clearance and new construction of public housing, but his amendment to the bill played into the hands of real estate interests that wanted to restrict the total number of housing units in order to enhance rents and profits.[66] Such conflicting goals and provisions have afflicted housing legislation ever since.

All these changes empowered the BHA to borrow and to receive subsidies from the federal government, determine what was substandard, plan and clear slums, and acquire land or take it by eminent domain. Sensitive to problems of site selection, the authority noted that a site should only be chosen "with the fullest appreciation of the importance of the relationship between a low-rent housing program and the long-range city plan."[67] Between 1937 and 1940 the BHA created projects in Charlestown, South Boston, East Boston, and built the Mission Hill, Lenox Street, and Orchard Park projects in Roxbury. The authority chose not to build in the West, South, or North Ends because the cost for land acquisition in those districts would have been too high.[68]

As the housing issue shows, the quest for solutions to urban problems increasingly moved to the state and federal levels. James Michael Curley operated on these levels, despite several lengthy interruptions to his

....

*James
Michael
Curley
and the
Old Boston*

148

political career. After serving a two-year term as governor, he was defeated by Henry Cabot Lodge for the U.S. Senate in 1936, and stood by as his successor in city hall, Frederick W. Mansfield, served from 1934 to 1938. (Mansfield, like Curley the son of Irish immigrants, had taken a far different route to the mayor's post. A lawyer, Mansfield was elected the first Democratic state treasurer in 1914 and long served as counsel to the American Federation of Labor and the Roman Catholic hierarchy in the state. Mansfield was the "Goo-Goo" candidate who lost to Curley in 1929 but beat former Mayor Malcolm Nichols in the 1933 election.[69] During the Mansfield administration the city constructed a new city hospital building, the George Wright Golf Course, and seven schools, but Mansfield was better known for austerity budgets and an enduring hostility to Curley.) Curley also lost the 1937 mayoral election—to Maurice Tobin of Mission Hill—and entered a low point in his career. Tobin, once a Curley protegé, was a former state representative and chairman of the Boston School Committee who in the mid-1930s established an independent base of power and urged voters to "repudiate bossism" when he challenged Curley for control of city hall. Other former Curley aides (including future mayor John B. Hynes) joined the revolt and Tobin "became the standard-bearer of a coalition of Bostonians determined to keep Curley out of office."[70] During Tobin's seven-year mayoralty he followed a conservative fiscal policy, cutting expenditures and the city debt.[71] Tobin also defeated Curley in the 1941 election rematch, but left city hall to become governor in early 1945. He served one two-year term on Beacon Hill, lost a reelection bid (in 1946), and went on to be President Truman's secretary of labor.

Curley, meanwhile, had returned to Washington and served in the House of Representatives from 1943 to 1945. Then began a most peculiar period in Boston's remarkable political history. When Maurice Tobin took up the governorship in 1945, special legislation allowed city council president John E. Kerrigan to be elected by his fellow councilors to finish the last year of Tobin's term as mayor. Kerrigan ran in the popular election in the fall of 1945 but was defeated by Curley, who won despite the fact that he faced imminent indictment on charges of conspiracy and using the postal service to defraud. Curley won 45 percent of the vote in a five-way race and began his fourth and final term as mayor. It is a popular misconception, often repeated in print, that Curley was in prison when he was elected mayor. He was not.

When Curley assumed office in January 1946, he was seventy-one years old and facing a controversial trial in Washington. The basic issue was influence-peddling, based on Curley's brief association with a firm run by

....

James
Michael
Curley
and the
Old Boston

149

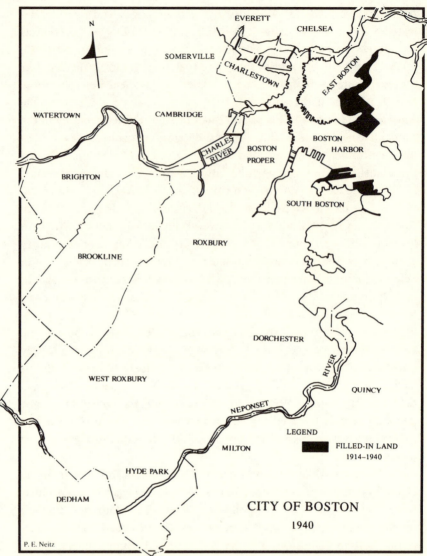

Map 6.3 City of Boston, 1940, showing landfill. The shores of East Boston extended into the harbor in the 1920s to allow for the runways of the new municipal airport, a process continued over the next half-century as Logan International Airport grew.

....

James

Michael

Curley

and the

Old Boston

150

a swindler who used Curley's name and congressional prestige to secure government contracts. Curley's biographer, Joseph F. Dineen, asserted that Curley never received any money from the scheme and historian Mark Gelfand writes "of the many legal problems that marked Curley's political career, this one least merited prosecution. Curley's involvement was marginal at most; he became the target not for what he did but for who he was."[72] The trial lasted only two days and on January 18, 1946, just two months after being elected mayor, Curley was convicted of ten counts of using the mail to defraud. After repeated unsuccessful appeals, Curley was finally sentenced on June 26, 1947, to a term of six to eighteen months in the federal penitentiary at Danbury, Connecticut. He promptly began his term; during Curley's incarceration the city was administered by City Clerk John Hynes.

President Harry Truman pardoned the mayor after Curley spent five months in prison. Returning to City Hall the day after Thanksgiving, the mayor announced a series of policy initiatives, including the installation of 5,000 parking meters in the city. Curley also called for continued pressure on the legislature for a harbor bridge to East Boston and a "waterfront skyway" (elevated highway) instead of a second tunnel and Central Artery Highway. The bridge to East Boston was never built; instead the second harbor (Callahan) tunnel was constructed in the fifties. Unfortunately Curley was not content to talk plans and issues but went on to ridicule temporary mayor John Hynes's stewardship of the city, saying "I have accomplished more in one day than has been done in the five months of my absence." Hynes offered no immediate response to Curley's insult, claiming that his stewardship of the city left him "not even slightly interested in running for mayor under any circumstances."[73] It wasn't long, however, before he decided to run against Curley in the next election using the slogan "A New Boston." He beat the old man and served as Boston's mayor for the next decade. With this "last hurrah" Curley's long political career ended and Boston's most famous mayor spent his last years observing the creation of a "New Boston." Though Curley mounted lackluster campaigns against Hynes in 1951 and 1955, the tumultuous Boston he represented was rapidly disappearing when he died in 1958. The world was changing and even old Boston was bound to catch up.

The New Boston first stirred even before Curley began his last mayoral term in 1946. Curley had been away from city hall for over a decade, yet some Bostonians felt the old city was in desperate need of decisive action and continued to hold Curley responsible. No one had been able to extricate Boston from the depression and a deep gloom had settled over the city. The attitude was so extreme, despite the World War II economic boom, that in 1944 William Roger Greeley, a prominent architect, stood up in Faneuil Hall and claimed that Boston had not shared with London the "advantage" of widespread destruction by aerial bombardment, which would clear out the old city and make way for the new.[74]

Greeley chaired the Boston Contest of 1944, which, despite his extraor-

Figure 6.5 Aerial view of Scollay Square, world-famous symbol of the Old Boston. This is a reduced size photograph from a series taken by Curtis-Wright Flying Service and shows the famous vaudeville, burlesque, and entertainment center to the left, running from Court and Cornhill Streets off to the left. The State House is in the lower left corner and the Samuel Adams Statue is in the center of Dock Square to the upper right, in front of Faneuil Hall. Old City Hall is on School Street in the front center. New City Hall was built in the 1960s in the area along Brattle Street toward the right. (Courtesy of the Archives of the City of Boston.)

....

James
Michael
Curley
and the
Old Boston

152

dinary rhetoric, was a creative and thoughtful attempt to address the planning needs of Boston and the region. The contest, designed to elicit a workable program for improving Boston, was initiated by the Boston Society of Architects, administered by Boston University, sponsored by Governor Leverett Saltonstall and Mayor Tobin, and supported by the Chamber of Commerce, MIT, and Harvard University. It drew scores of individuals and teams, and boasted a panel of judges that included Lewis Mumford, the famous urbanist. A team headed by Harvard political scientist Carl Friedrich won the contest by arguing that the metropolitan area had "become ill, decaying at the core, because its vitality has not been a common concern of all those having a stake in it." Friedrich deplored the business exodus from Boston's downtown, blaming the city's tortuous street patterns and lack of highways. Friedrich and his colleagues proposed that all communities within a twenty-five mile radius of the city join in a federation under the name "The Boston Metropolitan Authority," or District.[75] For this suggestion they won $5,000 but little else; support for a metropolitan solution appealed mainly to the already converted. It was, moreover, a solution proposed and disposed of before the first World War because of ethnic political conflict and the desire for local governmental autonomy. With Curley's return to city hall in 1946, such feelings were reinforced and the metropolitan solution had no more likelihood of success than Curley's nomination for an honorary degree from Harvard.

Along with Curley's defeat, a few more nails in the coffin of the old Boston were hammered in during 1949. Another milestone in the story of federal involvement in America's cities was the Housing Act of 1949, which proposed a national commitment to the principle of a "decent home and a suitable living environment for every American family."[76] Congress never matched the rhetoric with appropriate funding, but over succeeding decades it set federal and local policy and had a marked effect on both Boston and the nation. Principally the 1949 act cleared the way for the demolition of Boston's West End and the onset of a new style of "urban renewal." Attention returned to Boston's downtown in the fifties, a time when neighborhoods were again given short shrift.

Curley's opponent in 1949 adopted the same slogan, a "New Boston," that had been used by the Boston–1915 movement when Curley was an ambitious young politician first eyeing the mayoralty. Much had changed but much was the same. The metropolitan scheme of the Boston Contest of 1944 echoed the solution proposed by Filene and his associates three decades before. More significantly Hynes's call for a New Boston promised that political change would bring about the city's long-awaited revival. But Hynes and most observers focused on Curley and ignored other factors in explaining Boston's decline during the first half of the twentieth century. While Curley's political appeals to class and ethnic prejudice clearly harmed the social fabric of the city, the absence of economic and physical growth downtown is neither Curley's fault nor an adequate measure of city planning. Curley is credited with both too much and too little.

It is only in the long-term that Curley's impact can be understood. He came to political power in a city run by an established elite hostile to the Irish and other ethnic groups and unwilling to cooperate with their leaders. In his first two terms, Curley, like Fitzgerald before him, cooperated with the city's economic power structure when possible, as exemplified by his campaign for the 1924 zoning plan. Furthermore, Curley allowed the City Planning Board to continue as a preserve of traditional

Yankee leadership and an enclave for professionals, but the Great Depression called for a new approach and Curley's activist form of government, though still severely circumscribed, earned a freer rein.

The economic and physical problems of Boston during these decades resulted not just from disharmony between the Yankees and the Irish or personality conflicts among key players. The years during which Boston government moved definitively into a leading role in planning and directing the growth of the city coincided with depression in the nation and a general economic sluggishness in American cities. Boston's stagnation was part of the American urban story and nothing unique. During the postwar years and Curley's last term in office, fundamental social and economic changes swept the nation. Federal aid for home ownership and for highway construction hastened the suburbanization of a rapidly growing segment of America's population: commuters who continued to work in the urban core but no longer contributed to the city's tax and population base. Like other American cities, Boston simultaneously faced problems of competition, economic decline, and the obsolescence of housing, problems which cannot be laid at Curley's feet.

The crucial problem facing those involved in planning Boston during this era was the city's lack of credibility, and for this Curley was indeed responsible. But even here it would be wrong to make Curley's role the most significant factor. Certainly Curley's tax policy discouraged corporate investment in Boston and fostered the hostility of the business community, but the enmity between the private sector and city hall predated Curley's mayoralty. In fact, the public-private cooperation which had traditionally shaped Boston failed to survive even the Fitzgerald years. The private sector offered no leadership and shunned cooperation with Curley. Equally important, old Boston money had long since exited the city. Merchant princes may well have had more at stake in the city, but after the collapse of Filene's Boston–1915 movement they ceased to exert much muscle until the 1950s, when Curley's successor proved more amenable to business interests.

When the private sector abandoned planning leadership, the public sector assumed a more important role. The government was no longer handmaiden to the capitalists who shaped the city. Indeed, planning in Boston evolved during the Curley years into one of the most vital of all roles for city government. Curley changed the basic thrust of city planning by directing attention to the neighborhoods and by inviting government interest in new areas. Although the resulting physical changes to Boston were not of heroic proportions, they were nevertheless momentous. Streets, highways, parkways, tunnels, housing, schools, beaches,

....

James
Michael
Curley
and the
Old Boston

154

libraries, municipal buildings, and fire stations all required massive planning and construction, as did the national policy of accommodating the automobile and the dramatic regional population growth. Curley supported these projects partly to put people to work; in any case, planning was directed less by private-sector interests and more by public need and popular wishes. Although less dramatic, planning of this sort is more democratic and is Curley's legacy.

....

James
Michael
Curley
and the
Old Boston
155

7

Collins,
Logue,
and the
"New Boston"

The "New Boston" of the 1960s was dramatically different from the shabby, stolid, and tired old city of the first half of the century. Boston became a startling example of new architecture, city planning, and intense government activity. Picking up speed slowly in the fifties and then rapidly in the sixties, Boston emerged as a thriving economic center of the New England region. Thanks to extensive planning, the city could ride the waves of changing economic trends, some of which crested only in the seventies and eighties.

The term "New Boston" dates from the beginning of the century, when it served as a magazine title for the Boston–1915 movement. John Hynes adopted the slogan when he ran for mayor against James Michael Curley in 1949, and Hynes's supporters ran a New Boston Committee in the 1950s, but the Collins administration of the 1960s deserves recognition for making "New Boston" a reality as well as a watchword. As mayor, John F. Collins invoked an old theme in calling for the creation of a "New Boston"; his development administrator, Ed Logue, infused it with raw energy and brought it success.

Boston in the middle of the twentieth century desperately needed such energy. The city faced a slew of problems in the 1950s, including economic stagnation and a population decrease of over 100,000. Boston's economic slide, begun earlier in the century and intensified by the depression of the 1930s, was not yet over. During the 1950s Boston's conspicuous loss of vitality stemmed mainly from the much earlier downturn of New England's textile industry; many factories had moved to the South in the 1920s, and although the regional textile industry temporarily revived during World War II, it collapsed soon after. In 1947, 280,000 people worked in New England textile plants; by 1954 this number had dropped to 170,000, and by 1964, to 99,000.[1] Boston money financed many of the New England mills and the steady exodus from the region cut into the dividends of old Boston families. The economic slide of the region and Boston, its capital city, was also reflected in the diminished status of Boston banking. In 1900 the city ranked fourth in the nation. By 1965 the city ranked tenth.[2] Another measure of failing fortunes was the nose dive of the fishing industry, long an important part of the Boston economy. Between 1950 and 1963 the number of New England fishermen decreased by almost one-third as imports of frozen fish cut into domestic markets.[3]

But Boston also possessed some strengths. The city moved into a "service-based economy" of finance, insurance, and law in the late 1940s while the rest of New England still relied heavily on manufacturing. Boston's percentage of "service jobs" was twice that of the New England region. In 1948, 29 percent of Boston jobs were in manufacturing and 23 percent were in services, while 55 percent of the jobs in New England were in manufacturing and 12 percent were service-based.[4] Few appreciated the growing strength in services at the time. Rather, many Bostonians thought the loss of manufacturing jobs signaled the downfall of the city and region. Relatively speaking, Boston and New England were indeed declining. World War II spurred the growth of aircraft and other war-related industries in southern California; this trend continued into the 1950s. In addition, the development of air conditioning aided the growth of the Sun Belt and facilitated the movement of population from older northeastern cities such as Boston.

The attraction of sunnier climes and Boston's continuing stagnation alarmed many local business and political leaders. Boston seemed to be in a state of permanent economic decay. There were signs of hope, however, as the same defense-related growth which transformed southern California also fueled the economy of metropolitan Boston. The trailblazing Massachusetts Institute of Technology, across the Charles River in Cambridge, stimulated growth in the local defense industry. MIT had been crucial to the war effort and "its myriad scientists and technicians . . . became a catalyst for the renaissance of a Boston that had already begun to stir."[5] Over the years some one hundred companies evolved out of MIT, including Raytheon, the state's largest corporation, which itself spun off one hundred and fifty companies. Entrepreneurs like An Wang and Kenneth Olsen set up computer companies in the 1950s and strengthened

....

Collins,
Logue, and
the "New
Boston"

158

another vital component of the emerging postindustrial economy of Massachusetts.

At the center, however, stood Boston, still a city in need of initiative and growth. The city's business and political leadership realized that Boston had to revitalize the central business district in order to return to prosperity and to a position of leadership among American cities. This meant bucking the larger trends of 1950s-era America. Veterans' Administration mortgages and the expansion of federally funded highways revolutionized the nation's landscape. Suburbanization, aided by these policies, became increasingly important in determining the future of Boston and its environs. The U.S. Housing Act of 1949, however, most directly affected how Boston and other cities solved the conundrums of housing and downtown rejuvenation. This act and the revisions implemented by the 1954 Housing Act set federal policy in urban affairs in the 1950s. In this decade, Boston created both failures and foundations for future growth.

The main target of federal policy in the 1950s was urban blight. Throughout the United States in the 1940s and 1950s urban policy emphasized income-producing, tax-paying physical construction programs as a means of revitalizing the cities.[6] To revitalize the city, experts believed that "blighted" areas should be removed and homes for the middle-class built. The federal strategy called for cities to purchase slum property, with Washington paying two-thirds of the cost. The city would clear the land and then sell it to a private developer below market price. Poor neighborhoods near the business district were prime targets for renewal and the result was a massive loss of low-income housing.

The 1949 Housing Act provided for local public authorities, known as LPAs, to administer urban development programs. These LPAs, by statute, were given the power of eminent domain and had to be independent of the city government. Boston designated its housing authority as the local LPA, which allowed it to assemble strategically located, blighted residential areas for redevelopment for business or industrial use at prices attractive to developers. Boston's Planning Board took the first steps to revive the city even before the land was acquired. The 1949 act required that any renewal and housing project be part of a general plan for the whole community. Boston's Planning Board, therefore, issued a *General Plan for Boston* in 1950, proposing redevelopment of 20 percent of the city's land area over a period of twenty-five years.[7] All together, some 2,700 acres were designated for clearance and redevelopment.

Despite its good intentions, Boston planning in the 1950s became notorious for its insensitivity toward poor residents, which was typified

....
*Collins,
Logue, and
the "New
Boston"*
159

by the demolition of the West End. The destruction of this old immigrant neighborhood and its replacement with an upper-income enclave of apartment buildings that many consider ugly epitomizes the folly of urban renewal in America in the 1950s. The West End was destroyed because business and political leaders of the city wanted to restore Boston's greatness by creating a downtown development that would attract upper-income people, an approach entirely consistent with national trends and legislation.

Political leadership in Boston was a key ingredient in the drive to revitalize and reshape the city. The old Boston of the Curley years gave way to a new city of cooperation between the private and public sectors, although progress came slowly at first. The New Boston began in 1949 with the election of John Hynes and continued through the 1960s under his successor, John F. Collins. Mayor Collins's appointment of Edward J. Logue as the city's development administrator was critical because it was Logue, above all others, who planned and created the New Boston.

John B. Hynes defeated James Michael Curley in 1949 and served as Boston's mayor through the fifties, an unprecedented tenure in the city's history. Hynes worked in city hall for four decades, rising through the ranks of the municipal bureaucracy from junior clerk to mayor.[8] After serving as Boston's "temporary mayor" during the five months in 1947 when Curley was in Danbury Federal Prison, Hynes won the 1949 election and promised, in his inaugural address, to face up to some of Boston's worst problems. He vowed to stop the overassessment game that characterized the Curley regime, and although before long lawyers closely associated with Hynes appeared before the courts as tax abatement specialists,[9] leaders in the private sector welcomed the possibility of change in the new mayor's administration. The Boston Municipal Research Bureau, for example, prepared a brief report in 1950 which argued that "Boston is not adequately prepared to plan the shape of its future physical development." Noting that the Hub, "once a pioneer in the field of city planning," had "been lagging during the past generation," the research bureau called for an improved planning law and proposed making the Planning Board an integral part of city administration.[10] The suggestions went nowhere for years, and until 1957 city planning was divided between the Planning Board and the Boston Housing Authority.

Several other private organizations attacked Boston's economic decline. The Boston College Citizens Seminars, founded in 1954 under the direction of the Reverend W. Seavey Joyce, S.J., provided an academic forum for discussion of problems confronting Boston and the metropolitan area.[11] These seminars were a hopeful sign of the budding cooperation between Yankee businessmen and Irish politicians. The distrust and hostility between the two groups had endured for so long that one banker recalled, "there was a feeling that Boston was in the hands of supercrooks. Nobody had ever seen an honest Irishman."[12] In this atmosphere Father Joyce's seminars were novel. As historians Andrew Buni and Alan Rogers observe, "bringing together leaders from banking, the utilities, industry, and politics to discuss the common problems of the city sounds obvious in retrospect, but it was a precedent-shattering move in 1954." Once the ice was broken, other meetings and organizations followed. One such organization, the Greater Boston Economic Study Committee, was a mix of academics and businessmen. Formed in 1957, the committee concluded that despite the great need, "office buildings cannot be built for rent in downtown Boston" owing to confiscatory property taxes and lagging public confidence in the downtown area's future.[13] These groups and others worked hard to mobilize public opinion in support of a more aggressive effort in city planning; ultimately they succeeded.

Ever since the Irish takeover of city hall in the late 1800s the Commonwealth of Massachusetts had taken power away from the city, but when the Democratic party won control of the state legislature in the 1950s and 1960s this tendency was reversed. In 1948 Thomas P. O'Neill, Jr., of Cambridge became the first Democratic Speaker of the House since the Civil War. On the other side of Bulfinch's State House, the election of South Boston's Johnny Power as Senate president immeasurably assisted Boston during the fifties. These and other Democrats worked with the city and in 1957 the state legislature created the Boston Redevelopment Authority (BRA). All other Massachusetts cities and towns were already allowed to have separate redevelopment authorities, but Boston had been exempted until this time. Kane Simonian, head of the BHA's redevelopment division since 1951, obtained Mayor Hynes's backing to create a separate authority and the bill passed the legislature.[14] The Boston Housing Authority was stripped of its redevelopment power and the new agency given this responsibility. Simonian headed the new Boston Redevelopment Authority from its inception on October 4, 1957, and took along nearly the entire redevelopment division of the Housing Authority. The BRA is directed by a semi-autonomous, five-member board, with four members appointed by the mayor and one by the state.[15] Mayor Hynes's initial appointees included a journalist, a union leader, a businessman, and Monsignor Francis J. Lally, editor of the archdiocesan newspaper *The Pilot.* Lally's appointment was widely regarded as an attempt to put a human face on urban redevelopment, an endeavor both necessary and successful.

....

Collins,

Logue, and

the "New

Boston"

161

The BRA sorely needed a public relations coup. The two major "renewal" projects it took over were actually "slum-clearance" programs and major disasters for the city's image. Both the West End and the New York Streets redevelopment projects were initially directed by the Housing Authority and funded by the federal government. The city's original intent in these projects—to build new housing—crumbled in 1954 when changes in federal policy permitted up to 30 percent federal funding for nonresidential projects, thus making residential projects less attractive.[16] The altered federal policy allowed the city to transform the New York Streets area (just south of today's Massachusetts Turnpike extension at East Berkeley Street, Harrison Avenue, and Shawmut Avenue) from a residential neighborhood into an industrial no man's land.

The New York Streets area had long been a target for redevelopment and the city expected the project to attract industrial and commercial enterprises and bring in additional tax revenues.[17] Planners believed the New York Streets area was an ideal industrial site because of its easy access to major roads, the railroad, the Fort Point Channel, and the proposed Southeast Expressway. But African-American community activist Mel King, writing about the human side of this multi-ethnic neighborhood, recalls that: "On Seneca Street, where I lived with my parents, there were also Irish, Portuguese, Albanians, Greeks, Lithuanians, Armenians, Jews, Filipinos, Chinese, and a few (very few) Yankees. Across the tracks were Syrians and Lebanese and a larger number of Chinese. Although our buildings were pretty well sorted out by color and ethnic background, the street belonged to all of us." King tells how his family and others in the neighborhood, forced to move so that the "slum" could be "renewed," received minimal assistance and faced higher rents. King also points out that a *Herald-Traveler* series, which had portrayed the nearby Dover Street district as a "Skid Row," depersonalized the issue and "blotted out any understanding of the impact urban renewal would have on the lives of the people." Further obscured was the "fact that the *people* living in the area had significantly fewer options than other groups by virtue of their color, national background, and economic status."[18] Despite such sentiments—expressed publicly many years after the fact—there was no effective protest in 1955 when the BHA began purchasing and demolishing buildings. By September 1957 the job was done. The destruction of the New York Streets neighborhood to make way for industry (including a new plant for the *Herald-Traveler*) aroused little attention.

In contrast, the demolition of the West End quickly gained national notoriety. The West End clearance symbolized all that was wrong with city planning in the 1950s because it bulldozed the homes of poor people

....

Collins,
Logue, and
the "New
Boston"

162

Figure 7.1 Cleared land for Government Center and Charles River Park, looking toward the Charles River and Cambridge. Few structures remained after the demolition of the old West End neighborhood and high-rises for the wealthy took their place but the New England Telephone Building and Saint Joseph's Church can be seen. Note the foundations for the John F. Kennedy Federal Building. The Green Line Rapid Transit runs diagonally under New City Hall and can be seen in this picture. The Orange Line Rapid Transit can be seen in the forefront. (Courtesy of the Library of the Boston Redevelopment Authority.)

....
Collins,
Logue, and
the "New
Boston"

163

and replaced them with an enclave for the wealthy. The West End, one of Boston's most crowded neighborhoods, had been a colorful center of immigrant life for over a century and was targeted for "renewal" early in the twentieth century. Once home to a large black population and long under the political control of the famous Martin "Mahatma" Lomasney, the West End had increasingly become a multi-ethnic community, although the population dropped from 23,000 in 1910 to 12,000 in 1950. In the 1950s Italians predominated, accounting for 46 percent of the district's population, while Poles, Jews, and Irish made up 11, 10, and 5 percent respectively.[19]

The Boston Housing Authority applied to the federal government in 1950 for money to make preliminary plans for the clearance project. The study began the next year and in April 1953 the city announced the plan to redevelop the West End. The federal and state governments approved the plans in 1956 and by July of the next year the city council and Mayor Hynes okayed the project. Shortly thereafter, the Boston Housing Authority surrendered control of the West End to the new Boston Redevelopment Authority, which began holding informal hearings in October 1957. Despite tremendous opposition to the West End plans, members of the BRA board assumed that the project had gone too far to stop.[20] The city and federal governments signed a contract for redeveloping the area in January 1958, with the city providing one-third of the funding and the federal government two-thirds. The city gave West End residents official notice of demolition plans in April 1958 and the pace of evacuation quickened—by November of that year 1,200 of 2,700 households were gone.[21] The exodus accelerated in 1959 and was completed by the summer of 1960. The neighborhood was razed. As Walter Muir Whitehill points out, the project gained few friends for the BRA because it "brutally displaced people, disrupted neighborhoods and destroyed pleasing buildings."[22] In recompense, the BRA reported paying $320,000 for moving expenses and personal property loss for those evicted.[23]

With the West End cleared of people the redevelopment was put out to bid. A trio of developers, including a politically influential Boston lawyer named Jerome Rappaport, was chosen. Suspicions immediately surfaced that the designation was a fix. The city sold the land to Rappaport at a greatly reduced rate in accordance with the standard practice of urban renewal, but because the only other bidder had dropped out of the competition rumors spread that Mayor Hynes had engineered the switch so that Rappaport, his former campaign organizer and assistant, would win the project.[24] Rappaport had been a student at Harvard in 1949 when he organized the New Boston Committee and worked for the election of Hynes. He had served as Hynes's personal secretary in the early years of the new administration and took a key part in the scheme to modernize the Planning Board. While Rappaport may have had little trouble winning the project, he had a great deal of difficulty getting the financial backing to carry it out. After being turned down by other financial institutions, the John Hancock Life Insurance Company finally agreed to back Rappaport's

....

Collins,
Logue, and
the "New
Boston"

164

Figure 7.2 Charles River Park rising around Harrison Gray Otis House and the Old West Church. Government Center begins with the Hurley Building shown in the lower right. The vacant lot in the extreme right corner remained empty over a quarter-century later. Ironically, Ed Logue returned to Boston and attempted to complete the site as a private developer with a proposal for Boston University Law School and housing. (Courtesy of the Library of the Boston Redevelopment Authority.)

proposed Charles River Park development. Rappaport credits Hancock's support to their competition with the Prudential Insurance Company, then planning construction of the landmark Prudential Center.[25]

Rappaport commissioned architect Victor Gruen to design the new Charles River Park to entice well-to-do suburbanites back into the city. Gruen's five "urban villages" can only be understood as well-intentioned but uninspired. He wanted to counteract the automobile's dominance and still attract suburbanites to the jumble of tall apartment buildings and townhouses, but Charles River Park today is a scar on Boston's skyline; even Rappaport shrugs at its appearance.

The first residents of Charles River Park moved in during January 1962 but low-income residents of the old West End were effectively excluded because the apartments were all high-rent luxury units. Thirty years later, the BRA and city still hoped to develop a solitary remaining empty lot of the old West End into low-income housing. Rappaport, however, brought suit against the BRA in 1985 and as late as 1990 was still hoping to complete his original plans for Charles River Park, but the final one and a half acres, at Lowell Square near North Station, remain empty. The long-running battle seemed over in 1990 when the Massachusetts Appeals Court finally ruled that Rappaport has no right to build on the site. Early in 1991 the BRA designated the Roman Catholic Archdiocese of Boston as the developer of 200 units of limited-equity co-op family housing on this location. The Archdiocese will reserve half the new housing units for low- and moderate-income families and will give priority to former West End residents when the units are sold. In addition a small West End Archives and Museum will be included in the development. A recent *Boston Globe* editorial suggested that none of these efforts will correct the mistakes made years ago "in the name of civic betterment, but it does suggest that the values underlying theories of urban redevelopment have advanced considerably in that time."[26] Indeed, the forced evictions in the New York Streets area and the West End were remarkably similar to those inflicted on residents of the immigrant haven, Fort Hill, in the late 1860s. In both cases the residents of a poor neighborhood adjacent to downtown were swept aside in the pursuit of higher property values and the economic vitality of the commercial core. But as Jane Jacobs observes in her famous treatise, *The Death and Life of Great American Cities,* "the economics of city rebuilding do not rest soundly on reasoned investment of public tax subsidies, as urban renewal theory proclaims, but also on vast involuntary subsidies wrung out of helpless site victims."[27] Until completion of the archdiocese's plan the empty lot remains a silent reminder of the expulsion of thousands of poor people and a monument to destruction in the name of salvation.

The ouster of West Enders and the devastation of their neighborhood, however, were only the most visible results of a decade of renewal and destruction. Another unsightly result of 1950s planning was the proliferation of city-owned parking garages in downtown Boston to serve office workers who increasingly used automobiles. In the late 1980s several of these municipal garages were torn down to make way for towering office buildings while one, at Post Office Square, was demolished in order to create a new park over a new underground parking garage. In similar fashion, the once-vaunted Travelers Insurance Building, a symbol of the

....

Collins,
Logue, and
the "New
Boston"

166

early stirrings of the New Boston, was also demolished in the late 1980s to make way for a newer and grander structure at 125 High Street. A later generation, ready to forge ahead, decimated prominent symbols of the fifties, a destructive era in Boston's history.

When the Travelers Building opened in 1959 it was extolled as the symbol of a city being revitalized. A sixteen-story structure faced with white and blue brick, it stood in bright contrast to the grimy old buildings nearby. The Travelers was the first downtown office building in thirty years, a point touted by the president of the insurance giant who spoke to a select dinner crowd at the Algonquin Club on the occasion of the building's dedication. He also noted that "we had heard reports of a downtown blight; of traffic problems; of the typical march to the suburbs. But we were also made witness to the hopes and plans of a dynamic City administration; vigorously supported by progressive Boston businessmen."[28]

Another symbol of the 1950s, most of which still stands, was the Boston Housing Authority's Columbia Point housing project in Dorchester. Columbia Point, the largest public housing development in New England when it opened in 1954, at one time provided 1,504 units of low-income housing, but by 1975 the project contained fewer than 400 families.[29] In the sixties, seventies, and early eighties residents poured out and crime flowed in; over time, the strategy of consolidating poor people in one isolated area was repudiated. In the late 1980s, hopeful city, state, and federal officials joined with a private developer and tenants to create the mixed-income area they renamed "Harbor Point." Other public housing projects developed in Boston during the fifties include Fidelis Way in Brighton (1950), Cathedral in the South End (1951), the extension to the Mission Hill Project (1952), Bromley Heath in Jamaica Plain (1954), and Franklin Field in Dorchester (1954). These and nine other public housing projects of the 1950s joined the ten earlier projects that had opened between 1938 and 1949. All told, they significantly altered the way of life for many thousands of Bostonians in the years after the New Deal.

Among the most hotly disputed legacies of 1950s-era planning is the John F. Fitzgerald Expressway, better known as the Central Artery. The Artery, in planning since the early 1920s, cleared a wide path through downtown in the 1950s. It cut off the North End and the city's waterfront from the rest of Boston and quickly earned a reputation as an outdated eyesore. Scarcely a decade after its opening, planners began to dream of tearing it down and replacing it with a tunnel between North and South Stations. This idea evolved into a serious but never implemented proposal in the 1970s and 1980s, and in the 1990s sinking the central artery remains a key planning issue for Boston.

....
Collins,
Logue, and
the "New
Boston"

167

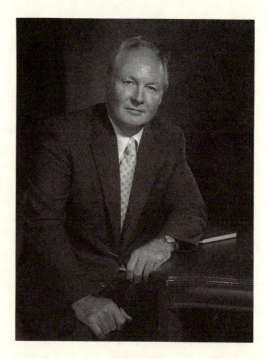

Figure 7.3 John F. Collins led Boston through its most dynamic period of urban redevelopment. He was described in a *Boston Globe* editorial (December 31, 1967) as "one of the three or four great chief executives of our city, if not the greatest" and "the man without whose leadership Boston might very well have sunk into permanent second class citizenship." (Courtesy of John F. Collins. Photography by Fabian Bachrach.)

....

Collins,

Logue, and

the "New

Boston"

168

But highways, housing projects, and parking garages were not all that Boston needed as it entered the 1960s. Despite a better relationship between city hall and the private sector, the city remained depressed in the late fifties and the Hynes administration failed to fulfill the promise of a new era. As the 1950s ended, "Boston seemed set in a downward drift. Neither the Curley style of confrontation nor the alternate politics of accommodation seemed to point a satisfactory way toward addressing the problems of the future."[30] Spending and taxation continued to be critical problems and confidence in the city treasury was almost nonexistent. But a decade later "the fantastically high property tax rate ($101 per thousand) is taken by many to be symptomatic of a fundamental disease in the Hub's body politic."[31] When Hynes beat Curley in 1949 the tax rate was only $56.80 per thousand.[32] In 1959, Moody's Investors' Service rated Boston bonds lower than those of any major city. In desperation, prominent business leaders Charles A. Coolidge and Ralph Lowell created a coordinating committee "to scoop up the pieces and act as receivers in the event of the financial collapse that seemed a distinct possibility."[33] Hynes had spent so much of his life in city hall that he was perhaps incapable of providing the fresh perspective and energy required in a time when government was increasingly responsible for the city's prosperity.

During the 1950s, despite good intentions and some solid accomplishments, Boston experienced "a period of sound planning remote from events, of piecemeal clearance projects displacing many people, of promising new development stymied by bureaucracy, and of spiraling taxes and declining population."[34] By 1960, when Ed Logue arrived to revamp the development office, the only tangible evidence of planning was the ruined West End. People in all levels of society were dismayed at what was happening to Boston.

At this point, the 1959 mayoral election delivered the political shock Boston needed. John E. Power, president of the Massachusetts State Senate and odds-on favorite to win in a field of lesser-known candidates, lost to John F. Collins, the Suffolk County register of probate. Physical shock followed the electoral upset as Collins and Edward J. Logue, his development director, substantially rebuilt Boston over the next eight years. Collins led Boston into one of its most turbulent and impressive periods. William Shannon, chronicler of the American Irish and keen observer of the local scene, writes that the emergence of John F. Kennedy as the Democratic presidential candidate in 1960 coincided with the development within Boston of "the capacity to renew itself, with politics

Figure 7.4 Edward J. Logue, the man Collins hired to run the city's redevelopment agency and build a revitalized city. Logue stands in front of the foundations for the New City Hall. Faneuil Hall and the Custom House Tower are behind. (Courtesy of Edward J. Logue. Photograph by Newsweek/James Coyne.)

....

Collins,

Logue, and

the "New

Boston"

169

as the catalyst."[35] Politics was indeed critical in initiating this era of change. Economic, technological, and social forces are also crucial, but at certain pivotal points politics is the key determinant of change.

The crux of political change was the newly elected mayor, John Frederick Collins, a Roxbury native well acquainted with Boston and its politics. Collins earned a law degree from Suffolk University at the age of twenty and was admitted to the bar at twenty-one. A veteran of World War II, he served two terms in the Massachusetts House of Representatives and two terms in the State Senate. Collins ran unsuccessfully for attorney general in 1954 and became a victim of polio the following year. He continued to campaign for the Boston City Council despite his illness and won. After brief service Collins resigned his post on the council in 1957 to accept gubernatorial appointment as Suffolk County register of probate. He won election to this post in 1958 before running for mayor in 1959.

Collins based his mayoral campaign on several simple tenets: Boston needed to limit its government and cut spending; municipal government relied too heavily upon the property tax; and the total clearance style of urban renewal was a failure. Looking back nearly thirty years later, Collins claimed that while running for office he had had a "mental model" of what the city needed, and asserted that "we changed the way urban renewal was done in this country."[36] The "we" includes Ed Logue, who in 1959 was in charge of the urban renewal program in New Haven. Logue, a graduate of both the college and the law school at Yale, clearly had the credentials to create and administer the massive urban renewal program Collins envisioned. Logue's work in New Haven, under Mayor Richard Lee, was already acknowledged a case study in success. According to Logue, "what was proposed could be delivered."[37] His achievements in New Haven encouraged more federal money to flow to the city and a *Fortune* magazine article on Mayor Lee and Logue concluded that the pair "wrote renewal history by accomplishing more with less cash than was done in almost any other U.S. city."[38]

Logue was lured to Boston in March 1960 at a salary of $30,000 a year ($10,000 higher than the mayor's) to prepare a comprehensive development program for the city. At that time, the city's program consisted of renewal projects in the New York Streets area, and the West End, and the Whitney Street project near Mission Church in Roxbury. Logue found a competent planning operation under Donald Graham, but "no overall plan or program to change the city and certainly no public or civic organization equipped to do it."[39] Logue set out to solve the problems of focus and organization, and spent most of his first year establishing his authority and consolidating power.

....

Collins,

Logue, and

the "New

Boston"

170

Logue's creation of a new and more powerful BRA, with the support and backing of Mayor Collins, was the true cornerstone of the New Boston. Logue crafted innovative legislation which merged the functions of the old City Planning Board into the BRA, creating a single agency responsible for both planning and implementing redevelopment. Consolidation of these two functions within one agency was unprecedented. It had never been attempted in Boston or elsewhere and posed a formidable challenge. The team of Collins and Logue, however, was nothing if not formidable. The BRA board (still dominated by Mayor Hynes's appointments) was reluctant to endorse their approach but Collins and Logue labored mightily to usher in the "New Boston" by going outside the board to win support from business leaders and the public.

Their most effective tactic was linking their agency reorganization proposal with the development of the Prudential Center. Boston needed an investment and construction boost and the Prudential could do the trick. In the late 1950s, the Prudential Insurance Company determined to combine a northeastern regional office with a major investment project in a downtown area. It chose Boston and announced plans to develop the site of the Boston and Albany Railroad yards (between the Back Bay and South End), but the city's outrageously high tax rate blocked a final commitment. Prudential executives and the Hynes administration reached an informal agreement by developing a special tax formula for the site and project; otherwise it would not have been undertaken. The Prudential broke ground in April 1959 even before receiving final written settlement of the tax question.

The Massachusetts Turnpike Authority emerged as a critical player at this juncture. The state's most important planner of the period, the legendary William F. Callahan, was an autocratic figure who had served as the Commonwealth's Department of Public Works (DPW) commissioner from 1933 to 1939 and from 1949 to 1952, and chairman of the Massachusetts Turnpike Authority from its inception in 1952. Callahan wanted to extend the turnpike from its terminus at Route 128 to downtown Boston but lacked the capital to finance the construction. After innumerable back-room conversations, Callahan was persuaded to draw on Turnpike Authority funds to acquire the Sumner Tunnel from the city, thus helping to remedy Boston's financial woes; to build a second tunnel under Boston Harbor (named after Callahan's deceased son); and to finance construction of the turnpike extension with bonds using the tunnel as collateral.[40] Callahan's maneuvers opened the way for the Turnpike Authority to acquire the Boston and Albany Railroad yards and for the Prudential project to begin. The new governor, Foster Furcolo, hoped

....

*Collins,
Logue, and
the "New
Boston"*

171

to persuade the insurance company to carry on with the project it had proposed to the Hynes administration, and filed legislation granting it the agreed-upon tax breaks. Recognizing potential legal problems, Furcolo sent the plan to the Massachusetts Supreme Judicial Court for an advisory opinion. The court rejected the proposed action by the Turnpike Authority and in August 1960 the Prudential halted work.

For Ed Logue, this situation posed both a hindrance and an opportunity. Meeting with some of Boston's business leaders, he discussed the possibility of using the urban renewal powers of the BRA to declare the site a blighted area so as to assert more control over its development. Soon afterward, the Supreme Judicial Court providentially issued another advisory opinion which rejected the Turnpike Authority's three-step solution to the Prudential tax agreement but endorsed action along the lines that Logue had privately suggested—namely to create new legislation that would address the needs of both the Prudential and the BRA. The General Court met in September 1960 in an atmosphere of crisis: city and state feared the Prudential Company would leave Boston if a legal solution failed to fall into place. Apprehension spurred the legislature, which had been emboldened by the court's opinions, to grant the insurance company giant tax breaks. The landmark legislation, known informally as the "Prudential bill" and formally as Chapter 121A, provided the Prudential Insurance Company with the tax concessions the firm felt were necessary to resume the project; the path to construction of the Prudential Center was cleared.[41] Charter 121A also helped create Logue's new and more powerful BRA. A rider attached to the "Prudential bill" abolished the City Planning Board, transferred its functions to the BRA, and granted the new agency the power to control urban renewal and development and to execute the plans.[42] Under the new law, the BRA issued a statement declaring the site blighted and determining that the Prudential project would be of practical use and beneficial to the community. The Prudential Center resumed construction in March 1962, three months after the Massachusetts Supreme Judicial Court upheld the BRA's findings. By the end of the year, forty-six of fifty-two stories were completed.[43]

Despite the importance of the Prudential Center in projecting a new image of Boston, the key feature of the legislation was not the tax abatement but the creation of a virtually new institution in Boston's government. To Ed Logue the paramount issue in 1960 was the authority to implement a redevelopment program; the Prudential project was secondary. The engine of change was now the new BRA, "the tool that rebuilt so much of Boston."[44] The extraordinary consolidation of functions and

....

Collins,

Logue, and

the "New

Boston"

172

power within the BRA is the most remarkable aspect of the entire era and one with incalculable ramifications for Boston in the decades since.

Collins and Logue garnered support for their renovation of the BRA by announcing an ambitious "Ninety Million Dollar Development Program for Boston" on September 22, 1960. They contended that "too much of Boston's greatness lies in its past. Today Boston has more than its share of slums and blights" and that this decay "is sapping the great strength and beauty, vitality and charm which it still possesses in such abundance."[45] The plan, written by Logue, called for renewal programs in ten separate areas: three downtown districts and seven residential neighborhoods. Collins and Logue were careful to stress their desire to preserve the North End from the fate that had befallen the adjoining West End. The program also noted that "luxury housing has its place . . . but there must be lower priced housing as well." Nearly 50 percent of the population and one-quarter of the city's land were located within the designated renewal areas. The plan also offered an agenda for financing, relocation, demolition, and public housing, and touched on the transportation question, asserting that "Boston seems to be suffering from too much action and not enough planning."

It was admittedly an ambitious program but Logue averred that "Rome was not built in a day and Boston will not be rebuilt in a day." The crucial element was money and Logue boldly professed that "Boston can afford a large-scale federally aided urban renewal program. There is no other comprehensive solution available and a patchwork solution is not good enough."[46] The Ninety Million Dollar Program recognized that local government would take the lead in rehabilitating the city. In many ways this was a new conception and an unprecedented extension of public power. Rather than devoting itself to public works projects and housing, the municipal government now proposed to organize and direct the revitalization of almost all phases of development in the physical city.

Collins's cordial relationship with the leadership of Boston's business community was key to winning approval of this program for the "New Boston." The powerful coordinating committee, an informal group of business leaders later known popularly as "The Vault" (after their meeting place at the Boston Safe Deposit and Trust Company) had backed John Power in the 1959 election but now worked effectively with Collins. Such willingness to cooperate, noticeably absent during the Curley years, had only begun under Hynes. Collins moved aggressively to work with business leaders like Charles Coolidge, a partner in the prestigious law firm Ropes & Gray and head of the coordinating committee, who were now

....

*Collins,
Logue, and
the "New
Boston"*

173

eager to aid Boston. At its biweekly meetings with the mayor the coordinating committee devised means of helping the city. One of its first measures was to reorganize the municipal assessing department. Several large corporations loaned personnel to assist in modernizing and professionalizing this crucial division, thus establishing confidence in an area of government which had long been a sore subject with the business community.

The board of the Boston Redevelopment Authority seemed happy to consider the Collins and Logue program and hoped to receive federal support, but it also supported the continued leadership of Kane Simonian, its first director. The passage of Chapter 121A, the resumption of work on the Prudential Center, and the popularity of the Ninety Million Dollar Program, however, all placed pressure on board members to accept Logue's leadership. On October 20, 1960, they accepted his proposal to appoint him development administrator for a ninety-day trial period while also continuing Simonian as director.[47] At the end of ninety days either Logue would be given full authority or he would quit. This odd arrangement served Logue's purposes, and during the trial period he and his staff worked frantically to prepare applications for federal funds. The BRA board, the city council, and the federal government all quickly approved his plans. Logue's contacts, vision, and successful track record in New Haven helped to win increased federal funding for Boston, and the Urban Renewal Administration soon announced a $20 million award to the city. Under Logue, Boston jumped up the list from seventeenth place to become the fourth largest recipient of federal urban renewal funds. A prominent element in Logue's game plan was the innovative use of federal regulations which allowed the city's capital investment to be calculated as its contribution to the total cost of the renewal process, with federal funding providing the remainder. This meant that the cost of capital improvements, which had to be made anyway, was included in the city's renewal formula.[48] State aid to Boston also increased in 1960 because the legislature voted to split the share of renewal costs with the city.[49] The upshot was that Boston paid only one-sixth of all capital improvement costs, a formula that Logue had also used successfully in Connecticut.

Given these successes, plus mounting political pressure, the BRA board voted on January 25, 1961, to hire Logue and to implement the reorganization he wanted.[50] This was a decisive and dramatic moment. Kane Simonian, director of renewal and redevelopment in Boston for over a decade, was pushed aside, signaling that the old ways of urban renewal had been discredited. Although Simonian retained control of the problem-riddled West End and New York Streets projects as well as responsibility

....

Collins, Logue, and the "New Boston"

174

for organizational matters that were non-planning in nature, the "New Boston" remained for Logue and his organization to create. Significantly, while Simonian and the BRA board remained at 73 Tremont Street, Logue and his staff moved into City Hall, cementing their close relationship with the mayor.[51]

Logue was now responsible only to the mayor and the BRA board. He could propose and execute renewal projects and develop comprehensive plans for the city as well as recommend capital improvements for all municipal departments.[52] Logue was granted full authority to hire and fire staff and set their salaries. He could also propose urban renewal plans and land-disposition agreements. The board could accept or reject his proposals but could not change them. The new legislation also prohibited any new personnel from gaining civil service tenure but it did not limit the size of the agency. During the Logue years, the BRA steadily expanded its staff, from 80 in early 1961 to 498 employees by the time he left in 1967.

As 1961 began, Boston was poised on the brink of an extraordinary epoch. As Harvard historian Stephan Thernstrom writes, the city possessed "a potent force for change: a brilliant and aggressive executive like Logue and a massive injection of outside funds to be devoted to the building of a New Boston along lines especially appealing to downtown businessmen, bankers, realtors, and newspaper editors."[53] The New Boston meant a commitment to lowering the tax rate, raising real estate values, and bolstering the financial health of the city. With the backing of Mayor Collins, Logue was given responsibility for the success of this program. Collins staked his political career on reviving Boston and had the good sense and self-assurance to hire the best available person and allow him the freedom to do the job. There were many reasons for the achievements of the New Boston, but Logue readily acknowledges "the one key absolutely indispensable ingredient was the mayor. Without the firm, unwavering, if often questioning support of John F. Collins, it would have been a very different story."[54] In terms of shaping Boston, this partnership was matchless. The only other comparable partnership in Boston's planning history had been that of Charles Bulfinch and Harrison Gray Otis. The earlier team, of course, worked primarily in the private sector while Collins and Logue worked in the public sector, a change that reflects a major shift in the locus of the planning process over a century and a half.

Logue personified the new approach to planning and showed tremendous energy and an unsurpassed ability to work with the city's civic and economic leaders. He also knew how to get federal funding. Ian Menzies, a former *Boston Globe* editor and longtime Boston watcher, suggests three

....
*Collins,
Logue, and
the "New
Boston"*
175

factors that account for Logue's success in administering the redevelopment agency in the 1960s. They were: a good relationship with Mayor Collins, a congenial relationship with the media, and the ability to "get something up to show them."[55] Above all, business and media leaders recognized that Boston had to be revived from its near-moribund condition and that Logue, who offered a workable scheme, was the man for the job.

The Collins–Logue era was in a multitude of ways the most consequential in Boston's planning history. Logue mounted an exceedingly active, savvy, and successful operation. Collins granted Logue the support necessary to withstand traditional patronage practices and Logue was able to attract the best available people. Logue gathered a talented staff and the BRA came to symbolize the optimum employment opportunity for planners during the 1960s. Among the attractions was the fact that although Logue retained firm grip on BRA planning and operations, he respected talent and delegated authority to project directors to an extraordinary degree. In the process he earned a devoted following.

One former leading BRA staff member recorded his recollections of meeting Logue:

> My impressions from that first meeting are still quite vivid. A man of moderate stature in his early 40s, Logue projected a tremendous aura of energy, power, and almost arrogant self assurance. One quickly felt certain of being in the presence of the top public development administrator in the nation, with the possible exception of Robert Moses of New York. At the same time Logue was able both to charm and disarm most new acquaintances through his deliberate, low-octave style of conversation and his casual Ivy League language and manners. At our first meeting I was introduced to apparent contradictions of his background which have always seemed to delight him—i.e., his origins in an Irish Catholic family of modest means in Philadelphia, his gentleman's education in Yale college and Law School, and his yen for the rough and tumble of ethnic urban politics in Boston and other Northern cities.[56]

....

Collins,

Logue, and

the "New

Boston"

176

Logue's public years in Boston brought him more than his share of the "rough and tumble" of politics and a good many detractors, despite his numerous supporters. Logue took the heat for the mayor in countless political battles and apparently enjoyed such conflict. One anonymous detractor claimed that Logue, who was "irascible and grating in personality . . . would go 10,000 miles to antagonize a friend."[57] Despite the hyperbole, even some of Logue's admirers concede that the remark captures something of his manner. A contemporary newspaper account once aptly characterized him as "a brilliant man with a quick mind—and he can be swiftly impatient with anyone, particularly on his staff, who can't follow his mental leaps. He is a charming man when he smiles his broad smile and his Irish face crinkles with amusement."[58] He is indeed a hard-driving and controversial figure, but whatever the impressions and assessments of personality, he must be recognized as the force who reshaped Boston in the 1960s and to whom the success of the New Boston redounds.

The first priority of the New Boston program was the construction of Government Center. The idea for such a center was not new and even the site, Scollay Square, had already been chosen, but Collins and Logue brought it to fruition. It was important that Government Center serve as a catalyst to the physical and psychological rejuvenation of Boston. Despite latter-day popular nostalgia for Scollay Square, Logue argued that the site, "a rundown and notorious skidrow, predominantly nonresidential, was the perfect vehicle to undertake a traditional clearance and redevelopment project."[59] Scollay Square, dear to the hearts of visiting sailors and long infamous for its ribald entertainments, had been deteriorating for years and clearly met the federal government's definition of a slum.

Memories of Scollay Square have lingered on in the hearts of many, but one Boston newspaper columnist effectively counters that nostalgia with the following description:

> wanderers have gone underground in Scollay Square for dozens of years. It used to be easy with all the low life there, the crooked and noisome alleyways, the confusing clatter of tattoo parlors, ginmills and girlie shows, the human wreckage of the city washed onto its grimy shores. . . . Scollay Square was the place where tattered vaude-villians clustered in lodging houses. There was the man . . . who played the violin with his teeth and a bulldog attached to the other end of the bow; and the one-man band and the old performer who always appeared on the street beaded like a costermonger, tiny fake pearls stitched to each part of his suit so that he looked like a walking waterfall. Scollay Square was the sailor's mecca and the sailor's curse. . . . Well, that was the Scollay Square we knew and, if not precisely loved, put up with. Its death knell did not find us throbbing with nostalgia. Despite the yeasty vigor of its raffish throngs, the place was also mean-spirited, sour, brutish and nasty.[60]

Proposals for a civic center to replace the bars, theaters, and tattoo parlors of Scollay Square had been floated for years. In the early 1950s,

....
*Collins,
Logue, and
the "New
Boston"*
177

for example, the Boston Planning Board, inspired by the shrinelike restoration of Independence Hall in Philadelphia, suggested locating a new city hall near Scollay Square, between Faneuil Hall and the Old North Church. In another report, the board proposed to simplify the street system in the area of Scollay Square and to clear the site for a government center.[61] The board hired the consulting team of Adams, Howard, and Greeley to create a blueprint for a new government center. In their 1956 report these consultants noted that the business center of the city had been creeping south for over a century and was now moving toward the Back Bay. "This slow persistent motion has left behind a wake of half-used buildings and . . . a tangle of narrow streets and odd-shaped plots of land"; Scollay Square itself was losing its entertainment activity and "is lapsing into sheer vacancy."[62] Their report echoed the call for new federal and state office buildings and a new city hall. The proposal won wide support and in 1958 the planning department received money to plan for the Scollay Square site.

The location of a federal office building in the Government Center was crucial. The federal government's General Services Administration had already purchased land in the Back Bay (where the John Hancock Tower now stands) and the mayor feared that the GSA planned a new thirty-story building there.[63] City officials lobbied the chief administrator of the GSA to choose Scollay Square for any major building projects, and succeeded only after enlisting the support of Representative John W. McCormack. The future speaker of the house exercised the requisite political muscle and persuaded the GSA administrator to accept the Scollay Square site, and the project was on its way.[64]

The Eisenhower administration made funds available to complete the plans in September 1960, and the state enacted legislation to build a new city hall.[65] The BRA then engaged the relatively unknown architectural firm of I. M. Pei and Associates which, in consultation with Walter Muir Whitehill, a noted Boston historian and the director of the Boston Athenaeum, prepared a plan for the location and scale of buildings in the Scollay Square district. Final plans for the sixty-acre site were unveiled in early 1963. It was a radical scheme: twenty-two streets were to be replaced by six. It was also innovative: Government Center project marked the first time in a urban renewal program in the United States that "early acquisition" of all the property was approved by the federal government before the official plan was accepted.[66] This allowed Logue to plunge ahead with his ambitious plans. Though unprecedented in size and scope, the project was reminiscent of Josiah Quincy's redevelopment of the marketplace that bears his name. The city assembled sites, demolished existing struc-

....

*Collins,
Logue, and
the "New
Boston"*

178

Figure 7.5 The BRA's plan for a new Government Center, most of which was built. The most conspicuous exception is the Motor Hotel (Number 4) which remains a parking lot for city employees. The Central Artery/Tunnel Project is slated to take and transform this lot into parking, stores, and vents for the depressed artery. (Courtesy of the Library of the Boston Redevelopment Authority.)

tures, held a national design competition, and coordinated federal and state governments and private construction. Despite these similarities, Government Center was a watershed in planning Boston.

The national design competition for the new city hall was won by a young and unknown architectural firm, Kallman, McKinnell and Knowles. Though its appearance was in stark contrast to every other Boston structure and was highly controversial then as now, the building won prestigious architectural awards. The Boston Society of Architects went on record in favor of the design, but a Citizens' Committee for a Bostonian City Hall organized an unsuccessful campaign to overturn the award panel's decision. City Hall's wide-open plaza and inverted pyramid appearance stand in dramatic contrast to old Scollay Square and convey the message of a bold new approach to city-building. Perhaps most important, this new City Hall shocked people into a new view of Boston: the Hub was no longer a provincial backwater, home of historical relics and corrupt politicians; to many, City Hall symbolized the spirit of a new and more confident Boston ready to face the future.

....

*Collins,
Logue, and
the "New
Boston"*

179

Figure 7.6 BRA head Ed Logue, Mayor John Collins, and BRA Chairman Monsignor Francis J. Lally at the groundbreaking for a state building (the Hurley) in Government Center. (Courtesy of Edward J. Logue.)

....

Collins,

Logue, and

the "New

Boston"

180

Groundbreaking took place on September 18, 1963, and it was ready for occupancy early in 1968, just as Mayor Collins turned the reins of power over to his successor. In the winter the plaza in front of City Hall is often windy and empty, a forlorn wasteland of public space. In summer it is devoid of shade, a hot, hard desert to cross, but at night it becomes an open-air concert hall. Numerous critics, visitors, and longtime Bostonians deplore it as an eyesore and periodically propose changes, but its historic significance in the development of Boston transcends its ungainly appearance.

More popular than City Hall was the new look for Boston's waterfront, the Hub's traditional window on the world. Logue readily appreciated the need to rehabilitate the Quincy Market area and commenced preparation of a waterfront plan. The Boston Chamber of Commerce worked with the city and in 1962 announced a $70 million plan to transform one hundred acres of Boston waterfront into a residential, historical, and recreational showplace. The plan, an outstanding example of public-private partnership, took eighteen months to prepare and included a "motor hotel" on Long Wharf, yacht clubs, museums, an aquarium, and restaurants. The chamber also proposed retail shops underneath adjacent portions of the elevated Central Artery to overcome the "psychological barrier" created by the highway. Frank S. Christian, a banker and chairman of the chamber's waterfront redevelopment division, said the effort "will demonstrate to the world that Boston is a city of great vitality and beauty," while Mayor Collins said that the proposal demonstrated what "a united community can accomplish when the leadership forces are working energetically and unselfishly toward common goals."[67] Such a view was unheard of during the Curley era.

The chamber turned its waterfront blueprints over to the BRA, which then secured federal money to flesh out the proposal, complete the engineering work, and—as Ed Logue put it—"push through some other bits of red tape."[68] The BRA also encouraged private development of the waterfront. The most obtrusive outcome was the I. M. Pei-designed Harbor Towers, a luxury apartment complex on India Wharf. At the planning stage, Logue underlined the contrast to the West End, where so many people had been forced from their homes, and assured people that the pattern would not repeat at Harbor Towers. There, he said, "Nothing is being displaced but the fish and we're preparing an aquarium for them next door."[69]

The old city aquarium in South Boston closed in 1953 and before long talk of a new, improved facility cropped up. One suggestion, in 1954, was to include an aquarium with the new Museum of Science on the Charles River.[70] The idea quietly died and the first few steps towards a new and separate aquarium were not taken until 1957. Boston businessman David B. Stone, later dubbed "Mr. Aquarium," led a group whose fundraising was so successful that the BRA turned Central Wharf over to them for the site in 1965 and New England Aquarium was on its way.[71] The new building opened in June 1969 and dramatically expressed the spirit of the New Boston by its modern design and extensive use of concrete.

By the end of 1967 most of the old waterfront had vanished. Boston's famous "T Wharf," a residential area after its fishing days were over, was condemned in 1962 and demolished in 1967. Gone, too, were the pilings and stones of the East Boston Ferry slip. After the opening of the Sumner Tunnel and Tobin Bridge, the city-operated ferry line fell on hard times and Mayor Hynes shut it down in 1952.[72] A connection with the colonial

....
Collins,
Logue, and
the "New
Boston"
181

past was cut, but only temporarily. In the 1980s a water shuttle to Logan International Airport restored the ancient link between downtown and East Boston.

The waterfront was the most striking example of private-public cooperation in the 1960s but not the only one. The Committee for the Central Business District forged a similar partnership with the city. Charles Coolidge headed the CBD committee, working closely with the mayor and the BRA. The staff of the City Planning Board had already drawn up plans for the district, but once again, action awaited Ed Logue's arrival. Inspired by progress on the waterfront, the CBD committee commissioned Victor Gruen Associates to suggest strategies to preserve the preeminence of the traditional downtown shopping area. Gruen's final report, in 1967, called for street closings and the creation of mall-like areas. By the mid-seventies much of this was accomplished and "Downtown Crossing" became a distinctive slice of the city.[73]

Another privately sponsored but unsanctioned contribution to planning in Boston in the 1960s came from the local architectural community. The Boston Society of Architects came up with the "Architects' Plan for Boston," which contained the "High Spine" concept of building the downtown out through the southerly portion of Back Bay. The report, inspired by Kevin Lynch, a local city-planning guru, proposed that "the existing line of business development from Faneuil Hall out toward Back Bay be continued as a 'High Spine' outward and upward as the future may require, circled by the ring of the Inner Belt."[74] Several buildings constructed since this report have partially fulfilled the idea, and although it was never officially adopted, it is another indication of the ferment stirred up by the New Boston.

In retrospect, it is clear that the sensational work of Edward J. Logue was the crucial element in the renaissance of Boston, but in 1962 questions arose about the effectiveness of his planning. An article in *The Boston Globe* noted that "several tons of plans and reports have come out of the Boston Redevelopment Authority . . . but aside from a lot of demolition and human displacement, and a few new building starts, there has been not enough evidence that a New Boston is with us."[75] Other newspapers carried alarming headlines about the "doubling" of redevelopment costs when Logue announced the Ninety Million Dollar Program would actually cost $173 million.[76] Despite the skepticism, urban redevelopment continued to garner support, primarily for economic reasons. Mayor Collins's address to the annual convention of the Massachusetts State Labor Council AFL–CIO in 1962 illustrates the power of the economic factor. He used a familiar-sounding argument for continued gov-

....

Collins,

Logue, and

the "New

Boston"

182

ernment efforts to reshape Boston and announced a $1 billion construction program, asserting "this construction will pump some $2.5 billion into the economy of the city with much of it going into worker's pay." Collins termed this "an unparalleled boom in the history of the city and probably unequalled in the nation."[77] He was right but it took time for buildings to materialize.

By the end of 1964, however, the New Boston was beginning to show its face. The one-hundred-acre Atlantic Avenue project, Government Center, and the Castle Square housing project were all begun that year, and the Prudential Center, the State Street Bank building, and the turnpike extension were nearly complete. The success of the State Street Bank building, with its name looming over the financial district, led other banks to clamor for their own signature buildings. In the years ahead the Bank of New England, the Bank of Boston, the Shawmut Bank, and others placed their own marks on the swiftly changing skyline. Outside the financial district, the old West End continued to sprout the ugly apartment buildings of Charles River Park and in April 1964, Boston's first redevelopment project, the New York Streets project, drew to a close under Kane Simonian's direction. Families long gone, the site was now devoted to light industrial and commercial purposes.[78] And Logue and Collins had hardly begun.

In 1964 Logue changed Boston's zoning code and drew up a general plan for the city. Up to this time all zoning for Boston was done by the state legislature. The legislature had authorized creation of the Boston Zoning Commission in 1956 but wrangling over the method of appointing members delayed the establishment of the commission until 1958.[79] The change of mayoral administrations and the creation of the BRA further slowed the work of writing a new zoning code until Logue turned his eye upon it. The new code eliminated building-height limitations and paved the way for the office towers delineating Boston's new skyline. The legislation also bolstered the power of the Zoning Commission. In addition, Logue's BRA kept a hand in the process through its recommendations on zoning appeals to the new Board of Appeal.[80] The Zoning Commission joined another city-sponsored organization in defining the city's appearance: in 1955 the state legislature had established the Beacon Hill Architectural Commission to protect the historic character of this lofty neighborhood. (A similar commission was created for the Back Bay in 1966.)[81]

Two Back Bay projects in the late 1960s, one at Copley Square and the other along Huntington Avenue toward Massachusetts Avenue, exemplify the New Boston in that neighborhood. In 1965, Copley Square was still

....

Collins,
Logue, and
the "New
Boston"

183

Figure 7.7 Copley Square. This photo was taken in preparation for the 1965 design competition to revamp this famous and challenging site. Traffic continued to go along Huntington Avenue through the center of the square although temporary barriers were erected at this time. The Boston Public Library is in the foreground. A municipal parking garage and several office buildings behind Trinity Church were later demolished to make way for the controversial new headquarters of the New England. (Courtesy of the Archives of the City of Boston.)

....
Collins,
Logue, and
the "New
Boston"

184

two triangular patches of grass separated by Huntington Avenue. The city sponsored a national competition to select a plan for a park on the site, and Sasaki Associates, an architectural firm from Watertown, Massachusetts, won the contest with a proposal for a sunken plaza. Ed Logue grandiloquently predicted "this exciting space will become a world-famous

Boston landmark, similar to the Piazza San Marco in Venice and St. Peter's Square in Rome."[82] But few Bostonians ever warmed up to the stark, treeless, dirty, and windswept plaza sunk below street-level. Hope springs eternal, especially at Copley Square, and the city sponsored yet another park competition in 1983. The latest face on Copley Square appeared in 1989.[83] The nearby Christian Science complex, adjacent to both the church headquarters and the Prudential Center, is another product of the sixties. The church hired I. M. Pei and Associates to develop plans for the area, which included a twenty-six-story administration building, an education building, underground garage, plaza, and reflecting pool.

Pei's imprint on Boston and its architecture is as stunning as it is controversial. From the blueprint for Government Center and City Hall Plaza, to the Christian Science Plaza, to Harbor Towers and the John Hancock Tower, Pei and his associates conceived a vision of Boston that greatly departs from the city's traditional materials, scale, form, and context. In the sixties, his designs were all the rage and the BRA encouraged his work. Bostonians today may be forgiven for deploring Pei's effect on the city, although few venture public remarks about the architectural legend. BRA director Stephen Coyle, however, is an exception; he once suggested that the U.S. Navy use Harbor Towers for target practice. Pei's design of the John Fitzgerald Kennedy Library in the 1970s is a more attractive expression of the architect's craft. Perhaps because it perches on the edge of Old Harbor in Dorchester, set off from other structures, Pei's design is permitted a more suitable context in which to be appreciated. In the city proper, however, many feel that the work of Pei and his associates intrudes disagreeably on the urban setting.

In 1965 the BRA published a general plan for Boston that treated social as well as physical renewal in areas throughout the city. The plan was "a city-wide attempt to treat both the causes and major symptoms of Boston's physical decline." It explicitly rejected the notion that government alone could plan for Boston and stated that the government's own plans "must be so designed, located, and timed as to have the maximum generating, guiding effect on privately planned and financed projects."[84] In the process, a balance was to be struck between change and preservation. The plan established a comprehensive, long-range standard with which land assembly and redevelopment projects had to comply. It offered a guideline for the revision of the city zoning map as well as for the development of public facilities. (The new Public Facilities Department, created in 1966, was part of the overall Logue strategy for Boston.)[85] Finally, the general plan laid down guidelines for various federal urban renewal projects.

The general plan was concerned with more than just physical development. It endeavored to stabilize the size of Boston's population while increasing its diversity; this meant reversing the trend toward the concentration of "low-income groups and nonwhites in the core city" by making "residential Boston attractive to families at the time when they acquire the economic means to move elsewhere." Thus, Logue continued, an "important objective of the Development Program must be to preserve the stability of residential neighborhoods in Boston and to make them, in as many respects as possible, competitive with surrounding cities and towns in housing, schools and public services."[86] The Collins and Logue approach from the beginning was to treat neighborhoods much more carefully than the West End had been treated under the previous administration. The BRA tried to include community groups in planning neighborhoods, much as it worked with business groups to plan the downtown. The BRA philosophy under Logue was "that neighborhoods will be planned by people living or working in those neighborhoods and that Redevelopment Authority personnel will act as co-workers in this planning." Logue called it "planning with people."[87] The first issue was to select the neighborhoods targeted for renewal and here again Logue built on antecedents.

Planning administrator Donald Graham credits Roxbury community leader Muriel Snowden with turning his attention and that of the city to renewal efforts in Roxbury in the late 1950s.[88] Muriel and Otto Snowden approached Graham at the Boston Planning Board and persuaded him to put Roxbury on the agenda. The result was the Washington Park project, which became the first full-scale residential renewal project under Collins and Logue. Washington Park was given top priority in 1961, according to the BRA, because the "city had a long-standing commitment to the people of the area to support their improvement efforts."[89] In his study of neighborhood planning in Boston, Langley Keyes points out that the population of Washington Park had changed dramatically in the fifties, from seventy percent white in 1950 to seventy percent black in 1960. Keyes also notes that influential citizens, both black and white, had been trying since the Housing Act of 1954 to use the program to deal with the area's mounting problems; these citizens were crucial to the plans for Washington Park.[90] Neighborhood leaders like Otto and Muriel Snowden, founders of the black community's Freedom House, wanted to halt decay and protect the residential character and quality of life in Washington Park. Others, however, felt that the Washington Park plan reflected middle-class aspirations, in opposition to other elements of the community. But unlike other examples of neighborhood renewal, Washington Park was

....

Collins,
Logue, and
the "New
Boston"

186

characterized by a close identity of goals and strategies between the BRA and at least some important elements of the community leadership. The city worked with the Snowdens and others and proposed to rehabilitate housing and construct new schools, recreational facilities, streets and utilities, "all leading to the restoration of the neighborhood." The BRA soon decided to expand the boundaries of the original Washington Park project up to the edge of Franklin Park, clearing 25 percent of the land and upgrading and rehabilitating the other 75 percent.[91]

Mayor Collins believed that this program in Roxbury, along with a second renewal project in Charlestown, provided a natural symmetry in the city's redevelopment efforts in terms of both geography and population. The mayor and the BRA characterized Charlestown, like Roxbury, as an area in decline. Hard numbers backed up this belief. The neighborhood's population dropped 40 percent in the 1950s and the value of all Charlestown property plunged from $48.4 million in 1930 to $34 million in 1960. Taking Burnham's adage seriously, the BRA under Logue would "make no little plans." The initial BRA scheme for Charlestown targeted over 90 percent of the homes for rehabilitation, the highest figure in the entire country.[92] But the BRA's desires were not to be consummated; the locals defied the agency. Charlestown residents had already endured a long history of government planning that damaged their neighborhood: in 1901 the state authorized the Boston Elevated to lay tracks up Main Street; in 1942 the Boston Housing Authority sliced off a substantial segment of the town for one of its projects; and in 1950 dozens of homes were bulldozed to make way for the Mystic–Tobin Bridge.[93] Charlestown had had enough and opposition to the BRA's plans for the neighborhood soon boiled over.

Logue's critics have charged that he would never risk a public hearing unless he was certain of a numerical advantage over opponents. If so, Charlestown was the exception, and "a junior Battle of Bunker Hill erupted" when residents protested BRA plans.[94] Monsignor Lally, chairman of the BRA and pastor of St. Mary's Church in Charlestown, was verbally attacked and another local pastor was punched when he spoke in favor of the BRA plans at a neighborhood hearing.[95] This raucous scene set the stage for a prolonged battle over renewal, and the strife was fueled by the fact that "Townies" had only to gaze across the mouth of the Charles to be reminded what renewal meant to working-class residents of the West End. Logue's work was stymied by the destruction wrought by his predecessors.

Langley Keyes concludes that Logue's expedition into Charlestown was complicated by the creation of an organized neighborhood association

....
Collins,
Logue, and
the "New
Boston"
187

opposing the BRA, meddling politicians who decided to make hay with the renewal plans, and the "eagle eye of the press seeking signs of further conflict."[96] By 1965, however, Logue garnered sufficient support to out-power the opposition, and he secured neighborhood approval of his revised plans. Key to the compromise between the BRA and the community was Logue's assurance that the elevated trains along Main Street would finally be torn down and that only 11 percent of the town's homes would be bulldozed. Logue won a great deal of what he sought to do in Charlestown but it had been a long, tough struggle. And it was not the last.

The controversial North Harvard Street project in Allston was another example of a fight between Logue's BRA and "the neighborhood." This decade-long conflict featured violent evictions, sit-ins, picketing, arrests, and a court battle all the way to the United States Supreme Court. BRA surveys contended that thirty of the fifty homes in the area were "substandard" and Logue concluded that the neighborhood was in a "particularly run-down condition."[97] The BRA's plan would have cleared homes from ten acres adjacent to the Harvard Business School and replaced them with a 300-unit apartment building. The BRA board declared the area "blighted" in September 1962 and the city council approved the clearance plans in December of that year. Harvard students and sundry politicians joined neighborhood opponents in the protest but the BRA continued to evict residents and tear down houses. Several families refused to move and a pitched battle broke out in August 1965. This nasty struggle was a public relations disaster and Mayor Collins asked a blue-ribbon panel to investigate the clash. The panel urged the BRA to rehabilitate the homes and restore former residents to the neighborhoods, but the federal Department of Housing and Urban Development refused to sanction this strategem. By the summer of 1966, the BRA plans were doomed, but only thirteen homes remained. The war outlasted Logue's tenure at the BRA and ended when a mixed-income housing development was finally built on the site in the 1970s.

This type of drawn-out conflict was something the BRA could ill afford. It was also a spur to encourage greater community involvement in planning. Logue had long recognized the importance of the social dimension in planning and was, in fact, a leader in incorporating community participation and social reform into the process of rebuilding the physical city. He often spoke about "planning with people" and created a social service agency with an agenda nearly as ambitious in its own realm as was the BRA in its domain. As Logue tells the story, he "conceived what became the nation's first antipoverty program in New Haven" and sold the

....

Collins,

Logue, and

the "New

Boston"

188

idea to Paul Ylvisaker at the Ford Foundation. Logue continues, "I told Paul in 1960 that I was going to Boston and asked him if I could get Ford help. He said yes and the result was ABCD."[98] The direct approach, excellent connections, and quick results typify the Logue style. ABCD, which stands for Action for Boston Community Development, was intended to become the vehicle for Boston to deal with the "human side of physical renewal" by promoting citizen participation in the planning process.[99] Despite the initial closeness of the BRA and ABCD, as time went on the two agencies found themselves increasingly hostile toward one another. Stephan Thernstrom of Harvard, in his account of ABCD, concluded that the "cold war" which ensued may have been inevitable because the goals of organizing neighborhoods and articulating their views often clashed with the goals of the city-wide redevelopment agency.[100] Such conflict between neighborhoods and the city presented a quandary for planners in the 1960s. Logue's political antennae were attuned to the private sector and established community leaderships, but less sensitive to the unorganized residents of poor neighborhoods. This surely is a factor in the political defeats suffered by both the mayor and BRA director in later years.

Collins and Logue hoped that the success of the New Boston would carry over into political advancement but each was disappointed. Collins handily won reelection as mayor in 1963 but fared poorly in Boston wards when he ran for the U.S. Senate in 1966. He decided not to run for a third term as mayor in 1967, and moved across the Charles River to MIT, where he taught urban studies. Collins also practiced law and engaged in a myriad of political, business, and civic activities. Logue left the BRA in August 1967, hoping to succeed Collins as mayor. He failed to survive the September preliminary election, leaving Louise Day Hicks and Kevin White to vie for the mayoralty in November. Logue then moved to New York and plunged into further controversy as head of the state's urban renewal program. He returned to Boston in the 1980s, however, to lecture at MIT and to run his own development company.

Logue's legacy is mixed. His strategy, innovative though it was, and a considerable advance over that of his predecessors, came to be characterized as a "top-down" approach that was no longer politically acceptable. Any criticism of Logue must, however, be seen in the context of the times. The 1960s was an era of stupendous social transformation, race riots, war, protests, and mounting disillusionment with government. Over the course of the decade, an increasing number of residents of city neighborhoods became bitterly opposed to urban renewal. Thus, although the decade proved a high-water mark of planning the physical city, it also

....

Collins,

Logue, and

the "New

Boston"

189

marked the infancy of another type of planning more directly concerned with the social realities of urban life. In fact, the very success of planning itself engendered change. As Thernstrom writes, Collins and Logue "were hungry for solutions to problems that could not be eliminated—that were indeed being aggravated—by the massive physical renewal program that was changing the face of the city."[101] Despite Logue's accomplishments many Bostonians maintain that the damage done to so many communities during the 1960s outweighs the positive aspects of the BRA's renewal program. But many observers also recognize the impressive achievements wrought by what the *Globe* termed "the nation's finest urban renewal program."[102]

Figure 7.8 An aerial view of Boston Common and Beacon Hill in the early 1960s when the scandal-plagued underground garage was under construction. See middle-left of the photograph for cranes and concrete forms. The Suffolk County Courthouse, to the right of the State House, remains the dominant building before the advent of the Saltonstall and McCormack Buildings within the decade. (Courtesy of the Library of the Boston Redevelopment Authority.)

Figure 7.9 Government Center Plaza. This view shows the New City Hall to the left and the Sears Crescent Building (1816) and Sears Block (1848) in the center in front of the financial towers of the Boston Company and the Bank of New England (1969) at left. Here the basic elements of the New Boston are in place—a massive public structure, an attempt at dramatic open space for pedestrians, preservation of old structures, and the huge demand for office space representing a revived economy. (Courtesy of the Library of the Boston Redevelopment Authority.)

....

*Collins,
Logue, and
the "New
Boston"*

191

In this dramatic era of Boston's history, municipal government came to be accepted as a powerful originator and agent of planning. Under John Collins, the city assumed a leadership role only hinted at in the past by remarkable figures like Frederick Law Olmsted. In some ways, Ed Logue's place in the city's planning history is similar to that of the great landscape architect: both understood the possibilities of urban development; both took existing plans and fashioned them into a package which they sold to Boston's movers and shakers. And both left a remarkable imprint on the city, although the Logue legacy is more heavily debated. *The Boston*

Sunday Herald, for example, once predicted that Logue would become "more controversial, more discussed, more fervently admired and fervently hated than any personality since James Michael Curley."[103] And the *Herald* was right. In his own way, each became a legend—a fact neither would deny. While Logue was on a journey through China in 1989, each member of his tour group was given a map inscribed in Chinese but accompanied by a legend printed in English. When a guide asked if everyone had a legend, Logue quipped, "Legend? I am a legend."[104]

Ed Logue and John Collins made their mark on Boston in a relatively short period, seven years. They inherited the foundations of the New Boston and began constructing it but left office before its fulfillment. Collins and Logue created a more powerful Redevelopment Authority, built Government Center, began redeveloping the waterfront and downtown shopping district, and stimulated office construction in the city. All told, their programs encompassed about one-quarter of the city's land area, and by the end of 1966, nearly $2 billion of public and private money had been invested in the BRA's urban renewal program.[105]

Their greatest achievement was the mobilization of both the public and private sectors. The pair demonstrated what energetic and articulate municipal leadership could do on a large scale: together, they sparked the rebirth of Boston, which flowered in the years ahead. Logue and Collins worked hard and achieved a great deal but they and the city also benefited by the improved economic climate of New England, and Boston in particular. The quiet revolution wrought by the computer was beginning to transform the workplace, and Boston as a center of this revolution was well-positioned for prosperity. Boston-based financial and legal firms provided the services needed by the growing computer industry, required more office space, and fueled the city's expansion. Similarly, banks and insurance companies contended for a better image by erecting grand new buildings in Boston, the capital of New England. The New Boston flourished because of a propitious combination of public-sector leadership and private-sector willingness to renew investments in the city, an opportunity that might have been lost had not Collins and Logue convinced investors of the advantages of Boston and the wisdom of enlarging their operations in the old city. Boston's prosperity in the 1970s and 1980s owed much to the confidence and energy that Logue and the city exuded during Collins's mayoralty.

8

....

Kevin White

and a

"World-Class

City"

In 1968, when Kevin White became mayor, Boston was financially secure, confident, and forward-looking. Old problems, however, still faced the city and new problems were just surfacing. Despite the success of Collins and Logue in renewing enthusiasm and investment in the city, a decline in population and manufacturing continued to threaten the future. Boston's population was draining into the suburbs. The national economic and social changes that boosted more people into the middle class emptied Boston and other cities. People who were "making it" were most often doing so by leaving the city.

Throughout Kevin White's mayoralty powerful social currents affected the city. Urban America went on a roller coaster ride of economic recession, political turmoil, and racial conflict. Although the busing controversy tarnished Boston's national reputation, the White years also saw a resurgence of civic pride and considerable favorable publicity for Boston. By the end of White's sixteen years, the city was in a much stronger position than at either the beginning or the middle of his reign.

Numerous efforts to improve upon the base established in the 1960s marked the White years. Projects planned and begun in the Collins administration were completed during White's term. The new administration also launched innovative measures to revitalize the city. Throughout the 1970s great strides were made by the increased use of the Chapter 121A tax incentive, the revival of neighborhood planning, and the resurgence of private development.

Demographic and economic trends circumscribed these efforts, however. An oil crisis and national recession in the mid-1970s hit New England especially hard. In addition, the Boston school desegregation order of 1974, which mandated busing and ignited years of conflict, impeded planning. In fact, Boston's history in the 1970s was dominated

Figure 8.1 This 1969 aerial view of Boston reveals the completed Prudential Center in the rear-middle with Government Center the dominant form in the front. The elevated Central Artery cuts off the North End and waterfront from the rest of the city. Few tall buildings are evident but two decades later the image is quite different. (Courtesy of the Library of the Boston Redevelopment Authority.)

by the busing controversy. The school desegregation order came in response to a long-standing denial of equal educational opportunity and the pattern of racism found deep in the city's psyche. As historian Ronald P. Formisano writes, some Boston politicians, "like Richard Nixon during these years, thrived on cultural, class, and racial resentments, and by the early 1970s Boston had become a cauldron of such animosities."[1] National television audiences were treated to images of hatred and violence with protesters and police fighting on the streets of Boston. The breakdown of community was obvious to all the world and the complexity of a multitude of racial, class, and political issues was reduced to a simplistic negative portrayal of the city. Judge W. Arthur Garrity's court ruling exacerbated tensions and proved counterproductive. Bostonians long suffered from his sincere but misguided attempt at social planning. The city was forced into a "crisis management" stance, preoccupied with putting out fires rather than planning to prevent them.

Moreover, the growth of the civil rights, black power, and women's movements of the 1960s, along with increasing student activism, helped to create a society in which people more freely expressed their opposition to the government and established ways. In Boston this spirit was manifested in community activism. Emerging from the turmoil and conflicts of the sixties, local activists played an increasingly vocal and more powerful role in shaping the city.

By the late 1970s, however, Boston seemed to have surmounted its problems and was becoming what Mayor White frequently called "a world-class city." The Bicentennial of the American Revolution focused the country's attention on Boston, which was beginning to gain recognition as a premier American city with unique historic character. Moreover, the changing national economy positioned Boston to take advantage of economic trends. The city once again became inviting to investors, who launched a period of spectacular growth.

To some, this was a period of unrestrained development, a building frenzy sponsored by an increasingly mercurial mayor. The latter White years saw a tremendous amount of construction, and a markedly changed skyline for the old city. Many decried the mayor's role in determining what buildings were to be constructed and even how they should look. Perhaps the most controversial was International Place. Architecture critic Robert Campbell of the *Boston Globe* was among those who strongly criticized the appearance and size of International Place, started toward the end of the White era on the former site of a city parking garage. Instead of blaming the project's architect, Philip Johnson, or the developer, Donald J. Chiofaro, Campbell held Mayor White responsible.

Figure 8.2 Kevin H. White served as mayor of Boston for sixteen years, longer than anyone else in the city's history. He presided over the fulfillment of the New Boston and imparted a sense of pride in "his city." (Courtesy of Kevin H. White.)

Campbell argued that "it's the fault of the planning process under Mayor Kevin White. All White cared about was selling the site . . . for all he could get. The more bulk the city permitted, the more bucks it got for the garage."[2]

The contentious debate over the appearance of International Place, coming as it did at the end of Kevin White's sixteen-year administration, effectively illustrates the controversial aspects of his role in planning Boston. The development of International Place indicates that there was a method to the process, and that White dominated it like no previous mayor, orchestrating the city's use of development to finance its normal budgetary expenses. The city had a marketable commodity, land, which it was willing to sell to the highest bidder.

The foundations of the 1960s New Boston proved sturdy enough to support a spectacular expansion of office and hotel space in the next several decades. Powerful forces were unleashed, and during the White years the question of who would control them came to the fore. Would it be the private sector, the BRA, the city's residents, or the mayor? The answer would be determined by politics, a game in which Kevin White excelled.

As Anthony Lukas writes in *Common Ground,* "if ever a man was bred for politics it was Kevin White."[3] Kevin Hagan White was born in Boston

....

Kevin White

and a

"World-Class

City"

196

in 1929 to a politically prominent family and married into another. His father, grandfather, and father-in-law all served terms as president of the Boston City Council. Kevin White attended Boston public schools, and graduated from Tabor Academy, Williams College, and Boston College Law School. In 1960, after four years as an assistant district attorney in Suffolk County, White was elected secretary of state for the Commonwealth of Massachusetts. He continued to hold this post until he ran for mayor in 1967 and defeated a number of well-known candidates in the preliminary election, including former BRA head Ed Logue.

White won the final election of 1967 against Louise Day Hicks, who was perceived as a segregationist, largely because the *Boston Globe* portrayed him as a moderate who would be able to mitigate the forces of reaction and racism personified by Hicks. Not since 1896 had the *Globe* endorsed a candidate for political office. In 1967 it abandoned neutrality, broke tradition, and endorsed White because of the importance it attached to the racial issue. White himself saw the election in less dramatic terms: he merely wanted to be mayor as a preliminary to running for governor in 1970. White recalls, "at first I didn't want to be mayor. It was the last thing I wanted to be. It was a stepping stone, and it became a lifetime job."[4] Thus, right from the beginning there was an element of haphazardness to the White years.

In announcing his first run for mayor in early 1967, White invoked a theme that would later find an echo in the 1983 campaign to select his successor. The Kevin White of 1967 resurrected the old conflict of neighborhoods versus downtown as a means of gathering support. He appealed to thousands of voters by criticizing his two immediate predecessors for ignoring the outlying districts. He blamed Boston's population drain on Mayors Hynes and Collins, although he acknowledged that the last two administrations had laid plans, constructed great new buildings, and revitalized the business community. He went on to charge, however, that "a great city is not only a place to work, it is a place in which to live and raise a family, and it is precisely here that we have failed."[5] Later in his campaign he argued that "Boston needs people programs to match the building program."[6]

White's position faithfully reflected public opinion on this issue. Many Bostonians were hostile to the BRA, which they believed had bulldozed a path through so many neighborhoods. Hale Champion, White's first BRA director, acknowledged that "our credibility in some of the communities we are attempting to serve is dangerously low."[7] Under Champion, the agency attempted to produce low-income housing. Although the Infill Housing program, which tried to erect low-cost housing on vacant lots

....

Kevin White

and a

"World-Class

City"

197

throughout the city, was a much-ridiculed failure, the seventies saw a net gain of 9,000 dwellings in Boston.[8]

White's Little City Hall program, based on the New York model created by Mayor John Lindsay, was more successful. Managers of these satellite offices were sometimes able to bring to the mayor matters of importance to the residents of their neighborhoods. One notable example is when Fred Salvucci, manager of East Boston's Little City Hall, persuaded the mayor to join the opposition to the Massachusetts Port Authority's plan to expand Logan Airport. Political scientist Martha Wagner Weinberg notes that this challenge to MassPort and the later fight against extending the interstate highway system through Boston neighborhoods were "direct responses to galvanized communities and . . . fashioned by staff members who advocate sensitivity to community concerns."[9]

The prominence of these staff members in advancing neighborhood causes within the loose framework provided by White shows that the mayor did not himself set out to champion neighborhoods against government agencies. He reacted rather than led. Looking back, twenty years after his first mayoral election, White acknowledged that the "neighborhood problems surfaced up to me."[10] Yet the focus on neighborhoods became closely identified with Kevin White early in his mayoralty.

The neighborhood problem with the greatest effect on the shape of Boston and long-term planning was the proposed junction of an Inner Belt Highway and Southwest Expressway. The idea of an Inner Belt highway originated in the Master Highway Plan of 1948 issued by the Massachusetts Department of Public Works. The state proposed to extend Interstate 95 from Route 128 in Canton through Hyde Park and Jamaica Plain and into the South End. The proposed Inner Belt would then cut through the city from the southern sections through the Fenway, across the Charles River and through portions of Cambridge. After the Federal Highway Act of 1956, the proposal mushroomed to include a five-story-high interchange in the South End connecting it with a new Southwest Expressway.[11] Opposition to this gargantuan project mounted gradually through the 1960s and came to a head in the early 1970s. Kevin White's political aspirations were, as usual, a critical factor in the controversy. South End residents worked with members of Urban Planning Aid, a group of city planners who opposed the highway, and managed to obtain a moratorium on further acquisitions of property by the BRA while the debate on the future of the highway went forward at the state and national levels of government.[12] Community activists scored a major victory for neighborhood opponents of government power and set an example for

....
Kevin White
and a
"World-Class
City"

198

others when they succeeded in stopping construction of the Inner Belt and Southwest Expressway.[13]

Several days after Republican Governor Frank Sargent, a former commissioner of the Massachusetts Department of Public Works, was sworn into office in January 1969, the "Greater Boston Committee (GBC) on the Transportation Crisis" led a "People Before Highways Day" march on the Boston Common. Founded in December 1968, the GBC was originally an alliance of people with an anti-highway, pro-mass transit view, but by this time it had grown to include those concerned about the environment, lack of housing, unemployment, and other social and economic issues related to transportation.[14] Governor Sargent met with the group and agreed to set up a task force headed by Professor Alan Altshuler of MIT to investigate the issue of highways.

Key aides to both Governor Sargent and Mayor White lobbied for their support of neighborhood and grass-roots organizations opposed to the Southwest Expressway.[15] Both White and Sargent sought to project a progressive image as they geared up to run for governor in 1970, and thus were especially vulnerable to pressure on the highway issue. But there was more to it than that. Mayor White recalled that he attended a slide presentation at a church hall showing the effects of the proposed expressway and went away a convert, concluding of the project, "this thing is ridiculous."[16]

Sargent imposed a partial moratorium on highway construction within the Route 128 region in February 1970 and established a $3.5 million Boston Transportation Planning Review headed by Altshuler.[17] Two years later, after beating Kevin White in the 1970 gubernatorial election, Sargent abandoned the highway plan entirely and launched an attempt, orchestrated by Altshuler, to fundamentally change federal highway funding policy. Since Massachusetts stood to lose the $600 million it had been allocated for the canceled highway, the state wanted the federal government to approve a transfer of these funds to mass transit programs. Fred Salvucci colorfully describes Governor Sargent's decision to terminate the expressway before getting federal approval for a transfer: "It was like he jumped off the top of the Prudential Center and hoped that Alan Altshuler would have a net woven to catch him by the time he got to the bottom."[18]

In fact, Altshuler did weave a safety net, with the cooperation of assorted Massachusetts and national political figures. The Interstate Transfer Option, approved by the Congress in 1973, allowed states to divert funds from highways to mass transit. It was not until 1978, however, that Governor Sargent's successor, Michael Dukakis, oversaw the start of construction on the new Southwest Corridor, which now provides rapid transit, commuter, and inter-city rail as well as parkland for Boston.[19]

Kevin White's Little City Hall program had its counterpart in a system of neighborhood or district planners within the city government. The BRA under Collins and Logue had focused on only one-third of the city—the South End, Roxbury, Charlestown, and downtown; under Kevin White all sections of the city received attention. Planners within the BRA advanced the notion of district planning to Hale Champion when he was the director of the agency, suggesting that the city be divided into ten districts, each with an average of 60,000 residents per planner.[20] Concurrently, the planners would create a Boston Urban Affairs Committee and local advisory committees. Champion persuaded the mayor to accept the proposals, and district planning was underway—despite objections from the Mayor's Office of Public Service, which ran the Little City Hall program and feared competition in dealing with neighborhoods.

The neighborhood advisory committees did not last long but district planning did. The status and strength of the district planning program varied depending on the degree of support accorded it by successive BRA directors and on the political climate. Robert Kenney, head of the BRA from 1971 to 1976, staunchly supported the concept.[21] During Kenney's tenure the district planners worked more cooperatively with the Little City Hall managers, then under the direction of David Davis (later director of the Massachusetts Port Authority). Kenney put John Weis in charge of the community planning program in 1973. Weis made planning districts coterminous with the boundaries of the Little City Hall districts.[22] With a staff of more than twenty, these planners increasingly acted as advocates for their neighborhoods. Newly available federal grant money also matched the needs of this program.

In the later years of White's administration the neighborhood planning program changed. The Mayor's Office of Program Development oversaw the dispersal of federal grant money and the Neighborhood Development Administration (NDA) took the district planning function away from the BRA, when critics charged that the neighborhood planners had become overly politicized.[23] Many of the planners themselves couldn't decide whether their loyalties lay with the mayor, the BRA, or the community. In the years after Kenney's departure from the BRA and Weis's move to the rival NDA, the BRA concentrated on downtown development, leaving neighborhood planning to the NDA. In 1971 the state created another agency with responsibilities for planning, the Boston Economic Development and Industrial Commission (EDIC), designed to spur the growth of industrial parks and to maintain manufacturing jobs in the city.[24]

Outside of city hall politics, the city's residents were often taking matters into their own hands. The most famous example was "Tent City," which heated up in the South End when people reacted angrily to a decade of relocation of poor families. The saga of Tent City began in April 1968 when a small group of South End residents protested what they saw as the city's wrecking-ball policy of demolishing homes in the name of urban renewal. They began with a three-acre site the city had cleared of homes and was using as a parking lot. The activists set up tents and makeshift houses and began a long battle to develop the site for affordable housing for the community.

In 1969, community activist Mel King led a group called Community Assembly for a United South End (C.A.U.S.E.) which denounced what they scathingly referred to as "the Boston Racist Authority." C.A.U.S.E. marched with placards on the BRA's South End office and five people nailed the office door shut at 72 Warren Avenue to protest the city's urban renewal policy.[25] At this point, the South End community split into factions which turned on each other, rendering the dispute more complicated than the straightforward community-versus-the-BRA argument it had originally been. The "Ad Hoc Committee for a South End for South Enders" clashed with the "Committee for a Balanced South End." The first group advocated maximum efforts for lower-income residents while the second favored a diversity of residents, including upper-income families.[26] This factionalism and controversy delayed by nearly twenty years the realization of the Tent City dream: a mixed-income housing development rose on the site in 1987.

Throughout the nation similar neighborhood activism altered how political leaders compete for power and effectively "ended large-scale clearance projects, drastically revised traditional planning practices by creating citizen review and participation procedures, and created a new policy emphasis on preservation and rehabilitation."[27] Fred Salvucci, a central figure in Boston planning for several decades, likens urban renewal and transportation plans of the fifties and sixties to childhood diseases for which there were once no antibodies.[28] In earlier years, projects like the Massachusetts Turnpike Extension and Logan Airport expansion displaced people, usually the poor, who had no protection. In the White years, effective antibodies to these diseases emerged as people with "middle-class skills and access" began to work against the harmful effects of such proposals.

But conflict in the neighborhoods exhausted the mayor, whose attention—like the BRA's—gradually shifted to the development of downtown Boston. Many observers attribute the change in focus to Kevin White's

....

*Kevin White
and a
"World-Class
City"*

201

tough reelection campaign in 1975. After repeated charges of corruption White lost interest in providing attention and services to residents of the neighborhoods. Furthermore, the nation's Bicentennial celebration spotlighted the city's historic sections, located in the heart of Boston; the neighborhoods receded from view.

The transformation of downtown Boston in the latter years of the White administration was nothing less than staggering. Novelist and columnist George Higgins writes that Kevin White

> presided over a breathtaking reclamation of an urban downtown unparalleled by any city not first laid waste by modern war. He did not finance it, as he has sometimes seemed to claim. What he did was to expedite it fiercely, midwifing the changes through the Byzantine bureaucracies, more than willing to cajole if that would do the job but quite willing to threaten—and to carry out his threats—when that seemed to become necessary.[29]

Indeed, downtown planning can best be described as a series of confrontations in which the mayor played a key role.

Kevin White waged his first great battle, the Park Plaza project, during his first term in office in the early 1970s. The initial Park Plaza proposal was a far cry from what was finally built in Park Square in the 1980s. The original project was the brainchild of developer and publisher Mortimer Zuckerman, who worked closely with Mayor White to arrange a privately financed redevelopment of this run-down commercial and office section bordering Boston Common and the Public Garden. Park Plaza was to be built in two stages and include a hotel, apartments, retail and office space, and a parking garage. First announced in 1970, the Park Plaza development sparked a donnybrook before Zuckerman finally surrendered to opposition by environmentalists, the BRA, state officials, and hostile competitors, and withdrew in 1974.

Mayor White had invited proposals for the Park Square area in May 1970 and by December of that year five companies had submitted plans. In July 1971 the BRA announced the selection of Zuckerman's Boston Urban Associates and the city council approved the plans in December. Opposition to the proposal quickly surfaced, and focused on many considerations besides the project's imposing size and lack of aesthetic quality. Chief among the complaints was that Zuckerman and his partner, Edward Linde, although experienced in real estate development, had no proven track record in their new firm.[30] Critics also opposed the municipal government's use of the powers of public domain and bonding authority for a private speculator; the financing of the package; the lack of

....

Kevin White
and a
"World-Class
City"

202

specific plans for the Combat Zone portion of the project; and the environmental impact on the Public Garden. Even BRA Director Robert Kenney disapproved the Zuckerman proposal. More serious opposition came from businesses and environmentalists. As Lukas writes, "like White, Zuckerman was an outsider, the object of Yankee condescension and obstruction. And like the mayor, he had beaten the Yankees at their own game."[31]

Despite the opposition, Mayor White dug in to fight for the Zuckerman proposal. Park Plaza was to have been the first major urban renewal project built without federal money: what Collins and Logue had done with government funds would be accomplished with private capital. Park Plaza has been described as Kevin White's first attempt to use the "master builder strategy" to enhance his reputation and increase his control within Boston's private sector.[32] The "master builder" strategy, as applied by John F. Collins and others, entails building large-scale public projects and providing other public services as a means of building and consolidating political support. But Kevin White faced problems unknown to his predecessors. The substantial federal funding available for urban renewal in the 1960s was not guaranteed to continue and by the early 1970s most major Boston banks and resident insurance companies had either built or planned new skyscrapers, thus leading the way in rebuilding the city. Nevertheless, this initial surge of construction was followed by a lull, and White jumped in with the Park Plaza scheme.

In order for the Zuckerman enterprise to pass muster, the BRA had first to submit the proposal to the state's Department of Community Affairs. Over the years this department had routinely approved urban renewal plans, but in this case the staff and a new department head balked at sanctioning what they felt was an inappropriate proposal.[33] Miles Mahoney, the commissioner, took office in the beginning of May 1972 and a month later announced that he would not approve the Zuckerman proposal. The mayor, the Boston newspapers, and organized labor all attacked Mahoney's decision, and the Greater Boston Trades Council organized thousands of workers to march on the State House in protest. Governor Sargent's leading staff advisers, Jack Flannery and Al Kramer, astonished by the overwhelming public response, set up a series of meetings to try to work out a compromise that would satisfy Mahoney and allow the project to continue. This proved impossible.

Kramer worried about the effect of the Park Plaza controversy on Sargent's upcoming announcement halting all highway construction in the Boston area. He believed the transportation issue was more important and should take precedence over Park Plaza. Feelings within the Sargent

....
*Kevin White
and a
"World-Class
City"*
203

administration ran high, especially after the governor announced in November 1972 that newly submitted Park Plaza revisions looked very promising. Within the government, Mahoney was increasingly isolated in his adamant opposition to the project. Finally, at the end of February 1973, Governor Sargent announced that Mahoney had rejected Park Plaza and then resigned. Years later, Sargent said he thought the project could benefit Boston and that in trying to get it approved, "I was sure that there would be some wiggling room, but it turned out there wasn't."[34]

Although Kevin White lost the Park Plaza battle, he clearly won the war. He emerged from the controversy with more power and a reputation for using the resources he had in hand to do battle.[35] From this point on, White exercised far greater control over development in Boston. His authority grew, as did his willingness to exert his influence in shaping the city.

Chief among the methods employed by the White administration to encourage development was Chapter 121A, first used with the Prudential Center. This state law, which applies only to areas designated as "blighted," allowed the mayor to make a two-pronged arrangement with developers. One provision waived zoning requirements and the other reduced tax liability. Chapter 121A was used extensively before Proposition 2 1/2, not simply to induce growth by reducing taxes but also to provide certainty for investors about what their tax rate would be.[36] This legislation, combined with other inducements to invest in Boston, promoted a flurry of construction. Public investment by the city, the Commonwealth, and the federal government in Kevin White's first ten years contributed mightily to the trend. Between 1968 and 1978 the city spent $674 million, the state spent $600 million, and the federal government invested $550 million.[37]

....

Kevin White
and a
"World-Class
City"

204

The mayor's personal intervention in the process of selecting developers met with increasing controversy but in one instance the results were widely applauded: the transformation of the Quincy Market area into Faneuil Hall Marketplace. The City of Boston still owned the central market building constructed by Mayor Josiah Quincy in the 1820s, while the North and South buildings flanking it were privately owned. All three structures had deteriorated badly and under Mayor Collins the BRA incorporated the district in plans for renewing the waterfront.

As Bernard Frieden and Lynne Sagalyn put it in a recent book, Boston's decision to build Faneuil Hall Marketplace "was more the result of close calls and lucky breaks than the calculated choice in city hall."[38] In 1956 the City Planning Board had marked the buildings for clearance but nothing happened and in the early sixties Ed Logue decided the buildings were worth saving. The city council approval of the Waterfront Plan made the preservation of Quincy Market official policy, but continued financial problems delayed completion of the project for over a dozen years. Finally, Ed Logue secured a $2.4 million grant from the U.S. Department of Housing and Urban Development (HUD) for the restoration.[39] Simultaneously, Cambridge architect Ben Thompson stressed rehabilitation in a blueprint he prepared for the area. A 1970 award by HUD allowed the BRA to accept bids for renovating the structures. Upheavals in the BRA and other political battles led Thompson's original partners to withdraw from the project, so in 1972 the BRA reopened the bidding and Thomp-

Figure 8.3 Faneuil Hall and Quincy Market. Taken from the roof of New City Hall, this photograph captures the scene of renovations (see the North Market Building roof at left) and Sam Adams in the midst of a street intersection before the wildly successful work of architect Benjamin Thompson and developer James Rouse transformed the locale into a model of the revitalized city. The State Street Bank Building, to the right, was a landmark structure of the Collins-Logue era in Boston, representing their success in attracting investment in Boston. (Courtesy of the Library of the Boston Redevelopment Authority.)

son teamed up with James W. Rouse of the Rouse Company to propose a plan for the market buildings. The Architectural Heritage Foundation also proposed a plan in collaboration with historian Walter Muir Whitehill that won the initial backing of the BRA. At this point Mayor White intervened and insisted on the selection of the Thompson-Rouse team.

Rouse was chosen to develop and manage the buildings under a ninety-nine year lease[40] and was granted a tax reduction as an incentive to undertake the project.[41] But another three years passed before Rouse could obtain funding for the project because of the eroding economic situation in both the nation and the region. Local bankers doubted that any venture of this magnitude could succeed without a single, large, major tenant. Finally, the logjam was broken in January 1975 when the Chase Manhattan Bank agreed to finance half the project if Boston banks would underwrite the other half. The resulting marketplace was a phenomenal success for Boston. Frieden and Sagalyn point out that "for professionals who work at planning and building cities, Faneuil Hall Marketplace is the outstanding city development project of an era."[42] It spurred similar restorations throughout the country.

In Boston the historic preservation movement, which has become such an integral part of the planning process, got another boost from the creation of the Boston Landmarks Commission.[43] Under the aegis of the BRA, this organization designates structures with historical or architectural significance, thus preserving them from alteration or demolition. The actions of this body may, however, be vetoed by the mayor, who also appoints the commission.

Kevin White may never have gotten the credit he deserves for making Faneuil Hall Marketplace such a resounding success, but he certainly gained notoriety when he intervened in the selection of a developer for the nearby hotel project.[44] The celebrated Long Wharf Hotel controversy erupted after the 1975 election and during the era sometimes called "Kevin II," when White's involvement in planning became both more intimate and more controversial. This particular battle ended when Robert Walsh, head of the BRA after Robert Kenney, opposed the mayor's decision and was forced out of office.

Many developers coveted the location because of Long Wharf's proximity to Faneuil Hall Marketplace. Walsh and the BRA hired an outside architectural adviser to select the most desirable proposal. Criteria for approval were the quality of architectural design, size of tax benefits to the city, adequacy of financing, and the amenities of the hotel. Although both the BRA staff and the outside adviser rated the submission by Mortimer Zuckerman last among the eight entries, Mayor White sup-

....

Kevin White
and a
"World-Class
City"

206

ported Zuckerman, forced another review of the submissions, and asked Walsh to make the choice final. Walsh refused and was fired. BRA's chairman flatly states that "the mayor saw a political process as well as a renewal process. Walsh didn't understand this."[45] The message to developers and others involved in planning was clear: Kevin White was a formidable adversary in the development process, willing to exercise independent judgment, stake out a position, and fight for it.

A similar conflict, again a victory for White, arose over the location of Boston's newest federal office building. The General Services Administration (GSA) wanted to consolidate office space for numerous federal agencies then housed in rental buildings throughout the city. It proposed locating the new building at the lower end of Washington Street and was supported by local commercial interests seeking a buffer between the department stores and the city's notorious home of "adult" entertainment, the Combat Zone.

Mayor White instead wished to stimulate development of the North Station area, and commissioned noted architect Moshe Safdie to develop a plan for the area that included a federal building. Safdie's imaginative proposal, including plans for a canal, never got off the ground because of opposition by downtown commercial interests that supported the Washington Street location. The mayor succeeded in placing the federal building on Causeway Street in the North Station area only after persuading executives of Allied Stores and its subsidiary Jordan Marsh to drop their opposition to the site. The GSA, in turn, reversed its position, and became amenable to the Causeway Street site.[46] The mayor also arranged for the city to acquire the needed land and grant it to the federal government. This struggle was only the latest in a long series of squabbles over the construction of federal buildings in Boston, all of which have substantially altered the cityscape.

Another branch of the federal government, unlike the GSA, brooked no interference in its plans and played a major role in extending the financial district down to the South Station area. This momentous movement began because of the inability of the Federal Reserve Bank to expand at its old site on Post Office Square. Frank Morris, president of the Federal Reserve Bank of Boston, moved quietly through a number of real estate brokers to acquire the parcels needed to build the bank at its present location on Atlantic Avenue across from South Station. With the bank now near South Station, other developers looked favorably on the district, which has since been transformed from the center of the leather industry to prime office space.[47]

Like the federal government, the Commonwealth of Massachusetts has

....
Kevin White
and a
"World-Class
City"

207

also shaped Boston by locating its office buildings and other facilities in Boston. The construction of a massive State Transportation Building in Park Square in the aftermath of the Park Plaza controversy led to substantial private investment and revitalization of the neighborhood. Similarly, the Massachusetts Port Authority stimulated development of the South Boston docks and Fort Point Channel districts by rebuilding roads and upgrading fish piers. Copley Place, an enclosed retail center with two hotels, offices, and parking, was yet another project controlled by the state of Massachusetts. In the early 1960s, the Massachusetts Turnpike Extension had cluttered a corner of Copley Square with an entrance to the Turnpike and ramps surrounded by grass and asphalt. In the 1970s and 1980s, the Commonwealth granted a ninety-nine-year lease on this property and its air rights to the Urban Investment Development Corporation, which created Copley Place.[48]

Another, more controversial aspect of the White years was the creation of an "Adult Entertainment District" in 1974. Bookstores, bars, and movie houses purveying what was euphemistically termed adult entertainment had already congregated on a section of lower Washington Street after the demolition of old Scollay Square. Popularly known as the Combat Zone, the district between Essex and Kneeland Streets was notorious for prostitution and violence, threatening adjacent businesses and residents of Chinatown. Calls to tear down the Combat Zone were opposed by residents and business people elsewhere in the city for fear that the striptease and pornography trades would simply relocate to other parts of town.

The City of Boston devised a solution through an amendment to the zoning code in 1974 that made "adult" entertainment forbidden everywhere in the city except the specially designated, two-block section of the existing Combat Zone. Flashing lights, prohibited elsewhere, were allowed in the zone and building owners were exempted from the controls of Boston's recently enacted and restrictive sign code. This distinctive and original approach to the issue of pornography was an attempt to isolate the activities and permit people to either avoid or seek out the area. The BRA also upgraded the area physically and planned a small pedestrian park, new sidewalks, and improved street lighting.[49] The number of businesses catering to the "adult entertainment" trade remained constant in the seventies and the effort to halt the Combat Zone's growth seemed successful. Before long, however, negative publicity over several infamous murders aroused public clamor for elimination of the zone. All during the 1980s the zone diminished in size and in 1990 there were only two sex-industry establishments, down from thirty-nine in 1977. Observers credit this remarkable decline to an aggressive effort to clear out

....

Kevin White
and a
"World-Class
City"

208

the district, led by the city's Licensing Board in the late 1980s, and to the availability of "adult" videotapes for home viewing, another example of the city being shaped by technology, and technological advances interacting with the economy.

The economy and the city's finances clearly affected planning Boston in the seventies. One yardstick was the amount of money the city allocated to schools, roads, and public facilities.[50] Paradoxically, the economy expanded after 1976 and the development boom accelerated after 1979, in the later White years, but the level of investment in the city's infrastructure declined after 1976 and virtually halted with the passage of Proposition 2 1/2 in November 1980.[51] This reduction in the amount of the city's property taxes was followed by a court decision which also cut Boston's revenue.

The first blow to the city treasury came in 1979 with the Tregor decision, in which the Massachusetts Supreme Judicial Court overturned Boston's traditional practice of assessing commercial property at a higher rate than residential property. By this decision the court forced the city to pay back millions of dollars to commercial property owners. The second blow hit in 1980 with the statewide imposition of a cap on property taxes, Proposition 2 1/2. Together, these measures crippled Boston financially. It took several years of concerted effort by city and state officials to restructure Boston's fiscal base and increase the state's contributions before the city could resume growth.

In 1981 Moody's Investors' Service suspended the city's bond rating, making it impossible to sell bonds for a year and slashing revenues by nearly half. Lafayette Place, a retail mall and hotel between the Combat Zone and Downtown Crossing, as well as other projects, were delayed for considerable lengths of time.[52] The cap on the property tax, imposed by the statewide referendum, along with reclassification imposed by the court decision in the Tregor case, drastically reduced the city's ability to provide services and led to deep cuts in personnel. To balance the budget, the mayor went hat-in-hand to the state legislature, which forced the city to sell property. The city-owned Hynes Convention center was transferred to the state as part of a legislative package that included state aid to Boston, and the city sold several municipal garages that had been constructed in the 1950s to developers who razed them and put up office buildings.

In November 1982 BRA Director Robert Ryan announced plans to sell garages at Fort Hill Square, Government Center, Kilby Street, and St. James Avenue.[53] The St. James garage in the Back Bay was leveled to make room for the controversial New England Life building designed by Philip

....

Kevin White
and a
"World-Class
City"
209

Johnson. Sale and demolition of another garage opened the way for International Place, the latest controversial project by Johnson. Both projects stemmed from a financial crisis rather than a master plan for the city. Similarly, events and circumstances rather than coherent plans propelled the redevelopment of the Charlestown Navy Yard into housing, office, and park space. In 1974, Nixon administration budget cutters closed the historic 133-acre naval facility, home of "Old Ironsides," two years after Massachusetts distinguished itself by being the only state to vote against Nixon. After the General Services Administration sold the land and buildings to the Boston Redevelopment Authority for a dollar, the city steered conversion of most of the buildings into housing and office space. An act of political vengeance and an economic blow to the city, especially to laid-off workers, ultimately turned into valuable assets: new land and buildings. Circumstances and luck operated in this case and many others, important determinants of the emerging shape of Boston during the years of Kevin White's mayoralty.

Kevin White's impulsive personality and charges of corruption obscure his role in the city's development just as similar problems hid the contribution of James Michael Curley to the evolution of a more democratic approach to planning. For many years after the 1975 election, charges of corruption hounded White and members of his administration. An infamous birthday party for the mayor's wife, Kathryn, scheduled for the Museum of Fine Arts in the spring of 1981, was canceled amid rumors of coercion and payoffs. The state's Ethics Commission and the U.S. attorney's office found evidence of a cash-laundering operation involving dozens of city employees and contractors but were never able to prove a link between the mayor and the illegalities. The U.S. attorney's office (under William Weld, who was elected governor of Massachusetts in 1990) spent years desperately trying to find evidence against White. Weld convicted more than a score of city officials and an equal number of businessmen before finally clearing the mayor's name five years after White left office.[54] In 1989 White characterized the investigation as an inept, wasteful exercise by "little tykes who wanted to be big shots,"[55] but a year later admitted on a local television show that "the party [for his wife] was an idea artificially hatched to make up for a problem. The problem was that I could barely survive on my salary."[56] Ironically, just when the federal prosecutors had cleared White's name on matters relating to the birthday party, another case captured public attention and raised additional, serious questions about the nature of Boston development and politics in the Kevin White years.

In 1989 an investigative team of the *Boston Globe* reported that in 1983

....

Kevin White
and a
"World-Class
City"

210

and 1984 former Massachusetts Attorney General Edward McCormack, nephew of the late Speaker John W. McCormack, built a real estate empire in Boston reckoned to be worth $41 million.[57] McCormack claimed that it was his legal skills, "image and reputation" that led developers to grant him partial ownership of ten major building projects, including 101 Arch Street, the Bostonian Hotel, 265 Franklin Street, Rowes Wharf, Harbor Point, 99 Summer Street, and Heritage on the Garden, but others attributed it to his connection to Mayor White. Both McCormack and White denied any collusion or secret financial deals but the fact that McCormack was transformed from a modest property-holder in 1982 into a multimillionaire by 1984 provided more ammunition for critics of Kevin White.

The charges of favoritism, cronyism, and corruption that permeated the latter portion of Kevin White's sixteen years in city hall were in marked contrast to John Collins's tenure as chief executive. Collins knew that a valuable opportunity to remake Boston would be lost if there were any hints of such shenanigans. Political connections and opportunities for corruption were, of course, nothing new in the story of this or any city, but the magnitude of the development projects and the fortunes to be had, combined with a more aggressive press, focused public attention on these issues during the years White ran Boston.

Contrasts abound between Kevin White and his immediate predecessor. Unlike John Collins, who wanted to make a mark on Boston when he ran for mayor in 1959, White had no "mental model" of what needed to be done to the physical city. But he didn't need one because the New Boston was already laid out and construction was under way. Only later in his lengthy rule over the new City Hall did White assume the role of arbiter of the city's appearance. While Collins had Ed Logue, White had a string of successively weaker BRA directors; the mayor himself was a greater force in determining public policy. As one student of the White administration observes, "under Mayor Collins, the BRA was Ed Logue. Under Mayor White, the BRA became Kevin White."[58] With interesting results.

Mark Gelfand writes of White and his mayoralty: "Dismissed by most political pundits in 1967 as cautious and shallow, White became the towering figure in Boston politics over the next sixteen years. As earlier with Curley, the politics of Boston between 1968 and 1983 essentially revolved around one man's personality; but if Curley had been a showman, White was enigmatic."[59] But both moved the process of planning in the same direction.

In many ways planning during the Kevin White years was more democratic than at any time in the past, while in others it was less democratic.

Figure 8.4 A view of the Custom House Tower and I. M. Pei's Harbor Towers with the Fan Pier in the distance. Rowes Wharf was later built on the parking lot along the water's edge. (Courtesy of the Library of the Boston Redevelopment Authority.)

Planning was one of many political activities that changed in the turbulent sixties. The general upheaval of the times demanded greater popular participation in the decisions of government, and the forcible removal of so many poor people in cities throughout the nation finally sparked concerted opposition to government "urban renewal" programs.

In addition to national trends, the peculiar development of Kevin White's political career sharply affected Boston. During his first two years in office he aimed at winning the state's gubernatorial election. When this ambition was thwarted it was replaced by a passion for national office; failing this, too, White at last devoted his attention to wielding power locally. He became the central figure in a city undergoing a transformation, and used popular discontent to strip planning bureaucrats of their power. At the same time, he consolidated his own control over the process. The mayor, and no appointed bureaucrat, became the central figure in decision-making. Although some critics say that Kevin White subjected the planning process to his whims, it actually became more democratic than in the past, and is a key part of the transition from the bureaucratic sixties to the unprecedented community participation of the late 1980s and 1990s.

The New Boston, started under Collins and Logue, became a reality during the White years and more than ever Americans viewed the Hub as an attractive and fashionable place to live and work. It was increasingly a

Figure 8.5 Boston skyline from John Hancock Tower. This photograph was taken after the Hancock Tower opened in 1975. The McCormack State Building is to the rear of the State House and One Beacon Street is to the right. By this time office buildings like the Bank of New England, One Boston Place, and 60 State Street (1977) towered over the Custom House Tower at right. More towers were to come. (Courtesy of the Library of the Boston Redevelopment Authority.)

national center of white-collar employment; combined with the city government's terrific cash shortage, this created the environment for an unprecedented and explosive building boom. Developers from all over the world scrambled to invest in America's hottest city. The transformation of the municipal and regional economy into one based on the provision of services goes a long way toward explaining the building frenzy of the early and mid-1980s.[60] Boston's premier position as a service-industry center, with over 1,000 institutions providing banking, brokerage, securities, real estate, and financial consulting services, required the expansion of office space. The worldwide transformation of finance, the restructuring of American industries, and the growth of the many high-tech firms in and around Boston helped fuel the demand for Boston's services. Furthermore, Boston's leadership in the worlds of education and medicine contributed to the prosperity of the city and region and added to the need for space.

Despite the powerful force exerted by this demand for expansion, it seems inconceivable that such a fantastic amount of building would have been approved without the cash crunch that threatened the viability of Boston's city government. Boston needed more tax revenues because of shocks to the city's tax structure created by the Tregor Case and Proposition 2 1/2. Both blows to the city treasury during the White years largely explain Mayor White's willingness to allow the phenomenal growth of buildings in downtown Boston. To pay its bills Boston had little alternative but to permit more buildings and to increase the tax base. The goals of the New Boston movement were at last achieved and even exceeded. Investors had apparently unlimited confidence in the future of the city, and the White administration gave them almost free rein. But Boston soon paid a price for success.

As the Kevin White years drew to a close in January 1984, Boston was a city remarkably transformed. The skyline had been dramatically altered and projects like Quincy Market were succeeded by even larger developments like Copley Place and Lafayette Place. Boston had become an attractive investment site for financiers throughout the world. But change in Boston was not limited to physical construction downtown. Momentous social changes rocked America during the years that Kevin White was mayor. The battle over Boston's school system and busing had sharply polarized the city. As whites fled the city, the black, Hispanic, and Asian populations swelled. In the late 1970s and early 1980s, Boston also felt the effects of free-spending baby boomers who began gentrifying areas like the South End and Charlestown with amazing speed. This influx of young professionals intensified the demand for housing and helped transform a housing surplus into a shortage.

By the eighties, affordable housing had all but disappeared and had become a critical issue in the neighborhoods and a major factor in the 1983 mayoral election. The effects of the downtown boom were just beginning to be felt, however, and it was left to White's successor, Raymond L. Flynn, to cope with both the problems posed by downtown success—too many tall buildings, traffic congestion, loss of manufacturing space—and the continuing needs of the neighborhoods. As the pace of change in Boston accelerated in the 1980s, the city and its newly elected mayor faced a challenge: to reconcile downtown prosperity with the needs of the neighborhoods.

....
Kevin White
and a
"World-Class
City"
215

9

....

Flynn,

Coyle,

and the

Boom

The 1983 mayoral election launched a new and explosive period in Boston planning. The race that year was wide open. Kevin White completed his fourth and final term in office and more than half a dozen candidates sought to replace him. The spectacular burst of downtown development during the later White years called forth criticism from a number of quarters, and the 1983 election was in part a reaction against the unanticipated success of those earlier planning efforts. Candidates campaigned against the excesses of downtown building, capitalizing on the widespread feeling that most Bostonians failed to share in the wealth created by the boom. To many, the most important problem facing Boston in 1983 was the overbuilding of downtown office space; others objected to the inequitable distribution of benefits deriving from the city's growth. The stark contrast between the opulence of the new Copley Place and the desolation of Dudley Square in Roxbury symbolized the gap between downtown wealth and neighborhood poverty.

The election therefore provided candidates and voters an opportunity to register their views on the future of planning in Boston. The seventy-eight candidate forums held throughout the city were "rock 'em sock 'em debates" that heightened interest in the outcome.[1] In the preliminary election in September voters eliminated well-known candidates like City Councilor Larry DiCara, School Committee President David Finnegan, and Suffolk County Sheriff Dennis Kearney, narrowing the choice to City Councilor Raymond L. Flynn of South Boston and Mel King of the South End. King, a longtime community activist, a former state representative, and an opponent of the BRA, was the first African American to run in a final election for mayor in Boston. Because both candidates campaigned on platforms that focused attention away from the downtown, the November election promised victory for the neighborhood interests of Boston as well as a new era of planning. King and Flynn share a populist concern with poverty and took similar positions on the campaign's major issues—neighborhood interests, housing, and increased economic assistance for the poor and disadvantaged.[2] For the two men these concerns came naturally from their backgrounds.

Raymond L. Flynn, a South Boston native "whose working-class credentials are impeccable," is the son of a longshoreman and a maid. "I didn't read about the problems of poverty and the struggles of hard-working families from some textbook," Flynn says, "I experienced them."[3] Flynn went to Providence College on a basketball scholarship and returned to Boston to marry Catherine Coyne and raise a family. The future mayor served in the Massachusetts House of Representatives and the Boston City Council and attracted considerable attention in the mid-1970s for his opposition to court-ordered busing. He later became an earnest advocate for binding the city together across racial and neighborhood lines; his political career came to be characterized by a vigorous effort to heal the wounds of racial conflict.

Flynn easily defeated King and in January 1984 succeeded Kevin White as mayor. Flynn's electoral success shocked veteran Boston-watchers, and predictions varied widely about the shape of his administration and the future of the city. Boston was at a crossroads. People wondered in what direction this relatively unknown mayor would take the city and how successful he would be. They wondered how he would deal with the power-wielders of the local business community. Flynn says, "I never made any deals to get to the mayor's office and with the history in this city of real estate interests, builders, and so on, that's something."[4] In contrast to his predecessor, Flynn notes, "my support was grass-roots level and I never forgot where I came from." After sixteen years of Kevin White, Bostonians had tired of his administration and were ready for change. Ray Flynn was markedly different. The increasingly distant and aloof White was replaced by the seemingly omnipresent Flynn. One man who served under both mayors observes that White was an "inside administrator" who kept tabs on the pulse of city hall while Flynn is an "outside administrator" who checks the pulse of the city; as "Jeep" Jones comments, "four walls would strangle Ray Flynn; four walls would protect Kevin White."[5]

Flynn's inexhaustible supply of energy became a hallmark of his efforts

....

Flynn,

Coyle,

and the

Boom

218

to grapple with the city's problems and to make himself accessible to all citizens. Late in Flynn's second term the *Globe* reported that "he has kept up for the last seven years an intense schedule of neighborhood meetings at schools, churches, and coffee shops as if he were never truly convinced that he had actually won his come-from-behind mayoral campaign in 1983. Considering that Flynn also continues to indulge a penchant for arriving first at major crime scenes and fires, it may well be that every voter in Boston has met the mayor at least once."[6] While Kevin White, too, had criticized his predecessors for ignoring the neighborhoods, sixteen years in office had transformed him into a "downtown mayor." After eight years no one could make that accusation about Ray Flynn.

When Flynn moved into the mayor's office in 1984, the city's greatest economic boom ever was under way but Boston still faced numerous intractable difficulties. All of Boston's residents did not share in the growth of the economy. In 1980 only forty-one percent of those who worked in Boston were city residents.[7] While the financial and managerial sectors of the service economy grew, all too many Bostonians were still mired in poverty or seeking jobs in the declining manufacturing sector. Ray Flynn set out to restore confidence to large numbers of Bostonians who felt left out of the mainstream prosperity. Within his first year in office one national publication reported that the new mayor had suc-ceeded in infusing the city "with a sense of optimism and renewal."[8]

Despite the populist rhetoric of the 1983 mayoral campaign, the city's new chief had to face the reality of the unprecedented growth of the downtown, which required the municipal government to work closely with developers, lawyers, construction interests, preservationists, archi-tects, planners, newspaper editors, and large-scale financial institutions. Nevertheless, as Robert L. Farrell, then chairman of the BRA, put it, "Flynn didn't pay the deference to the development community that Kevin [White] had."[9] According to one observer, businesspeople and developers feared Flynn would turn his back on the downtown. In order to assuage their fears, the mayor had the BRA board hire Stephen Coyle, "a man who spoke their language, who could understand their bottom line," to head the city's development agency.[10] Coyle's appointment may have reassured business, but it also reflected the mayor's concern for economic justice. Flynn says of Coyle, "we had the same political philoso-phy. Steve loves the politics of compassion."[11] Headed by the man Ian Menzies termed "the most innovative of BRA directors,"[12] Boston city planning entered a new era.

Coyle shares South Boston roots with Flynn but grew up in Waltham, Massachusetts, where he attended Brandeis University. He served on the

Figure 9.1 Stephen Coyle rests his arms on the towers of a city planning model. Coyle served as the head of the Boston Redevelopment Authority from July 1984 to January 1992, longer than any other chief executive officer since its creation in October 1957. (Photograph: © Larry Lawfer.)

....

Flynn,

Coyle,

and the

Boom

220

Waltham City Council in the 1970s while earning a degree at Harvard's Kennedy School of Government. Coyle also headed both the Dedham and Waltham Housing Authorities and ran for a seat in the Massachusetts Senate before going to Washington to serve as the executive assistant to the secretary of the Department of Housing and Urban Development and as deputy undersecretary of the Department of Health and Human Services during the Carter years. Coyle graduated from Stanford Law School and worked for an architectural and urban planning firm in San Francisco before returning to Boston and assuming the direction of the BRA. In his years in Boston he displayed the intellect, wit, vision, and energy to waltz through the astounding variety of interests and traps in Boston politics.

Coyle and the Flynn Administration in 1984 faced the prospect of an unprecedented number of new building projects because of the fantastic level of development activity begun during Kevin White's last year in office. A staggering amount of premium office space opened in 1984—over 3.4 million square feet.[13] Boston had gone from bust to boom. In 1974 the city had only 14 million square feet of premium office space but by the end of 1984 it had in excess of 25 million square feet and much more was planned. Flynn and Coyle decided to look at everything Mayor White had left in the development pipeline. As Coyle put it, "we were looking at 600-foot buildings. It was like [developers] were thinking, 'We better get something in before Flynn becomes mayor.'"[14] The two eventually approved only half of the projects they inherited, but the impact of the boom was substantial and changed Boston's skyline forever.

A couple of projects that originated in the White era aroused a tremendous outcry and the controversies altered the process of planning in Boston. Both the projects were designed by the famous architect Philip Johnson in association with John Burgee and in both, the second phase was changed to accord with the wishes of the city's planning agency. Both International Place and the New England became synonymous with conflict and compromise. International Place was a huge complex planned for the site of a city-owned parking garage on Oliver Street next to the Central Artery. Looking back at the original plans, Coyle acknowledges that it was approved too hastily by the BRA in the early days of the Flynn administration. Putting the best face on the matter, however, he points out that the design was a "magnificent expression of an older view as to how to solve the space problem in a peninsular city."[15] Even Philip Johnson later admitted that he had designed "two million goddam square feet that do not belong in this part of Boston."[16] The first phase, which included a forty-six-story tower containing over a million square feet of space, opened in 1987. Developer Donald Chiofaro shrugged off complaints about the building's immense scale and criticism of its countless Palladian windows and forged ahead with a second tower of 700,000 square feet.[17] The second phase had to be redesigned, however, because of state plans for depressing the adjacent Central Artery, and Coyle seized the opportunity to force a change in the appearance of the buildings.

A similar altercation forced changes in the two-phase Johnson-Burgee proposal for the new Back Bay corporate headquarters of the New England (formerly known as New England Life) building on Boylston Street. Once again, the first phase, a twenty-five-story office tower, enraged many concerned Bostonians because of their loathing for the architects, the design, and the impact of the building on the neighborhood. Angry citizens mobilized for a long drawn-out battle to stop the New England. Coyle approved the first phase only after the company agreed to dismiss Johnson and hire a new architect for the second tower. The *Boston Globe*'s

....

Flynn,

Coyle,

and the

Boom

221

architecture critic complained that the first phase was "so dreary, bulky, arrogant and life-denying as to make anyone despair of the future of Boston or of American Corporate architecture,"[18] but the second phase of the project, designed by Robert A. M. Stern, won support from local architects.

The two controversies, International Place and the New England, exemplify some of the problems of the Boston building boom of the 1980s and the way the public sector responded. After initial approval by the BRA and the subsequent outpouring of neighborhood opposition, each project was modified and scaled down. The Flynn administration, which had inherited the plans for these two projects, soon determined that any future proposals on such a large scale would have to be subjected to far more control from the outset.

The two projects also promised a sizeable tax yield for the city and point up one of the conflicts inherent in the BRA's position. It is committed to both redeveloping the city and increasing Boston's tax base as well as regulating the size and aesthetics of new buildings and the city. Some criticized Coyle's BRA "for sacrificing design standards and urban livability for profit, for using development as a revenue cow, for creating permanent (and towering) solutions to temporary fiscal problems"[19] and there is no doubt that the windfall revenues from new development were of the greatest significance (after state aid) to Boston's fiscal health in the 1980s.

The assessed value of taxable Boston real estate increased tremendously through the decade after the court-ordered updating of the city's assessment practices in the early eighties. Total taxable value of land and buildings in the city grew from $11.5 billion in 1984 to $22.5 billion in 1987, and to $34.2 billion two years later.[20] Revenues from property taxes account for about a third of Boston's city budget. Proposition 2 1/2 forced a reduction in the property tax levy estimated at nearly 50 percent (after accounting for inflation) between Fiscal Years 1981 and 1984.[21] The economic and development booms, however, led to a 45 percent growth in property tax revenues from Fiscal Year 1984 to 1989 ($334 million to $483.7 million). Of this revenue growth, 42 percent came directly from new construction of major commercial projects approved by the BRA which added millions to Boston's treasury every year.[22]

As the economic and fiscal tide turned in the mid-1980s, Boston's government became more financially secure, investors remained eager to put money into Boston, and the city was happy to exact a price from prospective developers. This situation differed radically from the 1960s and early 1970s when city officials had had to implore investors by

....

Flynn,

Coyle,

and the

Boom

222

offering tax incentives through Chapter 121A and other mechanisms. Boston city government now sat in the driver's seat and the private sector eagerly lined up to go along for the ride. During Flynn's first term in office, the city, courted by numerous suitors, could dictate terms regarding building downtown. Here Stephen Coyle played the key role. Kevin White controlled design issues, but Raymond Flynn leaves them to his BRA director. Coyle enjoyed his role as keeper of the gate and, as one observer said, "made developers dance." Dreamers and developers presented him with one proposal after another, most of which were turned down. Sometimes the suitor didn't own the land or someone else had a better idea or the building was better suited to somewhere else, "like Miami Beach or Mars. Some people complain about what got built," Coyle says. "They should see what didn't get built."[23] Coyle does not see the development of downtown solely as an urban design concern as many of his critics do but balances design issues with the economics of jobs, housing, and the city's future prosperity.

In 1984, Flynn and Coyle's first year in office, a major publication of the BRA summed up the state of development as "Downtown Projects: Opportunities for Boston." The document described ten private development projects which were modified to provide additional public benefits, both to the city as a whole and at the specific site of each. Coyle argued that through project review "the City has viewed each development proposal as a significant opportunity to help achieve its resident employment goals, to garner a wide range of public benefits, and to improve the design of the city."[24] Coyle and the BRA sought to channel new development into certain areas that they targeted for growth. Coyle denigrates the "rigid district-type planning" of Ed Logue, preferring to stretch downtown development into more distant corners of the city. Some corners were close to the center of downtown, such as South Station, others were farther away, such as the Charlestown Navy Yard.

Coyle's goal was to make Boston's downtown one of the finest in the country, one able to serve as the center of a commercial and service economy. He envisioned clusters of buildings and in his drive to create a "first-class downtown" for Boston, Coyle felt it should have "appropriately scaled buildings, be better designed, and decentralized."[25] One of the most admired achievements in city design during the Coyle era is the Rowes Wharf project, which includes condominiums, hotel rooms, office space, a marina, and a ferry boat launch. Architecture critic Robert Campbell praises the mixture of private uses and public space in this complex, asserting that "all this is wonderfully right as city-making. Buildings should be thought of not as elegant objects but as pieces of the

....

*Flynn,
Coyle,
and the
Boom*

223

city—pieces that join together to shape something much more important than themselves; the public realm, the network of outdoor rooms that are the streets and squares. Rowes Wharf's planners understand that truth."[26] Campbell credits not only the developer, Beacon Companies, but also the planners at the Boston Redevelopment Authority "who mandated many of Rowes Wharf's virtues" and helped "to create a better public world." Beacon Companies, a powerhouse developer in Boston for decades, won a 1983 BRA designation to develop the site (then used as a parking lot) a year before Coyle took the reins of the agency but Coyle pressured Beacon owner Edwin Sidman and architect Adrian Smith of Skidmore, Owings and Merrill to create a lower building, with more ornamentation and a classical dome over a fifty-foot-wide arch.[27] All of which made Rowes Wharf a "very creative and very expensive" undertaking according to Sidman, the man who paid for it.

Jane Holtz Kay, local preservationist and author, praises another example of good city-building, the creation of a park on the site of an old city-owned parking garage in Post Office Square. A squat, ugly structure built in the fifties was demolished in the late eighties to make way for a new and appealing public space in the city's financial district. The park, designed by the Halvorson Company, sits on top of a seven-level underground parking garage. Kay cites the new park's "eloquent openness" and lauds its developers, the Friends of Post Office Square (a group of area businesses led by the Beacon Companies) who "elevated the art of city-building by creating the most graceful open space in decades."[28]

These two examples of planning done in partnership between the public and private sector garnered much positive attention but Coyle had his eye on an entire city. He began with the announcement of new zoning guidelines for downtown development. Approved by the BRA and the zoning commission and signed into law by the mayor, the Interim Planning Overlay District (IPOD) strategy was based on the temporary imposition of regulations until permanent zoning controls could be devised and made law. The city's interim zoning plan incorporated height restrictions, design reviews, and historic preservation. It also stipulated open space, new environmental review procedures, rules on transportation management, and included incentives for housing as well as zoning control to protect manufacturing. The guidelines for new buildings established by the IPOD process—a corrective response to the White administration's project-by-project or building-by-building approach to development—was considered by many to be quite radical in the context of "Boston's longtime zoning-by-whimsy."[29] Rezoning the city represented a

....

Flynn,

Coyle,

and the

Boom

224

turn toward development according to rules and away from development on a deal-by-deal basis.

In 1987 Coyle took a bold step with the announcement of a new, updated plan called the Downtown Interim Planning Overlay District (Downtown IPOD). The most fascinating and innovative part of this plan calls for a cultural district to take form on twenty-seven city blocks as part of the rezoning process. John King, who wrote for the *Boston Globe* and was an insightful observer of Boston development in the 1980s, pointed out that three contemporary roles of the BRA are most visible in the proposal for the Midtown Cultural District. The BRA functions as the city's planning agency, as reviewer of development proposals, and as a department with social goals.[30] The necessary zoning provisions, passed in January 1989, spelled out not only height restrictions and design standards for new construction but also required the provision of day care facilities by developers. The new zoning offers density bonuses to developers for devoting space to nonprofit arts groups and earmarks money for the adjacent Chinatown community which has long suffered from city planning exercises like the Central Artery and the Combat Zone.

The Downtown IPOD concept exemplifies what the BRA under Coyle attempted throughout the city—to create a plan which meets the needs of the various neighborhoods and which is a true grass-roots effort. Throughout the city, Planning and Zoning Advisory Committees (PZACs) help formulate plans for individual districts. In some neighborhoods the BRA works with a PZAC, in others with a district council appointed by the mayor. In other places planning takes place without an IPOD because there are other controls, as in the North End where a fifty-five-foot building-height limit is in effect. The IPOD concept, although most publicized in the downtown, was conceived to meet the needs of a small section of Dorchester called Port Norfolk. This area between the Southeast Expressway and the mouth of the Neponset River faced many of the same problems as other sections of the city. Linda Bourque, assistant director of the BRA in charge of neighborhood planning and zoning, called it a "microcosm of zoning problems."[31] The mix of land originally zoned for residential and industrial purposes and the city's building boom fueled fears of future inappropriate development. The BRA found that neighborhood groups were not content to wait for the development of a grand master plan for the entire city but wanted their concerns about growth dealt with immediately. No other neighborhood wanted rapid development either and the IPOD strategy was applied early in the Flynn era to Roxbury, Allston-Brighton, and other sections of the city. The process involves

....

Flynn,
Coyle,
and the
Boom

225

community groups to an unprecedented extent. In Roxbury, for example, over 125 community meetings were held in developing the final plan. According to Linda Bourque, "we don't go in with a plan" but work with the community to develop one for that district. The BRA offers the community a team approach in which a district planner draws upon other staff for assistance in design, economic analysis, and environmental review.

Working with myriad community groups is an exhaustive and intensive approach but one dictated by practical necessity and the process of "planning with people" that has evolved over the last several decades. As Ed Logue found out in Charlestown and the South End, neighborhood groups will compete with one another and offer alternative visions of the future direction of the district. In the word of the BRA's Bourque, the responsibility of the professional planner and the BRA is to listen to the various groups and "to balance out and come up with a rational plan" for the IPOD district.

The central characteristic of neighborhood zoning and planning today is the variety of approaches to different districts and the corresponding diversity of plans. In the early 1990s there was little talk about a master plan for the city; rather, the BRA focused more on comprehensive planning for each district and the connection of each to the overall city. As Homer Russell, head of urban design for the BRA, explains it, other newer cities are easier to plan because they are more homogeneous. But 360-year-old Boston has more districts with unique characteristics. Russell's description of the goal is a "fine grain plan for each district, then a master plan with the focus on economic development, transportation and so on."[32] The master plan is ultimately completed but not in the orthodox manner. The BRA proceeds inductively rather than deductively; the resulting plan is the sum of the parts. To some extent, this process has grown out of a recognition of the diversity and unique qualities of the various neighborhoods of the city, but it also reflects the populist attitude of the Flynn administration. It is, in part, a fulfillment of the mayor's mandate to get the community involved in planning. And it is, in part, a manifestation of the Coyle approach to city-building.

Another example of the Coyle approach is the creation of the Boston Civic Design Commission (BCDC). This eleven-member commission, which became operative through an amendment to the city's zoning code, reviews projects of major significance throughout the city at the request of the mayor and the BRA. The BCDC role is twofold: to review the rules of planning (changes to zoning) and to review individual design plans. It may be too early to assess the commission's role but the preamble to the document creating the BCDC bears the unmistakable imprint of Stephen

Coyle and succinctly reveals the flavor of his approach to planning as well as the main functions of the BCDC:

> Since its settlement, Boston has evolved a vibrant urban form that gives this historic city its vivid sense of place. Boston today is a city with many remarkable historic structures, a visionary parks and open space system, and a richness and diversity of districts and neighborhoods that distinguish it from other American cities.
>
> A central concern to many Bostonians is how the design of new buildings affects what is called the public realm. The public realm is that aspect of the urban environment which is visible and accessible to the public, including both spaces and the building walls which frame them. The concept encompasses areas long thought of as public such as parks, tree-lined boulevards, sidewalks, and streets. It also includes some areas which are held in private ownership, but which are, in terms of their nature, function, or significance or their impact on the streetscape or existing historic context, truly public, such as the design of buildings, their lobbies, and connecting passageways. The principle of public realm rests on the belief that the public has a historic, necessary, and abiding interest in the way the city develops and changes because cities by their nature and function are public places as well as clusters of private property.[33]

This preamble, especially the final sentence excerpted, is an outstanding example of the ideas and rhetoric that Stephen Coyle brought to planning in the 1980s and 1990s and the way the definition of planning evolved under his aegis. To involve the community or the public to such an extent in design and other planning issues was simply unprecedented. One student of the process observed that "the public review process is so open that developers show several schemes to BRA planners and community groups, moving ahead only when a preference emerges."[34]

James K. Flaherty, a veteran member of the BRA board, praises the citizen access to planning decisions that is provided under the Flynn administration. Flaherty points out that "for a lot of years developers ran over people" and argues that although the planning process under Flynn and Coyle takes much longer, it is a great improvement over the past.[35] Development indeed took longer under the Flynn administration but it by no means stopped until the national and regional economic recession ended the downtown building boom. Yet during the boom Boston's growth was nothing short of sensational and the city grew by leaps and bounds. From 1984 to 1986 the city approved $3 billion in private downtown development projects, and employment growth quickly fol-

....

Flynn,
Coyle,
and the
Boom

227

lowed capital investment. In the financial, insurance, educational, medical and business, and professional sectors of the city, employment grew 26 percent from 1976 to 1986. Yet the vast majority of jobs and other economic benefits generated by this growth failed to reach Boston's low- and moderate-income residents, especially members of the city's minority groups.[36]

This situation troubles Ray Flynn. He was elected a "neighborhood mayor" and continues to feel that downtown development can be a powerful tool to help people in the neighborhoods. Flynn believes the effort to support growth and the downtown can be balanced with an emphasis on the neighborhoods. He sees the city in personal, even paternal terms, declaring, "I believe a city is like a family. I have six children and I can't just provide for four. The downtown is a member of the family and so are the neighborhoods. The relationship doesn't have to be antagonistic."[37] In accordance with this tenet, Flynn not only committed the city to a participatory planning process but also required that the fruits of the city's economic boom be shared with people from all of Boston's communities. As Michael F. Donlan, a Boston lawyer and BRA vice-chairman puts it, under Kevin White the imagery was of the mayor creating a few "instant millionaires" through his control of the development process, whereas Flynn works to secure benefits for the many.[38] Flynn set out to make good on his campaign platform of paying attention to neighborhood interests, providing affordable housing, and increasing economic assistance for the poor and disadvantaged. He attempted to preserve the character of the city while at the same time allowing development that advances his social agenda.

Flynn stated in May 1987 that Boston residents were getting a rare chance to sit at the "table of opportunity" but went on to caution that "a seat at the table is no guarantee development. Through these programs we seek to institutionalize the link between downtown growth and neighborhood revitalization."[39] Steve Coyle added, "the neighborhoods must be connected back to the economy, much more dramatically than they've been."[40] He publicly committed himself to the pursuit of the mayor's goal and stated "at the center of the public debate over Boston's growth policies is not the issue of the height, design, or massing of buildings, although these are important concerns. The criticial issue is economic justice."[41] This statement clearly highlights a remarkable phase in the history of planning in Boston. It is the neighborhood mayor's attempt to capture and distribute the benefits of the downtown boom, and to balance the benefits and burdens of growth.

Under Flynn and Coyle, the city implemented several "linkage pro-

....
Flynn,
Coyle,
and the
Boom

228

grams" which attempted to join the prosperity of the downtown to the needs of poorer neighborhoods and people. The linked housing and training programs aimed to supply Bostonians with jobs downtown and to provide downtown workers with housing in Boston. All of these linkage programs were predicated on the Flynn administration's desire to distribute the fruits of a healthy economy and investor interest in downtown Boston throughout the city. Although the roots of the linkage programs are buried in the White years, fulfillment came in the first Flynn administration. One of the initial housing linkage proposals won city council acceptance before Flynn's election, for example, but was vetoed by Mayor White. A month after Flynn's election the first linkage program was adopted. It required downtown developers to commit funds either to the direct creation of affordable housing or to a trust fund created for this purpose.[42] This housing linkage program required a developer to contribute five dollars for every square foot of floor space built over 100,000 square feet. The city also set up a jobs training linkage program which requires one additional dollar for every square foot of floor space built over 100,000 square feet.

In addition, Coyle engineered the parcel-to-parcel linkage program which stipulated, in two cases where the city owned valuable downtown property, that the developers of these sites must also develop another site in an overlooked Boston neighborhood. Upon Coyle's recommendation, the BRA board made a formal determination that minorities in Boston had been excluded from sharing the benefits of the rising prosperity of the city and that minority developers and business enterprise had not significantly benefited by major development in Boston. The BRA therefore proposed an "affirmative action remedy to increase opportunity for minorities in the predominately privately financed downtown development economy" by establishing a pilot linkage program.[43] The city explains that "linkage works by taking a portion of the value created by investment in areas undergoing substantial development, and directing that value to build affordable housing and job training in Boston's neighborhoods. The city's linkage policies represent a new social contract to build lasting bridges of economic opportunity between those areas of the city experiencing rapid growth and the people in Boston neighborhoods who, historically, have not shared in the benefits of that growth."[44]

The BRA pioneered the parcel-to-parcel linkage program for the development of the Kingston-Bedford Garage and another city-owned property in Park Square. The Kingston-Bedford Garage was linked with Parcel 18 at Roxbury's Ruggles Street and Park Square was linked with sites in the South End. The BRA required that the developer of the downtown site

....

Flynn,
Coyle,
and the
Boom

229

also prepare a proposal for developing the Ruggles Street site and stipulated that the project be jointly owned, with minorities controlling a 30 percent interest in the venture. This would, in the words of the BRA resolution, "create opportunities for minority developers and individuals to be equity participants in both downtown and neighborhood development." The BRA believes the program will also create more jobs, improve the quality of life, fulfill the community's vision for the Southwest Corridor, and expand housing opportunities.

Coyle also sees the linkage program with Ruggles Center as a response to "the great challenge" that came out of the 1983 mayoral campaign, when the marked contrast between the new mall at Copley Place and the rundown area near Dudley Square summarized the startling economic differences among neighborhood and ethnic groups. Mayor Flynn endorsed the parcel-to-parcel initiative in a letter that evoked the rhetoric of the 1983 campaign. He argued that development in downtown Boston "has been a very exclusive club of high and mighty buildings built by and for the high and mighty" and pointed out that "too many Boston neighborhoods have been left behind by growth." The city's job, said the mayor, "is to build bridges of opportunity that connect neighborhoods with the surging economy of the downtown, and link neighborhoods with one another."[45] In this case Chinatown, Roxbury, and the South End would be linked. Flynn and Coyle continued to fight for development of the Ruggles Center despite a major political battle over the site of the headquarters for the Massachusetts Water Resources Authority and a declining economy in the late 1980s, which stalled the effort. Cooperation between Governor Weld and the city in 1991, however, led to a compromise plan to relocate the Commonwealth's Registry of Motor Vehicles to the site.

The linkage policies adopted by Flynn and his administration represented an unusual and significant alternative to the usual public-sector solution to urban problems entailing a massive influx of public funds. Stephen Coyle refers to his plan as a "market orientation solution."[46] He argues that when investors in Boston gain a return on their capital greater than in comparable markets it is feasible to price in the cost of linkage. A linkage fee of five or six dollars paid over a period of seven years (which thereby reduced its value) was approximately 2 percent of the cost of development. In a decade when land values went up quickly, linkage fees were minimal and easily absorbed.[47] The net result was that linkage captured for the public a portion of the increase in land values that accompanied the economic boom of the 1980s. Coyle acknowledges that in a recession it is much harder to get linkage but remains confident in the assertion that developers "know it is part of doing business in Boston" and

....

Flynn,

Coyle,

and the

Boom

230

accept it as such. And to Coyle, it is impossible to separate these linkage programs from the issue of supply and demand. His policy in his first years at the BRA was to slow down the supply of future office space so that there would be a tight enough market by 1987 or 1988 to keep investors interested. He succeeded and by October 1989 developers of forty-one major commercial projects committed to pay over $76 million in housing linkage payments over the next decade.[48]

One of Mayor Flynn's priorities, providing affordable housing, received funds from the various linkage programs. This nonetheless proved to be one of the most intractable of the city's problems although nearly one thousand units were produced in one neighborhood, the South End, which had suffered the ravages of previous urban renewal or "people removal" efforts. In this neighborhood, numerous empty lots gave silent testimony to the ambitions and failures of the past. Coyle recalls visiting the South End with Mayor Flynn in 1984 and seeing lots that had been vacant for nearly two decades. Out of this visit came his determination to "settle a lot of ancient anger" felt by the community toward the BRA.[49] Principally, the BRA program known as the South End Neighborhood Initiative (SENHI) carried the ball for the Flynn administration on this issue.

SENHI began in 1986 with seven sites, including the long-awaited Tent City development. The local community forced the BRA to accept the principle that one-third of these housing units would be affordable to low-income households, one-third would be affordable to moderate-income households, and the remaining third would be sold or rented at market rates. Such proportions in housing required a massive commitment of public funds and the financing of SENHI reveals the complex arrangements needed to leverage limited resources into maximum return. Six and one-half million dollars came from linkage funds administered by the Neighborhood Housing Trust. The City of Boston put in a like amount (most of which came from Community Development Block Grant loans), while the BRA contributed another $8.6 million in the form of grants, loans, and real estate contributions.[50] The Massachusetts Housing and Finance Agency provided construction financing totaling $24.3 million, while local banks lent another $7.1 million. The sale of tax credits to several Boston institutions raised additional equity for the cooperative and rental developments. The complexity of this financing is a product of the federal retreat from housing and social welfare in the 1980s and is at the heart of planning near the end of the twentieth century.

City planning involves more people than ever before. City planners work with the private sector, financial institutions, labor organizations,

....

Flynn,

Coyle,

and the

Boom

231

architects, engineers, preservationists, environmentalists, the media, bureaucrats, and neighborhood leaders. It is a process vastly more complicated, time-consuming, and expensive than ever before. Planning in the
1980s became, in the words of Stephen Coyle, one "of negotiation and
contract and collective achievement of the vision."[51] During the first
Flynn administration the planning process came to include many participants for whom planning had always been a dirty word—one that had
meant government imposition of power. Hubie Jones, a prominent community leader and scholar who has observed Boston politics and planning
at close range for several decades, wrote in October 1987 that "residents
of the neighborhoods still do not trust the BRA or developers, because
historically and currently they have not been cut into the planning and
decision-making processes in real ways where their interests have as
much sway as the economic benefits at stake."[52]

Ray Flynn and Steve Coyle made a determined effort to change that
lingering hostility toward city planning efforts. To accomplish this they
produced policies designed to include a greater diversity of people and to
serve long-neglected or abused sections of the city. As Clarence "Jeep"
Jones, chairman of the BRA, says, the authority "today has the responsibility to be sure of inclusion rather than exclusion of all communities
across the city."[53] Jones's position as the first black chairman of the BRA is
itself a noteworthy example of inclusion, as is Flynn's appointment of
Consuelo Gonzales Thornell, the first woman and the first Hispanic to be
appointed to the BRA board.

Flynn and Coyle worked strenuously to earn the trust of the neighborhoods and to use government power to advance neighborhood and community interests. Never before had the city been so committed to such
strong citizen involvement, although the Flynn approach is a natural
extension of the ongoing evolution of more open and people-oriented
planning. Kevin White's Little City Hall program and the 1970s-era
"district planning" were steps forward in the evolution toward more
democratic planning but they were canceled out by the downtown focus
of the later White years. In any case, Flynn and Coyle went far beyond
these efforts and institutionalized community participation in planning.

The broadened process began early in the Coyle years at the BRA. The
battle over the design of the New England was one manifestation of
change and the controversy over planning for Dudley Square and Ruggles
Center in Roxbury was another. In mid-1985 word leaked out of a proposed $750 million office and high-tech center in the Dudley Station area
of Roxbury. Stephen Coyle termed the ensuing controversy "a cathartic
debate" which allowed greater community input and ultimately created a

....

Flynn,

Coyle,

and the

Boom

232

better proposal for the area.[54] Over succeeding years the Flynn administration fought through the parcel-to-parcel program to connect the downtown boom with the residents of Roxbury. The BRA also moved ahead on another front: in early 1988 it granted a nonprofit organization, the Dudley Street Neighborhood Initiative, the power of eminent domain and ability to control development in an area totalling thirty acres. This was the first time in the country that this power had been granted to such a nonprofit group.[55] Longtime BRA chairman Bob Farrell opposed the move (and soon resigned his position) because it gave "the most awesome power of government—taking away people's property—to private groups."[56] James Flaherty, another board member originally appointed by Kevin White, took a different view, suggesting that the controversial move by Flynn to give away the power of eminent domain "is a credit to his commitment to the South End and Roxbury community."[57] He stressed that it is rare that a mayor cedes such substantial power. It was also a rare instance when the mayor called the board to his office before they took a vote.

Only a vital matter would draw such attention and have such consequences. It was no less than a strenuous effort by Flynn to win support in the city's black community and an attempt to fulfill the campaign rhetoric promising empowerment to people in the neighborhoods. Some Roxbury community leaders had organized an unsuccessful movement to secede from Boston and create a separate minority-dominated city called "Mandela" but the Dudley initiative surely helped take the wind out of the sails of the separatist ship. Voters throughout the proposed new city rejected secession by a two-to-one margin in a referendum question. The issue of community power, however, remains far from settled.

Across the city, in Charlestown, Coyle grappled with another neighborhood with a long history of alienation from the BRA. The federal government shut down the Charlestown Navy Yard in 1974 and turned it over to the city. Federal guidelines on preservation established strong limits regarding what the BRA could do with the former federal property, but the agency under Coyle led the way in transforming the bulk of the Navy Yard, aside from the National Historic Park, into a new multipurpose district providing office space, housing (including many units of affordable housing), public access to the waterfront, and a significant site for medical research. BRA officials proudly point to the Navy Yard as the largest preservation project in the country and one which successfully integrates new development with valuable historic resources.[58] Furthermore, the BRA approved a plan for the New England Aquarium to move from Central Wharf in Boston to the Navy Yard in the 1990s. The decision

....

Flynn,

Coyle,

and the

Boom

233

to move the aquarium to the Navy Yard offers a parallel to that institution's part in the 1960s revitalization of the downtown waterfront—a role the BRA hoped it would replicate in Charlestown, although the recession and drop in real estate values apparently doomed the plan.[59]

Access to the city's entire waterfront became a priority for the BRA under Coyle: its most visible result is the lengthy Harborpark which aims at providing walkways and parks along the Boston waterfront from the Charlestown Navy Yard to the southern boundaries of the city and showcasing Boston's strengths. The park is made up of land along twenty-one miles of waterfront with exceptions for Fan Piers, the Boston Marine Industrial Park, East Boston, and MassPort property. The Harborpark District became a part of the city's zoning code in April 1990.[60] Its purposes include protection of the district from inappropriate uses, the promotion of balanced growth, and the extension of public access and use of the waterfront. It also stipulates, in certain situations and conditions, the creation of "affordable housing," water transportation facilities, cultural uses, open spaces, and day care facilities. The Harborpark District specifies differences within boundaries for discrete areas such as the North End and the Dorchester Bay/Neponset River Waterfront.

In November 1987 Raymond Flynn won reelection as mayor in the biggest margin of victory in Boston history and was given anew the challenges and opportunities of planning Boston. The first Flynn administration represents an unprecedented attempt to incorporate people into planning and to shape a city whose economy serves all people, but regional and state economic conditions changed drastically during Flynn's second term; the much vaunted "Massachusetts miracle" turned into an economic debacle and the context of planning in Boston underwent a significant change. Governor Michael Dukakis's defeat in the presidential election of 1988 (at the hands of George Bush, a native of neighboring Milton) seemed to mark the end of the good times in the Bay State as unemployment rates and business failures rose in succeeding years. Discouragement prevailed as the region's overheated economy cooled, banks lost hundreds of millions of dollars and were forced to close, and real estate prices plummeted.

Boston was no longer able to call the shots in a seller's market. The economic and building booms of the 1980s ended and planners had to accept the constraint of a shortage of capital. The city remained appealing to investors, but the glory days of winning expensive concessions from developers for the right to build in Boston were over. Boston could no longer assume that the private sector would continue to fund linkage programs and public benefits. Flynn and Coyle courted investors and were

....

Flynn,

Coyle,

and the

Boom

234

less certain that extravagant plans and promises would be met. Coyle acknowledges that "our role is changed from managing the boom to trying to encourage new investment."[61] The expansion of the office market slowed and few new buildings were contemplated in uncertain times as the unemployment rate and Boston office vacancy rates rose. Columnist David Nyhan of the *Globe* pointed out that "Ray Flynn ran Boston through its biblical span of seven years of fat" but now faces the first of a series of lean years.[62] Planning Boston in the early 1990s was dramatically different from the heady years of 1986 and 1987 and the city under Flynn turned to a traditional response—government spending.

In March 1991 the city released its sixth consecutive five-year capital plan, updating a $1.03 billion capital spending program and extending a program first begun in 1987.[63] Included in the massive capital planning program were funds for rebuilding Boston City Hospital, constructing a new police headquarters, and continuing physical improvements to the city's schools, parks, and roadways. Mayor Flynn expressed the classic faith in a positive role for the public sector when he stated "we move forward with the 'Rebuilding Boston' program each year with the firm belief that capital projects are good investments for our City, especially in this difficult economic climate. Capital projects not only preserve our neighborhoods, they will help to put our troubled economy back on its feet by putting the men and women of the construction industry back to work." Senator Edward M. Kennedy, U.S. Representative Joseph P. Kennedy II, and other officials joined Flynn in May 1991 to break the ground for a new Boston City Hospital, the most expensive capital project ever undertaken by the city of Boston, and the mayor proclaimed that "this is one of the most important days in Boston history." The new 356-bed hospital, scheduled to open in 1994, will be built with a federally guaranteed mortgage, the first time a publicly owned and operated hospital has secured such a loan.[64]

The BRA, although the chief agency involved in planning for the city, does not operate alone among the departments and agencies under the control of Boston's mayor. The Office of Capital Planning, which manages the five-year plan for "Rebuilding Boston," is a key player in determining the allocation of city funds for new and renovated municipal buildings. The Public Facilities Department (PFD) is another critical player. This department, which inherited the mission of the old Neighborhood Economic Development Administration, does far more than construct municipal buildings. It became actively involved in fulfilling the Flynn goals for affordable housing. It also served to rebuild neighborhood commercial centers and funnel Community Block Development Grants (CBDG)

Figure 9.2 Mayor Raymond L. Flynn is joined in 1991 by U.S. Representative Joseph P. Kennedy II and Senator Edward M. Kennedy, the great-grandson and grandson of another Boston mayor (John F. Fitzgerald), in laying bricks for the new Boston City Hospital. (Courtesy of the Boston Mayor's Office. Photograph by Gail Oskin.)

to assorted agencies and causes. This latter function has been administered since September 1990 by another agency, the Economic Development and Industrial Corporation (EDIC) of the City of Boston. EDIC, created in 1971, bears responsibility for maintaining industrial parks which help Boston preserve blue-collar manufacturing jobs. Under Flynn, EDIC also came to assume job-training programs and broadened its mission to meet the challenges of the city's economic future.

EDIC, the BRA, and others became actively involved in promoting Boston as a center of what has been termed "the New Economy," one founded on knowledge-based and technology-based industries. The city is aggressively courting educational, medical, and research institutions of all kinds to develop and expand new space, technologies, and jobs. This planning for the future of the Boston economy became an important function of city officials. Such economic development concerns increasingly came to occupy the mayor and his aides during his second term. Where once he and Coyle could choose among contestants for developments, they soon became salespeople targeting growth industries. Also, they looked more and more toward federal activity to alleviate urban woes.

....

Flynn,
Coyle,
and the
Boom

236

Ray Flynn assumed a leadership position among the nation's mayors in the late 1980s and early 1990s and became widely recognized as an advocate for the needs of American cities. In 1990 and 1991 he took to the national stage in a big way. At a mayors' summit meeting in New York in 1990, Flynn was reported "to have found the voice and soapbox to be one of the leading spokesmen for urban America."[65] His peers confirmed this stature in June 1991 when they elected Flynn to the presidency of the U.S. Conference of Mayors, a position not held by a Boston mayor since James Michael Curley. And after he won a stunning victory in Boston's preliminary elections in 1991, speculation about Flynn's national ambitions was fueled by the magnitude of his win.

Closer to home, Flynn and Coyle realized that Boston's fortunes would depend in large part on the fate of two gargantuan state-run public works projects in the 1990s: the construction of a depressed Central Artery and a third harbor tunnel, and the Boston Harbor cleanup mandated by a federal court and engineered by the Massachusetts Water Resources Authority. The Central Artery/Tunnel (CA/T) project, which "formally started" on May 13, 1991,[66] is a multibillion dollar project to build a tunnel under the harbor between South Boston and East Boston and to replace the existing elevated highway through the downtown area with a widened, underground roadway by the end of the decade. The CA/T Project (the roots of which reach back to at least 1968 when a third harbor tunnel was proposed) is designed to expand and improve two interstate highways in Boston: I-93 and I-90. Its planners intend it to replace the existing elevated section of I-93, known as the Central Artery, with a new eight-to-ten-lane underground roadway and to extend the Massachusetts Turnpike (I-90) via a new "Seaport Access Roadway" through the pier section of South Boston and underneath Boston Harbor to Logan Airport.

Plans for the depression of Central Artery date back to 1972. Supervised by Secretary of Transportation Fred Salvucci in the first Dukakis administration (1975–1979), these plans included a scheme for a railroad link between North and South Stations. In the years of the Edward J. King governorship (1979–1983) planners downplayed the Artery proposal but began the environmental review process for construction of a third harbor tunnel. Upon returning to the corner office in the State House in 1983, Dukakis permitted Salvucci to combine the depression of the Artery with the plan for a third harbor tunnel. House Speaker Thomas P. "Tip" O'Neill, Jr., guaranteed federal funds for these plans but also provided opponents with a highly visible target as they criticized the massive funding required to complete the project which they named "Tip's Tunnel."

....

Flynn,
Coyle,
and the
Boom

237

The project is seven-and-a-half miles long, stretching from Charlestown in the north to just south of Southampton Street and from Harrison Avenue in the west to Logan Airport and Route 1A in the east. It includes 3.7 miles of tunnel and 2.3 miles of bridges (the remainder will be surface streets and connections) and promises to open up twenty-seven acres of land long obscured by the massive elevated roadway in downtown Boston. These plans did not get put into action without further conflict. Battles erupted as soon as the state announced the proposal for the interchange between the Artery and Storrow Drive. This portion of the project proved to be a major bone of contention in 1990 and a rallying cry for critics of the entire project. Incredibly, the state's "Scheme Z" for the crossing (unveiled in late 1990) covered seventy acres and proposed to create as much elevated highway crossing the Charles River as was scheduled to be torn down in other sections. Wags pointed out that when the Artery was pushed down in one section it popped up in another. The opposition forced the state to create a special commission, which in June 1991 came up with an alternative proposal killing the notorious Scheme Z and allowing the CA/T to move forward.

Some environmental groups led the charge against Scheme Z, filing lawsuits designed to alter or stop the process, but other environmental associations support the CA/T and praise the opportunity to create spectacular open spaces including a "world-class botanical garden" in front of the Federal Reserve Bank. (The botanical garden is just one aspect of the plan for downtown Boston once the Central Artery is depressed.) The cleared land presents a unique opportunity to reverse earlier planning and to reknit the city's torn fabric and fashion a long swathe of parkland. Richard Taylor, secretary of transportation and construction in the Weld administration, took charge of the project in 1990 and pushed the idea of reconnecting the city with its historic waterfront, touting Boston's chance "to create a world-class boulevard."[67] He also praised the creation of 150 acres of parkland, including an extension of the Esplanade along the Charles River and over 100 acres of new land on Spectacle Island in Boston Harbor.

The state's Department of Public Works agreed to fund beautification of the Charles River basin, including new walkways and parks connecting the Esplanade with the U.S.S. *Constitution* in Charlestown. In response to environmentalists' concerns over the adverse impact of an improved highway system with an increased volume of traffic the Massachusetts Department of Environmental Protection approved the CA/T in 1991 but required traffic-mitigating actions like expanded commuter rail, more parking spaces at suburban transit stations, subsidized commuter boats

....

Flynn,

Coyle,

and the

Boom

238

across Boston Harbor, and other mass transit projects intended to keep the new Central Artery from being clogged with even more traffic. Massachusetts' secretary of environmental affairs Susan F. Tierney declared that these requirements ensure that the CA/T "will be an environmental as well as a transportation project."[68]

The BRA takes the same view. In its 1991 CA/T progress report the agency declared that "planning the reuse of this land requires citizens, planners, and business and political leaders to decide on what downtown Boston will be in the 21st century. The project is not just a transportation improvement, but is the biggest change to the downtown since the filling of the Back Bay."[69] Stephen Coyle was intensely aware of the potential of the Central Artery/Tunnel project in shaping the city and did not hesitate to invoke the name of Frederick Law Olmsted as he pursued his own vision for Boston. The "Boston 2000" plan points out that "not since the creation of Olmsted's Emerald Necklace has the City of Boston had such an opportunity to fundamentally change the image and identity of a significant portion of the city." The rhetoric of the city's Boston 2000 plan for the air rights over the new central artery perfectly evinces Coyle's spirit and style.

> The planning embodied in [the] Boston 2000 project reaffirms the tradition of city design and planning as illustrated by the City Beautiful movement, which highlighted the role of public infrastructure and open space projects in forming and ordering the city. The project joins other recent infrastructure and urban development projects— for instance, those in Barcelona—in postulating the forms of the 21st century city. Those forms include ordering the urban environment and extending the domain of pedestrians. The project also preserves, reclaims and articulates specific local physical attributes that are valued by the local community and envisions a restructuring of the larger civic environment. The urban design guidelines, in addition to reinforcing Boston's historic forms, translate the project's design vision into regulatory form by contemplating opportunities for contemporary urban design forms and elements which incorporate a mixture of architectural and landscape elements.[70]

The city's proposal for use of the air rights over the depressed artery illustrates the Coyle flair for encompassing myriad issues and points of view in a single planning document. It includes the creation of tree-lined boulevards, 1,000 new units of housing, and a network of streets to improve the pedestrian environment. Massive new office buildings are notably absent from the plan. Neither the aesthetics nor the economics of

....
*Flynn,
Coyle,
and the
Boom*

239

the early nineties allow this. Instead, the plan calls for a skating rink and neighborhood parks for Chinatown and the North End, and economic and residential development only where the historic context permits.[71]

The city's task in the 1990s is to work with all the community groups and the federal and state agencies involved to carry the project through to completion. Generally, despite partisan and other differences, state and local officials have come to see the need for close political cooperation and the city is working well with Governor Weld's administration to complete the project and secure benefits for both city and state.[72] The project had been closely associated with the previous Dukakis administration and might easily have been killed by the new Republican governor. Once Weld was persuaded of the value of the project, however, city-state relations smoothed out and the CA/T progressed.

One of the related projects (required by the state's environmental plan) is construction of a new mass transit system connecting the Fan Pier district of South Boston to downtown Boston. This stipulation dovetails with the federal government's announced intention of building a massive courthouse on a 4.6 acre site it purchased from restaurateur Anthony Athanas. U.S. Representative Joseph Moakley, a key player in selecting the site, proclaimed that "the new courthouse will serve as a catalyst for economic development in what is now a barren section of Boston."[73] Moakley, chairman of the House Rules Committee, helped direct federal funds to the Massachusetts Bay Transportation Authority to provide mass transit to the district. He also was instrumental in getting a fixed-span bridge to replace the Northern Avenue drawbridge, making the area more accessible. Summing up his work, Moakley said "When that mass transit comes down here, that bridge is completed, that courthouse is completed, this will be the hottest place in Boston. You will see hotels, office buildings. It'll be beautiful."[74] Athanas had spent decades unsuccessfully seeking to develop the site. He and his partners of the late 1980s proposed an immense project with offices, condominiums, and hotels but fell to bickering and suing one another, which killed the project. Some political and real estate observers suggested a plausible connection between the federal government's choice of the site and Athanas's longtime friendships with many Massachusetts politicians.[75] The General Services Administration maintained, however, that the Fan Pier property was chosen over downtown sites primarily because of its lower price.

The choice of this site for a new courthouse is merely one of the latest of countless decisions in Boston's history that have shaped the city. One may challenge the soundness or origins of the decision to site such an important government building away from the downtown but it offers

....

Flynn,

Coyle,

and the

Boom

240

another example of the process of determining the physical appearance and land use of the city. It is a political process, only in this case it is more obvious and direct. Planning involves politics, land, money, competing interests, and visions, and it creates future problems and opportunities. The city and state now have to come together to create an acceptable transportation solution to what will otherwise be an intolerable traffic problem. In the final analysis, the federal courthouse on Fan Pier may be evaluated on the basis of aesthetics and the transportation developments associated with it, but support for it and the drive to complete it are to be found in the mixture of politics and economics.

Similarly, the Central Artery/Tunnel has plausible aesthetic and engineering arguments in its favor but public testimony indicates that the economic argument for building the depressed artery and third harbor tunnel is the most significant. To many Bostonians, the goal above all is to stimulate the regional economy by bringing in the massive funds and jobs required to complete the project. Support for the CA/T comes from organized labor and business groups. The Greater Boston Chamber of Commerce joined with the media and other business and labor organizations supporting the project to help Boston retain a competitive position in the fields of commerce and services. The hope for thousands of construction and related jobs in the 1990s is a vital element in the coalition supporting the project and shows that Bostonians are once again turning to their government to secure economic goals for the community. Such hope represents continuity with earlier approaches to planning.

John F. "Honey Fitz" Fitzgerald tried to build a public-private partnership to create a "Bigger, Better, Busier Boston" in the first decade of the twentieth century. He sought the cooperation of the city's civic and business leaders but failed because of the ethnic, religious, and class cleavages that split the city. James Michael Curley recognized the importance of this conflict and, knowing that the fundamental splits in Boston's social structure prevented an effective public-private partnership, relied upon public works projects to aid Boston's people and economy in the 1930s. John Collins and Ed Logue, a generation later, dealing with a Boston no longer so bound by ethnic conflict, built the New Boston by the use of public funds in the 1960s and maintained a strong connection with the business community. Changes in the national political scene, however, shortly eliminated that sort of city-building and left succeeding administrations to contrive new solutions.

Under Flynn, the days of assured and fabulous federal funding were long gone. Gone too, is an economic region awash in prosperity and a state government willing to take up the slack left by the decline in federal

....
Flynn,
Coyle,
and the
Boom
241

funds. Flynn's mayoralty has, perforce, been an attempt to establish a strong public-private partnership of the sort that in the time of Fitzgerald was rejected, in the time of Curley was derided, and in the time of Collins was secured. In the 1980s and 1990s, Flynn and his administration work with the business community on several fronts to shape the community. Although the populist mayor never established a close and public relationship with business leaders such as characterized the Collins administration of the 1960s, Flynn knows how to work with the private sector.

Boston businesspeople came to regard Flynn positively, so much so that one journalistic account of Boston in the early 1990s characterizes their regard for the mayor as "almost touchingly positive. They admire him for keeping the city's finances in order. They appreciate the relatively predictable permitting process his development chief, Stephen Coyle, has created at the Boston Redevelopment Authority. They are impressed that his administration has been almost corruption-free. They value the role he has played as a racial healer, especially during his first term."[76] But Ray Flynn, who reached across the divide between the city's working-class neighborhoods and the glitzy offices of downtown, faces yet another chasm—that dividing Boston's white population from the minority communities, which are an ever-increasing proportion of the population.

Between 1980 and 1990 Boston's white population decreased while the black and Hispanic population jumped to new heights, a trend that poses new issues and opportunities for Boston's people, politicians, and planners. Ray Flynn, "the neighborhood mayor," worked hard to divert benefits from the downtown boom to the city's outlying areas but faced sharp criticism from some for failing to adequately address new needs arising from the demographic shifts. One observer writes "While Flynn's working-class heroics still played well with the rank and file in minority neighborhoods, his relations with many of their leaders was deteriorating."[77] This development may have begun with the infamous Carol Stuart murder in 1989 and continued through the next year's fight to abolish Boston's elected school committee. In the former case the mayor's police department was heavily criticized while in the latter Flynn was charged with grabbing power. Damage to the mayor seemed slight, however, and criticism of Flynn is nothing new.

James Green, a labor historian, criticized Flynn and his 1983 campaign advisers for making appeals for economic unity and ignoring divisive issues like racism, arguing that they had "repeated some past mistakes by assuming that racism and other forms of discrimination could be avoided as political issues and that economic reforms alone could bring people together. Such false idealism has never had much appeal to groups like

....

Flynn,

Coyle,

and the

Boom

242

Figure 9.3 An aerial view looking east to Boston. Taken in 1990, this photo allows one to imagine the old peninsula which is now largely covered by towers. The filling of land made Boston what it is today. Clockwise see the mudflats and fill of Logan International Airport in East Boston; Fan Pier and the Commonwealth Flats of South Boston; the uniform street alignment in the filled-in South End; the Prudential Center and Hancock Tower at the edge of the Back Bay, and the low-rise development of the Back Bay over to the Charles River. Beacon Hill is cheek by jowl with the old West End and Charlestown lies to the left, across the Charles River but much closer to Boston than when John Winthrop and company settled there in 1630. (Courtesy of Aerial Photos International.)

women and blacks whose oppression cannot be lifted just through economic reform."[78] Flynn's first two terms, however, were in large part a long-running effort to apply the strategy that Green had condemned and, judging by electoral results, scarcely a failure. Flynn won both the 1983 and 1987 elections and was successful in his bid for a third term in 1991 despite his pledge to serve no more than two terms. He argued that the city had made strides against many of the ills he inherited and that he "wanted to be there to preserve and protect the progress we made."[79] The voters agreed, turned down the candidacy of Edward Doherty, and in November 1991 overwhelmingly gave Flynn his third mayoral victory. Planning in his third term will be different, however, because the economic environment differs dramatically from the years when the neighborhood mayor could capture some of the downtown boom to fulfill his promises to the city's residents.

As his second term ended, Flynn's administration looked to the future and issued a planning document that offers an "agenda for economic development" and may be considered an "official preview" of the future. In it, the city identifies six goals: putting people to work; improving the business climate; building a more diversified, long-term economy; improving transportation systems; upgrading the quality of life for Bostonians; and providing the basis for a more equitable sharing of real economic opportunities among all the city's residents and neighborhoods.[80] Flynn and his aides advocate dozens of strategies for achieving this future and illustrate how they intend to (at least partially) shape the physical, economic, social environment of the city. Their vision of the future reveals optimism and determination, includes expectations of physical development remarkable for a city still suffering through a recession, and incorporates institutional, commercial, and governmental expansion projects.

....

*Flynn,
Coyle,
and the
Boom*

244

Building Boston's Economic Future boasts of major development projects underway, especially those in the medical research and health care sectors. In particular it points to the redevelopment of the Prudential Center and the development of Ruggles Center. Upcoming public facilities include a new Boston police headquarters, the new federal courthouse, and the South Station intermodal transportation facility for bus, subway, and rail connections. Hopes for private development include biotech manufacturing facilities, a new Boston Garden, hotels adjacent to both the Customs House and World Trade Center, and even a domed Boston stadium. Furthermore, the city's strategy for the nineties extends to promoting high-speed rail connecting Boston and New York and a visionary "Bioscience Line" providing a circumferential transit link for South

Station, the Newmarket area, Ruggles Center, Longwood medical area, Olmsted Plaza, and MIT with possible tie-ins to other sections of the city.[81]

This intentionally ambitious document not only points out the direction the city may take but it also may be used, in the years ahead, as a yardstick to measure the Flynn administration's success in shaping the city. Such a blueprint as an instrument of evaluation or scorecard, however, has its limitations. Planning is about goals, vision, strategies, and the physical development of the city, but it also concerns economic, social, and political forces, none of which can be so precisely measured, formulated, or predicted.

Evaluating planning requires more than going over a checklist of projects. The Flynn years in Boston are not over. The physical changes to the city that are taking place are already enormous, but the effect of the Flynn years on the planning process may be just as significant. Just looking at the skyline allows an evaluation of the physical transformation of Boston, but the Flynn-Coyle legacy in planning affects more than the skyline and will require the perspective of time to assess. Even before the completion of Ray Flynn's mayoralty, however, there is no question that Flynn and Coyle have dramatically shaped the city and the process of planning Boston. Steve Coyle left Boston early in 1992 to take a position in Washington. Adverse economic conditions and the absence of the mayor's star player pose formidable challenges for Ray Flynn and Bostonians in the 1990s.

Some might think a history of planning in Boston would make a slim volume, but the record shows that Boston is, in fact, a city with a long tradition of anticipating its future and planning its growth. This planning does not always mean the comprehensive and bureaucratic sort seen at the end of the twentieth century, but rather, planning of a broader type, which is the use of government power to advance the economic interests and to alter the physical appearance of the city. Planning is a political activity concerned with the allocation and regulation of a public resource, urban land. Planning is motivated, primarily, by economic interests. People congregate in cities essentially for economic reasons and develop an urban form that aims to expedite the pursuit of material advancement. Beyond this economic benefit, cities, of course, meet aesthetics and other cultural and social needs. These needs play a great part in modern planning, but they are subsidiaries to economic matters.

The evolution of Boston demonstrates continuity and growth in the process of planning as well as in the urban form. From its earliest days, Boston's local government shaped the community through the allocation and regulation of land use and the promotion and control of economic activity. To understand the development of the city we must consider decisions made, plans adopted, and courses of action followed within the framework of the time they occurred. People who shaped Boston have acted according to the circumstances, forces, ideas, interests, wishes, and foibles of their own time. Within the context of a capitalist society, Boston is a highly planned city, and like the man who was astonished to find he had been speaking prose all his life, Bostonians have always engaged in planning, although this use of the term is recent. City planning did not originate in the early twentieth century when the term and the profession of city planner emerged. Rather, the evolution of the physical Boston has been accompanied by the evolution of the practice of planning.

Boston had a definite and known point of origin and continued to grow during several centuries of the industrial era. It absorbed other towns and adapted itself to technological, economic, and social changes. What has occurred in Boston has been driven by these forces and, to a large extent, directed by the government through its planning function. The form of the city is a physical manifestation of decisions made by politicians, businesses, institutions, planners, and citizens to adapt to issues and problems of survival in an increasingly complicated world. In all of this, a vision of the future is necessary, although not sufficient.

Over the last two centuries a handful of visions for Boston were transformed into reality. Bulfinch's, as always, stands out. Though the fruits of his vision were often altered and sometimes eradicated, he achieved greater success than anyone else in realizing his dream of planning Boston. Josiah Quincy, "the Great Mayor," created Quincy Market less by artistic vision than by a program of action combined with the political power to implement it. Quincy's achievement was unique because he took the new form of city government and the post of mayor, infused them both with his views and energy, and imposed his program on a surprised business community. Quincy's primary motivation was not a grand vision of a new cityscape but a desire to rectify an intolerable situation—unsanitary meat markets and inadequate disposal of sewage and waste. The much-praised Quincy Market was essentially a practical solution to an unhealthful and disgusting problem, a remedy carried out with grace and beauty and one that established a high standard for city planning.

Another striking example of the positive role of government in shaping the city is the famous Back Bay. Early expectations for industrial development of the area were thwarted when railroads laid tracks across the Back Bay, interrupting the flow of the water and creating a smelly, dangerous cesspit. This unpleasant development forced the state to take corrective action. The state-controlled area was divided into the standard rectilinear pattern of streets seen everywhere in America. The state brushed aside proposals for parks and ponds and refused to integrate the Back Bay with the South End. From an abstract perspective, in fact, the South End can be considered a better example of city planning than the Back Bay. It has squares, public spaces, and a sense of intimacy that the Back Bay lacks. It is true that the South End also has problems with traffic circulation, but the Back Bay would have these too if it were not for the much later creation of Storrow Drive, which siphons traffic from Commonwealth Avenue and Beacon Street.

The Back Bay is graced with Commonwealth Avenue and has pleasing set-back and design requirements, but most of all it has beautiful buildings. That the Back Bay is such a gem owes more to architectural change in the nineteenth century and preservation in the twentieth than to any genius on the part of its planners. A brief consideration of the edges of the district illustrates this point. To the north, the banks of the Charles River were an eyesore until the Embankment was created in the early twentieth century. The joggers, strolling couples, bikers, and music lovers who enjoy the Esplanade today are the beneficiaries, not of the state planners of the nineteenth century, but of those later planners who were inspired to correct the aesthetic problems left by their forerunners. When we look to the western edges of the Back Bay we find the work of Frederick Law Olmsted. His masterful creation of the Back Bay Fens was, again, primarily a practical solution to another stinking problem, the overflow of the Muddy River and its sewage into the Charles River. Copley Square lies on the southern border of the Back Bay. This spot has troubled Bostonians for a century and only recently assumed an appearance remotely worthy of its reputation. Copley Square's significance has never resided in its public space, but in the beauty and importance of the buildings that border it. Trinity Church and the Boston Public Library came first and the square followed. The final edge of the Back Bay is dominated by the Prudential Center which, although highly criticized, is at least a step up from the dismal railroad yards that stood there until the middle of the twentieth century. The point is not to denigrate the glory of the Back Bay but to emphasize that it is not the result of the type of planning many believe it exemplifies. Rather, it is an example of a pragmatic correction of an earlier mistake. It is done exceptionally well, but it is not the result of any abstract vision. A creative response to a changing reality, it demonstrates the use of government power to advance economic interests and to alter the physical appearance of the city. It is, in short, planning.

City planning is not the realization of some grand plan or abstract scheme like Disneyland. Such creations are abstractions come to life in artificial situations, not models for city planners, despite their virtues of cleanliness, security, and excellent transportation systems. Theme park planning is, in fact, antithetical to traditional American values. In a society based on the concept of limited government, the expectation that a living organism, the city, will be created and directed according to the precepts that guide a commercial entertainment park is absurd. Yet such an expectation is often implicit in criticisms of the American city and its planning.

Planning a city is much more difficult than building a theme park. Planning is intimately tied to the political life of the American city. Those who dreamed of a better Boston succeeded only when they had political backing. In a democracy this is a sloppy process. Planning poses a dilemma in a society which wants the benefits of a rational and comprehensive city-planning process, but denies municipal government the power to achieve the results a master plan could produce.

The career of Robert Moses, the powerful empire-builder and creator of New York's parks, bridges, beaches, parkways, and housing projects, offers an insight into the problem of planning in a democracy. Moses was a man who "made himself indispensable to popularly chosen officials because of his ability to get things done. [He combined] a single-minded passion to accomplish what he thought ought to be done with exceptional financial and administrative skills, a knack for knowing the public's desires and for public relations, and the foresight to identify the automobile as the most important shaper of the urban environment."[1] Moses was a force to be reckoned with. He was a person with vision, the capacity to inspire the public, and the ability to carry out his plans. One can hardly conceive a better definition of an ideal planning type than this, but there is another side, as Robert Caro emphasizes in his biography, *The Power Broker: Robert Moses and the Fall of New York*. Moses derived a great deal of power from his position in state government and "coupled with the power he had obtained from his use within the city of federal money, it gave him considerable independence of the city's mayor. He was using forces outside the city to bend its highest elected official to his will. By emphasizing forces outside the city's control, he was remaking the city in certain crucial areas without allowing the city any say in that remaking."[2] In the end, Moses leaves a mixed legacy.

There is no evidence that Bostonians ever wanted a Robert Moses. The closest they came to having someone like this was Ed Logue in the 1960s. Logue's work in Boston is on a far smaller scale than Moses's in New York, but the idea was similar: to concentrate power, create an independent base of authority, and forge ahead. Moses may have accomplished more in absolute terms over many decades, but Logue transformed proportionally more of a smaller city in less than seven years. Moreover, Logue's achievement is perhaps more dramatic. He took a city in decline, worked with other visionaries to create a planning program, and wielded enough power to bring it to reality. Logue grasped the significance of economic, demographic, and social forces, and—most important of all—possessed an acute sense of political possibilities and realities. As MIT's Langley Keyes comments, "Logue is an action-oriented political pragmatist who has little use for general plans and city planners lacking the political power to realize their designs. For Logue, planning and politics are inseparable, planning being the art of the politically feasible, from the vantage point of City Hall."[3]

Logue succeeded in the 1960s because of his formidable talents, strong political backing, and a remarkable confluence of factors including federal generosity, a shifting economy, and plain luck. In the years after Logue, Boston rebounded as an economic force and center for the region, and its population began to increase; yet Boston's resurgence was also a reaction to another intolerable situation, economic despair. The grim reality of a deteriorating, nearly moribund city led to desperation, and by the time Logue arrived, he found a coalition willing and able to support a program of radical change. Political cooperation, engineered by Mayor Collins, proved decisive in getting the wheels of change in motion.

Such political cooperation has been key throughout the history of planning in Boston. Those with the most power to shape the city are by definition involved in politics. In recent years planning has come to incorporate neighborhood and community groups to an extent never dreamed of in earlier years, but this is fundamentally a result and reflection of changing political life. Bostonians no longer indulge in the grand schemes of anyone who would plan without working through a democratically based process. The challenge facing city officials today and in the future is to include community and neighborhood groups in planning in a positive manner. While such groups often feel the need to veto growth, they also need to be persuaded to accept change and accommodation in order to meet the future economic needs of the larger community.

Planning in Boston has always involved neighborhoods and local communities or factions as objects or subjects, but only recently have they been involved as participants in an institutionalized manner. Ed Logue touted "planning with people," but many saw his attack on poverty only as an attack on the poor. Logue and John Collins worked strenuously to transform the physical city in an attempt to change the social structure. They wanted to sweep away the poverty that was at the base of Boston, but too much physical change, destruction, and relocation were borne by too few. On the other hand, too much of the physical change seemed to benefit too few.

Boston's skyline changed dramatically under Kevin White. Of equal importance, however, was an increasing politicization of the planning process. Choosing not to have a strong head of the BRA, the mayor took decision-making into his own hands. He recognized the need for more community-based planning and greater sensitivity to social issues. Exhausted by other issues and forces, however, the mayor became the czar of downtown office-building design. Paradoxically, White's assertion of mayoral power so directly into urban design matters was a step toward greater democratization of the process. Where John Collins emphasized the rule of experts in design matters and allowed a special nonpartisan commission to select the winning architect for the new City Hall, Kevin White returned such decision-making rights to the office of mayor, where, at least in theory, the decisions were closer to popular influence and control. Whereas Collins removed significant urban design decisions from politics, White reasserted the primacy of politics in planning and design. Kevin White, in this sense, returned planning to its proper sphere where the citizenry could affect such decisions. In practice, however, White, in love with his city, but a loner, sought little input from other Bostonians so it was left to his successor to facilitate and institutionalize citizen input in the process of shaping the city.

In 1984 Ray Flynn and his development chief, Stephen Coyle, took over the reins of planning and began to form the city according to their own lights. They understood the process had to change and that the benefits of growth had to be distributed more widely than ever before. They also comprehended that the vision of one or two people or the concentration of decision-making in the hands of a few was no longer politically acceptable.

Yet opportunities to shape the physical city remain and the need for vision has not been eliminated. The task facing Flynn and others planning the future of Boston is to reconcile the need for vision with the realities of the marketplace, the possibilities of technology, and the social structure of Boston. The city faces one of its great planning opportunities in determining the future of downtown land to be opened up by the Central Artery/Tunnel project. It is in some ways a familiar situation. Nearly two centuries ago, Charles Bulfinch and Josiah Quincy planned and built on some portions of this land and, just as the Back Bay was planned to correct problems created in an earlier period, the Central Artery, the dream of one generation, quickly became the nightmare of another.

Boston continues to be reinvented. The design of Copley Square is one example; the land of the Central Artery is another. In yet another round of planning, competing interests will become involved to determine how this newly available downtown land should be used. This time around, some see the chance to make money, others to create parkland, and others to build housing. These people have different motives and visions, but all who wish to affect the shape of the city enter into the realm of planning which lies within the sphere of politics. How Boston looks will be decided in this realm and this sphere.

The challenge of politics—of planning—is to mediate among competing interests, to meet social needs, and to move forward. Politics and planning are inseparable, for politics allows—or impedes—the fulfillment of planning. Without political support a great deal of planning may take place but little can be accomplished. It is only through the art of politics that Bostonians over the years have had the chance to combine vision with economic realities to build their "city upon a hill."

A. Timeline of Boston Planning

1630	John Winthrop describes "a city upon a hill"; Thomas Graves plans Charlestown; Boston is settled
1634	Purchase of Boston Common
1635	Street system law
1640	Population of 1,200
1650	Population of 2,000
1652	Independent Roxbury commission lays out streets
1660	Population of 3,000
1670	Independent town of Charlestown surveys and records its streets
1673	Town grants entrepreneurs right to build seawall
1680	Population of 4,500
1690	Population of 7,000
1700	Population of 6,700
1707	Entrepreneurs granted right to develop Roxbury Neck
1710	Population of 9,000; private development of Long Wharf
1720	Population of 12,000
1730	Population of 13,000
1742	Population of 16,382; Faneuil Hall built at private expense
1760	Population of 15,631; Charlestown lottery to pay for street paving
1775	Population of 16,000; Battle of Bunker Hill

1776	Population of 3,000; British evacuation of Boston
1790	Population of 18,320
1793–96	Bulfinch develops Tontine Crescent
1795–98	Development of Bulfinch-designed State House; town vote to move workhouse and almshouse from Park Street
1799	Mount Vernon Proprietors adopt Beacon Hill street plan of Mather Withington
1800	Population of 24,937
1801	Street plan for Roxbury Neck adopted
1803	Town ordinance restricts height and style of Sentry Street building
1804	Bulfinch plan for developing park and promenades at Boston Common
1805	Bulfinch develops Park Street area
1807	Town agrees to allow private group to fill in Mill Pond, create Bulfinch Triangle between Haymarket and North Station
1810	Population of 33,787
	Bulfinch designs Colonnade Row built on Tremont Street
1817	Bulfinch leaves Boston for Washington, D.C.
1820	Population of 43,298
1821	Mill Dam (later Beacon Street) opens
1822	Boston assumes city form of government
1823	First Mayor Josiah Quincy begins plans for Faneuil Hall Marketplace
1826	S. P. Fuller plan for Louisburg Square; Faneuil Hall Marketplace (three buildings) opens
1829	Harrison Gray Otis elected mayor
1830	Population of 61,392; cows forbidden to graze on Boston Common
1833	South Cove Company forms to develop the emerging South End
1839	Work on Public Garden begins
1840	Population of 93,383
1844	Robert Gourlay offers plans for Boston and Back Bay
1846	Josiah Quincy, Jr., elected mayor
1850	Population of 136,881
1857	State begins to fill and develop Back Bay
1860	Population of 177,820
1866	City begins to clear out and level Fort Hill (near South Station)

1868	Roxbury annexed to Boston
1870	Population of 250,526
	Dorchester annexed to Boston
1872	Landfill creates Atlantic Avenue; Robert Copeland plan for Boston; Great Fire in the commercial district; Huntington Avenue laid out
1874	Charlestown, Brighton, and West Roxbury annexed to Boston
1875	Board of Park Commissioners created
1878	Frederick Law Olmsted begins work on Fens plan
1880	Population of 362,839
1882	City acquires Copley Square site; first report on park system by Frederick Law Olmsted
1884	First Irish-born mayor, Hugh O'Brien, elected
1886	Olmsted publishes notes and plans for Franklin Park
1887	West End Street Railway amalgamates all competition
1889	Boston's first electric streetcar operation begins; Metropolitan Sewer Commission created
1890	Population of 448,477; U.S. Congress approves use of Castle Island for park purposes
1891	Land-taking begun at Jamaica Plain
1892	Boston establishes 125-foot building-height limit; Chicago World's Fair opens, stimulates city planning
1893	Metropolitan Park Commission created
1894	Fens completed according to Olmsted plan; Jamaicaway completed; land taken for West Roxbury Parkway; legislature authorizes Boston Elevated Railway and Boston Transit Commission
1895	Third Mayor Josiah Quincy elected; Metropolitan Water Board created
1897	Tremont Street subways opens Park Street to Public Garden
1898	90-foot building-height limit set for Copley Square area; Park Street Subway extended to North Station
1899	Marine Park connected to Franklin Park by Columbia Road
1900	Population of 560,892; last horsecar line of the Boston Elevated Railway terminated
1901	Elevated transit lines open from Sullivan Square to Dudley Square via Tremont Street subway and along Atlantic Avenue; Metropolitan Water and Sewerage Board created (combines two predecessor agencies)

1903	Boston Elevated takes over street railway lines in West Roxbury
1904	City introduces first comprehensive building-height limits; streetcar operation begins in tunnel to East Boston
1905	John F. "Honey Fitz" Fitzgerald elected mayor
1907	Metropolitan Improvement Commission recommendations for development of port and civil center
1909	New Boston movement begins its four-year effort; Boston Elevated line opens to Forest Hills
1910	Population of 670,585
1912	Metropolitan Government proposal killed in legislature; legislature authorizes city planning boards; Park Street to Harvard Square subway opens
1914	City Planning Board created (one of fourteen in country); James Michael Curley elected for first of four mayoral terms
1915	Custom House tower addition completed
1916	New York zoning code enacted, serves as national model
1917	U.S. enters World War I
1918	Legislature takes over Boston Elevated Railway
1919	Metropolitan District Commission created (unifying parks commission with water and sewerage board); Boston Police Strike
1920	Population of 748,060
1921	Curley elected to second mayoral term
1922	First motor bus route established
1924	Boston creates a zoning plan; East Boston tunnel switches from streetcars to rapid transit
1928	Pyramid feature added to Boston zoning regulations for tall buildings; rapid transit to Ashmont opened
1929	Stock market crashes; Curley elected to third mayoral term
1930	Robert Whitten's Thoroughfare Plan
1930s	Completion of Summer Tunnel and Storrow Drive
1935	Creation of Boston Housing Authority (BHA); Planning Board proposes tearing down the elevated from Sullivan Station to Forest Hills; Curley becomes governor
1936	Trackless trolley line opened
1937	U.S. Housing Authority created; Maurice Tobin defeats Curley in mayoral campaign
1938	Elevated service along Atlantic Avenue ends
1940	Population of 770,816

1941	U.S. enters World War II; Huntington Avenue subway opens to Symphony Hall area
1944	Boston Contest to gather suggestions for revitalizing the metropolitan area
1945	Curley elected to fourth and final term as mayor
1947	Boston Elevated becomes Metropolitan Transit Authority
1949	Federal Housing Act calls for slum clearance; John B. Hynes defeats Curley in mayoral election
1950	Population of 801,444 (peak); Planning Board comes up with General Plan; Boston Housing Authority establishes Redevelopment Division
1952	East Boston rapid transit extended to Wonderland in Revere
1953	Plan for West End "renewal" announced
1957	Boston Redevelopment Authority (BRA) created; assumes West End and New York Streets projects from BHA; plans for Prudential Center announced
1958	Demolition of West End begins; Central Artery completed
1959	John F. Collins elected mayor; MTA opens service along former Newton Highlands branch of Boston and Albany Railroad
1960	Population of 697,197; demolition of West End completed; Ed Logue arrives in Boston as a consultant; Collins and Logue announce "Ninety Million Dollar Program"; Chapter 121A passes, allowing Prudential development, abolishing City Planning Board, and transferring its functions to BRA
1961	Logue appointed head of BRA; demolition of Scollay Square begins
1963	Capital improvement plan announced for twelve-year period
1964	Massachusetts Bay Transportation Authority created; MTA dissolves
1965	General Plan for Boston 1965–1975 announced; color coding of MBTA lines begins
1967	Logue leaves the BRA to run for mayor; Kevin H. White elected mayor
1968	Hale Champion appointed BRA administrator; neighborhood planning established; "Tent City" site occupied
1969	"People Before Highways" march against the Southwest Expressway

1970	Population of 641,071; Governor Sargent establishes moratorium on highway construction in metropolitan Boston; Park Plaza project announced
1971	Boston Economic Development and Industrial Corporation established; Commonwealth disapproves Park Plaza
1973	Interstate Transfer Option allows state to transfer federal highway funds to mass transit
1974	Boston School desegregation is ordered
1975	Elevated service from Haymarket to Everett ends
1976	Bicentennial celebration; Quincy Market reopens
1980	Population of 562,994; Proposition 2 1/2 passes
1983	Raymond L. Flynn elected mayor
1984	Stephen Coyle appointed director of the BRA
1985	Interim Planning Overlay District (IPOD) strategy becomes law
1986	South End Neighborhood Housing Initiative (SENHI) begins
1987	October crash of New York Stock Exchange; Raymond Flynn wins second term
1988	Dudley Street Neighborhood Initiative given power of eminent domain
1989	Midtown Cultural District Plan adopted
1990	Population of 574,823; Harborpark District becomes part of Boston Zoning Code
1991	Central Artery/Third Harbor Tunnel approved by Federal Highway Administration; Flynn wins third term
1992	Stephen Coyle leaves the BRA

....

Appendix A

B. Boston Population Trends, 1790–1990

Year	Population	Difference	% Change
1790	18,320		
1800	24,937	6,617	+36
1810	33,787	8,850	+36
1820	43,298	9,511	+28
1830	61,392	18,099	+42
1840	93,383	31,991	+52
1850	136,881	43,498	+47
1860	177,840	40,959	+30
1870	250,526	72,686	+41
1880	362,839	112,313	+45
1890	448,477	85,638	+24
1900	560,892	112,415	+25
1910	670,585	109,693	+20
1920	748,060	77,475	+12
1930	781,188	33,128	+4
1940	770,816	−10,372	−1
1950	801,444	30,628	+4
1960	697,197	−104,247	−13
1970	641,071	−56,126	−8
1980	562,994	−78,077	−12
1990	574,823	+11,829	+2

All population figures from U.S. Bureau of the Census

C. Chief Executive Officers of the Boston Redevelopment Authority

Kane Simonian	October 4, 1957, to January 25, 1961
Edward J. Logue	January 25, 1961, to August 4, 1967
Francis X. Cuddy	August 4, 1967, to January 15, 1968
Hale Champion	January 15, 1968, to August 31, 1969
John Warner	September 1, 1969, to January 6, 1971
Robert Kenney	January 25, 1971, to January 1, 1977
Robert Walsh	January 1, 1977, to July 11, 1978
Robert Ryan	September 1, 1978, to July 16, 1984
Stephen Coyle	July 14, 1984, to January 23, 1992

D. Board Members of the Boston Redevelopment Authority

Patrick J. Bocanfuso[1]	1968–1973
Paul J. Burns	1970–1975
James E. Cofield, Jr.	1976–1980
James G. Colbert	1957–1980
George P. Condrakes	1964–1969
Michael F. Donlan	1985–
Robert L. Farrell[2]	1969–1989
James K. Flaherty	1973–
Clarence J. Jones[3]	1981–
Francis J. Lally[4]	1957–1970
Joseph W. Lund[5]	1957–1961
Melvin J. Massucco	1957–1970
Stephen J. McCloskey	1957–1968
William A. McDermott, Jr.	1980–1985
Francis X. O'Brien	1989–
John P. Ryan	1961–1964
Consuelo Gonzales Thornell	1989–
Joseph J. Walsh[6]	1970–1989

[1]Chairman, November 1970 to February 1972
[2]Chairman, February 1972 to January 1989
[3]Elected Chairman, May 1989
[4]Chairman, April 1961 to November 1970
[5]Chairman, October 1957 to April 1961
[6]Chairman, January to April 1989

....

Appendix D

Introduction

1 Harold Lasswell's definition can be found in his *Politics: Who Gets What, When, How* (New York: Peter Smith, 1950), 3.

2 David Schuyler, *The New Urban Landscape: The Redefinition of City Form in Nineteenth-Century America* (Baltimore: The Johns Hopkins University Press, 1986), 15.

3 M. Christine Boyer, *Dreaming the Rational City: The Myth of American City Planning* (Cambridge: MIT Press, 1983), 67.

4 Sam Bass Warner, Jr., *The Private City: Philadelphia in Three Periods of Its Growth* (Philadelphia: University of Pennsylvania Press, 1968), x.

5 Eric H. Monkkonen, *America Becomes Urban: The Development of U.S. Cities and Towns, 1780–1980* (Berkeley: University of California Press, 1988), 218.

6 Melville C. Branch, "Goals and Objectives in Civil Comprehensive Planning," in *Urban Planning Theory*, ed. Melville C. Branch (Stroudsburg, PA: Dowden, Hutchinson, & Ross, Inc., 1975), 272.

7 Stanley K. Schultz, *Constructing Urban Culture: American Cities and City Planning, 1800–1920* (Philadelphia: Temple University Press, 1989), xii.

8 Kenneth T. Jackson, "The Impact of Technological Change on Urban Form," in *Technology, the Economy, and Society: The American Experience,* ed. Joel Colton and Stuart Bruchey (New York: Columbia University Press, 1987), 150.

9 Monkkonen, *America Becomes Urban,* 164, 161–62.

1 A City upon a Hill

1 Charles N. Glaab and A. Theodore Brown, *A History of Urban America,* 2d ed. (New York: Macmillan, 1976), 5. Also see Darrett Rutman, *Winthrop's Boston: Portrait of a Puritan Town* (Chapel Hill: University of North Carolina Press, 1965).

2 Walter Muir Whitehill's *Boston: A Topographical History,* 2d ed., enl. (Cambridge:

Belknap Press of Harvard University Press, 1975) remains the basic text for this aspect of Boston's history.

3 Albert P. Langtry, ed., *Metropolitan Boston: A Modern History,* 5v. (New York: Lewis Historical Publishing Co., Inc., 1929), 3:1044.

4 Whitehill, *Boston: A Topographical History,* 8; Glaab and Brown, *A History of Urban America,* 6.

5 John W. Reps, *The Making of Urban America: A History of City Planning in the United States* (Princeton: Princeton University Press, 1965), 141.

6 Elisabeth M. Herlihy, "The History of Boston's Street System," in *Report on a Thoroughfare Plan for Boston,* ed. Robert Whitten (Boston: City of Boston Planning Board, 1930), 154. In 1786 the Charlestown ferry was replaced by the Charles River Bridge and Harvard received annual compensation of two hundred dollars for some forty years. In 1854 the other two ferries went under private management but in 1870 the city of Boston returned them to the public domain. After folding in the 1950s, ferry service between Boston and East Boston resumed in the late 1980s with a shuttle connection between Rowes Wharf and Logan International Airport.

7 Daniel J. Boorstin, *The Americans: The Colonial Experience* (New York: Vintage Books, 1958), 29.

8 Sam Bass Warner, Jr., *The Urban Wilderness: A History of the American City* (New York: Harper & Row, 1972), 7.

9 Herlihy, "Boston's Street System," 150.

10 Other examples of planning in Puritan New England did occur; e.g., Cambridge was originally laid out in a gridiron street pattern. See Charles W. Eliot, Donald M. Graham, and David A. Crane, "Boston: Three Centuries of Planning," *A.S.P.O. Newsletter: American Society of Planning Officials* 30 (1964):43.

11 Elisabeth M. Herlihy, "Planning for Boston: 1630–1930," *City Planning Quarterly* 6 (1930):3–4.

12 Josiah Quincy, *A Municipal History of the Town and City of Boston during the Two Centuries from September 17, 1630 to September 17, 1830* (Boston: C. C. Little Brown and J. Brown, 1852), 4–5.

13 Quoted in Langtry, *Metropolitan Boston,* 3:1946.

14 Bernard Bailyn, *The Peopling of British North America: An Introduction* (New York: Alfred A. Knopf, 1987), 67.

15 Edmund S. Morgan, *The Puritan Dilemma: The Story of John Winthrop* (Boston: Little, Brown & Co., 1958), 65, 175–176.

16 Herlihy, "Boston's Street System," 157.

17 Whitehill, *Boston: A Topographical History,* 8.

18 Quincy, *Municipal History,* 5.

19 Justin Winsor, ed., *The Memorial History of Boston, including Suffolk County, Massachusetts 1630–1880,* 4 vols. (Boston: James R. Osgood & Co., 1881), 4:493–494.

20 Province Law of 1692, Chapter 32; now Chapter 3, Section 3 of the General Laws.

21 State Street Trust Co., *Boston's Growth: A Bird's-Eye View of Boston's Increase in Territory and Population from Its Beginning to the Present* (Boston: Walton Advertising and Printing Co., Inc., 1910), 18–20.

22 Whitehill, *Boston: A Topographical History,* 11.

23 James A. Henretta, "Economic Development and Social Structure in Colonial Boston," in *Cities in American History,* ed. Kenneth T. Jackson and Stanley K. Schultz (New York: Alfred A. Knopf, 1972), 68.

....

Notes to

A City

upon

a Hill

264

24 Gerald B. Warden, *Boston 1689–1776* (Boston: Little, Brown & Co., 1970), 68.

25 Caleb H. Snow, *A History of Boston: The Metropolis of Massachusetts from Its Origin to the Present Period with Some Account of the Environs,* 2d ed. (Boston: Abel Bowen, 1828), 160–161; Whitehill, *Boston: A Topographical History,* 19–20; Warden, *Boston 1689–1776,* 68.

26 Monkkonen, *America Becomes Urban* 65.

27 Ford Worthington Chauncey, ed., "Communications of Two Documents Protesting against the Incorporation of Boston," *Publications of the Colonial Society of Massachusetts* 10 (1904–1906):346.

28 Warden, *Boston 1689–1776,* 116–121.

29 Frank C. Brown, "John Smibert, Artist, and the First Faneuil Hall," *Old Time New England* 36 (1946):61–63.

30 Quincy, *Municipal History,* 11. Another prominent citizen's death bequest had led to the erection of the first townhouse for government use in 1657.

31 Jon C. Teaford, *The Municipal Revolution in America: Origins of Modern Urban Government, 1650–1825* (Chicago: University of Chicago Press, 1975), 43.

32 State Street Trust Co., *Boston's Growth,* 6.

33 Quincy, *Municipal History,* 7.

34 Sam Adams's comments appeared in the *Massachusetts Centinel and Republican Journal;* cited in Teaford, *The Municipal Revolution,* 68.

35 Herlihy, "Boston's Street System," 160–165.

2 The Great Selectman

1 Ellen Susan Bulfinch, ed., *The Life and Letters of Charles Bulfinch* (Boston: Houghton Mifflin, 1896), 59.

2 Workers of the Writers Program of the Works Progress Administration [WPA] on the State of Massachusetts, *Boston Looks Seaward: The Story of the Port, 1630–1940,* foreword and epilogue by William M. Fowler, Jr. (Boston: Northeastern University Press, 1985), 66–86.

3 Samuel Eliot Morison, *The Maritime History of Massachusetts, 1783–1860* (Boston: Houghton Mifflin Co., 1941), 125.

4 Writers of the WPA, *Boston Looks Seaward,* 71. Originally called the Charlestown Navy Yard, the name was changed in 1874 after Charlestown was annexed to Boston. It was called the Boston Navy Yard until 1945 when the name was again changed, this time to the Boston Naval Shipyard. See Bettina A. Norton, *The Boston Naval Shipyard, 1800–1974* (Boston: The Bostonian Society, 1975), 2.

5 Joseph L. Eldredge, ed., *Architecture Boston* (Barre, MA: Barre Publishing Co., 1976), 3.

6 Harold Kirker and James Kirker, *Bulfinch's Boston* (New York: Oxford University Press, 1964), 3–5, 40.

7 Quincy, *Municipal History,* 28–29. See also Bulfinch, *The Life and Letters of Charles Bulfinch,* 136, for Bulfinch's comments on his own contribution to the state law "giving power to the selectmen to widen streets and regulate pavements." Among today's streets widened during his tenure are Congress, Court, State, Hanover, Beacon, and Exchange.

8 John D. Forbes, "The Port of Boston, 1783–1815" (Ph.D. dissertation, Harvard University, 1936), 112.

9 Nathaniel B. Shurtleff, *A Topographical and Historical Description of Boston* (Boston:

Rockwell & Churchill, 1891), 355–356. Thirty years later the town had to pay $55,000 to repossess the land.

10 Kirker and Kirker, *Bulfinch's Boston,* 88, 40.

11 Christopher Tunnard and Henry Hope Reed, *American Skyline: The Growth and Form of Our Cities and Towns* (Boston: Houghton Mifflin Co., 1955), 62.

12 Douglass Shand-Tucci, *Built in Boston: City and Suburb 1800–1950* (Amherst: University of Massachusetts Press, 1988), 6.

13 Charles A. Place, *Charles Bulfinch: Architect and Citizen* (Boston: Houghton Mifflin Co., 1925), 56–69.

14 Kirker and Kirker, *Bulfinch's Boston,* 75.

15 Jane Holtz Kay, *Lost Boston* (Boston: Houghton Mifflin Co., 1980), 96.

16 Both the Massachusetts Historical Society, now located in the Fens, and the successor Boston Public Library, at Copley Square, exemplified the western migration of cultural institutions later in the century.

17 Place, *Charles Bulfinch,* 58–61, 40; Marjorie Drake Ross, *The Book of Boston: The Federal Period, 1775 to 1837* (New York: Hastings House Publishers, 1961), 86.

18 William M. Fowler, Jr., *The Baron of Beacon Hill: A Biography of John Hancock* (Boston: Houghton Mifflin Co., 1980), 278–279.

19 Carl Seaburg and Stephen Paterson, *Merchant Prince of Boston: Colonel T. H. Perkins, 1764–1854* (Cambridge: Harvard University Press, 1971), 119.

20 The threat of American involvement in European wars subsided, business began to return to normal, and by 1798 all of the homes in the Tontine Crescent were sold. Place, *Charles Bulfinch,* 71.

21 Samuel Eliot Morison, *Harrison Gray Otis, 1765–1848: The Urbane Federalist* (Boston: Houghton Mifflin Co., 1969), 219. The great Harvard historian was descended from Otis and his work is the basic account of Otis.

22 Matthew Edel, Elliott D. Sclar, and Daniel Luria, *Shaky Palaces: Home Ownership and Social Mobility in Boston's Suburbs* (New York: Columbia University Press, 1984), 198. This book analyzes the career of Otis, the history of developer Henry Whitney in the late nineteenth century, and the projects undertaken by Cabot, Cabot & Forbes in the 1950s and 1960s.

23 Morison, *The Urbane Federalist,* 372, 79. Morison suggests that Otis's aversion to the sea came from losses suffered by Otis's father and uncle.

24 Frederic Cople Jaher, "The Politics of the Boston Brahmins: 1800–1860," in *Boston 1700–1980: The Evolution of Urban Politics,* ed. Ronald P. Formisano and Constance K. Burns (Westport, CT: Greenwood Press, 1984), 69; Walter Firey, *Land Use in Central Boston* (Cambridge: Harvard University Press, 1947), 44.

25 Place, *Charles Bulfinch,* 67–68. Bulfinch had already designed the Connecticut state capitol in Hartford.

26 Harold Kirker, *The Architecture of Charles Bulfinch* (Cambridge: Harvard University Press, 1969), 104.

27 Morison, *The Urbane Federalist,* 76.

28 Whitehill, *Boston: A Topographical History,* 62; Kirker and Kirker, *Bulfinch's Boston,* 150.

29 Ross, *The Book of Boston: Federal Period,* 101; Kirker and Kirker, *Bulfinch's Boston,* 151, 158. Included among these homes was No. 85 Mount Vernon Street, designed by Bulfinch for Otis.

30 Whitehill, *Boston: A Topographical History,* 111.

31 Morison, *The Urbane Federalist,* 299, 219–220.

....

Notes to

The

Great

Selectman

266

32   Firey, *Land Use in Central Boston,* 46.

33   Morison, *The Urbane Federalist,* 219.

34   Robert Means Lawrence, *Old Park Street and Its Vicinity* (Boston: Houghton Mifflin, Co., 1922), 45–46; Nathaniel B. Shurtleff, *A Topographical and Historical Description of Boston* (Boston: Rockwell & Churchill, 1891), 309.

35   Kirker and Kirker, *Bulfinch's Boston,* 177.

36   Lawrence, *Old Park Street,* 30.

37   Allen Chamberlain, *Beacon Hill: Its Ancient Pastures and Early Mansions* (Boston: Houghton Mifflin Co., 1925), 188–189, 199–200. Louisburg Square was actually closed to traffic for a period in the 1850s in order to emphasize and assert the private way. Twenty years later barriers were again raised, and finally in another twenty years, 1895, this was recorded in the Suffolk County Deeds Office.

38   Kirker and Kirker, *Bulfinch's Boston,* 200.

39   Margaret Supplee Smith, "Between City and Suburb: Architecture and Planning in Boston's South End" (Ph.D. dissertation, Brown University, 1976), 28.

40   Whitehill, *Boston: A Topographical History,* 72. Site of present Blackstone and Franklin Squares.

41   Tunnard and Reed, *American Skyline,* 63–64; Herlihy, "Boston's Street System," 159–160.

42   Elizabeth Blackmar, *Manhattan for Rent, 1785–1850* (Ithaca: Cornell University Press, 1989), 97.

43   Laurence C. Gerckens, "Historical Development of American City Planning," in *The Practice of Local Government Planning,* ed. Frank S. So et al. (Washington, D.C.: International City Management Association, 1988), 26.

44   Schuyler, *The New Urban Landscape* 22.

45   Cited in Whitehill, *Boston: A Topographical History,* 74–75.

46   Winsor, *Memorial History of Boston,* 4:31.

47   Herlihy, "Boston's Street System," 165; Whitehill, *Boston: A Topographical History,* 77–78.

48   Kirker and Kirker, *Bulfinch's Boston,* 192–193.

49   Whitehill, *Boston: A Topographical History,* 76.

50   Place, *Charles Bulfinch,* 100; Whitehill, *Boston: A Topographical History,* 76–78; Morison, *The Urbane Federalist,* 223.

51   *Petition to the General Court for a Free Dam or Bridge from Wheeler's Point to South Boston* (Boston, 1805), 20. Manuscript copy in the Library of the Boston Athenaeum.

52   *Petition for a Free Dam or Bridge,* 21.

53   The great success of the first bridge was in providing a promenade for Bostonians seeking a fresh sea breeze and a panoramic view of the city. It was especially popular with young couples in courtship. The bridge was sold to the city two years after Otis completed his term as mayor of Boston.

54   Albert Lowell Cummings, "The Beginnings of India Wharf," *Proceedings of the Bostonian Society* 52 (1962):18–19.

55   John B. Blake, *Public Health in the Town of Boston, 1630–1822* (Cambridge: Harvard University Press, 1959), 222.

56   Whitehill, *Boston: A Topographical History,* 79–84.

57   Whitehill, *Boston: A Topographical History,* 79; Kirker and Kirker, *Bulfinch's Boston,* 186–187.

....

Notes to

The

Great

Selectman

267

58 Boston Town Records, August 3, 1807. *Boston City Document No. 115, 1807* (Boston: Municipal Printing Office, 1905), 224.

59 Place, *Charles Bulfinch,* 103.

60 Kirker and Kirker, *Bulfinch's Boston,* 91. Bulfinch's police role consisted of supervising two assistant police officers, seventeen constables, and thirty watchmen.

61 To provide some context to this matter, consider the case of Bulfinch's contemporary, the wealthy merchant Nathan Appleton. A man worth several hundred thousand dollars by 1815, he went to court in 1819 over a debt of $616.40 and forced a widow of a dry-goods merchant to turn over rental of her property to him and to go to jail. See Frances W. Gregory, *Nathan Appleton: Merchant and Entrepreneur, 1779–1861* (Charlottesville: University of Virginia Press, 1975), 137, 122.

62 Bulfinch, *The Life and Letters of Charles Bulfinch,* 128.

63 Kirker and Kirker, *Bulfinch's Boston,* 196.

64 Place, *Charles Bulfinch,* 199; Kirker and Kirker, *Bulfinch's Boston,* 86.

3 The Growth of a Metropolis

1 Robert Varnum Spalding, "The Boston Mercantile Community and the Promotion of the Textile Industry in New England, 1813–1860" (Ph.D. dissertation, Yale University, 1963), 11–13.

2 Robert F. Dalzell, Jr., *Enterprising Elite: The Boston Associates and the World They Made* (Cambridge: Harvard University Press, 1987), 43.

3 Writers of the WPA, *Boston Looks Seaward,* 93–94.

4 Stanley L. Kutler, *Privilege and Creative Destruction: The Charles River Bridge Case* (Baltimore: The Johns Hopkins University Press, 1971), 11.

5 Kutler, *Privilege and Creative Destruction,* 13.

6 Henry F. Graff, "The Charles River Bridge Case," in *Quarrels that Have Shaped the Constitution,* rev. and exp. ed., ed. John A. Garraty (New York: Harper & Row, 1987), 74–75.

7 Glaab and Brown, *A History of Urban America,* 23; Firey, *Land Use in Central Boston,* 91.

8 Henry C. Binford, *The First Suburbs: Residential Communities on the Boston Periphery, 1815–1860* (Chicago: University of Chicago Press, 1985), 10.

9 John Koren, *Boston 1822–1922: The Story of Its Government and Principal Activities During One Hundred Years* (Boston: City of Boston Printing Department, 1923), 10.

10 Robert McCaughey, "Josiah Quincy, 1772–1864" (Ph.D. dissertation, Harvard University, 1970), 264, 294. In 1823 Otis was busy running for governor and left the field clear for Quincy to win with a majority of 121 out of 4,766 votes cast.

11 Quincy, *Municipal History,* 376.

12 Koren, *Boston 1822–1922,* 11.

13 Richard G. Hewlett, "Josiah Quincy, Reform Mayor of Boston," *New England Quarterly* 24 (1951):195.

14 Thomas H. O'Connor, *South Boston: My Hometown, The History of an Ethnic Neighborhood* (Boston: Quinlan Press, 1988), 31.

15 Barbara Meil Hobson, *Uneasy Virtue: The Politics of Prostitution and the American Reform Tradition* (New York: Basic Books, 1987), 13–24.

16 Place, *Charles Bulfinch,* 114.

17 Quincy, *Municipal History,* 76.

18 Quincy, *Municipal History,* 76–82, 121.

....

Notes to

The

Great

Selectman

268

19 Cited in McCaughey, "Josiah Quincy," 289–295.

20 William Endicott, Frederick Stahl, Roger Webb, and Walter Muir Whitehill, *Faneuil Hall Markets Report* (Boston: Architectural Heritage Inc. and the Society for the Preservation of New England Antiquities for the Boston Redevelopment Authority, 1968), iii, 38, and Appendix C.

21 Robert A. McCaughey, *Josiah Quincy 1772–1864: The Last Federalist* (Cambridge: Harvard University Press, 1974), 112.

22 *Bowen's News Letter and City Record,* April 8, 1826, cited in McCaughey, "Josiah Quincy," 290.

23 Snow, *A History of Boston,* 377.

24 Samuel Adams Drake, *Old Landmarks and Historic Personages of Boston,* rev. ed. (Rutland, VT: Charles E. Tuttle Company, 1971), 128.

25 Oscar Handlin and Mary F. Handlin, *Commonwealth: A Study of the Role of Government in the American Economy: Massachusetts 1774–1861,* rev. ed. (Cambridge: Harvard University Press, 1969), 239.

26 Fern L. Nesson, *Great Waters: A History of Boston's Water Supply* (Hanover, NH: Published for Brandeis University by University Press of New England, 1983), 6.

27 Morison, *Urbane Federalist,* 1.

28 Morison, *Urbane Federalist,* 456–457.

29 Margaret Supplee Smith, "Between City and Suburb," 77–79. The second chapter of Smith's excellent study is devoted to planning in the South End and provides the basis for much of the following discussion.

30 Smith, "Between City and Suburb," 35.

31 Firey, *Land Use in Central Boston,* 60–63.

32 William H. Pease and Jane H. Pease, *The Web of Progress: Private Values and Public Styles in Boston and Charleston, 1828–1843* (New York: Oxford University Press, 1985), 38.

33 Morison, *Urbane Federalist,* 459.

34 Pease and Pease, *The Web of Progress,* 39.

35 Committee on Public Lands, "Estimates of the Values of the City Lands," *Boston City Document No. 45,* 1849, 2.

36 Kay, *Lost Boston,* 173–174.

37 Smith, "Between City and Suburb," 35, 41.

38 Smith, "Between City and Suburb," 10, 19, 42.

39 Stanley K. Schultz, *The Culture Factory: Boston Public Schools, 1789–1860* (New York: Oxford University Press, 1973), 249, 220.

40 Firey, *Land Use in Central Boston,* 63; for Smith's comments see his inaugural address in *Boston City Document No. 5,* 1854, and for more details on his administration see Joseph J. Fahey, *Boston's Forty-Five Mayors* (Boston: City Record, 1975), 13.

41 Whitehill, *Boston: A Topographical History,* 117, 174–175; Oscar Handlin, *Boston's Immigrants: A Study in Acculturation,* rev. and enl. ed. (New York: Atheneum, 1975), 93–94.

42 Schultz, *The Culture Factory,* 212.

43 Handlin, *Boston's Immigrants,* 89, 93–114.

44 *Report of the Committee on the Expediency of Providing Better Tenements for the Poor* (Boston: Eastburn's Press, 1846), 6.

45 Kay, *Lost Boston,* 212.

46 John P. Marquand, *The Late George Apley* (New York: Washington Square Press, 1963), 19.

....

Notes to

The Growth

of a

Metropolis

269

47 Lewis Mumford and Walter Muir Whitehill, *Back Bay Boston: The City as a Work of Art* (Dayton: Craftsman Type, Inc., 1969), 23. Whitehill's *Boston: A Topographical History* should be consulted for the story of nineteenth-century expansion of the land of Boston. See also chapter eight of Bainbridge Bunting's *Houses of Boston's Back Bay: An Architectural History, 1840–1917* (Cambridge: Belknap Press of Harvard University Press, 1967), which is devoted to the story of city planning in the Back Bay, and *Past Futures: Two Centuries of Imagining Boston* (Cambridge: Harvard University Graduate School of Design, 1985) by Alex Krieger and Lisa J. Green, which contains pictures of plans for the Back Bay.

48 Christopher R. Elliot, "The Boston Public Garden," *Proceedings of the Bostonian Society* 12 (1939), 29.

49 Robert Fleming Gourlay, *Plans for Beautifying New York and for Enlarging and Improving the City of Boston: Being Studies to Illustrate the Science of City Building* (Boston: Crocker & Brewster & Saxton Pierce, 1844).

50 Eliot, Graham, and Crane, "Boston: 300 Years of Planning," 43.

51 Gourlay, *Plans for Boston*, 8–12.

52 *Acts and Resolves of Massachusetts of 1856, Chapter 76*; Herlihy, "Boston's Street System," 154.

53 Whitehill, *A Topographical History*, 129.

54 Bunting, *Houses of Boston's Back Bay*, 389.

55 Mumford and Whitehill, *Back Bay Boston*, 20.

56 Cynthia Zaitzevsky, *Frederick Law Olmsted and the Boston Park System* (Cambridge: Belknap Press of Harvard University Press, 1982), 15.

57 Firey, *Land Use in Central Boston*, 66; *Acts and Resolves of Massachusetts of 1859, Chapter 183*, sec. 3 & 5.

58 James L. Bruce, "Filling in of the Back Bay and Charles River Development," *Proceedings of the Bostonian Society* 12 (1940), 27.

59 Firey, *Land Use in Central Boston*, 67.

60 M. Denman Ross, *Estimate of the Financial Effect of the Proposed Reservation of Back Bay Lands* (Boston: J. Wilson & Son, 1861), 19–20; see also Firey, *Land Use in Central Boston*, 68.

61 Reps, *The Making of Urban America*, 290.

62 Robert Morris Copeland, *The Most Beautiful City in America: Essay and Plan for the Improvement of the City of Boston* (Boston: Lee & Shephard, 1872), 10–12.

63 Copeland, *Essay and Plan*, 16.

64 Copeland, *Essay and Plan*, 22, 26, 36.

65 Copeland, *Essay and Plan*, 21–22, 46.

66 Sam Bass Warner, Jr., *Streetcar Suburbs: The Process of Growth in Boston, 1870–1900* (New York: Atheneum, 1972), 14, 18–19.

67 Jon C. Teaford, *City and Suburb: The Political Fragmentation of Metropolitan America, 1850–1970* (Baltimore: The Johns Hopkins University Press, 1979), 54–55.

68 *Acts and Resolves of Massachusetts of 1867*, Chapter 359.

69 Teaford, *City and Suburb*, 56.

70 *Boston Daily Advertiser*, June 22, 1869; *Acts and Resolves of Massachusetts of 1869*, Chapter 349.

71 *Acts and Resolves of Massachusetts of 1851*, Chapter 250; *Acts and Resolves of Massachusetts of 1873*, Chapter 314.

72 *Roslindale: Boston 200, Neighborhood History Series* (Boston: City of Boston, 1975), 1.

....

Notes to

The Growth

of a

Metropolis

270

73 *Acts and Resolves of Massachusetts of 1873,* Chapters 303 and 286.

74 Leo F. Schnore and Peter R. Knights, "Residence and Social Structure: Boston in the Ante-Bellum Period," in *Nineteenth-Century Cities: Essays in the New Urban History* ed. Stephan Thernstrom and Richard Sennett (New Haven: Yale University Press, 1969), 249 (table 2).

75 Kenneth T. Jackson, *Crabgrass Frontier: The Suburbanization of the United States* (New York: Oxford University Press, 1985), 149.

76 Koren, *Boston 1822–1922,* 155–159.

77 Charles P. Huse, *The Financial History of Boston, from May 1, 1822 to January 31, 1909* (Cambridge: Harvard University Press, 1916), 129; Whitehill, *Boston: A Topographical History,* 219.

78 Walter H. Kilham, *Boston after Bulfinch* (Cambridge: Harvard University Press, 1946), 85.

4 Building Downtown and around Town

1 Françoise Choay, *The Modern City: Planning in the Nineteenth Century* (New York: G. Braziller, 1970), 7.

2 Robert A. Woods and Albert J. Kennedy, *The Zone of Emergence: Observations of the Lower-Middle- and Upper-Working-Class Communities of Boston, 1905–1914,* 2d ed., abridged and edited with a preface by Sam Bass Warner, Jr. (Cambridge: MIT Press, 1969), 166–167; 122–123; 189.

3 Teaford, *The Unheralded Triumph: City Government in America, 1870–1900* (Baltimore: The Johns Hopkins University Press, 1986), 311–312.

4 Teaford, *The Unheralded Triumph,* 289–293.

5 Robert A. Silverman, "Nathan Matthews: Politics of Reform in Boston, 1890–1910," *New England Quarterly* 50 (1977):631.

6 Warner, *Streetcar Suburbs,* 4, 7.

7 Sam Gurvitz, quoted in *The North End: Boston 200, Neighborhood History Series* (Boston: Boston 200 Corporation, City of Boston, 1975), n.p.

8 Martin E. Marty, *Righteous Empire: The Protestant Experience in America* (New York: The Dial Press, 1970), 155–157.

9 Sam Bass Warner, Jr., *The Province of Reason* (Cambridge: Belknap Press of Harvard University Press, 1984), 98.

10 Kay, *Lost Boston,* 211.

11 John Harris, ed., "The Great Boston Fire, 1872, A Disaster with a Villain: Old Style Politics," *Boston Sunday Globe,* November 12, 1972, 71–72.

12 Harold Murdock, editor, *Letters Written by a Gentleman in Boston to his Friend in Paris Describing the Great Fire* (Boston: Houghton Mifflin Co., 1909), 46–47, 32.

13 Harris, "The Great Boston Fire," 25, 11.

14 Mumford and Whitehill, *Back Bay Boston,* 88.

15 Christine Rosen, *The Limits of Power: Great Fires and the Process of City Growth in America* (New York: Cambridge University Press, 1986), 179–182.

16 Rosen, *The Limits of Power,* 183–184.

17 Kilham, *Boston After Bulfinch,* 73.

18 Rosen, *The Limits of Power,* 187–190.

19 Warner, *The Urban Wilderness,* 22; Herlihy, "Boston's Street System," 159; Huse, *Financial History of Boston,* 130.

....

Notes to

Building

Downtown

and around

Town

271

20 Rosen, *The Limits of Power,* 201.

21 *Proceedings of the Boston City Council of 1872.* November 18, 1872, 357.

22 Henry L. Pierce, *The Inaugural Address of Henry L. Pierce, Mayor of Boston, to the City Council, January 6, 1873* (Boston: Rockwell & Churchill, City Printers, 1873), 11, 16.

23 Fahey, *Boston's Forty-Five Mayors,* 18.

24 Herlihy, "Boston's Street System," 168.

25 Rosen, *The Limits of Power,* 206.

26 Rosen, *The Limits of Power,* 207.

27 Rosen, *The Limits of Power,* 245, 236–237.

28 Marjorie Drake Ross, *The Book of Boston: The Victorian Period, 1837–1901* (New York: Hastings House Publishers, 1964), 91.

29 Robert A. Silverman, *Law and Urban Growth: Civil Litigation in the Boston Trial Courts, 1880–1900* (Princeton: Princeton University Press, 1981), 83.

30 Krieger and Green, *Past Futures,* 47.

31 Whitehill, *Boston: A Topographical History,* 171–172.

32 See Doreve Nicholaeff, "The Planning and Development of Copley Square," (M.A.A.S. thesis, Massachusetts Institute of Technology, 1979), especially 8–9, 27, 57, 69.

33 Winsor, *Memorial History,* 4:488.

34 Nicholaeff, "The Planning and Development of Copley Square," 75, 102.

35 Edel, Sclar, and Luria, *Shaky Palaces,* 198, 195, 264.

36 Warner, *Streetcar Suburbs,* 4, 37, 124.

37 Warner, *Streetcar Suburbs,* 31, 155–156.

38 Teaford, *The Unheralded Triumph,* 134–135, 6.

39 Warner, *Streetcar Suburbs,* 33.

40 Stephen Hardy, *How Boston Played: Sport, Recreation, and Community, 1865–1915* (Boston: Northeastern University Press, 1982), 83, 69–71.

41 Jon A. Peterson, "The Impact of Sanitary Reform upon American Urban Planning, 1840–1890," in *Introduction to Planning History in the United States,* ed. Donald A. Krueckeberg (New Brunswick, NJ: The Center for Urban Policy Research, Rutgers University, 1983), 29.

42 Richard E. Foglesong, *Planning the Capitalist City: The Colonial Era to the 1920s* (Princeton: Princeton University Press, 1986), 111.

43 Cynthia Zaitzevsky, *Frederick Law Olmsted and the Boston Park System* (Cambridge: Belknap Press of Harvard University Press, 1982), 51, 3.

44 Thomas Bender, *Toward an Urban Vision: Ideas and Institutions in Nineteenth-Century America* (Lexington: The University of Kentucky Press, 1975.

45 Geoffrey Blodgett, "Frederick Law Olmsted: Landscape Architecture as Conservative Reform," *Journal of American History* 62 (1976):872; see also Schultz, *Constructing Urban Culture,* 157.

46 Melvin Kalfus, *Frederick Law Olmsted: The Passion of a Public Artist* (New York: New York University Press, 1990), 272.

47 Laura Wood Roper, *F.L.O.: A Biography of Frederick Law Olmsted* (Baltimore: The Johns Hopkins University Press, 1973), 383.

48 Irving D. Fisher, *Frederick Law Olmsted and the City Planning Movement in the United States* (Ann Arbor, Michigan: UMI Research Press, 1986), 31.

49 Blodgett, "Olmsted," 884.

50 See the plans of Uriah Crocker (1869), Robert Copeland (1872), and the Parks Commission (1876) in Krieger and Green's *Past Futures,* 35.

....

Notes to

Building

Downtown

and around

Town

272

51 Dana F. White, "Frederick Law Olmsted, the Placemaker," in *Two Centuries of American Planning*, ed. Daniel Schaffer (Baltimore: The Johns Hopkins University Press, 1988), 101.

52 Hardy, *How Boston Played*, 82.

53 Roy Lubove, ed., *The Urban Community: Housing and Planning in the Progressive Era* (Englewood Cliffs, NJ: Prentice Hall, Inc., 1967), 4.

54 Mellier Goodin Scott, *American City Planning since 1890* (Berkeley: University of California Press, 1969), 17–20.

55 *Acts and Resolves of Massachusetts of 1892*, Chapter 342; *Acts and Resolves of Massachusetts of 1893*, Chapter 407.

56 Scott, *American City Planning Since 1890*, 23; Merino, "A Great City and Its Suburbs," 59.

57 Schuyler, *The New Urban Landscape*, 66–67.

58 Stanley K. Schultz and Clay McShane, "To Engineer the Metropolis: Sewers, Sanitation, and City Planning in Late-Nineteenth Century America," *Journal of American History* 65 (1978):395.

59 Metropolitan District Commission, "Origin, Development and Activities of the Metropolitan District Commission" (Boston: Commonwealth of Massachusetts, 1964), 2.

60 Huse, *Financial History of Boston*, 32.

61 Scott, *American City Planning Since 1890*, 19; *Acts and Resolves of Massachusetts of 1889*, Chapter 439.

62 *Acts and Resolves of Massachusetts of 1895*, Chapter 488; *Acts and Resolves of Massachusetts of 1901*, Chapter 168.

63 *Acts and Resolves of Massachusetts of 1919*, Chapter 350.

64 O'Connor, *Bibles, Brahmins, and Bosses*, 132–133.

65 Lawrence W. Kennedy, "Power and Prejudice: Boston Political Conflict, 1885–1895" (Ph.D. dissertation, Boston College, 1987), especially 120–129.

66 Hugh O'Brien, *Inaugural Address of Hugh O'Brien, Mayor of Boston, before the City Council, January 5, 1885* (Boston: Rockwell & Churchill 1885), 35.

67 O'Brien, *Inaugural Address of 1885*, 32–33; 61.

68 C. E. Norton to Frederick Law Olmsted, March 5, 1885, Olmsted Papers.

69 Thomas K. McCraw, *Prophets of Regulation: Charles Francis Adams, Louis D. Brandeis, James M. Landis, Alfred E. Kahn* (Cambridge: Belknap Press of Harvard University Press, 1984), 17.

70 Warner, *Streetcar Suburbs*, 23.

71 Charles W. Cheape, *Moving the Masses: Urban Public Transit in New York, Boston, and Philadelphia, 1880–1912* (Cambridge: Harvard University Press, 1980), 109–112.

72 Cornelius Dalton, John Wikkala, and Anne Thomas, *Leading the Way: A History of the Massachusetts General Court, 1629–1980* (Boston: Office of the Massachusetts Secretary of State, 1984), 176; Cheape, *Moving the Masses*, 115, 117–118.

73 Samuel Eliot Morison, *One Boy's Boston, 1887–1901* (Boston: Houghton Mifflin Co., 1962), 25.

74 Cheape, *Moving the Masses*, 119–120.

75 Cheape, *Moving the Masses*, 127–129.

76 Cheape, *Moving the Masses*, 131.

77 Brian Cudahy, *Change at Park Street Under: The Story of Boston's Subways* (Brattleboro, VT: S. Greene Press, 1972), 12. The vote was 15,369 to 14,928. Cheape, *Moving the Masses*, 142–143.

....

Notes to

Building

Downtown

and around

Town

273

78   Cudahy, *Change at Park Street Under,* 17.

79   Cheape, *Moving the Masses,* 145–146, 152.

80   Geoffrey T. Blodgett, "Josiah Quincy, Brahmin Democrat," *New England Quarterly* 38 (1965):435.

81   Silverman, *Law and Urban Growth,* 82, 92.

82   Lubove, *The Urban Community,* 2.

83   Glaab and Brown, *History of Urban America,* 150.

84   Michele M. Hilden, "The Mayors Josiah Quincy of Boston" (Ph.D. dissertation, Clark University, 1970), 133.

85   Blodgett, "Josiah Quincy," 443. Woods, interestingly, was committed to the concept of neighborhood planning at a time when most contemporary reformers viewed urban problems from a citywide perspective. See Christopher Silver, "Neighborhood Planning in Historical Perspective," *Journal of the American Planning Association* 51 (1985):162.

86   Hardy, *How Boston Played,* 94–95.

87   Scott, *American City Planning Since 1890,* 10.

88   See the street superintendent's complaint that "this practice is very objectionable" in the *Annual Report of the Street Department for the Year 1897. City Document No. 34, 1898.*

89   Blodgett, "Josiah Quincy," 440.

90   Blodgett, "Josiah Quincy," 450.

91   Josiah Quincy, *Valedictory Message of Josiah Quincy, Mayor of Boston, 1896–1899* (Boston: Municipal Printing Office, 1900), 37–38.

5   "A Bigger, Better, Busier Boston"

1   Russell B. Adams, *The Boston Money Tree* (New York: Thomas Y. Crowell Co., 1977), 203–211.

2   Robert W. Eisenmenger, *The Dynamics of Growth in the New England Economy, 1870–1964* (Middletown, CT: Wesleyan University Press, 1967), 19; Writers of the WPA, *Boston Looks Seaward,* 192–193, 209.

3   Writers of the WPA, *Boston Looks Seaward,* 151–170.

4   M. Christine Boyer, *Dreaming the Rational City,* 90.

5   Writers of the WPA, *Boston Looks Seaward,* 179–180; Whitehill, *Boston: A Topographical History,* 220.

6   Among the finest accounts of the era is Robert Wiebe's, *The Search for Order, 1877–1920* (New York: Hill & Wang, 1967).

7   Richard Hofstadter, *The Age of Reform: From Bryan to F.D.R.* (New York: Alfred A. Knopf, 1956).

8   Kenneth Fox, *Better City Government: Innovation in American Urban Politics, 1850–1937* (Philadelphia: Temple University Press, 1977), 42–53.

9   O'Connor, *Bibles, Brahmins, and Bosses,* 138.

10   The only in-depth treatment of Collins was done by M. Jeanne d'Arc O'Hare, C.S.J., in "The Public Career of Patrick Andrew Collins," Ph.D. dissertation completed at Boston College in 1959.

11   Steven P. Erie, *Rainbow's End: Irish-Americans and the Dilemmas of Urban Machine Politics, 1840–1985* (Berkeley: University of California Press, 1988), 46.

12   Patrick A. Collins, *Inaugural Address of Patrick A. Collins, Mayor of Boston, to the City Council, January 4, 1902* (Boston: Municipal Printing Office, 1902), 8.

....

Notes to

Building

Downtown

and around

Town

274

13 Shand-Tucci, *Built in Boston,* 188.

14 Michael Holleran and Robert Fogelson, "'The Sacred Skyline': Boston's Opposition to the Skyscraper, 1891–1928," (Cambridge: MIT Center for Real Estate Development, Working Paper #9, August, 1987), 9–13.

15 Holleran and Fogelson, "The Sacred Skyline," 16.

16 *Acts and Resolves of Massachusetts of 1892,* Chapter 419.

17 Holleran and Fogelson, "The Sacred Skyline," 20, 23.

18 Shand-Tucci, *Built in Boston,* 106.

19 *Acts and Resolves of Massachusetts of 1896,* Chapter 313.

20 *Acts and Resolves of Massachusetts of 1898,* Chapter 458.

21 Holleran and Fogelson, "The Sacred Skyline," 24–26.

22 *Acts and Resolves of Massachusetts of 1899,* Chapter 457; *Acts and Resolves of Massachusetts of 1902,* Chapter 543.

23 *Acts and Resolves of Massachusetts of 1904,* Chapter 333.

24 Lubove, *The Urban Community,* 9. Some believed that the architectural inspiration for the Columbian Expositions was Boston's new Public Library building at Copley Square, designed by McKim and White. McKim aided Olmsted in laying out the Exposition. Kay, *Lost Boston,* 246.

25 Howard P. Chudacoff and Judith E. Smith, *The Evolution of American Urban Society,* 3d ed. (Englewood Cliffs, NJ: Prentice-Hall, 1988), 195.

26 Chudacoff and Smith, *The Evolution of American Urban Society,* 196–197.

27 Foglesong, *Planning the Capitalist City,* 125.

28 Paul Boyer, *Urban Masses and Moral Order in America, 1820–1920* (Cambridge: Harvard University Press, 1978), 262; 272.

29 Henry Greenleaf Pearson, *Son of New England: James Jackson Storrow, 1864–1926* (Boston: Thomas Todd Co., 1932), 37.

30 *Report of the Metropolitan Improvement Commission* (Boston: Wright & Potter, 1909), 36; see also *Acts and Resolves of Massachusetts of 1907, Resolves,* Chapter 108.

31 *Report of the Metropolitan Improvement Commission,* 260, 45, 264–265.

32 Shurtleff, or Shurcliff, as he later renamed himself, was born in Boston in 1870 and earned degrees from MIT and Harvard. He was a pupil and colleague of Charles Eliot of Metropolitan Park fame. Shurtleff set out on his own and became Boston's leading landscape architect and an influential consultant to many towns, cities, and schools. His work included the redesign of Boston Common in 1918, Storrow Memorial Embankment, a major study of the Boston park system in 1925, and the gardens of the restored Williamsburg, Virginia.

33 *Report of the Metropolitan Improvement Commission,* 188.

34 Boston Society of Architects, *Report Made to the Boston Society of Architects by its Committee on Municipal Improvement* (Boston: Alfred A. Mudge & Son, 1907), 1.

35 For the pier scheme, see *Report Made to the Boston Society of Architects,* 25–26. For the island plan, see 11–14. Here too the committee made many comparisons to other cities which had islands similarly situated in famous rivers.

36 *Report Made to the Boston Society of Architects,* 8–9, 2.

37 *Report Made to the Boston Society of Architects,* 2.

38 See Herbert Marshall Zolot, "The Issue of Good Government and James Michael Curley: Curley and the Boston Scene from 1897–1918" (Ph.D. dissertation, State University of New York–Stony Brook, 1975), 23.

39 O'Connor, *Bibles, Brahmins, and Bosses,* 135–136.

....

Notes to

"A Bigger,

Better,

Busier

Boston"

275

40 Writers of the WPA, *Boston Looks Seaward*, 180.

41 Kay, *Lost Boston*, 274.

42 Francis Russell, *The Great Interlude: Neglected Events and Persons from the First World War to the Depression* (New York: McGraw-Hill Book Co., 1964), 176.

43 Doris Kearns Goodwin, *The Fitzgeralds and the Kennedys: An American Saga* (New York: Simon & Schuster, 1987), 134–135.

44 Hyde Park was incorporated as a town on April 22, 1868. It was annexed to Boston on January 1, 1912, *Acts and Resolves of Massachusetts of 1911*, Chapter 469 and 583.

45 *Hyde Park: Boston 200, Neighborhood History Series 7*, 16.

46 Koren, *The Story of Boston, 1822–1922*, 14.

47 Edward C. Banfield and Martha Derthick, *A Report on the Politics of Boston* (Cambridge: Joint Center for Urban Studies of MIT and Harvard University, 1960), 2:2.

48 Paul U. Kellogg, "Boston's Level Best: The '1915 Movement' and the Work of Civic Organizations for Which It Stands," *The Survey*, June 5, 1909, 382–395.

49 *New Boston* (May 1910), 5–10.

50 *New Boston* (May 1910), 7, 10–11, 13–15.

51 Fogelsong, *Planning the Capitalist City*, 126.

52 Glaab and Brown, *A History of Urban America*, 243–244.

53 Frederick Law Olmsted, Jr., "Address on City Planning," Second National Conference on City Planning, Rochester, NY, May 1910, in Lubove, ed. *The Urban Community*, 81.

54 *New Boston* (December 1910), 345.

55 Boston Chamber of Commerce, *"Real Boston": The 'Get Together' Spirit Among Cities and Towns* (Boston: Boston Chamber of Commerce, 1911), 2–4.

56 Scott, *American City Planning since 1890*, 116; Merino, "A Great City and Its Suburbs," 88.

57 Scott, *American City Planning since 1890*, 116.

58 *Acts and Resolves of Massachusetts of 1911*, Chapter 607.

59 Roy Lubove, *Community Planning in the 1920s* (Pittsburgh: University of Pittsburgh Press, 1964), 6.

60 *Report of the Homestead Commission* (Boston: Wright & Potter Printing Co., 1913), 36–38.

61 *Report of the Homestead Commission*, 42.

62 *Acts and Resolves of Massachusetts of 1913*, Chapter 494, Chapter 41; General Laws, Sections 70, 71, 72; Boston Ordinance, Chapter 6, 1913, approved January 27, 1914.

63 *First Annual Report of the City Planning Board*, 1915, 2, 17.

....

Notes to

"A Bigger,

Better,

Busier

Boston

276

6 James Michael Curley and the Old Boston

1 Shaun O'Connell, *Imagining Boston: A Literary Landscape* (Boston: Beacon Press, 1990), 121.

2 Ian Menzies, "Where's Boston? Is America's 'In' City Losing Its Soul?" *Bostonia* 61 (September/October 1987):30.

3 William Leuchtenberg, *The Perils of Prosperity, 1914–1932* (Chicago: The University of Chicago Press, 1958), 183.

4 O'Connor, *Bibles, Brahmins, and Bosses*, 148.

5 *East Boston: A Survey and Comprehensive Plan* (Boston: City of Boston Printing Department, 1916).

6 Glaab and Brown, *A History of Urban America*, 269. Although abandoned at the end of

the war these housing projects affected consideration of the housing issue and provided some precedent for the New Deal programs of the 1930s.

7   *Seventh Annual Report of the City Planning Board,* 1921, 28–29.

8   Lubove, *The Urban Community,* 14.

9   Boyer, *Urban Masses and Moral Order,* 268, 276.

10 Fogelsong, *Planning the Capitalist City,* 206.

11 Scott, *American City Planning since 1890,* 156–160; Glaab and Brown, *A History of Urban America,* 265.

12 Warner, *Streetcar Suburbs,* 122.

13 Article 60 of the Massachusetts Constitutional Amendments. The popular vote in the state was 161,214 in favor and 83,095 against while the corresponding figures in Boston were 34,953 in favor and only 8,673 against. Frederic H. Fay, "The Planning of a City," in *Fifty Years of Boston: A Memorial Volume Issued in Commemoration of the Tercentenary of 1930,* ed. Elisabeth M. Herlihy (Boston: Boston Tercentenary Committee, 1932), 50.

14 Chapter 40 of the General Laws, Sections 25–30.

15 *Acts and Resolves of Massachusetts of 1924,* Chapter 488.

16 Fay, "The Planning of a City," 51.

17 *Acts and Resolves of Massachusetts of 1923,* Chapter 462, Section 18.

18 *Acts and Resolves of Massachusetts of 1928,* Chapter 137. According to the legislation, a building could rise above 155 feet if the total building volume did not exceed the number of square feet of buildable area of the lot multiplied by 155 feet. It further required "that every part of such building or structure above a height equal to two and one half times the effective width of the street, but not exceeding one hundred and twenty-five feet, shall set back from every street and lot line one foot for each two and one half feet of additional height."

19 Michael Southworth and Susan Southworth, *The Boston Society of Architects' A.I.A. Guide to Boston* (Chester, CT: The Globe Pequot Press, 1987), 95. I also wish to acknowledge the research and assistance of Ann Pilcher, one of my students at Boston College, who wrote a paper titled "The United Shoe Machinery Corporation Building," Dec. 1987.

20 Sam Bass Warner, Jr., *The Private City,* 207.

21 Marc A. Weiss, *The Rise of the Community Builders: The American Real Estate Industry and Urban Land Planning* (New York: Columbia University Press, 1987), 54.

22 Scott L. Bottles, *Los Angeles and the Automobile: The Making of the Modern City* (Berkeley: University of California Press, 1987), 197.

23 Herlihy, *Fifty Years of Boston,* 53, 61.

24 Langtry, *Metropolitan Boston,* 3:1046.

25 Albert Bushnell Hart, ed., *Commonwealth History of Massachusetts, Colony, Province and State,* 5 v., 5:63, 89; Herlihy, "Boston's Street System," 163.

26 Charles Trout, *Boston: The Great Depression and the New Deal* (New York: Oxford University Press, 1977), 37; Hart, *Commonwealth History,* 5:89.

27 Herlihy, *Fifty Years of Boston,* 54.

28 See the *Tenth Annual Report of the City Planning Board,* 1923, Appendices 4–6.

29 Robert Whitten, ed., *Report on a Thoroughfare Plan for Boston* (Boston: City of Boston Planning Board, 1930), 14.

30 *Twenty-fifth Annual Report of the City Planning Board,* 1938, 20. *Sixteenth Annual Report of the City Planning Board,* 1929.

....

Notes to

James

Michael

Curley and

the Old

Boston

277

31 *Sixteenth Annual Report of the City Planning Board,* 1929, 8.

32 See Arthur Shurtleff, *A Special Report to the Boston Park Department* (Boston: City of Boston Park Department, 1925), 25–28.

33 Herlihy, *Fifty Years of Boston,* 57.

34 *Acts and Resolves of Massachusetts of 1929,* Chapter 229; *Acts and Resolves of Massachusetts of 1938,* Chapter 453.

35 Charles H. Trout, "Curley of Boston: The Search for Irish Legitimacy," in Formisano and Burns, *Boston 1700–1980,* 179.

36 Trout, "Curley of Boston," 181.

37 O'Connor, *Bibles, Brahmins, and Bosses,* 145.

38 Michael J. Ryan, "Where Did Curley Get the Cash?" *Boston Sunday Globe,* April 17, 1988, 91.

39 O'Connell, *Imagining Boston,* 125.

40 James Michael Curley, *I'd Do It Again: A Record of All My Uproarious Years* (Englewood Cliffs, NJ: Prentice-Hall, Inc., 1957), 220–221.

41 *Boston Herald,* July 11, 1946.

42 Banfield and Derthick, *A Report on the Politics of Boston,* 6:8–9.

43 Curley, *I'd Do It Again,* 220.

44 O'Connor, *Bibles, Brahmins, and Bosses,* 146–147.

45 For a useful discussion of the City Council, see William P. Marchione, Jr., "The 1949 Boston Charter Reform," *New England Quarterly* 44 (1976):373–398.

46 Trout, *Boston: The Great Depression,* 28–29.

47 Fahey, *Boston's Forty-Five Mayors,* 31.

48 Trout, *Boston: The Great Depression,* 98.

49 J. Joseph Huthmacher, *Massachusetts People and Politics, 1919–1933* (Cambridge: Harvard University Press, 1959), 218.

50 Trout, *Boston: The Great Depression,* 117.

51 Trout, *Boston: The Great Depression,* 142.

52 *Twenty-first Annual Report of the City Planning Board,* 1934.

53 Trout, "Curley of Boston," 186.

54 Trout, "Curley of Boston," 186–188.

55 See Marc Weiss, "The Origins and Legacy of Urban Renewal," in *Federal Housing Policy and Programs: Past and Present,* ed. J. Paul Mitchell (New Brunswick, NJ: Rutgers Center for Urban Policy Research, 1985), 253–276 for a fine debunking of some myths about the roots of urban renewal programs.

56 Cudahy, *Change at Park Street Under,* 50.

57 Trout, *Boston: The Great Depression,* 150–151; *Twenty-sixth Annual Report of the City Planning Board,* 1939, 9–10.

58 Mumford and Whitehill, *Back Bay Boston,* 26; William P. Marchione, *The Bull in the Garden: A History of Allston-Brighton* (Boston: Trustees of the Public Library of the City of Boston, 1986), 117.

59 Mark I. Gelfand, *A Nation of Cities: The Federal Government and Urban America, 1933–1965* (New York: Oxford University Press, 1975), 59; Glaab and Brown, *A History of Urban America,* 269–273.

60 Trout, *Boston: The Great Depression,* 14.

61 Glaab and Brown, *A History of Urban America,* 272–275.

62 *Twenty-second Annual Report of the City Planning Board,* 1935, 47.

63 Trout, *Boston: The Great Depression,* 152–153.

....

Notes to

James

Michael

Curley and

the Old

Boston

278

64 *Acts and Resolves of Massachusetts of 1933,* Chapter 364; *Acts and Resolves of Massachusetts of 1935,* Chapter 449, Section 262.

65 Glaab and Brown, *A History of Urban America,* 276; *Acts and Resolves of Massachusetts of 1938,* Chapter 484; Boston Housing Authority, *A Review of the Activities of the Boston Housing Authority, 1936–1940* (Boston, 1941), n.p.

66 Timothy L. McDonnell, S.J., *The Wagner Housing Act: A Case Study of the Legislative Process* (Chicago: Loyola University Press, 1957), 334–337.

67 Boston Housing Authority, *A Review of the Activities of the BHA,* n.p.

68 The United States Housing Authority (USHA) regulations established a maximum of $1.50 per square foot. Costs in these three Boston districts ranged from two to four dollars.

69 Fahey, *Boston's Forty-five Mayors,* 35.

70 Vincent A. Lapomarda, "Maurice Joseph Tobin: The Decline of Bossism in Boston," *New England Quarterly* 43 (1970):365.

71 Fahey, *Boston's Forty-five Mayors,* 36.

72 Joseph F. Dineen, *The Purple Shamrock: The Honorable James Michael Curley of Boston* (New York: W. W. Norton & Company, 1949), 291; Mark I. Gelfand, "Boston: Back to the Politics of the Future," in *Snowbelt Cities: Metropolitan Politics in the Northeast and Midwest since World War II,* ed. Richard M. Bernhard (Bloomington: Indiana University Press, 1990), 43; *Boston Globe,* January 19, 1946.

73 *Boston Globe,* November 29, 1947.

74 Adams, *The Boston Money Tree,* 305.

75 *The Boston Contest of 1944* (Boston: Boston University Press, 1944), 3; 10–15; 8.

76 Glaab and Brown, *A History of Urban America,* 281.

7 Collins, Logue, and the "New Boston"

1 Eisenmenger, *The Dynamics of Growth in the New England Economy,* 9.

2 Michael P. Conzen and George K. Lewis, *Boston: A Geographical Portrait* (Cambridge: Ballinger Publishing Company, 1976), 31.

3 Eisenmenger, *The Dynamics of Growth in the New England Economy,* 18.

4 Joint Center for Urban Studies of MIT and Harvard University, *Future Boston, Patterns and Perspectives* (Cambridge: Joint Center for Urban Studies, 1982), 13.

5 Adams, *The Boston Money Tree,* 278, 284.

6 Gelfand, *Nation of Cities,* 208, 164.

7 *General Plan for Boston: Preliminary Report* (Boston: City of Boston Planning Board, 1950), 63, 9.

8 Fahey, *Boston's Forty-five Mayors,* 38–40.

9 Banfield and Derthick, *Report on the Politics of Boston,* VI:9–10. See also *Christian Science Monitor,* August 9, 1954.

10 Boston Municipal Research Bureau, *Bulletin No. 158* (April 10, 1950), 1.

11 O'Connor, *Bibles, Brahmins, and Bosses,* 160.

12 Andrew Buni and Alan Rogers, *Boston: City on a Hill, An Illustrated History* (Woodland Hills, CA: Windsor Publications, Inc., 1984), 137–138.

13 Greater Boston Economic Study Committee, *Report on Downtown Boston* (Boston, 1959), n.p.

14 The BRA was created under former Massachusetts General Law (MGL), Chapter 121.

....

Notes to

Collins,

Logue, and

the "New

Boston"

279

In 1969, Chapter 121B of the MGL replaced MGL Chapter 121. *Acts and Resolves of Massachusetts of 1957,* Chapter 150.

15 *Forty-fourth Annual Report of the City Planning Board,* 1957, 9–10.

16 U.S. Housing Act of 1954, Title III. The 1954 legislation also substituted the term "urban renewal" for "urban development" and required a "Workable Program" with a land-use plan, zoning, relocation of displaced persons, building codes, and citizen participation.

17 *Thirty-ninth Annual Report of the City Planning Board,* 1952, 11; *Forty-second Annual Report of the City Planning Board,* 1955, 8.

18 Mel King, *Chain of Change: Struggles for Black Community Development* (Boston: South End Press, 1981), 21.

19 Marc Fried, *The World of the Urban Working Class: Boston's West End* (Cambridge: Harvard University Press, 1973), 53.

20 Author's interview with Monsignor Francis J. Lally on June 3, 1987, three months before Lally's death.

21 Herbert Gans, *Urban Villagers: Group and Class in the Life of Italian Americans,* up. and rev. ed. (New York: Free Press, 1982), 324–327.

22 Whitehill, *Boston: A Topographical History,* 201.

23 *1960 BRA Annual Report,* 4.

24 Gans, *Urban Villagers,* 324–325.

25 Author's interview with Jerome Rappaport, November 6, 1987.

26 *Boston Globe,* July 11, 1990, and March 18, 1991.

27 Jane Jacobs, *The Death and Life of Great American Cities* (New York: Vintage Books, 1961), 5.

28 Press release of The Travelers Insurance Company, September 17, 1959. The Travelers Historical Resource Center, Hartford, Connecticut.

29 Boston Housing Authority, *"Meeting the Promise,"* The BHA *1987 Annual Report* (Boston: Boston Housing Authority, 1987), 6.

30 William V. Shannon, "Boston's Irish Mayors: An Ethnic Perspective," in Formisano and Burns, *Boston 1700–1980,* 211.

31 Murray Levin, *The Alienated Voter: Politics in Boston* (New York: Holt, Rinehart and Winston, 1960), 1–2.

32 *City of Boston and County of Suffolk, Auditing Department Annual Report for the Fiscal Year Ending December 31, 1960* (Boston: City of Boston Printing Department, 1961), Schedule G-2, 114.

33 Adams, *The Boston Money Tree,* 307.

34 Eliot, Graham, and Crane, "Boston: Three Centuries of Planning," 46.

35 William V. Shannon, "Boston's Irish Mayors: An Ethnic Perspective," 211.

36 Author's interview with John F. Collins on September 23, 1987.

37 Author's interview with Edward J. Logue on November 23, 1987.

38 Walter McQuade, "Boston: What Can a Sick City Do?" *Fortune* 69 (June 1964):136.

39 Edward J. Logue, "Boston, 1960–1967: Seven Years of Plenty," *Proceedings of the Massachusetts Historical Society* 84 (1972): 86. Logue also pointed out that Graham, who left a year after Logue's program got under way, never got the credit he deserved for the basic work he began.

40 Joseph Slavet, at the time director of the Boston Municipal Research Bureau, was encouraged by Henry Shattuck, the chairman of the bureau, to aid in these successful negotiations. Author's interview with Joseph Slavet, September 23, 1987. Inter-

....

Notes to

Collins,

Logue, and

the "New

Boston"

280

estingly, another cross-harbor connector, the Mystic–Tobin Bridge, had been constructed and opened by a separate authority in 1949 and was subsequently taken over by yet another group, the Massachusetts Port Authority.

41 An Act Concerning the Development and Redevelopment of Blighted Open Areas, Decadent Areas and Sub-Standard Areas by Urban Redevelopment Corporations with Special Provisions for Projects in the City of Boston, Massachusetts General Law Chapter 121A, Chapter 652 of the Acts of 1960. Chapter 121A had been in effect since 1946 and allowed housing in blighted areas. The 1960 revision noted here allowed for commercial development in a designated blighted area. Other early 121A projects in Boston were the Tremont-Mason Building, a twenty-eight-story luxury apartment building overlooking the Common (completed in 1966) and the Jamaicaway Tower, a thirty-story residential tower. Edward J. Logue, *Seven Years of Progress: A Final Report* (Boston: Boston Redevelopment Authority, 1967), 87–88. Incidentally, the Tremont-Mason building was built, in part, on the site of four buildings owned by the George Robert White Fund, the sale of which was to provide an annual income to the city. *1962 Annual Report of the Boston Redevelopment Authority,* 19.

42 The legislation also removed the requirement of state or city council involvement in the granting of Chapter 121A tax agreements. These 121A agreements were now subject only to the approval of the mayor.

43 *1961 Annual Report of the Boston Redevelopment Authority,* 9; ii.

44 Author's interview with Edward J. Logue, November 23, 1987; and Logue, "Seven Years of Plenty," 90.

45 "The Ninety Million Dollar Development Program for Boston," *City Record,* September 24, 1960 (Vol. 52, Number 39), 759–774. The Plan was presented to the city council as a crisis issue and the council was reluctant to be seen as obstructionist. *Boston Traveler,* May 29, 1962.

46 "The Ninety Million Dollar Program," 760, 761, 772.

47 *Boston Herald,* October 21, 1960.

48 *1962 Annual Report of the Boston Redevelopment Authority,* 34–35.

49 *Acts and Resolves of Massachusetts of 1960,* Chapter 776.

50 *City Record,* January 28, 1961.

51 Kane Simonian, the first executive director and head of the BRA, had gone to court charging that the January 25 action of the board was a violation of the Civil Service Tenure Law guaranteed to all redevelopment authority staffers in the state. The Massachusetts State Supreme Court dismissed Simonian's suit in May 1961, stating that because the BRA had been reorganized with the Chapter 121A legislation, the granting of the post of BRA administrator to Logue was not a demotion for Simonian. Simonian was still with the BRA, as secretary to the board, into the 1990s.

52 *1961 Annual Report of the Boston Redevelopment Authority,* 2.

53 Stephan Thernstrom, *Poverty, Planning, and Politics in the New Boston: The Origins of A.B.C.D.* (New York: Basic Books, 1969), 6–7.

54 Edward J. Logue, "A Look Back at Neighborhood Renewal in Boston," *Policy Studies Journal* 16 (1987):344.

55 Author's interview with Ian Menzies on October 5, 1987.

56 David A. Crane, "Mayor Richard S. Daley Lights the Way for the Boston Renaissance," draft article for celebration of the Graduate School of Fine Arts, University of Pennsylvania, dated August 4, 1989, 5.

57 Anonymous, quoted in Michael D. Appleby, *Logue's Record in Boston: An Analysis of*

....

Notes to
Collins,
Logue, and
the "New
Boston"

281

His *Renewal and Planning Activities,* (New York: Council for New York Housing and Planning Policy, 1966), 15.

58   *Boston Sunday Herald,* December 5, 1965.

59   Logue, *Seven Years of Progress,* 11, 139. When the Scollay Square clearance began the West End was still essentially empty and the two projects created a gigantic cut through the city from the Charles River across to Faneuil Hall. See also Logue, "Seven Years of Plenty," 92.

60   Robert Taylor, "The Roving Eye," *Boston Herald,* July 31, 1962.

61   *Fortieth Annual Report of the City Planning Board,* 1953, 5–6; *Forty-third Annual Report of the City Planning Board,* 1956, 3.

62   Adams, Howard, and Greeley Inc., *Government Center—Boston 1959* (Boston: Prepared for the City Planning Board, 1959), 6.

63   H. D. Hodgkinson, "Miracle in Boston," *Proceedings of the Massachusetts Historical Society* 84 (1972):71–75.

64   Author's interview with John F. Collins, November 3, 1987. Another advocate for placing the federal building in the Scollay Square site was West End developer Jerome Rappaport who felt the Government Center project was critical to the success of his Charles River Park enterprise. Author's interview with Jerome Rappaport on November 6, 1987.

65   *1960 Annual Report of the Boston Redevelopment Authority,* 5.

66   Logue, "Seven Years of Plenty," 93. The Government Center project, which required relocation of a subway line, was also the first instance in the nation where the federal government subsidized a capital improvement in mass transit. Eliot, Graham, and Crane, "Boston: Three Centuries of Planning," 48.

67   *Boston Herald,* June 27, 1962.

68   *Boston Globe,* June 26, 1962.

69   *Boston Herald,* March 17, 1967.

70   Editorial in *Boston Herald,* October 26, 1954.

71   Supplement to *Boston Sunday Globe,* June 15, 1969.

72   *Boston Sunday Globe,* December 3, 1967.

73   Whitehill, *Boston: A Topographical History,* 102–103. Some of Gruen's more radical proposals, such as a second-story level walkway along West Street, failed to garner sufficient support and did not receive much attention from Mayor Collins. The committee was largely funded through the efforts of Edward Mitton, the head of Jordan Marsh, and H. D. Hodgkinson, the head of Filene's. Hodgkinson, "Miracle in Boston," 77.

74   "The Architects' Plan for Boston," *Journal of the American Institute of Architects,* January 1, 1962, 39.

75   *Boston Sunday Globe,* September 23, 1962.

76   See, e.g., *Record-American,* June 7, 1962.

77   *Traveler,* October 2, 1962.

78   Logue, *Seven Years of Progress,* 85. An earlier BRA publication claimed that this project "is proof that renewal can serve as a vehicle of private industrial and commercial development." *1962 Annual Report of the Boston Redevelopment Authority,* 16.

79   The Zoning Enabling Act was in *The Acts and Resolves in Massachusetts of 1956,* Chapter 665. It was amended by Chapter 77 of the Acts of 1957 to require city council approval of all members and to expand the number of commission members from nine to eleven.

····

Notes to

Collins,

Logue, and

the "New

Boston"

282

80   The zoning code was adopted by the Zoning Commission on March 29, 1963, and became effective December 31, 1964. The mayor appoints members of the Zoning Commission from among candidates proposed by a wide variety of professional and business organizations including the Associated Industries of Massachusetts, the AFL-CIO, the Greater Boston Real Estate Board, the Boston Society of Architects and others. For commentary on the BRA's continued involvement, see Logue, *Seven Years of Progress*, 137.

81   *Acts and Resolves of Massachusetts of 1955,* Chapter 616; *Acts and Resolves of Massachusetts of 1966,* Chapter 625.

82   Logue, *Seven Years of Progress,* 88.

83   The firm of Clark and Rapuano won the competition in 1984, construction began in late 1987, and the revamped park was reopened in June 1989.

84   *1965–1975 General Plan for the City of Boston and the Regional Core* (Boston: Boston Redevelopment Authority, 1964), 1.

85   *Acts and Resolves of Massachusetts of 1966,* Chapter 642.

86   *1965–1975 General Plan,* 53.

87   *1961 Annual Report of the Boston Redevelopment Authority,* 6; Logue, *Seven Years of Progress,* I.

88   Author's interview with Donald M. Graham on October 30, 1987.

89   *1961 Annual Report of the Boston Redevelopment Authority,* 21, 24. Lower priority areas were identified as East Boston, Jamaica Plain, South Boston, and the Back Bay, all of which lost population in the 1950s.

90   Langley C. Keyes, *The Rehabilitation Planning Game: A Study in the Diversity of Neighborhood* (Cambridge: MIT Press, 1969), 145, 159–160.

91   *1964 Annual Report of the Boston Redevelopment Authority,* 9. Among the efforts of the BRA in these early years of the Washington Park project was to arrange for mortgages for area residents through the Boston Banks Urban Renewal Group, which was composed of local savings and cooperative banks as well as federal loan associations. The BRA arranged for two employees of this group to be located at the site Rehabilitation office. *1963 Annual Report of the Boston Redevelopment Authority,* 1:2–3.

92   For population and property value estimates, see the *1962 Annual Report of the Boston Redevelopment Authority,* 10; for the initial redevelopment plans, see the *1963 Annual Report of the Boston Redevelopment Authority,* 5:1.

93   Keyes, *The Rehabilitation Game,* 99–100.

94   *Record-American,* January 15, 1963.

95   Author's interview with Monsignor Francis J. Lally on June 3, 1987.

96   Keyes, *The Rehabilitation Game,* 118–119, 129, 136–137.

97   *Record-American,* January 23, 1963.

98   Correspondence to the author dated May 31, 1988.

99   Thernstrom, *Poverty and Planning,* 9.

100   Thernstrom, *Poverty and Planning,* 128.

101   Thernstrom, *Poverty and Planning,* 163.

102   Editorial in *Boston Globe,* June 7, 1967.

103   *Boston Sunday Herald,* December 5, 1965.

104   Quoted in "Lots & Blocks" by Jerry Ackerman and Matt Carroll, *Boston Sunday Globe,* July 1, 1990.

105   *Herald Traveler,* July 30, 1967.

....

Notes to

Collins,

Logue, and

the "New

Boston"

283

8 Kevin White and a "World-Class City"

1   Ronald P. Formisano, *Boston Against Busing: Race, Class, and Ethnicity in the 1960s and 1970s* (Chapel Hill: University of North Carolina Press, 1991), 58.

2   *Boston Globe,* October 27, 1987.

3   Anthony J. Lukas, *Common Ground: A Turbulent Decade in the Lives of Three American Families* (New York: Alfred A. Knopf, 1985), 589.

4   Interview with Kevin White by John Robinson, *Boston Globe,* February 7, 1991, 8.

5   *Boston Globe,* February 15, 1967.

6   *Boston Globe,* June 12, 1967.

7   *City Record,* July 20, 1968. Vol. 60. No. 29.

8   Research Department, Boston Redevelopment Authority, *Boston Present and Future; Background Information for Infrastructure Planning* (Boston: Boston Redevelopment Authority, 1983), 14.

9   Martha Wagner Weinberg, "Boston's Kevin White: A Mayor Who Survives," in Formisano and Burns, *Boston 1700–1980,* 222–223.

10 Author's interview with Kevin H. White, November 13, 1987.

11 Alan Lupo, Frank Colcord, and Edmund P. Fowler, *Rites of Way: The Politics of Transportation in Boston and the U.S. City* (Boston: Little, Brown & Co., 1971), 14.

12 The BRA was responsible for land acquisition for the highway because of the area's inclusion in the urban renewal program.

13 This successful effort too saw a major resolution in 1987 when the rapid transit and park project of the Southwest Corridor opened in the spring.

14 Lupo, Colcord, and Fowler, *Rites of Way,* 60. Fred Salvucci characterized this group as rhetorically pro-transit but increasingly and more deeply rooted in an attitude of opposition to the disruption of local communities, Author's interview with Frederick Salvucci, December 18, 1987.

15 Lupo, Colcord, and Fowler, *Rites of Way,* 46.

16 Author's interview with Kevin H. White, November 13, 1987.

17 Former Governor Volpe was furious at his successor and refused to speak to Sargent for six months. Volpe felt that the rail and highway were both badly needed and since land was already taken, people relocated, and houses destroyed, the project should be completed. Kathleen Kilgore, *John Volpe: The Life of an Immigrant's Son* (Dublin, NH: Yankee Books, 1987), 183.

18 Author's interview with Frederick Salvucci on December 18, 1987. Also see *Boston Globe,* December 6, 1987.

19 Other legacies of the Boston Transportation Planning Review included the state assumption of MBTA deficits and the creation of local mass transit authorities throughout the state. Salvucci interview.

20 Judeth Van Hamm Wiers, *Facts and Fictions of Community Participation: The Boston Experience* (Boston: Boston Redevelopment Authority, 1973), 3. Champion served as director of the BRA for less than two years, following F. X. Cuddy, who had succeeded Ed Logue. Cuddy had been Mayor Collins's assessment commissioner and was seen as an interim administrator. John Rosenblum, "The Boston Redevelopment Authority" (Case study: Harvard Business School, 1969).

21 Kenney, a Harvard M.B.A. who was a management consultant with Price, Waterhouse, had served eighteen months within city hall as director of the Public Facilities Department. *Christian Science Monitor,* January 15, 1971.

....

Notes to

Kevin White

and a

"World-Class

City"

284

22 Author's interview with John Weis, November 18, 1987.

23 Ian Menzies column, *Boston Globe,* December 1, 1980; Barbara Ferman, *Governing the Ungovernable City: Political Skill, Leadership, and the Modern Mayor* (Philadelphia: Temple University Press, 1985), 118; Author's interview with Phil Zeigler on November 5, 1987.

24 *Acts and Resolves of Massachusetts of 1971,* Chapter 1097.

25 *Boston Globe,* April 24, 1968.

26 Abt Associations, *Financial Settlement, South End Urban Renewal Project (Mass. R-56): Final Environmental Impact Statement.*" Prepared for the Boston Redevelopment Authority and Office of Federal Compliance, City of Boston, 1979.

27 John H. Mollenkopf, *The Contested City* (Princeton: Princeton University Press, 1983), 210.

28 Author's interview with Frederick P. Salvucci, December 18, 1987.

29 George V. Higgins, *Style Versus Substance: Boston, Kevin White and the Politics of Illusion* (New York: Macmillan Publishing Company, 1984), 144–145.

30 Colin S. Diver, "Park Plaza" (Case Program, Kennedy School of Government, Harvard University), (A) 4.

31 Lukas, *Common Ground,* 621.

32 Ferman, *Governing the Ungovernable City,* 177–178.

33 Diver, "Park Plaza," (A) 5–9.

34 Diver, "Park Plaza," (B) 1–4; (C) 1.

35 Ferman, *Governing the Ungovernable City,* 180–181. White was largely effective in keeping the opposition to Park Plaza from doing battle in the legal arena and Ferman argues he scared the business interests on issues such as taxing, zoning, and assessing powers.

36 Author's interview with Robert Kenney on November 18, 1987.

37 Christopher Carlaw, *A Decade of Development in Boston* (Boston: Boston Redevelopment Authority, 1979), 25.

38 Bernard J. Frieden and Lynne Sagalyn, *Downtown, Inc.* (Cambridge: MIT Press, 1989), 107.

39 Ian Menzies, "The Faneuil Hall Marketplace: Window on New England," *Blair and Ketchum's Country Journal* (April 1979), 50–51.

40 *Boston Globe,* May 17, 1974.

41 A tax letter of agreement gave a three-year property tax abatement after which the property taxes would be set at 25 percent of gross rental income. As economist Jeff Brown concluded in the late 1980s, "Although this would be a giveaway by today's standards, the circumstances of the time called for a strong incentive to the private developer." Jeffrey P. Brown, "Boston" in *Cities Reborn,* ed. Rachelle Levitt (Washington, DC: Urban Land Institute, 1987), 30.

42 Frieden and Sagalynn, *Downtown, Inc.,* 173.

43 *Acts and Resolves of Massachusetts of 1975,* Chapter 772.

44 Another example might be 60 State Street which was a hole in the ground for several years until Cabot, Cabot, & Forbes finally met the mayor's desires and was allowed to construct the present office building.

45 Ferman, *Governing the Ungovernable City,* 182. It has been suggested by at least one observer that this conflict was needless as the BRA's own studies indicated the need for at least a dozen hotels. Much energy by many potential hotel developers was wasted over just this one site. The Robert L. Farrell quote is from author's interview on April 17, 1991.

....

Notes to

Kevin White

and a

"World-Class

City"

285

46 Author's interview with Kevin White, November 13, 1987.

47 The BRA furthered this development in the 1970s by encouraging and assisting other companies, most notably Stone and Webster, to locate in this section of Boston. Kenney interview, November 18, 1987. This BRA effort continued in the late 1980s with zoning proposals to encourage building at either South Station or North Station rather than in the more built-up central business district.

48 Jeffrey P. Brown, "Boston," in *Cities Reborn,* ed. Rachelle L. Levitt (Washington, D.C.: Urban Land Institute, 1987), 38.

49 *Boston's Adult Entertainment District* (Boston: City of Boston, 1976), n.p.

50 Gregory W. Perkins, *Twenty-Two Years of Boston's Fiscal Record: A Review of Expenditure and Revenue Trends for Boston City Government, 1960–1982* (Boston: Boston Redevelopment Authority, 1983), 2.

51 BRA, *Boston Present and Future,* 1.

52 The plan for Lafayette Place was for the city to build a garage and then lease it to Mondev developers, but when the city lost its bond rating and the site continued to be a hole in the ground, the developer finally built the garage and sold it back to the city, which now leases it back to the developer.

53 *Boston Globe,* November 20, 1982.

54 *Boston Globe,* April 14, 1989.

55 *Boston Globe,* April 22, 1989.

56 *Boston Globe,* May 28, 1990. Former prosecutors felt that White's statement was the missing link in the investigation although beyond the statute of limitations for any charges.

57 *Boston Globe,* January 29 and 30, 1989.

58 Tilo Schabert, *Boston Politics: The Creativity of Power* (New York: Walter de Gruyter, 1989), 304.

59 Mark I. Gelfand, "Back to the Politics of the Past," 54.

60 See Alexander Ganz, "Where Has the Urban Crisis Gone? How Boston and Other Large Cities Have Stemmed Economic Decline," *Urban Affairs Quarterly* 20 (1985):449–468.

9 Flynn, Coyle, and the Boom

1 Author's interview with Raymond L. Flynn, April 24, 1991.

2 Thomas H. O'Connor, *South Boston, My Home Town: The History of an Ethnic Neighborhood* (Boston: Quinlan Press, 1988), 231.

3 John Powers, "In Like Flynn," *Boston Globe Magazine,* January 13, 1991, 22.

4 Author's interview with Raymond L. Flynn, April 24, 1991.

5 Author's interview with Clarence "Jeep" Jones, April 25, 1991. Jones served as deputy mayor to Kevin White who later appointed him to the BRA board. Under Flynn, Jones became chairman of the BRA in May 1989.

6 *Boston Globe,* April 25, 1991.

7 See Jeffrey P. Brown, *Who Works in Boston: Commuting Patterns in the Boston Metropolitan Area, 1980* (Boston: Boston Redevelopment Authority, 1984), 4.

8 Mindy Blodgett, "A Fresh Start in Boston, Too," *Progressive* 49 (June 1985):23.

9 Author's interview with Robert L. Farrell, April 17, 1991.

10 John Powers, "Boston's 21st Century Man: BRA Director Stephen F. Coyle," *Boston Globe Magazine,* June 1, 1986, 32, 24.

....

Notes to

Kevin White

and a

"World-Class

City"

286

11 John King, "How the BRA Got Some Respect: Boston Redevelopment Agency Believes in Doing It All," *Planning*, May 1990, 7.

12 Author's interview with Ian Menzies, October 5, 1987.

13 Robert Amatruda, *The Boston Class-A Office Market, Year-End 1990 and Quarterly Projections, 1991–1996* (Boston: Boston Redevelopment Authority, 1991), Table 6.

14 Powers, "Coyle," 26.

15 Quoted in *Boston Globe*, October 27, 1987.

16 John Powers, "Sky King: International Place Developer Don Chiofaro," *Boston Globe Magazine*, May 13, 1990, 18.

17 *Boston Globe*, October 24, 1987.

18 Robert Campbell, "Commentary," *Boston Globe*, January 22, 1988.

19 Powers, "Coyle," 24–26.

20 Source: City of Boston Assessing Department.

21 John Avault, Memorandum to Stephen Coyle, February 9, 1989, "The Role of Development Property Tax Revenues in Boston City Budget: Is the City Dependent on Development Revenues?"

22 In Fiscal Year (FY) 1985 the additional revenue from these new projects equaled $11.9 million. The additional tax levy on such new construction of major commercial projects in FY 1986 was $11.7 million. New construction of major commercial projects added $6.2 million to city tax revenues in FY 1987. New construction projects swelled tax revenues for Boston by $9.4 million in FY 1988. The FY 1989 total was $8.7 million and even with a recession in 1990 new construction added another $9.7 million to the city's tax revenues. The total additional property tax revenue for new construction of major projects in FY 1991 came to $6.2 million. John Avault, memorandum to Alexander Ganz, February 22, 1991, "Estimates of Boston Building Permit and Tax Revenue Attributable to BRA Managed Development" (draft).

23 John Powers, "Unbuilt Boston," *Boston Globe Magazine*, December 30, 1990, 14.

24 BRA, *Downtown Projects: Opportunities for Boston* (Boston: Boston Redevelopment Authority, 1984), 79.

25 Author's interview with Stephen Coyle, February 26, 1991.

26 Robert Campbell, column in *Boston Globe*, October 13, 1987.

27 Margaret Pantridge, "City By Coyle," *Boston Magazine*, July 1988, 54–55.

28 Jane Holtz Kay column, *Boston Globe*, December 30, 1990.

29 Jane Holtz Kay, "The Limits of Growth: Boston's Downtown Plan," *Progressive Architecture* 66 (October 1985):29.

30 King, "How the BRA Got Some Respect," 9.

31 Author's interview with Linda Bourque, June 26, 1990.

32 Author's interview with Homer Russell, May 7, 1991.

33 Article 28 of the Boston Zoning Code, Section 28–1.

34 King, "How the BRA Got Some Respect," 5.

35 Author's interview with James K. Flaherty, May 7, 1991.

36 "Resolution of the Boston Redevelopment Authority regarding disposition policies for the Kingston-Bedford Garage, Essex Street Lot, and Parcel 18," *BRA Document No. 4805*, September 25, 1986.

37 Author's interview with Raymond L. Flynn, April 24, 1991.

38 Author's interview with Michael F. Donlan, October 31, 1991.

39 Address of Mayor Raymond L. Flynn, "New Zoning and Development Rules: A Blueprint for Boston's Future," delivered at John Hancock Hall, Boston, May 11, 1987.

....

Notes to

Flynn,

Coyle, and

the Boom

287

40 Richard Green, "Coyle in Command: A Candid Interview with Stephen Coyle, the Outspoken Director of the Boston Redevelopment Authority," *S/F: New England's Real Estate Magazine,* August 1987, 22.

41 BRA, *Downtown Projects II: Opportunities for Boston,* 2.

42 W. Dennis Keating, "Linking Downtown Development to Broader Community Goals," *Journal of the American Planning Association* 52 (Spring 1986): 136–137.

43 *BRA Document No. 4805,* September 25, 1986, 9.

44 *Linkage: Building Affordable Homes* (Boston: City of Boston, 1991), n.p.

45 Letter of Raymond L. Flynn, mayor of Boston to Robert L. Farrell, chairman, Boston Redevelopment Authority, September 25, 1986. Attached to *BRA Document No. 4805,* September 25, 1986.

46 Author's interview with Stephen Coyle, February 26, 1991.

47 Calculations by John Avault, deputy director, Policy Development and Research, Boston Redevelopment Authority.

48 *Linkage: Building Affordable Homes,* 6.

49 Author's interview with Stephen Coyle, February 26, 1991.

50 Source: Office of Neighborhood Housing and Development, Boston Redevelopment Authority, March 1991.

51 Green, "Coyle in Command," 22.

52 Hubie Jones column, *Boston Herald,* October 25, 1987.

53 Author's interview with Clarence Jones, April 25, 1991.

54 Author's interview with Stephen Coyle, February 26, 1991.

55 Norman Boucher, "The Death and Life of Dudley: A Lesson in Urban Economics," *Boston Globe Magazine,* April 8, 1990, 53.

56 Author's interview with Robert L. Farrell, April 17, 1991.

57 Author's interview with James K. Flaherty, May 7, 1991.

58 Author's interview with Homer Russell, May 7, 1991.

59 *Boston Globe,* September 6, 1991; *Boston Business Journal* September 30, 1991.

60 Boston Zoning Code, Article 42A, Amendment.

61 "Boston According to Coyle: A Q&A with the City's Chief Planner," *Boston Globe,* January 27, 1991.

62 David Nyhan, "Assessing the Mayor," *Boston Globe,* May 7, 1991.

63 *City Record,* 83, no. 11 (March 18, 1991): 1.

64 *Boston Globe,* May 7, 1991.

65 *Boston Globe,* November 14, 1990.

66 *Boston Globe,* May 14, 1991. Ceremonies honoring the formal start of what is termed "the $5 billion Central Artery/Third Harbor Tunnel Project" were held on C Street near Northern Avenue in South Boston. Governor William Weld, Mayor Raymond L. Flynn, Senator John Kerry, and other public officials participated.

67 Richard Taylor, address at the *Boston Herald* Forum on the Central Artery/Tunnel Project, Federal Reserve Bank of Boston auditorium, May 3, 1991.

68 *Boston Globe,* July 11, 1991.

69 *Boston 2000: A Plan for the Central Artery Progress Report* (Boston: Boston Redevelopment Authority, 1991), 1.

70 *1991 Summary Boston 2000: A Plan for the Central Artery Air Rights* (Boston: City of Boston, 1991), n.p.

71 *Boston 2000: A Plan for the Central Artery,* 2.

72 Author's interview with Stephen Coyle, October 11, 1991.

....

Notes to

Flynn,

Coyle, and

the Boom

288

73 *Boston Herald,* June 11, 1991.

74 Joseph Moakley, quoted in Daniel Golden, "Massachusetts Muscle," *Boston Globe Magazine,* September 29, 1991, 24.

75 *Boston Globe,* June 12, 1991.

76 Margaret Pantridge, "The Power Failure," *Boston Magazine,* October 1991, 93.

77 John Strahinich, "How Fast is Ray Flynn?" *Boston Magazine,* September 1991, 118.

78 James Green, "The Making of Mel King's Rainbow Coalition: Political Changes in Boston, 1963–1983," in *From Access to Power: Black Politics in Boston,* ed. James Jennings and Mel King (Rochester, VT: Schenkman Books, 1986), 126–127.

79 *Boston Globe,* July 28, 1991.

80 *Building Boston's Economic Future: An Agenda for Economic Development* (Boston: City of Boston, 1991), 1–4.

81 *Building Boston's Economic Future,* 36.

Conclusion

1 Mark I. Gelfand, "Rexford G. Tugwell and the Frustration of Planning in New York," *Journal of the American Planning Association* 51 (Spring 1985): 156.

2 Robert Caro, *The Power Broker: Robert Moses and the Fall of New York* (New York: Alfred A. Knopf, 1974), 467.

3 Keyes, *The Rehabilitation Game,* 28.

Bibliography

....

A. Primary Source Material

1. Government Documents

Boston Housing Authority. *Meeting the Promise: The BHA 1987 Annual Report.*
————. *A Review of the Activities of the Boston Housing Authority, 1936–1940.* Boston, 1941.
Boston Redevelopment Authority. *Annual Reports: 1959–1964, 1966.*
————. *Boston's Adult Entertainment District.* 1976.
————. *Boston 2000: A Plan for the Central Artery.* 1991.
————. *Downtown Projects: Opportunities for Boston.* 1984.
————. *1965–1975 General Plan for the City of Boston and the Regional Core.* 1965.
————. *Planning Boston's Next Decade of Development, 1980–1990.* 1980.
Boston City Council. Committee on Public Lands. *Report of a Subcommittee of the Committee on Public Lands.* Boston City Document No. 45, 1849.
————. *Proceedings of the City Council, 1872.*
Boston City Planning Board. *Annual Reports of the City Planning Board, 1914–1959.*
————. *General Plan for Boston: Preliminary Report.* 1950.
————. *Zoning for Boston: A Survey and Comprehensive Plan.* 1924.
————. *Building a Better Boston: Renewal for Roxbury.* 1958.
————. *East Boston: A Survey and Comprehensive Plan.* 1916.
Boston Street Department. *Annual Report of the Street Department for the Year 1897. Boston City Document No. 34,* 1898.
Champion, Hale. *Final Report of Hale Champion, Director, Boston Redevelopment Authority, to Kevin H. White, Mayor of Boston.* Boston: Boston Redevelopment Authority, August 28, 1969.
City of Boston. *A Volume of Records Relating to the Early History of Boston Containing Boston Town Records, 1796 to 1813.* Boston: Municipal Printing Office, 1905.
City of Boston and Suffolk County. Auditing Department. *Auditing Department Annual*

Report for the Fiscal Year ending December 31, 1960. Boston: City of Boston Printing Department, 1961.

Clarke, Eliot C. *Main Drainage Works of the City of Boston.* Boston: Rockwell & Churchill, City Printers, 1885.

Collins, John F. "The Ninety Million Dollar Development Program for Boston." *City Record,* September 24, 1960 (Vol. 52, Number 39): 759–774.

Collins, Patrick A. *Inaugural Address of Patrick A. Collins, Mayor of Boston, to the City Council, January 4, 1902.* Boston: Municipal Printing Office, 1902.

Committee on the Expediency of Providing Better Tenements for the Poor. *Report of the Committee on the Expediency of Providing Better Tenements for the Poor.* Boston: Eastburn's Press, 1846.

Commonwealth of Massachusetts. *Acts and Resolves of the General Court.* (Annual publication of the Massachusetts Secretary of State.)

Flynn, Raymond L. *A Blueprint for Boston's Future: New Zoning and Development Rules.* Boston: Address delivered at the John Hancock Hall, May 11, 1987.

Homestead Commission. *Report of the Homestead Commission.* Boston: Wright & Potter Printing Co., 1913.

Logue, Edward J. *Seven Years of Progress: A Final Report.* Boston: Boston Redevelopment Authority, 1967.

Metropolitan Improvement Commission. *Report of the Metropolitan Improvement Commission.* Boston: Wright & Potter Printing Co., 1909.

O'Brien, Hugh. *Inaugural Address of Hugh O'Brien, Mayor of Boston, before the City Council, January 5, 1885.* Boston: Rockwell & Churchill, 1885.

Pierce, Henry L. *The Inaugural Address of Henry L. Pierce, Mayor of Boston, to the City Council, January 6, 1873.* Boston: Rockwell & Churchill, 1873.

Quincy, Josiah. *Valedictory Message of Josiah Quincy, Mayor of Boston, 1896–1899.* Boston: Municipal Printing Office, 1900.

Shurtleff, Arthur A. *Special Report to the Boston Parks Department.* Boston: City of Boston Parks Department, 1925.

Smith, Jerome V. C. *Inaugural Address before the Boston City Council.* Boston City Document No. 5, 1854.

Whitten, Robert, ed. *Report on a Thoroughfare Plan for Boston.* Boston: City of Boston Planning Board, 1930.

2. *Planning Proposals and Papers*

Abt Associates. *Financial Settlement, South End Urban Renewal Project* (Mass. R-56): Final Environmental Impact Statement. Prepared for the Boston Redevelopment Authority and Office of Federal Compliance, City of Boston, 1979.

Adams, Howard and Greeley, Inc. *Government Center–Boston 1959.* Boston: Prepared for the City Planning Board, 1959.

Boston Chamber of Commerce. *"Real Boston:" The 'Get Together' Spirit among Cities and Towns.* Boston: Chamber of Commerce, 1911.

———. *Report on City Planning in Relation to the Street System in the Boston Metropolitan District.* Boston: Chamber of Commerce, 1914.

———. *Report on the Street System.* Boston: Chamber of Commerce, 1914.

The Boston Contest of 1944. Boston: Boston University Press, 1944.

Boston Municipal Research Bureau. "Bulletin No. 158," April 10, 1950.

Boston–1915 Committee. "A Plan for a Boston Plan," *The Survey* 22 (June 5, 1909): 396.

Boston Society of Architects. *Report Made to the Boston Society of Architects by its Committee on Municipal Improvements*. Boston: Alfred Mudge & Sons, Inc., 1907.

Copeland, Robert Morris. *The Most Beautiful City in America: Essay and Plan for the Improvement of the City of Boston*. Boston: Lee & Shephard, 1872.

Endicott, William, Frederick Stahl, Roger Webb, and Walter Whitehill. *Faneuil Hall Markets Report*. Boston: Prepared for the Boston Redevelopment Authority by Architectural Heritage, Inc. and the Society for the Preservation of New England Antiquities, 1968.

Gourlay, Robert Fleming. *Plans for Beautifying New York and for Enlarging and Improving the City of Boston: Being Studies to Illustrate the Science of City Building*. Boston: Crocker & Brewster & Saxton Pierce, 1844.

Greater Boston Chamber of Commerce. *Perspectives on Boston's Growth*. Boston: Greater Boston Chamber of Commerce, 1987.

Greater Boston Economic Study Committee. *Report on Downtown Boston*. Boston: Greater Boston Economic Study Committee, 1959.

Olmsted, Frederick Law. Papers. Microfilm collection, Francis Loeb Gund Library, Graduate School of Design, Harvard University.

Petition to the General Court for a Free Dam or Bridge from Wheeler's Point to South Boston. Boston, 1805. Manuscript copy in the Library of the Boston Athenaeum.

Ross, M. Denman. *Estimate of the Financial Effect of the Proposed Reservation of Back Bay Lands*. Boston: J. Wilson & Son, 1861.

Snelling, George H. *Memorial, with Remarks and Letters, in Favor of a Modification of the Back Bay Plan*. Boston: Damrell & Moore, 1860.

Sturgis, Robert S. "The Architects' Plan for Boston." *Journal of the American Institute of Architects* (January 1962): 35–39.

3. *Interviews conducted in Boston by the author*

Avault, John	March 11, 1991
Bourque, Linda	June 26, 1990
Champion, Hale	November 13, 1987
Collins, John F.	September 23, 1987; November 3, 1987
Coyle, Stephen	February 26, 1991
Curley, Frank X.	August 13, 1991
Donlan, Michael F.	October 31, 1991
Farrell, Robert L.	April 17, 1991
Flaherty, James K.	May 7, 1991
Flynn, Raymond L.	April 24, 1991
Gambon, Jill	May 11, 1990
Ganz, Alexander	June 3, 1987
Goody, Joan	May 22, 1991
Graham, Donald M.	October 30, 1987
Jones, Clarence	April 25, 1991
Jones, Hubie	December 10, 1987
Kenney, Robert T.	November 18, 1987
Lally, Msgr. Francis J.	June 3, 1987
Levine, Mel	October 26, 1987
Logue, Edward J.	November 23, 1987

McCann, Paul   November 10, 1987
Memolo, Ralph   September 25, 1987
Menzies, Ian   October 5, 1987
Morrison, Kevin J.   March 11, 1991
Nolan, Martin F.   February 17, 1988
Perkins, Gregory W.   November 19, 1987
Rappaport, Jerome   November 6, 1987
Russell, Homer   May 7, 1991
Salvucci, Frederick P.   December 18, 1987
Simonian, Kane   October 15, 1987; February 22, 1991
Slavet, Joseph   September 23, 1989
Weis, John   November 18, 1987
White, Kevin H.   November 13, 1987
Zeigler, Philip   November 5, 1987

B. Secondary Source Material

1. Unpublished Studies

Arnone, Nancy Rita. "Redevelopment in Boston: A Study of the Politics and Administration of Social Change." Ph.D. diss., Massachusetts Institute of Technology, 1965.

Burns, Constance K. "The Irony of Progressive Reform in Boston." Ph.D. diss., Boston College, 1985.

Crane, David A. "Mayor Richard S. Daley Lights the Way for the Boston Renaissance." Draft article for celebration of the centennial celebration of the Graduate School of Fine Arts, University of Pennsylvania, dated August 4, 1989.

Culver, David M. "Tenement House Reform in Boston, 1846–1898." Ph.D. diss., Boston University, 1972.

Forbes, John D. "The Port of Boston, 1783–1815." Ph.D. diss., Harvard University, 1936.

Gordon, Jacques. "Case Study: Faneuil Hall Marketplace, Boston." Department of Urban Studies and Planning, Massachusetts Institute of Technology, Revised March 1986.

Gupta, Vineet Kumar. "The Use of Zoning Mechanisms for Growth Management: Downtown Boston in the 1980s." M.C.P. and M.S.A.S. thesis, Massachusetts Institute of Technology, 1988.

Hilden, Michele M. "The Mayors Josiah Quincy of Boston." Ph.D diss., Clark University, 1970.

Kennedy, Lawrence W. "Power and Prejudice: Boston Political Conflict, 1885–1895." Ph.D. diss., Boston College, 1987.

Larson, Leslie. "A History and Analysis of the Development of Central Boston." Draft report prepared for the Boston Redevelopment Authority, 1988.

McCaughey, Robert. "Josiah Quincy, 1772–1864." Ph.D. diss., Harvard University, 1970.

Merino, James Anthony. "A Great City and Its Suburbs: Attempts to Integrate Metropolitan Boston, 1865–1920." Ph.D. diss., University of Texas, 1968.

Nicholaeff, Doreve. "The Planning and Development of Copley Square." M.A.A.S. thesis, Massachusetts Institute of Technology, 1979.

O'Hare, M. Jeanne d'Arc, C.S.J. "The Public Career of Patrick Andrew Collins." Ph.D. diss., Boston College, 1959.

Pikielek, Frederick. "Planning in Boston: The Historical Record." Draft report prepared for the Boston Redevelopment Authority, 1972.

Pilcher, Ann T. "The United Shoe Machinery Corporation Building." Course paper, Boston College, 1987.

Rudnik, Dianne Tarmy. "Boston and the Fire of 1872: The Stillborn Phoenix." Ph.D. diss., Boston University, 1971.

Rudsten, Daniel. "City-State Conflict: A Study of the Political Relationship Between the Core City of Boston and the Massachusetts State Legislature." Ph.D. diss., Tufts University, 1973.

Smith, Margaret Supplee. "Between City and Suburb: Architecture and Planning in Boston's South End." Ph.D. diss., Brown University, 1976.

Spalding, Robert Varnum. "The Boston Mercantile Community and the Promotion of the Textile Industry in New England, 1813–1860." Ph.D. diss., Yale University, 1963.

von Hoffman, Alexander C. "The Making of the Modern City: The Development of Jamaica Plain, Massachusetts, 1632–1920." Ph.D. diss., Harvard University, 1986.

Weismantel, William. "Collision of Urban Renewal with Zoning: The Boston Experience, 1950–1967." Ph.D. diss., Harvard University, 1969.

Wells, Barbara Alice. "The Development and Social Implications of City Planning in the City of Boston." M.S. thesis, Simmons College, 1941.

Zolot, Herbert Marshall. "The Issue of Good Government and James Michael Curley: Curley and the Boston Scene from 1897–1918." Ph.D. diss., State University of New York-Stony Brook, 1975.

2. *Published Case Studies and Research Reports*

Amadon, Elizabeth Reed. *Faneuil Hall: Historical Report.* Boston: Architectural Heritage, 1970.

Amatruda, Robert. *The Boston Class-A Office Market, Year-End 1990 and Quarterly Projections, 1991–1996.* Boston: Boston Redevelopment Authority, Research Department Report No. 403, 1991.

Appleby, Michael D. *Logue's Record in Boston.* New York: Council for New York Housing and Planning Policy, 1966.

Banfield, Edward C., and Martha Derthick. *A Report on the Politics of Boston.* Cambridge: Joint Center for Urban Studies of MIT and Harvard University, 1960.

Boston Redevelopment Authority, Research Department. *Present and Future; Background Information for Infrastructure Planning.* Boston: Boston Redevelopment Authority, Research Department Report No. 136, 1983.

Brown, Jeffrey P. *Who Works in Boston: Commuting Patterns in the Boston Metropolitan Area, 1980.* Boston: Boston Redevelopment Authority, Research Department Report No. 157, 1984.

Carlaw, Christopher. *A Decade of Development in Boston.* Boston: Boston Redevelopment Authority, Research Department Report No. 92, 1979.

Diver, Colin S. *Park Plaza.* Cambridge: Case Program of the John F. Kennedy School of Government, Harvard University, 1975.

Holleran, Michael and Robert Fogelson. "The Sacred Skyline: Boston's Opposition to the Skyscraper." Cambridge: MIT Center for Real Estate Development, Working Paper #9, August 1987.

Howell, James M. *The Boston and Regional Economy into the 1990s: The Prospects for Economic Recovery.* Boston: Boston Redevelopment Authority, 1990.

Joint Center for Urban Studies of MIT and Harvard University. *Planning Metropolitan Boston.* Cambridge: Harvard University Press, 1967.

————. *Future Boston, Patterns and Perspectives.* Cambridge: Joint Center for Urban Studies of MIT and Harvard University, 1982.

Metropolitan District Commission. *Origin, Development and Activities of the Metropolitan District Commission.* Boston: Commonwealth of Massachusetts, 1964.

O'Brien, Thomas. *A History of Boston's Government Center.* Boston: Boston Redevelopment Authority, Research Department Report No. 22, 1982.

Perkins, Gregory W. *Boston's Waterfront: A Storied Past and a Brightening Future.* Boston: Boston Redevelopment Authority, Research Department Report No. 268, 1986.

————. *An Overview of Boston's City-Funded Capital Expenditures, 1960–1980.* Boston: Boston Redevelopment Authority, Research Department Report No. 144, 1983.

————. *Twenty-Two Years of Boston's Fiscal Record: A Review of Expenditure and Revenue Trends for Boston City Government, 1960–1982.* Boston: Boston Redevelopment Authority, Research Department Report No. 151, 1983.

Rosenblum, John. *The Boston Redevelopment Authority.* Boston: Case Study of the Harvard Business School, 1969.

Sanborn, George, comp. *Chronicle: The Boston Transit System.* Boston: Massachusetts Bay Transportation Authority, 1989.

Staunton, John. *Urban Renewal and Planning in Boston: A Review of the Past and a Look at the Future.* Boston: Boston Redevelopment Authority, 1972.

Wiers, Judeth Van Hamm. *Facts and Fictions of Community Participation: The Boston Experience.* Boston: Boston Redevelopment Authority, 1973.

3.   Books and Articles

Abrams, Charles. *The City Is the Frontier.* New York: Harper & Row, 1965.

Adams, Russell B. *The Boston Money Tree.* New York: Thomas Y. Crowell Co., 1977.

Anderson, Martin. *The Federal Bulldozer: A Critical Analysis of Urban Renewal, 1949–1962.* Cambridge: MIT Press, 1964.

Anderson, Peter. "West End Story: A Neighborhood in Exile and Its Effort to Go Home." *Boston Globe Magazine,* 24 May 1987.

Babcock, Richard F. *The Zoning Game: Municipal Practices and Policies.* Madison: University of Wisconsin Press, 1966.

Bailyn, Bernard. *The Peopling of North America: An Introduction.* New York: Alfred A. Knopf, 1987.

Bender, Thomas. *Toward an Urban Vision: Ideas and Institutions in Nineteenth Century America.* Lexington: University of Kentucky Press, 1975.

Bergen, Philip. *Old Boston in Early Photographs, 1850–1918: 174 Prints from the Collection of the Bostonian Society.* New York: Dover Publications, Inc., 1990.

Binford, Henry C. *The First Suburbs: Residential Communities on the Boston Periphery, 1815–1860.* Chicago: University of Chicago Press, 1985.

Black Bostonia: Boston 200 Neighborhood History Series. Boston: Boston 200 Corporation, City of Boston, 1975.

Blackmar, Elizabeth. *Manhattan for Rent, 1785–1850.* Ithaca: Cornell University Press, 1989.

Blake, John B. *Public Health in the Town of Boston, 1630–1822.* Cambridge: Harvard University Press, 1959.

Blodgett, Geoffrey. "Frederick Law Olmsted: Landscape Architecture as Conservative Reform." *Journal of American History* 62 (1976): 869–889.

——. *The Gentle Reformers: Massachusetts Democrats in the Cleveland Era.* Cambridge: Harvard University Press, 1966.

——. "Josiah Quincy, Brahmin Democrat." *New England Quarterly* 38 (1965): 435–453.

Blodgett, Mindy. "A Fresh Start in Boston, Too." *Progressive* 49 (June 1985): 23.

Boorstin, Daniel J. *The Americans: The Colonial Experience.* New York: Vintage Books, 1958.

"Boston." *Architectural Forum* 120 (June 1964), Special Issue.

Bottles, Scott L. *Los Angeles and the Automobile: The Making of the Modern City.* Berkeley: University of California Press, 1987.

Boucher, Norman. "The Death and Life of Dudley: A Lesson in Urban Economics." *Boston Globe Magazine,* 8 April 1990.

Boyer, M. Christine. *Dreaming the Rational City: The Myth of American City Planning.* Cambridge: MIT Press, 1983.

Boyer, Paul. *Urban Masses and Moral Order in America, 1820–1920.* Cambridge: Harvard University Press, 1978.

Branch, Melville C. "Goals and Objectives in Civil Comprehensive Planning." In *Urban Planning Theory,* edited by Melville C. Branch. Stroudsburg, PA: Dowden, Hutchinson & Ross, 1975.

Brighton: Boston 200 Neighborhood History Series. Boston: Boston 200 Corporation, City of Boston, 1975.

Brown, Frank C. "John Smibert, Artist, and the First Faneuil Hall." *Old Time New England* 36 (1946): 61–63.

Brown, Jeffrey P. "Boston." In *Cities Reborn,* edited by Rachelle L. Levitt. Washington, DC: Urban Land Institute, 1987.

Bruce, James L. "Filling in of the Back Bay and Charles River Development." *Proceedings of the Bostonian Society* 12 (1940): 25–38.

Bugbee, James M. "The City Government of Boston." In *Johns Hopkins University Studies in Historical and Political Science,* vol. 5, edited by Herbert B. Adams. Baltimore: The Johns Hopkins University Press, 1887.

Bulfinch, Ellen Susan, ed. *The Life and Letters of Charles Bulfinch.* Boston: Houghton Mifflin Co., 1896.

Buni, Andrew, and Alan Rogers. *Boston: City on a Hill, An Illustrated History.* Woodland Hills, CA: Windsor Publications, Inc., 1984.

Bunting, Bainbridge. *Houses of Boston's Back Bay: An Architectural History, 1840–1917.* Cambridge: Belknap Press of Harvard University Press, 1967.

Bunting, W. H. *Portrait of a Port: Boston, 1852–1914.* Cambridge: Belknap Press of Harvard University Press, 1971.

Buttenwieser, Ann L. *Manhattan Water-Bound: Planning and Developing Manhattan's Waterfront from the Seventeenth Century to the Present.* New York: Columbia University Press, 1987.

Caro, Robert. *The Power Broker: Robert Moses and the Fall of New York.* New York: Alfred A. Knopf, 1974.

Chamberlain, Allen. *Beacon Hill: Its Ancient Pastures and Early Mansions.* Boston: Houghton Mifflin Co., 1925.

Charlestown: Boston 200 Neighborhood History Series. Boston: Boston 200 Corporation, City of Boston, 1975.

Cheape, Charles W. *Moving the Masses: Urban Public Transit in New York, Boston, and Philadelphia, 1880–1912.* Cambridge: Harvard University Press, 1980.

Choay, Francoise. *The Modern City: Planning in the 19th Century.* New York: G. Braziller, 1970.

Chudacoff, Howard P., and Judith E. Smith. *The Evolution of American Urban Society.* 3d ed. Englewood Cliffs, NJ: Prentice Hall, 1988.

Conzen, Michael P., and George K. Lewis. *Boston: A Geographical Portrait.* Cambridge: Ballinger Publishing Co., 1976.

Cudahy, Brian. *Change at Park Street Under: The Story of Boston's Subways.* Brattleboro, VT: S. Greene Press, 1972.

Cummings, Abbott Lowell. "The Beginnings of India Wharf." *Proceedings of the Bostonian Society* 52 (1962): 17–24.

————. "Charles Bulfinch and Boston's Vanishing West End." *Old-Time New England* 52 (1961): 31–47.

Curley, James Michael. *I'd Do It Again: A Record of All My Uproarious Years.* Englewood Cliffs, NJ: Prentice Hall, Inc., 1957.

Cushing, George M., Jr. *Great Buildings of Boston: A Photographic Guide,* with text by Ross Urquhart. New York: Dover Publications, 1982.

Cutler, John Henry. *"Honey Fitz": Three Steps to the White House.* Indianapolis: Bobbs-Merrill, 1962.

Dalton, Cornelius, John Wikkala, and Anne Thomas. *Leading the Way: A History of the Massachusetts General Court, 1629–1980.* Boston: Office of the Massachusetts Secretary of State, 1984.

Dalzell, Robert F., Jr. *Enterprising Elite: The Boston Associates and the World They Made.* Cambridge: Harvard University Press, 1987.

Dineen, Joseph. *The Purple Shamrock: The Honorable James Michael Curley of Boston.* New York: W. W. Norton & Company, 1949.

Dorchester: Boston 200 Neighborhood History Series. Boston: Boston 200 Corporation, City of Boston, 1975.

Drake, Samuel Adams. *Old Landmarks and Historic Personages of Boston.* Rev. ed. Rutland, VT: Charles E. Tuttle Co., 1971.

Edel, Matthew, Elliott D. Sclar, and Daniel Luria. *Shaky Palaces: Home Ownership and Social Mobility in Boston's Suburbs.* New York: Columbia University Press, 1984.

Eisenmenger, Robert W. *The Dynamics of Growth in the New England Economy, 1870–1964.* Middletown, CT: Wesleyan University Press, 1967.

Eldredge, Joseph L., ed. *Architecture Boston.* Barre, MA: Barre Publishing, 1976.

Eliot, Charles W., Donald M. Graham and David A. Crane. "Boston: Three Centuries of Planning." *A.S.P.O. Newsletter: American Society of Planning Officials* 30 (1964): 43–48.

Elliott, Christopher R. "The Boston Public Garden." *Proceedings of the Bostonian Society* 12 (1939): 27–47.

Erie, Steven P. *Rainbow's End: Irish-Americans and the Dilemmas of Urban Machine Politics, 1840–1985.* Berkeley: University of California Press, 1988.

Fahey, Joseph J., ed. *Boston's Forty-five Mayors: From John Phillips to Kevin H. White.* Boston: City Record, 1975.

Ferman, Barbara. *Governing the Ungovernable City: Political Skill, Leadership, and the Modern Mayor.* Philadelphia: Temple University Press, 1985.

Firey, Walter. *Land Use in Central Boston*. Cambridge: Harvard University Press, 1947.

Fisher, Irving D. *Frederick Law Olmsted and the City Planning Movement in the United States*. Ann Arbor: UMI Research Press, 1986.

Fogelsong, Richard E. *Planning the Capitalist City: The Colonial Era to the 1920s*. Princeton: Princeton University Press, 1986.

Ford, Worthington Chauncey, ed. "Communication of Two Documents Protesting against the Incorporation of Boston." *Publications of the Colonial Society of Massachusetts* 10 (1904–1906): 345–352.

Formisano, Ronald P. *Boston Against Busing: Race, Class, and Ethnicity in the 1960s and 1970s*. Chapel Hill: University of North Carolina Press, 1991.

Formisano, Ronald P., and Constance K. Burns, eds. *Boston 1700–1980: The Evolution of Urban Politics*. Westport, CT: Greenwood Press, 1984.

Fowler, William M., Jr. *The Baron of Beacon Hill: A Biography of John Hancock*. Boston: Houghton Mifflin Co., 1980.

Fox, Kenneth. *Better City Government: Innovation in American Urban Politics, 1850–1937*. Philadelphia: Temple University Press, 1977.

Freiberg, Malcolm, comp. *The Changing Face of Boston over 350 Years*. Boston: Massachusetts Historical Society, 1980.

Fried, Marc. *The World of the Urban Working Class: Boston's West End*. Cambridge: Harvard University Press, 1973.

Frieden, Bernard J., and Lynne B. Sagalynn. *Downtown, Inc.: How America Rebuilds Cities*. Cambridge: MIT Press, 1989.

Frieden, Bernard J., and Marshall Kaplan. *The Politics of Neglect: Urban Aid from Model Cities to Revenue Sharing*. Cambridge: MIT Press, 1975.

Gans, Herbert. *Urban Villagers: Group and Class in the Life of Italian Americans*. Rev. ed. New York: The Free Press, 1982.

Ganz, Alexander. "Where Has the Urban Crisis Gone? How Boston and Other Large Cities Have Stemmed Economic Decline." *Urban Affairs Quarterly* 20 (1984): 449–468.

Gelfand, Mark I. "Boston: Back to the Politics of the Future." In *Snowbelt Cities: Metropolitan Politics in the Northeast and Midwest since World War II.*, edited by Richard M. Bernard. Bloomington: Indiana University Press, 1990.

———. *A Nation of Cities: The Federal Government and Urban America 1933–1965*. New York: Oxford University Press, 1975.

———. "Rexford G. Tugwell and the Frustration of Planning in New York City." *Journal of the American Planning Association* 51 (Spring, 1985): 151–160.

Gerckens, Laurence C. "Historical Development of American City Planning." In *The Practice of Local Government Planning*, edited by Frank So, et al. Washington, DC: International City Management Association, 1988.

Glaab, Charles N., and A. Theodore Brown. *A History of Urban America*. 2d ed. New York: Macmillan, 1976.

Golden, Daniel. "Massachusetts Muscle." *Boston Globe Magazine,* 29 September 1991.

———. "Wheeler and Dealer." *Boston Globe Magazine,* 19 March 1989.

Goodwin, Doris Kearns. *The Fitzgeralds and the Kennedys: An American Saga*. New York: Simon & Schuster, 1987.

Graff, Henry F. "The Charles River Bridge Case." In *Quarrels that Have Shaped the Constitution*. Rev. ed., edited by John A. Garraty. New York: Harper & Row, 1987.

Green, James R., and Hugh Carter Donahue. *Boston's Workers: A Labor History*. Boston: Trustees of the Public Library of the City of Boston, 1979.

Green, Richard. "Coyle in Command: A Candid Interview with Stephen Coyle, the Out-spoken Director of the Boston Redevelopment Authority." *S/F: New England's Real Estate Magazine* (August 1987): 22–27, 44–49.

Gregory, Frances W. *Nathan Appleton: Merchant and Entrepreneur, 1779–1861.* Charlottes-ville: University Press of Virginia, 1975.

Hancock, John L. "Planners in the Changing American City, 1900–1940." *Journal of the American Institute of Planners* 33 (1967): 290–304.

Handlin, Oscar. *Boston's Immigrants: A Study in Acculturation.* Rev. ed. New York: Atheneum, 1975.

Handlin, Oscar, and Mary F. Handlin. *Commonwealth: A Study of the Role of Government in the American Economy, Massachusetts, 1774–1861.* Rev. and enl. ed. Cambridge: Har-vard University Press, 1969.

Hardy, Stephen. *How Boston Played: Sport, Recreation, and Community 1865–1915.* Boston: Northeastern University Press, 1982.

Harris, John. *Historic Walks in Old Boston* 2d ed. Chester, CT: Globe Pequot Press, 1989.

———, ed. *The Great Boston Fire: 1872, A Disaster with a Villain: Old Style Politics. Boston Sunday Globe,* 12 November 1972. (Special insert)

Hart, Albert Bushnell, ed. *Commonwealth History of Massachusetts, Colony, Province and State.* 5 vols. New York: The States History Company, 1930.

Herlihy, Elisabeth M. "Planning for Boston, 1630–1930." *City Planning Quarterly* 6 (1930): 1–13.

———, ed. *Fifty Years of Boston: A Memorial Volume Issued in Commemoration of the Tercentenary of 1930.* Boston: Tercentennary Committee, 1932.

Hewlett, Richard G. "Josiah Quincy, Reform Mayor of Boston." *New England Quarterly* 24 (1951): 179–196.

Higgins, George V. *Style Versus Substance: Boston, Kevin White and the Politics of Illusion.* New York: Macmillan Publishing Company, 1984.

Hobson, Barbara Meil. *Uneasy Virtue: The Politics of Prostitution and the American Reform Tradition.* New York: Basic Books, 1987.

Hodgkinson, H. D. "Miracle in Boston." *Proceedings of the Massachusetts Historical Society* 84 (1972): 71–81.

Hofstadter, Richard. *The Age of Reform: From Bryan to F.D.R.* New York: Alfred A. Knopf, 1956.

Hultman, Eugene C. "The Charles River Basin." *Proceedings of the Bostonian Society* 12 (1940): 39–48.

Huse, Charles P. *The Financial History of Boston, from May 1, 1822 to January 31, 1909.* Cambridge: Harvard University Press, 1916.

Huthmacher, J. Joseph. *Massachusetts People and Politics, 1919–1933.* Cambridge: Harvard University Press, 1959.

Hyde Park: Boston 200 Neighborhood History Series. Boston: Boston 200 Corporation, City of Boston, 1975.

Jackson, Kenneth T. *Crabgrass Frontier: The Suburbanization of the United States.* New York: Oxford University Press, 1985.

———. "The Impact of Technological Change on Urban Form." In *Technology, the Economy, and Society: The American Experience,* edited by Joel Colton and Stuart Bruchey. New York: Columbia University Press, 1987.

Jackson, Kenneth T., and Stanley K. Schultz, eds. *Cities in American History.* New York: Alfred A. Knopf, 1972.

Jacobs, Jane. *The Death and Life of Great American Cities*. New York: Vintage Books, 1961.

Jamaica Plain: Boston 200 Neighborhood History Series. Boston: Boston 200 Corporation, City of Boston, 1975.

Jennings, James, and Mel King, eds. *From Access to Power: Black Politics in Boston*. Rochester, VT: Schenkman Books, Inc., 1986.

Kalfus, Melvin. *Frederick Law Olmsted: The Passion of a Public Artist*. New York: New York University Press, 1990.

Kay, Jane Holtz. "The Limits of Growth: Boston's Downtown Plan." *Progressive Architecture* 66 (October 1985): 29.

———. *Lost Boston*. Boston: Houghton Mifflin Co., 1980.

Keating, W. Dennis. "Linking Downtown Development to Broader Community Goals." *Journal of the American Planning Association* 52 (Spring 1986): 133–141.

Kellogg, Paul U. "Boston's Level Best: The 1915 Movement and the Work of Civic Organizations for Which It Stands." *The Survey* 22 (5 June 1909): 382–395.

Keyes, Langley C., Jr. *The Boston Rehabilitation Program: An Independent Analysis*. Cambridge: Joint Center for Urban Studies of MIT and Harvard University, 1970.

———. *The Rehabilitation Planning Game: A Study in the Diversity of Neighborhood*. Cambridge: MIT Press, 1969.

Kilgore, Kathleen. *John Volpe: The Life of an Immigrant's Son*. Dublin, NH: Yankee Books, 1987.

Kilham, Walter H. *Boston after Bulfinch*. Cambridge: Harvard University Press, 1946.

King, John. "How the BRA Got Some Respect: Boston's Redevelopment Agency Believed in Doing It All," *Planning* (May 1990): 4–9.

King, Mel. *Chain of Change: Struggles for Black Community Development*. Boston: South End Press, 1981.

Kirker, Harold. *The Architecture of Charles Bulfinch*. Cambridge: Harvard University Press, 1969.

Kirker, Harold, and James Kirker. *Bulfinch's Boston*. New York: Oxford University Press, 1964.

Koren, John. *Boston, 1822 to 1922: The Story of Its Government and Principal Activities During One Hundred Years*. Boston: City of Boston Printing Department, 1923.

Krieger, Alex, and Lisa J. Green. *Past Futures: Two Centuries of Imagining Boston*. Cambridge: Harvard University Graduate School of Design, 1985.

Krueckeberg, Donald A., ed. *Introduction to Planning History in the United States*. Piscataway, NJ: The Center for Urban Policy Research, Rutgers University, 1983.

Kutler, Stanley L. *Privilege and Creative Destruction: The Charles River Bridge Case*. Baltimore: The Johns Hopkins University Press, 1971.

Langtry, Albert P., ed. *Metropolitan Boston: A Modern History*. 5 v. New York: Lewis Historical Publishing Co., 1929.

Lapomarda, Vincent A. "Maurice Joseph Tobin: The Decline of Bossism in Boston." *New England Quarterly* 43 (1970): 355–381.

Lasswell, Harold. *Politics: Who Gets What, When, How*. New York: Peter Smith, 1950.

Lawrence, Robert Means. *Old Park Street and Its Vicinity*. Boston: Houghton Mifflin Co., 1922.

Leuchtenberg, William. *The Perils of Prosperity, 1914–1932*. Chicago: University of Chicago Press, 1958.

Levin, Mel. *Bureaucrats in Collision: Case Studies in Area Transportation Planning*. Cambridge: MIT Press, 1971.

Levin, Murray. *The Alienated Voter: Politics in Boston*. New York: Holt, Rinehart & Winston, 1960.

Logue, Edward J. "Boston, 1960–1967: Seven Years of Plenty." *Proceedings of the Massachusetts Historical Society* 84 (1972): 82–96.

———. "A Look Back at Neighborhood Renewal in Boston." *Policy Studies Journal* 16 (1987): 335–346.

Lubove, Roy. *Community Planning in the 1920s*. Pittsburgh: University of Pittsburgh Press, 1964.

———. *Twentieth Century Pittsburgh: Government, Business and Environmental Change*. New York: John Wiley & Sons, 1969.

———, ed. *The Urban Community: Housing and Planning in the Progressive Era*. Englewood Cliffs, NJ: Prentice Hall, 1967.

Lukas, Anthony J. *Common Ground: A Turbulent Decade in the Lives of Three American Families*. New York: Alfred A. Knopf, 1985.

Lupo, Alan. *Liberty's Chosen Home*. Rev. ed. Boston: Beacon Press, 1988.

Lupo, Alan, Frank Colcord, and Edmund P. Fowler. *Rites of Way: The Politics of Transportation in Boston and the U.S. City*. Boston: Little, Brown & Co., 1971.

McCaughey, Robert A. *Josiah Quincy 1772–1864: The Last Federalist*. Cambridge: Harvard University Press, 1974.

McCraw, Thomas K. *Prophets of Regulation: Charles Francis Adams, Louis D. Brandeis, James M. Landis, Alfred E. Kahn*. Cambridge: Belknap Press of Harvard University Press, 1984.

McDonnell, Timothy L., S.J. *The Wagner Housing Act: A Case Study of the Legislative Process*. Chicago: Loyola University Press, 1957.

McKelvey, Blake. *The Urbanization of America, 1860–1915*. New Brunswick, NJ: Rutgers University Press, 1963.

———. *The Emergence of Metropolitan America, 1915–1966*. New Brunswick, NJ: Rutgers University Press, 1968.

McQuade, Walter. "Boston: What Can a Sick City Do?" *Fortune* 69 (June 1964): 132–137, 163–164, 166, 169–170.

Marchione, William P. *The Bull in the Garden: A History of Allston-Brighton*. Boston: Trustees of the Public Library of the City of Boston, 1986.

———. "The 1949 Boston Charter Reform." *New England Quarterly* 49 (1976): 373–398.

Marquand, John P. *The Late George Apley*. New York: Washington Square Press, 1963.

Marty, Martin E. *Righteous Empire: The Protestant Experience in America*. New York: The Dial Press, 1970.

Menzies, Ian. "The Faneuil Hall Marketplace: Window on New England." *Blair and Ketchum's Country Journal* (April 1979): 48–51.

———. "Where's Boston? Is America's 'In' City Losing Its Soul?" *Bostonia* 61 (September/October 1987): 28–35.

Meyerson, Martin, and Edward C. Banfield. *Boston: The Job Ahead*. Cambridge: Harvard University Press, 1966.

Mollenkopf, John H. *The Contested City*. Princeton: Princeton University Press, 1983.

Monkkonen, Eric H. *America Becomes Urban: The Development of U.S. Cities and Towns, 1780–1980*. Berkeley: University of California Press, 1988.

Morgan, Edmund S. *The Puritan Dilemma: The Story of John Winthrop*. Boston: Little, Brown & Co., 1958.

Morison, Samuel Eliot. *Harrison Gray Otis, 1765–1848: The Urbane Federalist*. Boston: Houghton Mifflin Co., 1969.

———. *The Maritime History of Massachusetts, 1783–1860*. Boston: Houghton Mifflin Co., 1941.

———. *One Boy's Boston 1887–1901*. Boston: Houghton Mifflin Co., 1962.

Mumford, Lewis, and Walter Muir Whitehill. *Back Bay Boston: The City as a Work of Art*. Dayton: Craftsman Type, Inc., 1969.

Murdock, Harold, ed. *1872: Letters Written by a Gentleman in Boston to his Friend in Paris Describing the Great Fire*. Boston: Houghton Mifflin Co., 1909.

Nesson, Fern L. *Great Waters: A History of Boston's Water Supply*. Hanover, NH: Published for Brandeis University by the University Press of New England, 1983.

North End: Boston 200 Neighborhood History Series. Boston: Boston 200 Corporation, City of Boston, 1975.

Norton, Bettina A. *The Boston Naval Shipyard, 1800–1974*. Boston: The Bostonian Society, 1975.

O'Connell, Shaun. *Imagining Boston: A Literary Landscape*. Boston: Beacon Press, 1990.

O'Connor, Thomas H. *Bibles, Brahmins, and Bosses: A Short History of Boston*. 2d ed., revised. Boston: Trustees of the Public Library of the City of Boston, 1984.

———. *Fitzpatrick's Boston, 1846–1866: John Bernard Fitzpatrick, Third Bishop of Boston*. Boston: Northeastern University Press, 1984.

———. *South Boston, My Home Town: The History of an Ethnic Neighborhood*. Boston: Quinlan Press, 1988.

Pantridge, Margaret. "City by Coyle." *Boston Magazine* (July 1988): 54–59.

———. "The Power Failure." *Boston Magazine* (October 1991): 60–61, 93–98.

Pearson, Henry G. *Son of New England: James Jackson Storrow, 1846–1926*. Boston: Thomas Todd Co., 1932.

Pease, William H., and Jane H. Pease. *The Web of Progress: Private Values and Public Styles in Boston and Charleston, 1828–1843*. New York: Oxford University Press, 1985.

Place, Charles A. *Charles Bulfinch: Architect and Citizen*. Boston: Houghton Mifflin Co., 1925.

Powers, John. "Boston's 21st Century Man: BRA Director Stephen F. Coyle." *Boston Globe Magazine*, 1 June 1986.

———. "In Like Flynn." *Boston Globe Magazine*, 13 January 1991.

———. "Sky King: International Place Developer Don Chiofaro." *Boston Globe Magazine*, 13 May 1990.

———. "Unbuilt Boston." *Boston Globe Magazine*, 30 December 1990.

Quincy, Josiah. *A Municipal History of the Town and City of Boston during the Two Centuries from September 17, 1630 to September 17, 1830*. Boston: C. C. Little and J. Brown, 1852.

Reps, John W. *The Making of Urban America: A History of City Planning in the United States*. Princeton: Princeton University Press, 1965.

Roper, Laura Wood. *F.L.O.: A Biography of Frederick Law Olmsted*. Baltimore: The Johns Hopkins University Press, 1973.

Rosen, Christine M. "Infrastructural Improvement in Nineteenth-Century Cities: A Conceptual Framework and Cases." *Journal of Urban History* 12 (1986): 211–256.

———. *The Limits of Power: Great Fires and the Process of City Growth in America*. New York: Cambridge University Press, 1986.

Roslindale: Boston 200 Neighborhood History Series. Boston: Boston 200 Corporation, City of Boston, 1975.

Ross, Marjorie Drake. *The Book of Boston: The Federal Period, 1775 to 1837.* New York: Hastings House Publishers, 1961.

———. *The Book of Boston: The Victorian Period, 1837 to 1901.* New York: Hastings House Publishers, 1964.

Russell, Francis R. *The Great Interlude: Neglected Events and Persons From the First World War to the Depression.* New York: McGraw-Hill Book Co., 1964.

Rutman, Darret. *Winthrop's Boston: Portrait of a Puritan Town.* Chapel Hill: University of North Carolina Press, 1965.

Ryan, Dennis P. *Beyond the Ballot Box: A Social History of the Boston Irish, 1845–1917.* Amherst: University of Massachusetts Press, 1989.

Sagalyn, Lynne B. "Measuring Financial Returns When the City Acts as an Investor: Boston and Faneuil Hall Marketplace." *Real Estate Issues* 14 (Fall/Winter 1989): 7–15.

Schabert, Tilo. *Boston Politics: The Creativity of Power.* New York: Walter de Gruyter, 1989.

Schaffer, Daniel, ed. *Two Centuries of American Planning.* Baltimore: The Johns Hopkins University Press, 1988.

Schnore, Leo F., and Peter R. Knights. "Residence and Social Structure: Boston in the Ante-Bellum Period." In *Nineteenth Century Cities: Essays in the New Urban History,* edited by Stephan Thernstrom and Richard Sennett. New Haven: Yale University Press, 1969.

Schultz, Stanley K. *Constructing Urban Culture: American Cities and City Planning, 1800–1920.* Philadelphia: Temple University Press, 1989.

———. *The Culture Factory: Boston Public Schools, 1789–1860.* New York: Oxford University Press, 1973.

Schultz, Stanley, and Clay McShane. "To Engineer the Metropolis: Sewers, Sanitation, and City Planning in Late-Nineteenth Century America." *Journal of American History* 65 (1978): 389–411.

Schuyler, David. *The New Urban Landscape: The Redefinition of City Form in Nineteenth Century America.* Baltimore: The Johns Hopkins University Press, 1986.

Scott, Mellier Goodin. *American City Planning since 1890.* Berkeley: University of California Press, 1969.

Seaburg, Carl, and Stephen Paterson. *Merchant Prince of Boston: Colonel T. H. Perkins, 1764–1854.* Cambridge: Harvard University Press, 1971.

Shand-Tucci, Douglass. *Built in Boston: City and Suburb, 1800–1950.* Amherst: University of Massachusetts Press, 1988.

Shannon, William V. *The American Irish: A Political and Social Portrait.* 2d ed. Amherst: University of Massachusetts Press, 1989.

Shurtleff, Nathaniel B. *A Topographical and Historical Description of Boston.* Boston: Rockwell & Churchill, 1891.

Silver, Christopher. "Neighborhood Planning in Perspective." *Journal of the American Planning Association* 51 (Spring 1985): 161–174.

Silverman, Robert A. *Law and Urban Growth: Civil Litigation in the Boston Trial Courts, 1880–1900.* Princeton: Princeton University Press, 1981.

———. "Nathan Matthews and the Politics of Reform in Boston, 1890–1910." *New England Quarterly* 50 (1977): 626–643.

Snow, Caleb H. *A History of Boston: The Metropolis of Massachusetts From its Origin to the Present Period with Some Account of the Environs.* 2d ed. Boston: Abel Bowen, 1828.

South Boston: Boston 200 Neighborhood History Series. Boston: Boston 200 Corporation, City of Boston, 1975.

South End: Boston 200 Neighborhood History Series. Boston: Boston 200 Corporation, City of Boston, 1975.

Southworth, Michael, and Susan Southworth. *The Boston Society of Architects' A.I.A. Guide to Boston*. Chester, CT: Globe Pequot Press, 1987.

Stanley, Raymond W., ed. *Mr. Bulfinch's Boston*. Boston: Old Colony Trust Company, 1963.

State Street Trust Co. *Boston's Growth: A Bird's-eye view of Boston's Increase in Territory and Population from its Beginnings to the Present*. Boston: State Street Trust Company, 1910.

Steinbach, Carol. "Tapping Private Resources: The Linkage Trend." *Journal of Housing* 44 (July–August 1987): 111–115.

Stout, Glenn. "A Garden Blooms." *Boston Magazine* (November 1988): 133–139.

Strahinich, John. "How Fast is Ray Flynn?" *Boston Magazine* (September 1991): 100–120.

Sutcliffe, Anthony, ed. *The Rise of Modern Urban Planning, 1800–1914*. New York: St. Martin's Press, 1980.

Teaford, Jon C. *City and Suburb: The Political Fragmentation of Metropolitan America, 1850–1970*. Baltimore: The Johns Hopkins University Press, 1979.

———. *The Municipal Revolution in America: Origins of Modern Urban Government, 1650–1825*. Chicago: University of Chicago Press, 1975.

———. *The Twentieth-Century American City: Problem, Promise, Reality*. Baltimore: The Johns Hopkins University Press, 1986.

———. *The Unheralded Triumph: City Government in America, 1870–1900*. Baltimore: The Johns Hopkins University Press, 1984.

Thernstrom, Stephan. *The Other Bostonians: Poverty and Progress in the American Metropolis, 1880–1970*. Cambridge: Harvard University Press, 1973.

———. *Poverty, Planning, and Politics in the New Boston: The Origins of A.B.C.D*. New York: Basic Books, 1969.

Trout, Charles. *Boston: The Great Depression and the New Deal*. New York: Oxford University, 1977.

Tunnard, Christopher, and Henry Hope Reed. *American Skyline: The Growth and Form of Our Cities and Towns*. Boston: Houghton Mifflin Co., 1955.

Vasu, Michael Lee. *Politics and Planning: A National Study of American Planners*. Chapel Hill: University of North Carolina Press, 1979.

Warden, Gerald B. *Boston 1689–1776*. Boston: Little, Brown & Co., 1970.

Warner, Sam Bass, Jr. *The Private City: Philadelphia in Three Periods of Its Growth*. Philadelphia: University of Pennsylvania Press, 1968.

———. *The Province of Reason*. Cambridge: Belknap Press of Harvard University Press, 1984.

———. *Streetcar Suburbs: The Process of Growth in Boston 1870–1900*. New York: Atheneum, 1974.

———. *To Dwell Is to Garden: A History of Boston's Community Gardens*. Boston: Northeastern University Press, 1987.

———. *The Urban Wilderness: A History of the American City*. New York: Harper & Row, 1972.

———. *The Way We Really Live: Social Change in Metropolitan Boston Since 1920*. Boston: Trustees of the Public Library of the City of Boston, 1977.

Weiss, Marc A. "The Origins and Legacy of Urban Renewal." In *Federal Housing Policy and Programs: Past and Present* edited by J. Paul Mitchell. New Brunswick, NJ: Rutgers Center for Urban Policy Research, 1985.

————. *The Rise of the Community Builders: The American Real Estate Industry and Urban Land Planning*. New York: Columbia University Press, 1987.

West Roxbury: Boston 200 Neighborhood History Series. Boston: Boston 200 Corporation, City of Boston, 1975.

Whitehill, Walter Muir. *Boston: A Topographical History* 2d ed. enl. Cambridge: Belknap Press of Harvard University Press, 1975.

————. *Boston in the Age of John Fitzgerald Kennedy*. Norman: University of Oklahoma Press, 1966.

Wiebe, Robert. *The Search for Order, 1877–1920*. New York: Hill & Wang, 1967.

Winsor, Justin, ed. *The Memorial History of Boston, including Suffolk County, Massachusetts, 1630–1880*. 4 v. Boston: James R. Osgood & Co., 1881.

Woods, Robert A. and Albert J. Kennedy. *The Zone of Emergence: Observations of the Lower-Middle- and Upper-Working-Class Communities of Boston, 1905–1914*. 2d ed. Abridged, edited, and with a preface by Sam Bass Warner, Jr. Cambridge: MIT Press, 1969.

Workers of the Writers Program of the Works Projects Administration in the State of Massachusetts. *Boston Looks Seaward: The Story of the Port, 1630–1940*. Foreword and epilogue by William M. Fowler, Jr. Boston: Northeastern University Press, 1985.

Zaitzevsky, Cynthia. *Frederick Law Olmsted and the Boston Park System*. Cambridge: Belknap Press of Harvard University Press, 1982.

....

Index

314